Man and His Physical Universe

Man and His

Physical Universe

Richard Wistar

Professor of Chemistry, Mills College

Second Edition

John Wiley & Sons, Inc. New York • London

Library of Congress Catalog Card Number: 63-11456
Printed in the United States of America

Preface

THIS TEXT is designed to provide a sound foundation in the physical sciences for those students who have not decided to major in science. If the student eventually chooses a career in science, this broad view will have provided a helpful perspective. If he decides to major in some other field, he will have an introduction to science that is sufficient for him to continue as an informed layman.

The twin problems of content and treatment are particularly critical for the author of a textbook in physical science: the amount of material that could legitimately be included would fill several volumes; and the treatment must be sound without being too technical. My decisions on content started from the conviction that students will learn more readily and retain more effectively material with which they have a continuing association. The weather, photography, the stars, and geological formations are examples of such material and are important aspects of physical science. The intelligent layman encounters articles about recent progress in atomic theory, the basis for Nobel prize awards, and the findings of space research. Not only in the physical sciences but also in the life sciences, current explanations are being given more and more on the molecular level. Some understanding of chemical change and atomic structure is necessary for the modern citizen. There are many gaps in the field, but the teacher must remember that if he

v

does his job well the student will continue to learn after classes are over.

In the presentation of these subjects I have tried to keep the technical details of special vocabulary and symbols to a minimum. This can be done without sacrificing accuracy. I have tried to be moderate in what was excluded as well as what was included. There are some formulas and symbols, and some use is made of high-school-level mathematics in order to avoid circumlocutions that would insult the student.

The usual order of treatment is to begin with facts of everyday experience, then to go on to facts that can be presented by demonstration, then to present additional factual material in the text, and, from all this, to develop the models and theories that are currently accepted as the best representations of the nature of the physical world. To the extent that it is possible, modern scientific developments are explained in terms of these models and theories. To a limited extent, subjects are put in their historical and cultural setting.

There has been no attempt to segregate the subject matter of the different branches of physical science. Chemistry and physics are introduced wherever appropriate in all the units. Astronomy is mostly confined to the unit on the solar system and geology to the unit on the geological history of the earth. Weather forecasting and photography, treated broadly, serve to introduce many important scientific subjects. There are many small problems, rather than one central one, covered in the unit on electricity and magnetism, and the subject of atomic structure draws on a wide background. The scientific process and critical thinking are emphasized frequently, but it

seems useful to devote a special chapter to these subjects at the midpoint of the course; at that time they can be treated in the context of the course, familiar examples can be evoked, and the stage can be set for further examples.

In this second edition, the order of the units has been changed and each unit has been completely rewritten. The subject of the weather starts the student off on familiar ground and introduces many fundamental concepts that are developed and used in later units. The units on the solar system and geology have been moved to the end of the book, so that more explanations in terms of physics and chemistry could be included. Chemical symbols and equations have been introduced and used sparingly. Every topic has been refreshed, with new findings and interpretations replacing outdated ones.

In one of the several outside book reports required each year from my students in this course, I found the following comment: "The book I am reviewing is written a great deal in the manner of a textbook. It is completely factual with little attempt to bring out any great interest. It is my earnest hope that such a criticism is not deserved by this book. A textbook for physical science should be interesting and exciting—certainly the subject is. It is also hoped that those students who read this book will gain a new respect for scientists and their contributions to our culture, and that they will have a developing interest in and an understanding of science as they go through life.

Oakland, California
January, 1963

RICHARD WISTAR

Contents

vii

viii

Unit One

Weather

Chapter 1

Our Atmosphere as a Gas

THE TOPIC of weather forecasting has been chosen to open this book because it is a subject that can lead us naturally and quickly from the known to the unknown. An understanding of this topic will draw on a broad background of important scientific principles, and your day-by-day practice of predicting will help keep these principles and their more general applications fresh in your mind. Many aspects of physical science will be developed carefully in an effort to show you how we arrived at our present ideas and what we still do not understand. The final results of this long inquiry are important, but a study of the path by which we reach them is even more so.

What we observe as the "weather" is the series of events occurring at the bottom of a sea of air many hundreds of miles deep. This sea is complex in structure and extremely complicated in behavior. Since we live at the bottom of the atmosphere we will talk about its height rather than its depth. Let us consider the problem of determining the height of the atmosphere. What evidence can we look for? We know that even moderate exercise makes us short of breath near a mountain top, and that explorers of really high mountains must take oxygen masks although they are only six miles above sea level. Man and animals in spacecrafts circling the earth at a few hundred miles up must be in completely sealed cabins. The friction of the atmosphere heats incoming meteors to incandescence at 185 miles, and the glow of the northern lights disappears above 600 miles.

The thin layer that lies within 30,000 to 40,000 feet of the surface is called the troposphere. Here the air is moving along the surface of the earth, churning up and down and swirling in great whirlpools. The temperature tends to decrease with altitude, reaching the freezing point below 20,000 feet. Above 40,000 feet the vertical mixing largely ceases, so it is the troposphere that we need to study to understand the weather. Since all of the atmosphere is a gas, we must study the behavior of gases; besides varying amounts of water vapor and dust, the air consists of 78% nitrogen, 21% oxygen, and 1% rare gases. Hurricanes and thunderstorms are obvious examples of the tremendous amounts of energy involved in weather phenomena; to understand these and many other aspects of the weather, it is first necessary to acquire a background in the basic elements of physics.

WEATHER LORE

It would be hard to find a field of public activity that equals that of weather forecasting in the mixture of truth, half truth, and falsehood that has been handed down in our folklore.

We have such sayings as:

An evening gray and morning red
Will send the shepherd wet to bed.
Evening red and morning gray
Two sure signs of one fine day.

And such signs as, "When rheumatic people complain of more than ordinary pains it will probably rain," "Smoke from the chimney descending to the ground means rain," "A ring around either the sun or the moon indicates rain within two days."

These are consistent with what we know to be dependable signs of good or bad weather.

Then we have Izaak Walton's (1593–1683) advice to fishermen:

When the wind is in the north,
The skillful fisher goes not forth;
When the wind is in the east,
'Tis good for neither man nor beast;
When the wind is in the south,
It blows the flies in the fish's mouth;
When the wind is in the west,
There it is the very best.

This could be true for some parts of the country, but it would be false for many others.

Finally, there are sayings which do not contain a grain of truth:

In this month is St. Swithin's day [July 15]
On which, if that is rain, they say
Full forty days after it will
Or more or less some rain distill.

"If the new moon appear with the points of the crescent turned up the month will be dry. If the points are turned down it will be wet." The direct opposite of this is also quoted. The fact that the crescent of the new moon never does point down has apparently escaped the attention of the people who perpetrate this one. A final example of nonsense that is still believed in by many people is the rule:

Go plant the bean when the moon is light,
And you will find that this is right;
Plant the potatoes when the moon is dark,
And to this line you always hark.

The development of science has enabled us to predict the weather with a considerable degree of accuracy. The results still leave much to be desired, but as our understanding of the situation increases the dependability of the forecasts becomes greater. Today the United States Weather Bureau collects data from stations all over the country and from ships at sea. After analyzing this information it advises owners of farms and stores about coming storms, freezes, hot spells, etc. Farmers have learned the value of using these forecasts in deciding whether to work late to get in a crop, to light their smudge pots, to insulate fruit in freight cars, etc. Stores plan sales campaigns; power companies, airlines, and road crews plan their work; small boats look for storm warnings; and you and I decide upon a picnic on the basis of the weather forecast we read in the paper or listen to over the radio.

AIR PRESSURE AND THE BAROMETER

Observing Air Pressure

We are not ordinarily aware of the atmosphere around us. We breathe it in and out subconsciously. We walk around in it without hindrance. Nevertheless, however invisible they may be, stiff winds uproot trees. Steam from boiling water condenses and then disappears—it must go somewhere. On a cold winter day the window panes collect moisture on the inside—it must come from the atmosphere.

The air around you weighs about 1.20 grams per liter (1.2 ounces per cubic foot) at room temperature and normal atmospheric pressure. This value can be determined rather easily by using a precision balance to weigh a glass container (a separatory funnel) before and after removing the air from it with a vacuum pump. The air in an ordinary two-story house would weigh close to a ton, because of the column of air pressing down on us that reaches high above the earth. Another example of atmospheric pressure can be seen when you turn a partly filled glass of water upside down in a dishpan, the water inside the glass can be made to

stand higher than the level of the water in the pan (Figure 1–1). What is holding up this column of water? If the pressure at *D* and *C* are not the same, water will be pushed from the place where the pressure is greater to the one where it is less. Since the water is free to travel, between *C* and *D*, and it is not doing so, we can assume that the pressure is the same in both places. The atmospheric column several hundreds of miles high is pressing down at *D*. At *C*, the pressure is the combination of that exerted by the column of water, *B*, and that of the air trapped above it at *A*. We can repeat the experiment with the glass completely full of water, and the whole column of water will still be held up. Is there any limit to the height of a column of water which would stay up in a glass tube under these circumstances? According to this analysis, the downward pressure of the column of water cannot be greater than the downward pressure of the atmosphere.

The Greeks and the medieval scientists did not approach the problem this way. They said that if a glass tube was filled

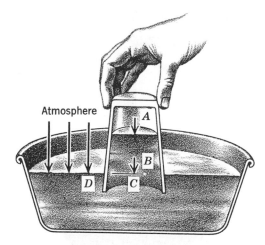

Figure 1–1.   The atmospheric pressure at D exactly equals the pressure at C, which is made up of the sum of the pressure of the trapped air, A, and the column of water, B.

with water and inverted into a bowl of water and the level in the tube dropped, then the space above the water would be empty. They argued that it was a logical absurdity to say that a space was filled with nothing, hence it could not happen. This was epitomized in the saying, "Nature abhors a vacuum." Many a farmer and miner had observed that a lift pump would not raise water more than 34 feet and Galileo was probably the first scientist to remark, rather caustically, that nature's abhorrence of a vacuum seemed to be limited to 34 feet of water.

Measuring Air Pressure

Torricelli (1608–1647), a pupil of Galileo, approached the problem much as we

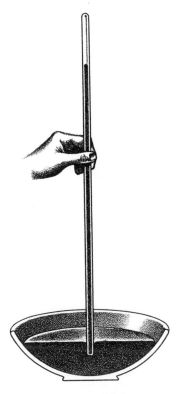

Figure 1–2. Toricelli's barometer.

have. He used mercury instead of water, because its specific gravity (see next section) is 13.6. In this way he could get the same downward pressure with a much shorter, more convenient column. A tube filled with mercury would have to be only a little over

$$\frac{34 \text{ feet} \times 12 \text{ inches/foot}}{13.6} =$$

30 inches long

He found that no matter how much longer the tube was, the atmosphere would support a column of mercury only about 30 inches high (Figure 1–2). In this way he invented the first barometer in 1644.

Pascal (1623–1662) carried on the work in this subject and performed some spectacular experiments with long glass tubes, using water and wine for liquids. He had his brother-in-law take a mercury barometer to the top of Puy de Dôme (4805 feet high). He found that the mercury level dropped. It stood at 59 cm at the top. When he returned, a second barometer, left as a control with an observer at the base of the mountain, had not varied from its reading of 70 cm. Pascal published a description of this and other experiments and concluded with the remark:

Nature has no repugnance for the void; she makes no effort to avoid it. All the effects that have been attributed to this horror proceed from the weight and pressure of the air, and that is the sole and veritable cause; it is from ignorance of it that the imaginary horror of the void was invented, to make an explanation. This is not the only circumstance wherein, man's weakness having failed to find the true causes, he has expressed (the causes) by specious names which fill the ear and not the mind.[1]

Pascal foresaw the usefulness of a barometer in measuring altitude and forecasting the weather.

[1] Morris Bishop, *Pascal, the Life of Genius*, Reynal and Hitchcock, New York, 1936.

UNITS

Some unfamiliar terms (gram, liter, specific gravity, etc.) were introduced in the preceding section, and they must be defined. Sometimes terms such as these will be defined precisely, at other times a simplified definition will be given, and there will also be situations where a working definition will be introduced and the concept will be refined and improved as ideas about it develop. Science is a pragmatic activity and it frequently happens that definitions are altered in the light of increased knowledge about the subject.

The definition of the term meter is a case in point. This is a unit of length and it is approximately 39 inches. It was originally intended to be 1/10,000,000 of the distance between the North Pole and the equator. Until recently the precise definition stated that it was the distance between two scratches on a certain metal bar kept in a vault in Paris. Accurate copies of this bar were kept in several parts of the world, but they were really secondary standards and the task of comparing them with the original was cumbersome. The presently accepted definition of a meter is that it is 1,650,763.37 times the wave length of the orange-red line in the spectrum of krypton 86. Thus the primary standard is generally available in interested laboratories around the world.

The standard mass is a metallic cylinder that is defined as a kilogram. This, too, has many replicas around the world. The method by which a standard and an unknown are compared will be discussed later (page 18). One method that is simple but lacks the highest precision is to use an equal arm balance. There are a thousand grams in a kilogram.

The standard of volume is, of course, in terms of length. A cubic centimeter (cc) is the volume occupied by a cube that is one centimeter on a side. Another unit of volume is the liter. A liter is the volume occupied by 1000.027 cc, and it can be considered 1000 cc for our purposes.

The term specific gravity refers to the weight of any volume of a substance compared to the weight of the same volume of water. A cubic centimeter of mercury weighs 13.6 grams, and the same volume of water weighs 1 gram, so the specific gravity of mercury is

$$\frac{13.6 \text{ grams per cc}}{1 \text{ gram per cc}} = 13.6$$

The units cancel out and specific gravity is only a number, a ratio. Density, on the other hand, is the weight of some generally accepted unit of volume. In the metric system this volume is usually the cubic centimeter for solids and liquids and the liter for gases.

TEMPERATURE AND THE THERMOMETER

The human nervous system is unreliable both qualitatively and quantitatively as an indicator of temperature. To convince yourself of this, try leaving a small block of wood in the refrigerator until it has reached the same temperature as the metal shelves. Then touch the wood and the shelf and notice how much colder one of them feels than the other.

Galileo constructed an instrument for measuring temperature (Figure 1–3) which was, in reality, a barometer that was unusually sensitive to temperature. He made no effort to establish a scale, and apparently used his device merely to tell whether the temperature was going up or down. The early workers with barometers noticed that the temperature affected the instrument slightly, and it was common

Figure 1–3.   Galileo's thermometer.

knowledge that substances, in general, expanded and contracted with changing temperature.

How does one go about constructing two thermometers that give comparable readings? A scientist in Italy might wish to correspond with a colleague in England concerning the proper temperature to grow a certain kind of plant. The temperature scales and their two thermometers must be set up according to some common system. There must be a standard range in temperature just as there is a standard meter in distance. A little thought on the subject will convince you that there must be two fixed points on the scale and that the interval must be divided into some arbitrary number of degrees.

However, it is rather difficult to decide on the temperatures that can serve as the fixed points until a temperature scale has been developed, and several experiments (preferably repeated in different labora-

tories) have shown that these points are, in fact, fixed. Science was fortunate that preliminary experiments were made with water, and that the freezing point and boiling point of water are reasonably constant under normal variations in laboratory conditions. Newton observed that a mixture of snow and water always gave the same reading on his thermometer, and Amontons found that water always boiled at the same temperature, no matter how long he boiled it or how hot the fire was. These two points of reference were the basis for the centigrade scale invented by Celsius in 1742. He divided the interval into 100°. This is the scale used throughout most of the world and by scientists everywhere. Fahrenheit developed a scale which was sensible in that it tried to avoid negative numbers, but it was most illogical otherwise. He took for his zero the coldest temperature he could obtain by mixing ice and salt. For his upper reference point he chose body temperature, and called it 96°. In this scale, the boiling point of water turned out to be 212°. For some strange reason, the English-speaking countries have clung to this way of recording temperature.

There are numerous ways of changing back and forth from the centigrade to the Fahrenheit scales. Since $32°F = 0°C$, always subtract 32 from any Fahrenheit reading. Between the freezing and the boiling points of water, the centigrade scale has 100° and the Fahrenheit has 180°. Thus, there are $180/100 = 9/5$ (nearly 2) Fahrenheit degrees for every centigrade degree:

$$68°F = (68 - 32) \, 5/9 = 20°C$$
$$104°F = (104 - 32) \, 5/9 = 40°C$$
$$15°C = 15 \times 9/5 + 32 = 59°F$$

For very high temperatures the centigrade reading is slightly more than half the Fahrenheit reading.

GAS LAWS

Boyle's Law

Since the air around us is a gas that is constantly changing in temperature and pressure, we shall have to see what influences these factors have on the behavior of gases. The quantitative treatment that was made possible by these researches was essential for the development of the atomic theory that followed soon after. We all know that increasing the pressure on a gas decreases its volume, and that as we decrease the pressure the gas tends to spring back to its original volume. Robert Boyle (1627–1691) investigated this situation quantitatively.

The type of experiment performed by Boyle is illustrated in Figure 1–4. A volume, V_1, of gas is confined in the short arm of a J-shaped tube. Its pressure is P_1 (Figure 1–4a). The pressure of the gas is counterbalanced by the pressure of the atmosphere, P_4, and the pressure of the mercury, P_5, which stands higher in the long arm than in the short arm. $P_1 = P_4 + P_5$. In part b of this figure, more mercury has been added to the long arm, so that the pressure of the mercury is now P_6, and the atmospheric pressure, P_4, remains the same. The gas has been compressed to V_2 and it is now exerting a pressure $P_2 = P_4 + P_6$. In part c, the gas has been further compressed to V_3, and it is exerting a pressure P_3. $P_3 =$

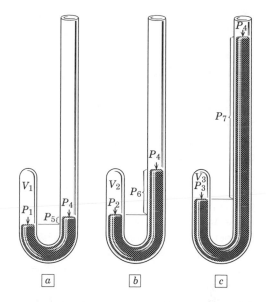

Figure 1–4.   *An experiment to demonstrate Boyle's law.*

$P_4 + P_7$. Expressing the volume in cubic centimeters and the pressure in centimeters of mercury, Table 1–1 shows the type of data that Boyle obtained in his experiments.

In analyzing his results he found that, in any one series of experiments, if he multiplied the pressure of the gas by its corresponding volume ($P_1 \times V_1 = 800.0$, $P_2 \times V_2 = 797.9$, $P_3 \times V_3 = 805.8$) the product was a constant within the limits of accuracy of the experiment. This can be generalized into $P \times V = k$, or $V = k/P$, or $V \propto 1/P$. For a given amount of

Table 1-1

	a	b	c
Atmospheric pressure in cm of mercury	$P_4 = 76$	76	76
Pressure of mercury	$P_5 = 4$	$P_6 = 25$	$P_7 = 82$
Total pressure on gas	$P_1 = 80$	$P_2 = 101$	$P_3 = 158$
Volume of gas in cc	$V_1 = 10.0$	$V_2 = 7.9$	$V_3 = 5.1$

gas at constant temperature, the volume is inversely proportional to the pressure.

Charles' Law and Absolute Zero

The earliest thermometers made use of the expansion of air that was kept at constant pressure. This behavior was studied quantitatively by Charles (1746–1823) and Gay-Lussac (1778–1850), and they discovered that for a given amount of gas kept at constant pressure the fractional increase in volume with increasing temperature was a constant. This is better illustrated with an example. Starting with 273 cc of any gas at 0°C, and increasing or decreasing the temperature by 1°C, the resulting volume would be 274 or 272 cc, respectively. At constant pressure, the change in volume was ⅟₂₇₃ for every degree change of temperature.

The figures in Table 1–2 raise the question of what would be the resulting volume if we lowered the temperature of 273 cc of gas from 0°C to −274°C, keeping the pressure constant all the time. According to the law of Charles and Gay-Lussac, there would be no volume left at −273°C. This was the first indication that there might be a bottom to the temperature scale. This lowest possible temperature, −273°C (?°F), is called absolute zero. On the absolute scale, water freezes at +273° and boils at 373°. It is this absolute temperature that is represented by T, and centigrade temperature

Table 1-2

INITIAL VOLUME, CC	CHANGE IN TEMPERATURE, °	FINAL VOLUME, CC
273	+1	274
273	−1	272
273	−10	263
273	−100	173
273	−274	(?)

by t. The law of Charles and Gay-Lussac can now be stated as $V \propto T$, or $V = kT$. The two gas laws can be combined in an equation $V = kT/P$ or $PV = kT$, where k is a constant. The value of k depends on the units used for the other three terms.

SUMMARY

1. Weather lore is extremely unreliable as a basis for predicting the weather.
2. The lowest layer of the atmosphere is called the troposphere. Significant vertical mixing and weather phenomena are confined to this layer.
3. The normal pressure of the atmosphere at sea level will support a column of water 33.8 feet high, or a column of mercury 29.92 in. (76.0 cm) high.
4. Variations in atmospheric pressure are measured by the barometer.
5. The unit of length is the meter, and it is defined as 1,650,763.37 times the wave length of the orange-red line in the spectrum of krypton 86.
6. The unit of mass is the kilogram and there is a metal cylinder that is the standard.
7. Specific gravity is the ratio of the weight of any volume of a substance compared to the weight of the same volume of water.
8. Density is the weight of a standard volume of a substance. This is usually the weight in grams per cubic centimeter.
9. The fixed points on the centigrade temperature scale are the freezing point of water taken as 0° and the boiling point of water taken as 100°.
10. The Fahrenheit temperature scale uses the same two fixed points but assigns them the values of 32° and 212° respectively.
11. Interconversion between the centigrade and Fahrenheit scales may be made by using the formula $(°F − 32) \frac{5}{9} = °C$.
12. Boyle's law states that for a given quantity of gas at constant temperature the volume is inversely proportional to the pressure.
13. There is a lowest possible temperature called absolute zero. It is −273.18°C.

14. Charles' law states that for a given quantity of gas at constant pressure the volume is directly proportional to the absolute temperature.
15. The two gas laws can be combined in the equation $P \times V = k \times T$.

QUESTIONS AND EXERCISES

1. Explain the action of a siphon.
2. If a balloon had a volume of 1 cubic foot at the base of Puy de Dôme, what volume would it have at the top of the mountain if there was no change in temperature?
3. Calculate an approximate value for the weight of a cubic foot of air at the top of Puy de Dôme.
4. Calculate the approximate height in inches of Pascal's barometer column at the top of Puy de Dôme.
5. If the atmospheric pressure was 76 cm of mercury, what would have been the height of Pascal's barometer column when it was filled with wine (density = 0.984 g per cc)?
6. Make the following temperature conversions: $100°C = ?°F$, $0°F = ?°C$, $-40°C = ?°F$.
7. Is 20°C twice as hot as 10°C? Is 473°C twice as hot as 100°C? Explain.
8. Calculate the change in volume of a balloon having a volume of 5 cubic feet, if the temperature changes from 20°C to 30°C.
9. Calculate the volume of the balloon in Problem 2 if the temperature at the base of the mountain was 20°C and at the top 10°C.
10. What is the weight of air in an automobile tire whose volume is 4 cubic feet when the air is under a pressure of three times atmospheric?

Chapter 2

The Evidence for Atoms

THERE are a number of important concepts that we now take for granted, but which evolved only slowly to their present form. The idea of a pure substance is a case in point. A pure substance has nothing else mixed with it. Different samples of the same pure substance have the same physical properties of color, melting point, boiling point, etc. Water can be purified by distillation, and it was purified water that was used to establish the reference points on the temperature scale. Sea water would have given different values. White table sugar (sucrose) is purer than brown sugar.

CONSTANT COMPOSITION AND THE CONSERVATION OF MASS

Different samples of a pure substance also have the same composition. The techniques used in chemical analysis will be considered later, but in the meantime we shall examine the results of some analyses. A sample of pure methane (natural gas) always analyzes for 75% carbon and 25% hydrogen. The analysis of pure sucrose shows 42.1 + % carbon, 51.4 + % oxygen, and 6.4 + % hydrogen.

The idea that matter is indestructible, that it can neither be created nor destroyed, is fundamental to any quantitative study. Yet, the common experience of watching a heavy log burn down to a light pile of ashes seems to contradict the law of the conservation of mass. The great French chemist, Lavoisier (1743–1794), carried out a significant experiment involving the oxidation of tin. He placed a weighed quantity of tin in a large glass vessel and sealed it off. He then weighed the vessel, heated it for several hours until the tin had turned into tin oxide, and weighed it again. Next, he broke the glass seal, noticed that air rushed in, and re-weighed the flask. Finally he weighed the tin oxide that was formed. With letters to represent the weights actually recorded, his experiment can be outlined as follows:

1. Weight of tin $= a$
2. Weight of tin + air + flask before heating $= b$
3. During the heating the tin changed to tin oxide
4. Weight of tin oxide + air + flask after heating $= b$
5. Flask opened and air rushed in
6. Weight of flask and contents after opening $= b + c$
7. Weight of tin oxide $= a + c$

Steps 2 and 4 show that there is no change in weight during the reaction. The weight of the air that rushed into the flask, c, was the same as the weight of the air that combined with the tin when it changed to tin oxide. From a bookkeeping point of view, everything is accounted for. In this experiment Lavoisier not only made out a good case for the law of the conservation of mass but he also used a technique, the quantitative approach, that was absolutely essential for the developments that were to come. Our confidence in the law of the conser-

vation of mass is based in innumerable experiments that have been carried out with the highest possible degree of precision.

ELEMENTS

Lavoisier also helped to make clear our present-day meaning of the word element. For thousands of years mankind had been trying to show that the many different substances that we encounter around us were made up of varying combinations of a few simple units. A pile of bricks, mortar, and water can be combined into such diverse structures as a pavement, a wall, a bridge, a house, or a tower. Might it not be that stones, leaves, water, and air could be broken down into a few basic building materials?

By gently heating a crystal of "blue stone," crystalline copper sulfate, we can observe a clear liquid collecting near the top of the tube and the white powder that is left behind (Figure 1–5). The identity of the liquid can be determined by measuring appropriate physical properties, boiling point and freezing point, for instance. It turns out to be water. After the white powder has cooled it will become blue once more when a few drops of water are placed on it. The products of the change brought about by heating are obviously simpler than the original crystalline material. Can these products be further simplified? Passing an electric current through water breaks it up into two gases, hydrogen and oxygen. These can be recombined to produce water, so water is complex.

In making lime we heat limestone. A gas, carbon dioxide, is driven off, and lime is left behind. Burning charcoal in oxygen produces carbon dioxide, and burning the metal calcium in oxygen

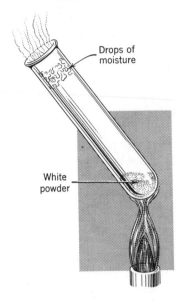

Figure 1–5.   Heating bluestone in a test tube breaks it up into a white powder and water.

Labels in figure:
Drops of moisture

White powder

produces lime. Hence limestone, carbon dioxide, and lime are complex substances. They can be broken down into simpler parts, or they can be built up out of simpler parts. The word element refers to the relatively few basic substances that cannot be broken down or built up from other things. Since the evidence is all negative, it is extremely difficult to demonstrate that a substance is an element.

Lavoisier stated the problem in the above terms and compiled a list of substances that he thought were elements. Most of these have stood the test of time, but a few have been found to be compounds, and many more elements have since been discovered.

DALTON'S ATOMIC THEORY

John Dalton (1766–1844), while trying to picture how one gas could diffuse through another, hit upon the idea that each gas might be composed of particles that had a characteristic size and shape. This would allow any one particle to jostle its way through the crowd. He drew pictures of these particles, which he called atoms, showing how similar ones could not interpenetrate but different types could. He assumed that all the atoms of a given element had the same properties of size, shape, and possibly, weight. There were many chemical analyses available and he turned to these figures for support for his new theory.

The two common oxides of carbon are carbon monoxide and carbon dioxide. In carbon monoxide 12 parts by weight of carbon are associated with 16 of oxygen. In carbon dioxide 12 parts of carbon are combined with 32 of oxygen. The ratio of the weights of oxygen which combine with the same weight of carbon is $16/32 = 1/2$. This is a ratio of small whole numbers. To illustrate this further, 32 grams of oxygen combine with 4 grams of hydrogen to form water and with 2 grams of hydrogen to form hydrogen peroxide. Here, again, the ratio of the weights of hydrogen that combine with the same weight of oxygen is $4/2 = 2/1$.

In methane (the main constituent of natural gas) we find 12 grams of carbon combined with 4 grams of hydrogen. We now have a three-cornered relationship. The same weight of oxygen (32 grams) that combines with 12 grams of carbon also combines with 4 grams of hydrogen, and these two elements combine with each other in exactly this proportion by weight. This is diagramed below.

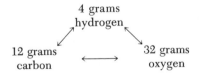

4 grams
hydrogen

12 grams   32 grams
carbon   oxygen

The above figures are merely a sample of the vast amount of analytical data that was available and that continued to accumulate. It all made sense to Dalton and the other scientists of his time if they assumed that each element was made up of atoms that were all alike in size and weight, but were different from the atoms of any other element. In preparing a table of the characteristic weights of the elements it was realized that these atoms must be extremely small and that it would be out of the question to weigh a single, isolated one. The important thing was to compare the weights of the different kinds. Since hydrogen was the lightest substance known (and still is), they placed its atomic weight at 1 and figured the rest of the atomic weights with hydrogen as a standard of comparison. For reasons of convenience we have been using the atomic weight of oxygen as 16.000 as the standard for many years. There were many pitfalls along the path, and it was fifty years before the scheme was put on a rational basis. But, with all its faults, Dalton's atomic theory gave science an acceleration and a direction for advance. Recently, circumstances have made another standard even more practical and this will be introduced later. This recently adopted standard makes only a minute difference in the numerical values of the atomic weights.

MOLECULES

Applying Dalton's atomic theory to the data we just considered, we get information about the make-up of the molecules of carbon monoxide, carbon dioxide, water, hydrogen peroxide, and methane. A molecule is the smallest stable unit that contains more than one atom. If all carbon atoms have a weight of 12 units and the oxygen atoms a weight of 16, then carbon monoxide would have 1 atom of each element and carbon dioxide would have 1 atom of carbon and 2 of oxygen. Since 32 grams of oxygen combine with 4 grams of hydrogen to form water, we would expect that it contained 2 atoms of oxygen and 4 of hydrogen. This caused considerable confusion at the time, and it was considerably later that other lines of evidence showed that a molecule of water is actually half this size, with 1 atom of oxygen to 2 of hydrogen—or H_2O, as it is written in a chemical formula. Hydrogen peroxide has 2 atoms of hydrogen to 2 of oxygen, and methane has 1 atom of carbon to 4 of hydrogen, as we would expect. An atom (the word means indivisible) is the smallest particle of an element, and a molecule is the smallest particle of a substance whose particles contain more than one atom. Some molecules contain only 2 or 3 atoms, CO and H_2O, for instance. The atoms may be different or the same element as in O_2 and N_2.

CHEMICAL CHANGE

In earlier parts of this chapter there have been several examples of chemical change, or chemical reaction, mentioned. The formation of tin oxide from tin and oxygen and the decomposition of crystalline copper sulfate to form water and anhydrous copper sulfate were two of the reactions described. When there is a change in the arrangement of the atoms so that certain combinations are broken up or new ones formed, this is called a chemical reaction. Later on, when we have developed a short-hand language for referring to the elements and describing the molecules, these will be much easier to think about. Both the formation of water from hydrogen and oxygen and the decomposition of limestone into lime and carbon dioxide are examples of chemical reaction.

It is clear from the sample reactions mentioned that a rearrangement of the atoms may involve great changes in the superficial properties of the substances concerned. The shiny metal, tin, and the colorless gas, oxygen, form the white powder, tin oxide. When oxygen combines with hydrogen, the clear liquid, water, is formed. Crystalline copper sulfate is blue and the anhydrous form is white. A study of the chemical and physical properties of compounds challenges the chemist to learn how to build new ones with desirable properties.

SUMMARY

1. Different samples of the same pure substance have the same chemical composition and physical properties.
2. The law of the conservation of matter may be stated in the following terms: in any transformation there is no change in the total amount of matter.
3. An element is a substance that cannot be broken down or built up from other substances.
4. A molecule is the smallest stable unit that contains more than one atom.
5. The smallest particles that matter can be broken down into by chemical means are called atoms.
6. The atoms of each element have chemical and physical properties that are characteristic of that element.
7. The atomic weight of an element is the weight of some convenient number of its atoms compared to the weight of the same number of atoms of some arbitrarily chosen standard.
8. A chemical change, or reaction, involves a change in the arrangement of the atoms.

QUESTIONS AND EXERCISES

1. Was Lavoisier's experiment any help in deciding whether tin is an element or a compound?
2. If Lavoisier had used an open flask instead of a sealed one during his experiment, which one of the weights would have been different?
3. Calculate the per cent hydrogen in hydrogen peroxide.
4. Name four elements that can be bought in a jewelry store.
5. Suppose you pour vinegar over a substance in a test tube and observe bubbling and a gas given off. Does this prove that the substance is a compound?
6. If you have 100 cc of a liquid that you suspect is water, how can you identify it? (Do not taste anything in the laboratory.)
7. How many meanings can you give to the symbol for an element, C, for instance?
8. To each of the following attach one or more of the terms atom, molecule, element, compound: CH_4, H_2, CaO, Ca, CO, He.

Chapter 3

Motion and Energy

WHEN an object is at rest, does it tend to remain at rest unless something happens to it? When an object is moving, does it remain in motion unless something happens to it? The idea that it takes a force to change the state of motion of an object took a long time to develop. Experimenting with an object like a hockey puck and giving it the same strength push each time over substances of differing smoothness, one would find that it traveled a few feet on concrete, many feet on a bowling alley surface and even farther on slick ice. Reducing the frictional resistance between the puck and the surface over which it is traveling results in it continuing its motion for a greater distance. It tends to continue in its forward motion and we are forced to explain why it stops. We also observe that the forward motion is in a straight line unless we hit the puck sideways or it strikes something.

THE FIRST LAW OF MOTION

Sir Isaac Newton (1642–1727) arrived at a concise and generalized description of the motion of objects in his first law of motion, that states:

A body tends to remain at rest or in uniform motion in a straight line unless acted upon by some force.

This description has come to be accepted

as accurate and we now use it principally to detect and observe forces. If an object either increases or decreases its speed or changes its direction of motion, we consider that this is evidence that a force has been acting.

The first law of motion describes the property of matter called inertia. When you are sitting still you have no feeling of motion, yet you know that the earth is rotating on its axis and traveling around the sun at a speed of several miles per second. When a smoothly running car stops suddenly, you are not "thrown" forward, you tend to keep going forward at the same speed the car was traveling. The sieve-like basket of an automatic washing machine holds the clothes and forces them to travel in circles; but the water can escape through the holes, and it moves, as both it and the clothes tend to do, in straight lines.

To measure the speed of an object that is moving in a straight line one observes the time that it takes to travel a measured distance. The result is expressed in centimeters per second, miles per hour, etc. The idea of velocity includes both speed and direction. The velocity of a car is given by the statement that it is traveling west with a speed of 40 miles per hour. We could, for instance, observe that it traveled along a road going west for a distance of 10 miles in 15 minutes. Clearly, this figure of 40 miles per hour is an average velocity. No car can maintain an absolutely uniform speed for that distance, nor could it be steered in a perfectly straight line. All of our velocity

measurements are of this type; all of our track records are like this.

If the velocity is changing, we say that the motion is accelerated. The common use of this word implies an increase in speed, but, using the word precisely, it applies to any change in velocity.

Acceleration is defined as the rate of change of velocity. This would be expressed in such units as meters per second per second (m per sec^2), for instance. If a car is going 5 miles per hour and 10 seconds later it is going 25 miles per hour, it has changed its speed by 20 miles per hour in 10 seconds. Its acceleration is 2 miles per hour per second or 2 miles per hour $\times$ seconds.

THE SECOND LAW OF MOTION

Newton's second law of motion gives a quantitative description of the acceleration of an object. It states that when a force acts on an object, the acceleration is proportional to the force and inversely proportional to the mass of the object, and the acceleration is in the direction that the force is acting. The first part of this can be summarized in the equation $a = f/m$ or $f = am$.

Newton's second law provides us with our most accurate measure of mass and an operational definition of force. The standard mass was discussed on page 7. The unit of force, a newton, is a force that will give a mass of one kilogram an acceleration of one meter per second per second. A dyne is the force that will give a mass of one gram an acceleration of one centimeter per second per second. Therefore 10^5 dynes equal one newton. To compare a mass M_2 with a standard mass M_1, the experiment illustrated in Figure 1–6 would be used. The force of the compressed spring is the same in both directions, so that

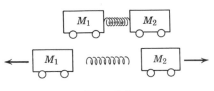

Figure 1–6.

$$a_1 M_1 = f = a_2 M_2$$

$$M_2 = \frac{M_1 a_1}{a_2}$$

The two accelerations can be measured and the value of M_2 obtained. There are other ways of carrying out this comparison, but this method serves to illustrate the principle.

THE THIRD LAW OF MOTION

The third law of motion states that to every action there is an equal and opposite reaction. Forces occur in pairs, never singly. Some applications of this law are fairly obvious, but others require more thought to follow through. If someone dives from the back of a rowboat, he travels in one direction and the boat travels in the opposite one. As he sits in a chair, his downward push on the chair is matched by its upward push on him. When a gun is fired, the recoil represents the backward thrust on the gun that is equal and opposite to the forward thrust on the bullet.

Another term, momentum, can be conveniently introduced at this point. Any moving mass has momentum and the amount of momentum is defined as the product of the mass and the velocity. A mass of 30 grams, moving in a straight line with a velocity of 12 cm per sec has a momentum = 30 grams × 12 cm per sec = 360 gram cm per sec.

WORK AND ENERGY

After a precise treatment of a few more common terms we can begin to make the quantitative study of gases that is necessary for an understanding of the weather. Work is one of those terms in common use that has a somewhat different meaning in science. For work to be done, a force must act through a distance; and the amount of work is defined as the force multiplied by the distance through which it acts. Work = force × distance. Figure 1–7 illustrates this point. It is "hard work" to stand still and hold a fifty-kilogram mass, but this is not work in the scientific sense. Energy is an extremely important word that is in common use—atomic energy, solar energy, kinetic energy, electrical energy, etc. Energy is defined as the ability to do work. Innumerable experiments have established the fact that energy can be neither created

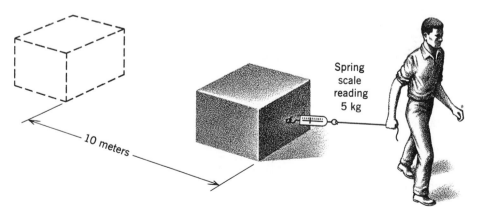

Figure 1–7. Work equals force times distance.
This illustration shows 5 kilograms × 10 meters = 50 kilogram meters of work being done.

nor destroyed. This statement is known as the law of the conservation of energy. (The interconversion of mass and energy will be discussed later.) From this law of the conservation of energy we can get some help in calculating how much energy a system has. How much work is a two-pound book able to do in dropping three feet to the floor? In other words, what is its energy because of its position (potential energy)? If we calculate the amount of work that would have to be done on the book to raise it from the floor to its present position, the law of the conservation of energy tells us that this will be the amount of work that it is able to do in returning to the floor. This amount of work would be 3 feet $\times$ 2 pounds = 6 foot-pounds.

In the old-fashioned grandfather's clock in which the weights are wound up once a week, the potential energy of the weights is slowly transformed into the energy of the moving parts of the clock, of the sound waves of the ticking, and of the striking bell. Each weekend, when the clock is wound up, we do as much work on the weights in a few seconds as they do in seven days. The rate of doing work is very different. The term that applies to the rate of doing work is power. The familiar unit of power is horsepower. One horsepower is 550 foot-pounds per second.

A substance can do work because it is in motion. The energy that a substance has because of its motion is called kinetic energy; erosion by wind and by running water are examples of the results of kinetic energy. If we know the mass, m, and the velocity, v, of a substance, we can calculate its kinetic energy from the equation: kinetic energy = $\frac{1}{2}mv^2$. There are several other types of energy that we will encounter in this book, but it will be better to discuss them when we encounter them.

SPECIFIC HEAT

There was a great deal of confusion in the early nineteenth century about the use of the word heat. What was the difference between two bars of iron, one of which was hotter than the other? Some said that there must be a substance, which they called caloric, that could flow from one thing to another. The amount of caloric in a body was thought to determine how hot it was. While supervising the boring of cannon in Munich, Count Rumford became impressed with the tremendous amount of heat evolved by the process. There seemed to be no limit to the quantity of heat that could be generated, and he suggested (1798) that the heat came from friction and that it was an evidence of motion.

Because gases were so much more compressible than liquids or solids, it was assumed that the particles in gases were relatively far apart. The particles in liquids were thought to be touching each other but free to roll around like marbles in a box. In a solid, the particles were considered to be held in a fixed position with respect to each other. It was the motion of these particles that constituted heat. They were hotter when they moved faster.

The following experiments describe one aspect of the problem of heat that was very confusing to the early scientists and is of considerable importance for our study of the weather. If equal weights of water and dry sand are placed on an electric hot plate to warm up, the temperature of the sand will increase more rapidly than that of the water. If 100 grams of sand at 20°C is poured into 100 grams of boiling water (100°C) and the mixture is stirred, the temperature of the mixture reaches about 80°C. If 100 grams of water at 20°C is mixed with 100 grams of boiling water, the temperature comes to about 60°C. Using equal weights of the components in each case, the water dropped 40° as it heated water by 40°, but it dropped only 20° as it heated sand up 60°. It takes less heat to produce a given change in temperature in sand than in water. The term specific heat refers to the amount of heat necessary to change the temperature of 1 gram of a substance by 1°C. The unit of heat, the calorie, is defined as the amount necessary to raise the temperature of 1 gram of water by 1°C (more precisely, from 15°C to 16°C). In cooling from 100°C to 80°C, the 100 grams of water gave up 20° × 100 grams × 1 cal per g deg = 2000 cal. This amount heated 100 grams of sand through 60°, so the specific heat of sand is

$$\frac{2000 \text{ cal}}{100 \text{ grams} \times 60°} = 0.33 \text{ cal per g deg}$$

SUMMARY

1. Every object in the universe has inertia, which means that it tends to remain at rest or in uniform motion in a straight line unless acted upon by a force.
2. The term velocity includes the idea of direction as well as speed.
3. Acceleration is the rate of change of velocity.
4. The force required to accelerate a body is proportional both to its mass and to its acceleration, and the direction of the acceleration is the same as that of the force.
5. The unit of force is a newton. This is the force that will give a mass of one kilogram (1 kg) an acceleration of one meter per second per second (1 m per sec²).
6. To every action there is an equal and opposite reaction.
7. Momentum: mass × velocity.
8. Work: force × distance.
9. Energy: ability to do work.
10. Power: rate of doing work.
11. Potential energy: energy possessed by a body because of its position.
12. Kinetic energy: energy possessed by a body because of its motion.
13. Calorie: the amount of heat needed to raise the temperature of 1 gram of water 1°C.
14. Specific heat: the number of calories needed to raise the temperature of a substance 1°C.
15. Energy can be neither created nor destroyed.

QUESTIONS AND EXERCISES

1. Explain how it is that you can take a bucket partly filled with water and whirl it around in a vertical plane without spilling any water.
2. Is there anything that is truly at rest?
3. Determine the specific heat of lead BB shot by the technique described in this section. What are a few serious sources of error in this experiment?
4. How far would you have to lift a 50-pound weight in 1 second in order to be exerting 1 horsepower?
5. One British thermal unit (Btu) is the amount of heat needed to raise one pound of water 1°F. How many calories are there in a Btu?
6. What is the change in momentum when a ball weighing 100 grams and moving with a speed of 15 cm per sec strikes perpendicularly against a wall and rebounds with no loss in speed?
7. When you are sitting still, is your motion accelerated? (The answer to this may be either yes or no, and it requires an explanation.)
8. What is the kinetic energy of the ball mentioned in Problem 6?
9. Presume that you apply a force of 1 newton to an object, initially at rest, that weighs 2 kg for a distance of 3 meters, the object then slides for 10 meters and stops after a total of 10 seconds from the beginning of the experiment. How much work did you do?
10. Assuming no frictional resistance for the first three meters in Problem 9, what was the maximum speed acquired by the object?

Chapter 4

Kinetic Theory

and Change of Phase

ONE of the most fruitful techniques that mankind has developed for increasing his understanding of the world around him is the comparison of the behavior of simplified models with that of the real world. To the extent that they jibe, the model is probably an accurate one. The inevitable discrepancies between the model and nature reveal the flaws and the oversimplifications in our model, and suggest the modifications that will make it a closer imitation of reality.

THE IDEAL GAS

The work of Dalton and Rumford opened the way for the development of a model of matter that involved particles and motion. In a gas, the particles are the atoms and molecules. These are relatively far apart and their motion gives them kinetic energy. Since a gas can be made to do work by expanding when it is heated, temperature is a measure of the kinetic energy of the particles.

The kinetic-molecular picture of an ideal model gas can be outlined broadly as follows:

1. A gas is made up of molecules that are in rapid motion.
2. The molecules undergo frequent collisions.
3. The molecules move in straight lines between collisions.
4. The molecules are negligibly small

in comparison with the space occupied by the gas.

5. The molecules have no attraction for each other.

6. There is no loss of kinetic energy as a result of these collisions (the collisions are perfectly elastic).

Let us examine, very briefly, the way in which such a model would be expected to behave. Gases should diffuse—the fragrance of flowers is noticed at a distance. Gases exert pressure—blowing into a rubber balloon distends it. It is this pressure of the rapidly moving molecules in the air on the surface of the well of mercury that holds up the column in the barometer. It is this pressure on the surface of the water in a well that pushes the water to as high as (but no higher than) 34 feet in the pipe of a lift pump. An airplane wing is so shaped that, as it flies, the force of the molecules hitting the bottom side is greater than that of those which hit the top side. This, and this alone, keeps the plane from falling. The pressure of the atmosphere at sea level is 14.7 pounds per square inch.

Boyle's law can be understood in terms of this model. If we measure the volume and pressure of a certain amount of a gas and then compress the same number of molecules into half the volume, the particles will be hitting the piston twice as frequently. The pressure will be doubled.

We shall leave many of the consequences of this model till later, but it might be well to consider a few of the ways in which it turns out to be inadequate. According to point 4 above, repeated doubling of the pressure on a gas should halve its volume each time. Even in the neighborhood of 1 atmosphere pressure this is not strictly true, and as the pressure goes to several atmospheres the discrepancy between the calculated and measured volumes becomes greater. Molecules do have a volume. The word

"negligible" is relative and allowance for the volume of the molecules must be made in a more refined model. When a gas expands it does work in pushing back the atmosphere, and one would expect a cooling effect from the loss in kinetic energy. However, when this is taken into account, there is still a temperature effect unaccounted for. This indicates that point 5 is not strictly true. In the case where there is a small force of attraction between the molecules, they are slowed down as they move apart. This results in a lowering of the temperature. When a gas is both compressed and cooled, the molecules slow down and approach each other more closely, and the intermolecular forces assume increasing importance. The force of attraction between the molecules makes them coalesce into a liquid. This change of phase will be discussed in the next section.

CHANGE OF PHASE

Now let us extend this kinetic picture to include liquids and solids. As a gas cools, the molecules slow down. The order of magnitude of the motion involved can be seen from the fact that the speed of the average water-vapor molecule at 100°C is about 700 m per sec. At a temperature which is unique (depending on the pressure) for each gas, the speed is not great enough to overcome the force of attraction between the molecules, and they stick together. What we observe is that the gas condenses to a liquid. There is still plenty of motion; the molecules are darting around among each other, but they are always touching several neighbors.

As the liquid is cooled the motion becomes slower. Again, another temperature (which again depends upon the pressure) is reached, which is peculiar for each substance, at which the speed is not sufficient to allow a molecule to pull away from the attraction of those around it. The whole mass of the liquid begins to set, like a jelly, into a fixed pattern. We say that it has solidified, or frozen. There is still motion. The particles vibrate about a given point like a leaf caught in a spider web. This motion becomes less and less frantic with dropping temperature until it ceases altogether at absolute zero.

Let us reverse the process and follow the changes as a solid is heated. The motion of the molecules becomes more and more agitated. Occasionally a molecule on the surface of a crystal may be hit so hard by the one below it that it is knocked completely out of place and darts off into space. This passage from the solid directly to the gas phase is called sublimation. Dry ice sublimes without melting and condenses from a gas to a solid without passing through the liquid phase (this is also referred to as sublimation). In dry, cold weather, snow sublimes. Usually, however, the solid remains intact. It expands, but remains solid until the melting point is reached. This is the same temperature as the freezing point. As energy is put into the molecules (or they are heated) their motion increases enough to overcome their mutual attraction, and they break out of the relatively fixed arrangement that was characteristic of the solid.

As the liquid is heated, the molecules move about more rapidly. Some of those at the surface will be hit from behind and knocked out of the liquid. Unless they have a high velocity they will be pulled back, but some will escape. We call this evaporation. Only the fastest moving molecules can evaporate. ("Fast moving" and "hot" mean the same thing.) The average speed of those that remain in the liquid is reduced by the loss of the fastest ones; or, to put it differently, evaporation produces a cooling effect—this is

readily observed when our hands are wet. The evaporation of a few drops of ether on our hands cools them even more than water, because ether evaporates much faster.

VAPOR PRESSURE

In the liquid, molecules dart about rapidly, although their motion is considerably restricted by the pull of their close neighbors. Above the liquid the molecules are relatively far apart. Like the nitrogen and oxygen molecules of the air, these vapor (evaporated liquid) molecules exert a pressure on everything they hit. It is impractical to build a pressure gauge to measure the pressure exerted by any one kind of molecule present in a gaseous mixture, but we can measure the pressure of water vapor by the technique shown in Figure 1–8. On the left (a) there is a regular barometer with the space above the mercury column containing only a relatively few molecules of mercury vapor. On the right (b) a drop of water has been introduced into the mercury column. It has risen to the top and part of it has evaporated. Since these water vapor molecules exert a downward pressure on the column of mercury, it does not stand quite so high as in a. The difference in height represents the vapor pressure of water.

In Figure 1–8, the rate at which the molecules are evaporating from the drop depends on their average speed; that is, it depends on the temperature. The rate at which the water-vapor molecules bump into the drop and condense back to a liquid will depend on their concentration in the vapor. As the concentration of vapor molecules builds up, the rate of condensation increases. Finally, the two rates become equal—as many are leaving as are entering the liquid in any one

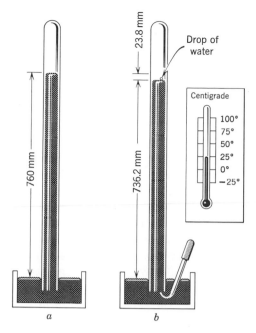

Figure 1–8. An experiment by which the vapor pressure of water may be determined.

second. A dynamic equilibrium is established. This situation may be compared to a busy store where the number of customers remains approximately constant although many are entering and leaving at any one time.

We can see from the above discussion that, for any given temperature, the equilibrium concentration of vapor molecules will have a certain value. The liquid will have a definite vapor pressure for that temperature. If the temperature is raised, the rate of evaporation will increase and more molecules will be in the vapor phase. With more vapor molecules, the rate at which they condense will increase and finally, the rates of evaporation and condensation will again balance. A new equilibrium will be set up at this higher temperature. When the new equilibrium is established there will be a higher concentration of vapor molecules, which means a higher vapor pressure. If we

carry out the experiment outlined in Figure 1–8 at two different temperatures we shall find a greater depression of the mercury column at the higher temperature. Table 1–3 gives the figures for the vapor pressure of water at several different temperatures.

As the temperature of a liquid is increased, its vapor pressure increases until, finally, the vapor pressure is equal to the atmospheric pressure above it. At this temperature the liquid boils. The atmospheric pressure above a liquid has a pronounced effect upon its boiling point. At Denver, Colorado, which is about a mile above sea level, water boils just below 200°F.

When a liquid evaporates, the vapor occupies a much greater volume than the liquid from which it came. For instance, 1 gram of water (how many cubic centimeters?) occupies a volume of about 1.4 liters when it evaporates at the boiling point. Energy in the form of heat must be supplied to the boiling liquid to do this work of expanding against atmospheric pressure. Energy is also required to overcome the mutual attraction of the molecules which are touching their neighbors in the liquid state. The energy that is required to evaporate a liquid at its boiling point without increasing its temperature is referred to as the latent heat of vaporization. This amounts to 539.5 (540 approximate value) cal per g for

Table 1–3   Vapor Pressure of Water in Millimeters of Mercury from 0°C to 100°C

t	vp	t	vp	t	vp
0	4.6	35	42.2	70	234
5	6.5	40	55.3	75	289
10	9.2	45	71.9	80	355
15	12.8	50	92.5	85	434
20	17.5	55	118	90	526
25	23.8	60	149	95	634
30	31.8	65	188	100	760

water. This is indeed a large amount compared to the 100 calories that are required to raise 1 gram of water from the freezing to the boiling point. When condensation (the reverse of evaporation) takes place, the molecules are speeded up (by their mutual attraction) as they approach the liquid, and consequently the average speed of the liquid molecules is increased. The atmosphere does work on the vapor in condensing it to a liquid, and the same amount of heat, 539.5 cal per g, is added to water by condensation.

A change in temperature or a change in phase is an example of physical change as contrasted with chemical change that was mentioned earlier. In a physical change the structure of the molecules is not altered. The difference between the two types of change is an arbitrary but useful one, and it can be illustrated by the difference between giving hair a permanent wave and shrinking wool by washing it in hot water. When hair is given a permanent wave some of the bonds between neighboring sulfur atoms are broken and the hair is held in the desired shape while new sulfur-sulfur bonds form to retain this shape. When wool shrinks it is because whole fibres slide past each other and are held in this new position by barb-like projections.

This detailed, mechanical picture of the gaseous, liquid, and solid states is the basis for understanding much of our ability to predict the weather.

CRYSTALLIZATION

When a liquid solidifies at its freezing point, the particles may assume a random, disordered arrangement; or, more commonly, they may be lined up in a three-dimensional pattern. This ordered arrangement is called a crystal. Salt, sugar, snow flakes, and quartz are common examples of crystals. The solid particles have well-defined faces, and the angles between the faces are characteristic of the substance. This large-scale symmetry results from the way in which the particles at the atomic level build up layer after layer of a repeated pattern as the solid grows from the liquid.

Each crystal, with its typical arrangement of particles, has a characteristic density. Sometimes the particles are less closely packed in the crystal than they are in the liquid. Ice, for instance, has a density of 0.917 g per cc; and the fact that ice floats instead of sinking in water has extremely important consequences. However, crystals are usually more dense than the liquid from which they freeze.

Heat is always liberated when a liquid freezes, and the same amount of heat is absorbed when a solid melts. This is called the latent heat of fusion. This energy change is the result of the work done by the change in volume and that done by the forces between the particles. For water, the latent heat of fusion is 80 cal per g.

HUMIDITY

When we have some form of precipitation, such as rain, snow, hail or fog, water has been evaporated at some distant point, brought to where we are, and condensed. The principal sources of moisture for our atmosphere are the oceans and seas, which cover 70% of the area of the globe. There is not enough evaporation from rivers and lakes to affect more than a small area in their vicinity. Great forests contribute a moderate amount of moisture to the air. It has been estimated that an average of about 5000 tons of water evaporates every day from each square mile of well-watered forest land. As an aid in studying significant weather conditions, we need a quantitative way to express the amount of moisture present in the atmosphere. The humidity is the term used for this. When the vapor pressure of the water in the air is at the equilibrium value for its temperature (Table 1–3), it is called its saturated vapor pressure. The actual vapor pressure of water in any sample of air is usually less than this, and the fraction

$$\frac{\text{actual vapor pressure}}{\text{saturated vapor pressure}} \times 100$$

$$= \text{per cent relative humidity}$$

A value of less than 30% is considered very dry, and one of greater than 80% is very moist, or humid.

THE HEAT PUMP

The energy changes accompanying evaporation and condensation are put to practical use in electric refrigerators and freezers. A suitable liquid (usually Freon) that has been cooled by evaporating through an expansion valve is circulated in coils inside the refrigerator. It is colder than its surroundings, so it picks up heat. The gas is then compressed and condensed to a liquid. The warm liquid passes through coils outside the box and is cooled by (gives up heat to) the air in the room. After being cooled nearly to room temperature, the liquid then passes through the expansion cycle again. When a refrigerator is "running," what you hear is the motor that operates the pump and the fan that blows air over the radiator coils. The refrigerator mechanism may be regarded as a heat pump that removes heat from one place (the inside of the refrigerator) and delivers it to another (the outside of the refrigerator).

It has been obvious for many years that this mechanism could be used for air conditioning a house. By opening the appropriate valves, the coil conditioning the air inside the house can either be warmed by the gas as it condenses or cooled by the liquid as it evaporates. A coil outside of the house takes care of the other half of the cycle. Figure 1–9 shows such a system. During the heating cycle the compressor compresses and heats the gas. The gas circulates through the inside coil, warms the air in the house, and is, itself, cooled and condensed to a liquid. This liquid flows to the outside coil. Here it passes through an expansion valve and absorbs enough energy from the outside air to evaporate. The resulting gas moves to the compressor and goes through the cycle again.

Turning the four-way valve directs the recently compressed gas to the outside coil first, so that the heating takes place there and the cooling half of the cycle in the coil inside the house.

SUMMARY

1. The kinetic theory of an ideal gas includes the ideas: that the molecules are in rapid motion in straight lines between their frequent collisions; that their volume and the forces between them can be neglected; and that the collisions are perfectly elastic.

2. In an actual gas we find that the volume of the molecules and the forces between them must be taken into consideration, except at very low pressures.

3. The saturated vapor pressure of a liquid is the pressure of the vapor molecules when the liquid and vapor are in equilibrium.

4. The boiling point is the temperature at which the vapor pressure of a liquid is equal to the atmospheric pressure.

5. The freezing or melting point is the temperature at which the liquid and solid phases of a substance are at equilibrium with each other under normal atmospheric pressure.

6. Sublimation is the evaporation of a solid directly into the vapor phase, and the term also applies to the reverse process.

7. The latent heat of vaporization is the number of calories required to evaporate 1 gram of liquid at its boiling point.

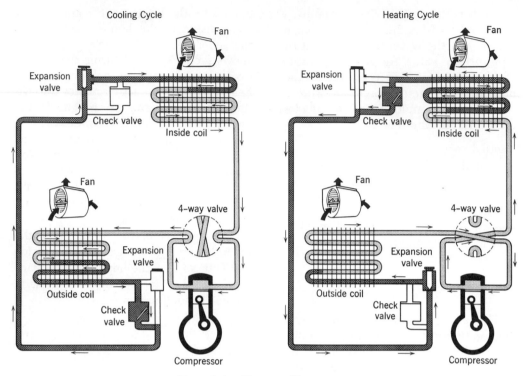

Figure 1–9. Diagram of heat pump.

8. The latent heat of fusion is the number of calories liberated when 1 gram of a substance solidifies at its freezing point.

9. In a crystal there is large-scale symmetry in the arrangement of the particles at the atomic level.

10. Per cent relative humidity of water vapor in the air at any given temperature

$$= 100 \frac{\text{actual vapor pressure}}{\text{saturated vapor pressure}}$$

QUESTIONS AND EXERCISES

1. Why does a balloon expand as it rises above the earth?

2. Why must an airplane be moving very fast before it can rise from the ground?

3. Using graph paper, plot the data supplied in Table 1–3.

4. What would be the boiling point of water at the top of Puy de Dôme? At the base of this mountain?

5. What would have been the height of the mercury column in Figure 1–8, part *b*, if the temperature had been 95°F?

6. If 100 grams of ice is placed in 100 grams of water at 25°C and left there until the water is cooled to 0°C, how much would the liquid water weigh?

7. Describe the action of a vacuum-return coffee maker in terms of the ideas in this chapter.

8. The mass of a water vapor molecule is about nine times that of a hydrogen molecule. If they are both at the same temperature, how would their speeds compare? What would be the average speed of a hydrogen molecule at 100°C?

9. Look up a description of the modern process for making liquid air and notice how it makes use of the principles discussed in this and the previous chapter.

10. If the air temperature is 30°C and the relative humidity is 29%, to what temperature would the air have to be cooled for the relative humidity to rise to 100%?

Chapter 5

Tools of

the Weather Forecaster

INSTRUMENTS to measure humidity are called hygrometers. We could make this measurement by using a drying agent to remove the moisture from a sample of outside air and comparing this with air that is saturated with moisture at the same temperature. This would be direct but too expensive and time-consuming to be practical. There are indirect methods that are more suitable.

FOR MEASURING HUMIDITY

One of these indirect methods makes use of the cooling effect of evaporation. In the wet-and-dry-bulb psychrometer, two thermometers are strapped together, one of which has a moistened wick around its bulb (Figure 1–10). Water is both condensing on and evaporating from the wick. Unless the humidity is 100% there is a net evaporation and cooling, and the lower the humidity the greater is the cooling. Tables have been constructed from which we can read off the humidity from the temperature of the dry bulb and the difference in temperature between the dry and the wet bulb. This method is convenient and precise and is the one used in weather-observation stations. Another method for measuring the humidity depends on the fact that certain fibers change their length with changing humidity. This is a familiar fact to sailors who work with ropes and to girls whose hair has a natural tendency to curl. The weather-bureau instruments use strands

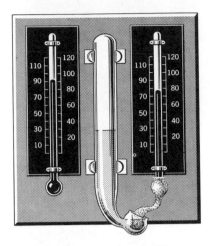

Figure 1-10.   Wet-and-dry-bulb psychrometer.

of naturally blond hair. They are wound around a small drum and fastened off to one side (Figure 1–11). The drum carries a pointer and is turned one way by a spring and the other way by the tension of the hair. Low humidity makes the hair shrink and swings the pointer over the scale. At high humidity the hair stretches and the spring pulls the pointer in the opposite direction. This instrument is capable of only a moderate degree of precision, but it is sufficiently accurate and is so convenient that it is employed for most home weather guides and in the weather-bureau radiosondes that will be described later.

Another method for measuring humidity makes use of the dew point. The dew point is the temperature to which air must be cooled to start condensation. At the dew point the vapor pressure of the water in the air is the same as the saturated vapor pressure for that temperature, as given in Table 1–3. To make this measurement, ice and water are placed in a shiny metal tumbler. The water is stirred with a thermometer, and as soon as the first film of condensed moisture appears on the outside, the temperature of the water is recorded. If this temperature turns out to be 10°C we know that the actual vapor pressure of the water in the air is 9.2 mm. If the actual air temperature is 20°C, then the saturated vapor pressure at this temperature is 17.5 mm and the per cent humidity is

$$\frac{9.2 \text{ mm}}{17.5 \text{ mm}} \times 100 = 52.6\%$$

Of course, air containing water vapor must be cooled to its dew point before rain can fall. But more of that later.

FOR MEASURING TEMPERATURE

Since we are sufficiently well acquainted with the ordinary thermometer, a description of it can be passed over. In order to get a continuous recording of the temperature, we need a revolving drum carrying ruled paper and pen and ink on the end of a lever arm, and a thermometer to actuate them (Figure 1–12). The thermometer is a curved tube filled with alcohol and sealed. With an increase in temperature the alcohol expands more than the metal and tends to straighten out the curve. This motion is transmitted to the lever arm so that the temperature is recorded on the graph paper. The drum moves so slowly that it makes only one revolution in one week.

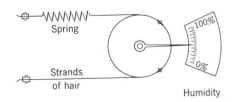

Figure 1-11.   Diagrammatic representation of a hair hygrometer.

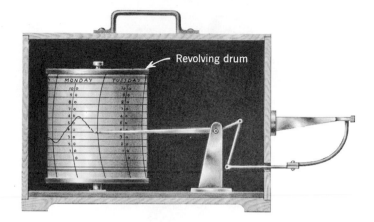

Revolving drum

Figure 1–12. A recording thermometer, or thermograph. The curved tube at the right changes shape with changing temperature.

FOR MEASURING PRESSURE

The mercury barometer has been described. For precise readings a temperature correction must be made, because the column of mercury, the glass tube, and the brass scale expand differently with increasing temperature. The unit now in use for recording atmospheric pressure is the millibar. This corresponds to a pressure of 1000 dynes per sq cm. At sea level the pressure normally varies from about 980 to 1040 millibars. The readings at stations above sea level are corrected for altitude so that they can all be compared. A portable type of barometer is called an aneroid barometer. An evacuated and sealed metal box with a corrugated tap expands and contracts as the outside pressure changes. The top of the box is connected to a pointer that indicates the pressure on a scale. Sometimes the scale is graduated to read in feet above sea level so that the instrument can be used as an altimeter in airplanes or by hikers on trips in the mountains. If the pointer is fitted with a pen that writes on a moving graph paper, the device is a recording barometer or barograph (Figure 1–13).

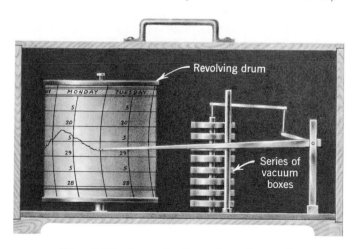

Revolving drum

Series of vacuum boxes

Figure 1–13. A recording barometer, or barograph.

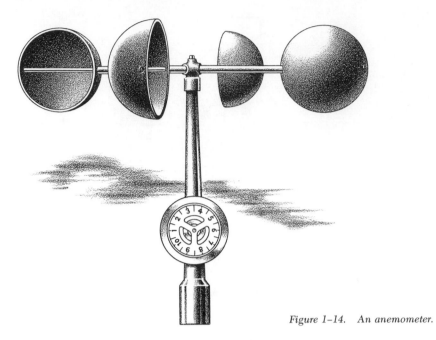

Figure 1–14.   An anemometer.

Beaufort Number	Map Symbol	Descriptive Words	Velocity	Guide For Estimating Velocities
0	∘	Calm	Less than 1	Smoke rises vertically.
1		Light air	1 to 3	Direction of wind shown by smoke but not by wind vanes.
2		Light breeze	4 to 7	Winds felt on face; leaves rustle; ordinary vane moved by wind
3		Gentle breeze	8 to 12	Leaves and small twigs in constant motion, wind extends light flag.
4		Moderate breeze	13 to 18	Raises dust and loose paper; small branches are moved.
5		Fresh breeze	19 to 24	Small trees in leaf begin sway; crested wavelets form on inland water.
6		Strong breeze	25 to 31	Large branches in motion; whistling heard in telegraph wires; umbrellas used with difficulty.
7		Moderate gale	32 to 38	Whole trees in motion; inconvenience felt in walking against the wind.
8		Fresh gale	39 to 46	Breaks twigs off trees; generally impedes progress.
9		Strong gale	47 to 54	Slight structural damage occurs (chimney pots and slate removed.)
10		Whole gale	55 to 63	Trees uprooted; considerable structural damage occurs.
11		Storm	64 to 75	Rarely experienced; accompanied by wide spread damage.
12		Hurricane	Above 75	Devastation occurs.

Figure 1–15.   The Beaufort scale. (From The Physics of Blown Sands and Desert Dunes, *by R. A. Bagnold, by permission of William Morrow and Co., New York.)*

FOR MEASURING WIND AND RAIN

The best way to measure the direction from which the wind is blowing is still the old-fashioned weather vane. For recording the speed of the wind, the most common instrument is the anemometer (Figure 1–14). The rate of revolution of the cups is a measure of the speed of the wind. The speed of the wind in miles per hour is translated into a number on the Beaufort scale and recorded on the weather maps by arrows, as indicated in Figure 1–15.

The amount of rainfall is observed by catching the water in a large can called a rain gauge (Figure 1–16). Figure 1–17 shows how this looks in cross section. The inside tube, A, has an area of 1/10 of the top of the funnel, and so the actual

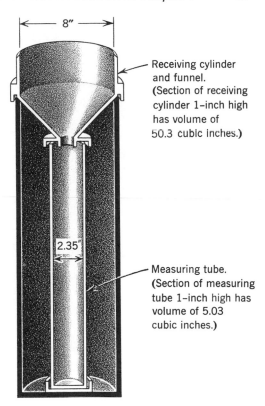

Receiving cylinder and funnel. (Section of receiving cylinder 1-inch high has volume of 50.3 cubic inches.)

Measuring tube. (Section of measuring tube 1-inch high has volume of 5.03 cubic inches.)

Figure 1–17.   Diagram of a rain gauge.

depth of rainfall is 1/10 the amount measured in A.

OBTAINING DATA FROM THE UPPER AIR

Only recently has it been realized that important information might be obtained by sampling the atmosphere up to as high as 50,000 feet. We now know that the first signs of a storm can be detected thousands of feet above us. Neither kites nor airplanes are practical for obtaining these data, so an extremely simple, light-weight radio set called a radiosonde was developed to be carried aloft by a balloon (Figures 1–18 and 1–19). The pressure, temperature, and humidity are reg-

Figure 1–16.   Rain gauge. (U.S. Weather Bureau.)

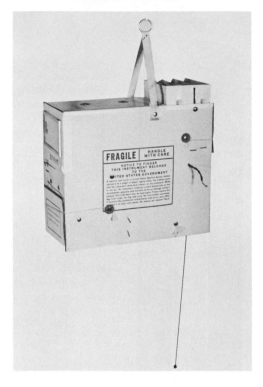

Figure 1–18.

tal United States and its possessions. In addition, hundreds of amateur observers make regular reports of the weather in their localities, and ships at sea send in data by radio. The country is divided into seven major forecasting districts where the data are assembled and forecasts prepared. As the data from any one station come in, they are recorded on a map in symbols such as is illustrated in Figure 1–20. For our purposes it will be necessary to consider only a few of the symbols. With the data pared down to the bone, the notations for the above station would appear as shown in Figure 1–21. From left to right, these mean that the temperature is 31°F, the wind is

istered continuously, and the signals from the small radio sender relay this information to the weather station at regular intervals. The whole apparatus must be simple and cheap enough to be expendable.

The Tiros satellites are an important part of our space study program. From a height of 100 miles or more they photograph large areas of the earth's surface and relay the pictures back to us. The cloud patterns observed in the pictures furnish valuable weather information, particularly over the oceans where surface data are scarce.

WEATHER MAPS

There are about two hundred regular weather stations throughout the continen-

Figure 1–19.

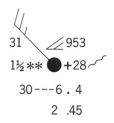

Figure 1–20. An example of the way that data are recorded for a single weather station.

blowing from the northwest with a force of 5 (19–24 miles per hour), and the barometric pressure is 995.3 millibars. In recording the pressure, the 10 or the 9 at the beginning of the number is omitted, so that 235 would mean 1023.5 millibars. The black circle at the point of the arrow means that the sky is completely covered with clouds at this station.

SUMMARY

1. Humidity is usually measured by a wet-and-dry-bulb psychrometer, a hair hygrometer, or a dew-point apparatus.
2. Dew point: the temperature to which air must be cooled to start condensation.
3. Temperature is usually measured by a mercury thermometer or a Bourdon gauge filled with alcohol.
4. Atmospheric pressure is usually measured by a mercury or an aneroid barometer.
5. The direction of the wind is observed by means of a weather vane.

Figure 1–21. A simplified version of Figure 1–20, showing only temperature, barometric pressure, wind direction and force, and cloud cover.

6. The velocity of the wind is measured by means of an anemometer.
7. The amount of rainfall is measured by a rain gauge.
8. A radiosonde is a balloon carrying weather-recording instruments and a radio to send the information back to the weather-bureau station.
9. Weather maps for the United States are prepared each day. On them are recorded in symbols the weather data collected at each of the regular weather stations. From these maps the weather forecasts are prepared.

QUESTIONS AND EXERCISES

1. Name and describe six instruments which are used to obtain weather data at a weather station.
2. If the dew point is within 2° of the air temperature, is the humidity very high or low?
3. What factor besides changing pressure would affect the reading of an aneroid barometer?
4. What two factors would you have to be careful about when using an aneroid barometer for an altimeter when mountain climbing?
5. What is the point of having the measuring tube of a rain gauge one-tenth the area of the catching funnel?
6. For as long as possible a radiosonde is tracked by radar. What additional information is thereby obtained?
7. Start cutting out and saving the weather maps from your local newspaper. As you study farther in this unit see if you can follow the tracks of storms across the country and try your hand at forecasting the next day's weather.
8. What number on the Beaufort scale represents a wind of 15 miles per hour? What would the arrow representing it look like?
9. If the air temperature is 77°F and the humidity is 38.7%, what is the dew point?
10. See how many simple but dependable weather instruments you can construct.

Chapter 6

Elements of

Weather and Climate

IT SHOULD be clear by now that one needs to draw on a wide background of scientific theory to understand and predict the weather. This chapter and the following three will be concerned primarily with the application of the theoretical ideas already presented to such aspects of weather as the seasons, clouds and precipitation, and the wind.

SEASONS

The changing angle at which the rays from the sun strike the earth is responsible for the changing seasons. As the sun is most nearly overhead at noon on June 21, we receive the greatest amount of heat

from it then. However, we know that June 21 marks the beginning of summer, not its height. The seasons lag behind the sun by 2 or 3 months along the seacoast and by a few weeks in the interior of the continent. This geographical difference points to the explanation. Water has a much greater specific heat than soil. Since the oceans heat up more slowly than the continents, even after the sun's warmth has started to wane in July and August the water is still being warmed. Of course, the water also cools off more slowly than the continent, and so the coldest time of winter is delayed along the coast until February. This relatively high specific heat of large masses of water gives coastal regions and islands a much more moder-

Figure 1–22.   Banner cloud. (U.S. Weather Bureau, C. D. Walcott.)

ate climate at all seasons. The water cools the air in summer and warms it in winter. A continental climate is characterized by a short lag of the seasons behind the sun, rapid and extreme changes in tempera-

ture, and great seasonal differences in temperature. For instance, for St. Louis, Missouri, the average July temperature is 80.2, the average January temperature is 32.9; for San Francisco, California (which

Figure 1–23a.   Cirrocumulus clouds. (U.S. Weather Bureau, U.S. Army.)

Figure 1–23b.   Cirrostratus clouds, with a few altocumulus clouds visible below the altostratus layer. (U.S. Weather Bureau, L. A. Boyd.)

Figure 1–23c.   Cirrus clouds. (U.S. Weather Bureau, F. Ellerman.)

is at about the same latitude), the same two average temperatures are 58.9 and 49.8.

CLOUDS

A cloud is only one of the many treasures of nature that most of us take for granted. In spite of the fact that each cloud is a unique and ever-changing entity, clouds have been classified into a few simple types. Once knowledge about these types has been acquired, it will be natural to observe them more carefully, and to use this knowledge in predicting the weather. First of all, how does a cloud form? Figure 1–22 shows a cloud

over Mt. Assiniboin; if we were on top of the mountain we would find the wind blowing hard, but the cloud remains stationary. As moist air rises up the side of the mountain its pressure drops, and it is cooled by expansion (page 23). When it is cooled below the dew point, the moisture condenses into droplets which form the cloud. The process of condensation releases heat (page 26) and the cloud is also warmed by the sun. The drops are carried a few miles through the cloud and eventually evaporate again. Thus, the cloud hangs over the peak, yet it is composed of a constantly changing population of drops that are forming at one edge and evaporating at the other. The conditions for the formation of a

Figure 1–24a.   Altostratus clouds near the horizon. (U.S. Weather Bureau, C. F. Brooks.)

cloud are the cooling of moist air below its dew point. We can see from this that very moist air will form clouds at a lower altitude than fairly dry air. For any given set of conditions of temperature and humidity, there will be a definite height at which cloud formation starts, and you will observe the flat bottom to cumulus clouds and large cloud formations.

Clouds are classified according to their altitude. The prefix alto- is placed before the names of clouds between 6500 and 20,000 feet, and cirro- before those above 20,000 feet. If the cloud formation is composed of individual clouds they are called cumulus clouds, and if they form a uniform layer across the sky they are called stratus clouds. Thus above the 20,000-foot level are (a) cirrocumulus clouds, which are commonly called mackeral sky; (b) cirrostratus clouds, which form a thin, milky sheet; and (c) cirrus clouds, which are the mare's tails, or thin, hooked wisps (Figures 1–23a, b, and c). Since at this altitude the temperature is always below the freezing point, these clouds are composed of ice crystals. The refraction of light through the ice crystals gives rise to the large ring around the sun or the moon.

Between 6500 and 20,000 feet are altostratus clouds, which usually form a thick, dark-gray blanket, and altocumulus clouds, which are large white or gray masses (Figures 1–24a and b). Below 6500 feet the cumulus clouds are the fleecy cotton puffs with flat bottoms. The low, gray layers of clouds (high fog, in the West) are called stratus, and the low, heavy masses of distinct units that practically cover the sky are given the hybrid name of stratocumulus. The word nimbus refers to a cloud from which rain is falling, and cumulonimbus to a huge thunderhead that towers from near the ground up to 30,000 feet or higher (Figure 1–25). Later, we shall see what sort of weather is associated with these types of clouds and how a sequence of them indicates the presence and nearness of a cyclone.

Figure 1–24b. Altocumulus clouds. (U.S. Weather Bureau, A. C. Lapsley.)

Figure 1–25.   Cumulonimbus cloud, with rain shower at its base. (U.S. Weather Bureau, U.S. Navy.)

The minute droplets in a cloud are usually too small to fall to earth as rain. If the moist air that was cooled to form the cloud is cooled further by being elevated, the drops grow in size and eventually become heavy enough to fall. The conditions which usually give rise to rain are the passage of warm moist air: (a) up the windward side of a mountain range, (b) from the warm ocean to cold land, (c) up over a wedge of cold air, and (d) up into the air on ascending currents. Condition (a) is responsible for the heavy rainfall on the western slopes of the Cascade range in Washington and Oregon. Much of the rain in California, the Middle West, and the East comes from conditions (b) and (c). The spring and summer rains in the North Central States and much of the tropical rainfall comes from conditions (d).

It has been found that condensation takes place on the surface of small particles that are able to react with water. The principal sources of these particles are the salts that are thrown into the air from the spray of breaking waves and the smoke from burning coal and petroleum products. Fine dust, except that from volcanoes, is not particularly effective as condensation nuclei. The long white trails left by jet planes are the result of moisture condensing on the particles in the exhaust fumes of the jets.

Figure 1–26. Microphotographs of snow crystals. (U.S. Weather Bureau, W. A. Bentley.)

Figure 1–27.   A cross-sectional view of a large hailstone, showing multilayered structure. (U.S. Weather Bureau.)

SNOW AND HAIL

When moisture condenses directly from the vapor to the solid phase (below 32° F) it forms snow. Snow crystals are characteristically hexagonal and beautiful in design when viewed under a low-powered microscope (Figure 1-26). It is a surprising fact that snow crystals, falling through a cloud of supercooled water droplets will grow very large and will initiate a heavy rainfall from an otherwise stable cloud. This is the basis for one of mankind's very few successes in controlling the weather. Seed nuclei of Dry Ice or silver iodide are introduced into suitable clouds where they trigger the formation of snow. Cloud seeding has been used to increase the rainfall near reservoirs for water and power and it has been suggested as a means of preventing a cloud from building up to serious storm proportions.

Hail is formed by the freezing of rain. When there is much turbulence in a cloud, raindrops may be swept up high enough to freeze. These balls of hail usually accumulate more moisture as they fall; if they make several round trips before finally hitting the ground, they have an onionlike structure and may be very large (Figure 1–27).

SUMMARY

1. The lag of the seasons behind the changing angle of the sun's rays is due to the specific heat of the earth.
2. Since water has a higher specific heat than soil, the lag of the seasons is greater along the coast than in the interior of the continents.
3. Coastal climates have a great seasonal lag and moderate temperature changes throughout the year.
4. Continental climates have a short seasonal lag and rapid and extreme changes of temperature.
5. Atmospheric moisture condenses into small drops to form clouds when air is cooled below its dew point and nuclei are present for the drops to form on.
6. Clouds are classified as cirrus, cirrostratus, and cirrocumulus above 20,000 feet altitude; altostratus and altocumulus between 6500 and 20,000 feet; and stratus, cumulus, stratocumulus, nimbus, and cumulonimbus below 6500.
7. We have rain when the air is cooled sufficiently to produce drops large enough to fall to earth.
8. Techniques have recently been developed for obtaining rain from clouds that would not otherwise have produced it.
9. Snow is formed when water vapor condenses directly to a solid. Snow crystal have a characteristic hexagonal shape.
10. Hail is formed by the freezing of raindrops.

QUESTIONS AND EXERCISES

1. Why do cumulus clouds usually have flat bottoms?
2. If you are in doubt about the height of a cloud, how could its apparent speed help you decide?
3. Would you expect Nevada to receive less rainfall than northern California? Why?
4. What type of cloud is indicated by a ring around the sun?
5. Keep a record for several days of the types of clouds that you see. If a storm comes during this period, compare the sequence of clouds with the description of a storm in Chapter 8.
6. Which of the conditions that produce rain is most important in your area?
7. Under what conditions would it be possible to have a humidity of 105%.
8. What are the three principal differences between a coastal- and a continental-type climate?
9. Discuss the legal complications that may very well develop from any widespread attempt at artificial rain-making.
10. Why is the hottest time of the year in the interior of our continent later than June 21?

Chapter 7

Winds

THE BLOWING of the wind is such a common occurrence that many may well have taken it for granted. But when we stop to think about the blanket of air which covers the globe the questions arise: "Why does the air move around? Where does it come from, and where does it go?"

GENERAL DISTRIBUTION OF WINDS AROUND THE EARTH

As the sunlight pours down on the earth, it heats the air in the tropics more than that in the polar regions. The warmer air in the tropics expands and rises, and the colder air flows toward the Equator

from the Poles. As the warm tropical air rises it continues to expand. As we learned earlier, a gas is cooled by expansion, and so the high-altitude tropical air flows poleward and sinks to replace the cold surface air which moved toward the Equator. This oversimplified scheme of circulation is shown in Figure 1–28. It resembles the circulation in a closed room heated by a single radiator. You can follow such air currents with a candle flame.

The actual pattern of prevailing winds is very different from this simple picture. The warm air that is rising near the Equator and traveling north (and south) is cooled enough to sink down again in the region of the Tropic of Cancer (or the Tropic of Capricorn). The cold air moving toward the Equator from the Polar regions is warmed by its passage over the earth and it starts to rise by the time it has reached a latitude of about 50°N (or S).

The Coriolis effect is another factor that must be taken into account in the general circulation of the winds. The Coriolis effect is an inertial one and results from the fact that different parts of the earth are moving eastward at different speeds. If we were observers on the moon looking at the earth, we would see that the surface features were moving from left to right across our field of vision. As the earth rotates, a spot on the Equator is moving eastward at a rate of 1050 miles per hour. The daily circular path through which St. Louis moves is only about 20,000 miles long, so a spot here is moving 830 miles per hour. At Nome, Alaska, the circular speed is slightly less than 420 miles per hour. The cold polar air moves southward with the rotational speed of the place from which it started, and it moves across land that has a constantly greater eastward speed. The north wind becomes a northeast and finally an east wind. In the northern hemisphere, the wind can be seen to veer to the right as we look in the direction in which it is moving.

Air from north of the Equator flows in to take the place of the heated air which has risen there. This southward-moving air curves in from the northeast just as the polar air did. The heated air rises and moves poleward to cool and descend again. By the time it has traveled approximately to the Tropic of Cancer (or the Tropic of Capricorn) it has cooled sufficiently to sink. It comes down and returns to the Equator along the ground.

In between these two circulating units in each hemisphere there is a third which is carried along by the other two. In the middle latitudes the air is moving north-

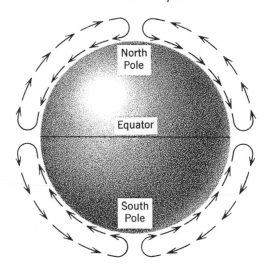

Figure 1–28. An oversimplified scheme of circulation of the winds.

ward along the ground. As it does so, it reaches latitudes that are rotating more slowly. It curves to the right and becomes a wind from the southwest. There are three circulating units in the southern hemisphere, and Figure 1–29 shows the prevailing winds in broad outline. The details of this broad picture are modified by the unequal heating of the oceans and the continents, by mountain barriers, and by the shifting of the sun with the changing seasons.

The line of contact between the polar easterlies and the stormy westerlies is called the polar front. This region of frequent storms shifts north into Canada during the summer, and south into the central United States during the winter. The horse latitudes are a region of gently settling air which is rather dry. The name comes from the days of the sailing vessels, which would frequently find themselves becalmed near the Tropic of Cancer. Any horses in the cargo would be thrown overboard to conserve the supply of drinking water. On the continents, the

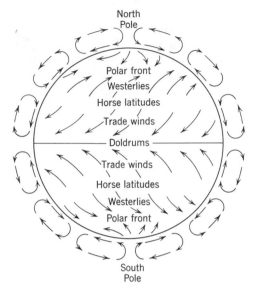

Figure 1–29. *The prevailing winds of the world, in broad outline. These are modified considerably by surface features.*

for the continental United States is the polar front. Here the warm air from the south meets the cold air from the north. The two masses are moving in nearly opposite directions, and a counterclockwise whirlpool of ascending air results. This is a low-pressure area and is given the name cyclone. Do not confuse this use of the word with its common meaning of a rapidly whirling, destructive wind. Tornado and hurricane are names applied to special kinds of cyclones. A descending mass of air with the surface winds blowing out from the center is characterized by high pressure, usually fair weather, and a generally clockwise distribution of wind direction, and is called an anticy-

horse latitudes are the typically dry regions: northern Mexico, North Africa, Arabia, and Central Australia.

Between the Tropic of Cancer and the Equator is the region of the northeast trade winds. This name also comes from the days of the sailing vessels. Here the skipper could count on a steady wind which would carry him nearly to the Equator. Once the ship was near the Equator, the sails would flap in the gently rising air. It was hot, humid, and showery, and no progress could be made for days on end. This region was named the doldrums—from a slang phrase meaning "dull." During the summer, all these regions in the northern hemisphere are compressed and shifted northward, and during the winter they shift southward and spread out. The wind roses in Figure 1–30 show the remarkable consistency of the northwest and southeast trade winds and the high percentage of calm periods in the doldrums.

The birthplace of much of the weather

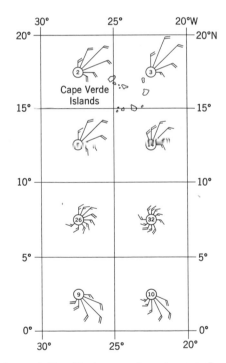

Figure 1–30. *Northeast and southeast trades and doldrums over the Atlantic Ocean, June 1922. The wind rose is given for each 5-degree square. Arrows fly with the wind. The length of the arrow is proportional to the frequency of the winds from that direction. The figure in the center gives the percentage of calms, light airs, and variable winds. (From U.S. Hydrographic Office Pilot Chart.)*

clone. We will examine the weather conditions associated with typical cyclones and anticyclones in the next chapter.

SPECIAL TYPES OF WINDS

A few special types of winds have been given special names and are of sufficient importance to be discussed here. Tornado, hurricane, and typhoon are names applied to the same kind of wind. It is marked by an extremely low pressure at the center, counterclockwise winds of very high velocity, and a heavy rainfall. These can be devastating in their destruction of trees, houses, and ships. Sometimes the destruction is limited to a narrow path of only a few hundred feet in length. Tornado is the name that usually applies to this type of storm. Sometimes the storm covers a front of more than a hundred miles and lasts for a week or more as it moves over the earth. The autumn hurricanes of the east coast are of this type. In mountainous regions there is a peculiar type of wind called a foehn or chinook. As air rushes up one side of a mountain range, it is cooled by expansion. When the cool-

ing carries the temperature below the dew point, there is condensation and rain. The condensation removes most of the moisture from the air and also warms it. When the partially warmed, dry air descends the range on the lee side, it is further warmed by compression, so that a hot, dry foehn wind results (Figure 1–31). In the West these are called chinook (or Santa Ana) winds, they are of considerable economic importance. They usually blow in the wintertime, and they can melt many feet of snow in a single day, thus uncovering feed and water for range cattle.

Along the coast and for a few miles inland there is generally a period of calm followed by a reversal of the wind direction at sunrise and sunset. The land heats up faster than the sea when the sun first strikes them in the morning, and it cools down faster in the evening. The warmed air rises above the land, and a sea breeze (from the sea toward the shore) sets in soon after sunrise. In the evening there is a calm at sunset and then a land breeze springs up. Of course, this is a small-scale phenomenon and it is easily overcome by a storm with strong prevailing winds.

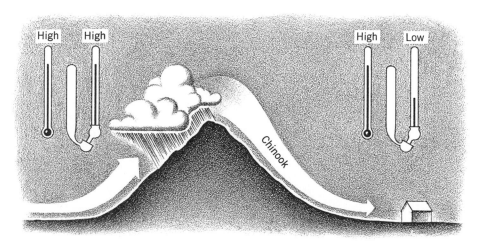

Figure 1–31. Diagram showing conditions necessary for the formation of a foehn, or chinook, wind.

SUMMARY

1. The northern hemisphere has three general systems of winds, which result from the unequal distribution of heat from the sun and from the rotation of the earth.

2. In one of these systems the wind moves southward from the Pole in an ever-increasing westerly direction to about the northern border of the United States.

3. In the second of these systems the settling air moves northward from about the Tropic of Cancer in an ever-increasing easterly direction.

4. In the third of these systems the settling air moves southward from the Tropic of Cancer in an ever-increasing westerly direction toward the Equator.

5. The polar front is the line of meeting of the northeast winds of the polar system with the southwest winds of the central system.

6. A cyclone is a low-pressure area with a counterclockwise system of winds blowing toward it.

7. An anticyclone is a high-pressure area with a clockwise system of winds blowing out from it.

8. A trade wind is a seasonal prevailing wind which blows consistently from a certain direction.

9. A wind system characterized by a very low-pressure area, high wind velocity, and heavy rainfall is variously called tornado, hurricane, or typhoon.

10. A foehn, or chinook, is a warm, dry wind flowing rapidly from a high to a low altitude.

QUESTIONS AND EXERCISES

1. Would you expect the humidity at the Tropic of Cancer and at the Equator to be about the same or very different?

2. Would you expect the equivalent of the trade winds to exist in the upper atmosphere? Would this be of any importance for intercontinental air travel?

3. Why are the conditions typical of a coastal climate less pronounced along the Atlantic Coast than along the Pacific Coast of the United States?

4. At what seasons of the year would the area called the doldrums be right at the Equator?

5. When you pull the plug out of the bathtub, which way does the water whirl as it goes down the drain? Why?

6. From what direction does a chinook wind usually blow?

7. The difference in specific heat between water and soil has been used to explain a number of different things. See how many of them you can list.

8. What determines where the Tropic of Cancer is drawn on the globe?

9. Would a cyclone or an anticyclone be found regularly in the neighborhood of the North Pole?

10. Why does a chinook wind have a high temperature and a low humidity?

11. Show that the rotation of the earth gives an eastward speed to any point on its surface that (in miles per hour) is approximately equal to $1000 \times$ the cosine of the latitude of that spot.

Chapter 8

The Interaction of Air Masses

IT WAS MENTIONED earlier that when a mass of warm, moist air blowing from the southwest meets a mass of polar air blowing from the northeast, a cyclone is developed. Figure 1–32 shows the sequence of events. The cooling of the warm, moist air as it rides up over the polar air results in an increasing amount of precipitation as the cyclone develops. Since the cyclones that affect the weather of the United States seem to originate somewhere in Siberia, they usually reach us in a fairly well-developed stage.

CYCLONE DEVELOPMENT

Figure 1–33 shows a horizontal section through a well-developed cyclone. The symbol ⌣⌣⌣ represents a warm front, which is the line between a mass of cold air and an advancing mass of warm air. The symbol ⋀⋀⋀ represents the cold front where the cold air mass is advancing toward the warm air. Since the cold front advances faster than the warm front, it eventually catches up with it. This situation is called an occluded front, and is indicated by the symbol ⋀⌣⋀ . The solid black lines are lines of equal barometric pressure, isobars, drawn at intervals of 2, 3, or 4 millibars, and they represent a typical distribution of pressures around a cyclone or a low-pressure area.

If a vertical section is taken between points X and Y we have Figure 1–34. Let us consider the series of changes that

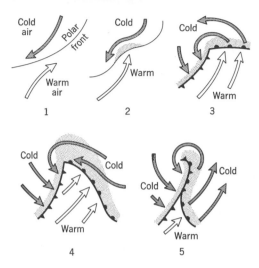

Figure 1–32.   *Five stages in the life of a cyclone. From a kink in the polar front, warm front and cold front develop. The dots represent areas of precipitation. At 4 the storm is at its height, at 5 the cold front is rapidly overtaking the warm front and the storm is dissipating. (After Trewartha.)*

would be observed at Y as the storm moves eastward from its present position. This is indicated by the successive positions of Y as Y1, Y2, Y3, Y4, Y5, and Y6. These changes are outlined in Table 1–4.

A storm of this type may cover an area of a thousand miles on a side, and the changes described may take place over a period of one to four days. If you are located north of the center of the low-pressure area, the storm is less severe and lasts for a shorter time, and there is no intermediate clearing. At the extreme south end of the storm there is very little precipitation.

ANTICYCLONES

An anticyclone, or high-pressure area, consists of a mass of descending air that spreads out along the surface with a dis-

tribution of winds rotating in a clockwise direction. Since this mass of air is descending from an altitude of 30,000 or 40,000 feet, it is rather dry to begin with and the increase in pressure warms it. Therefore, fair weather usually accompanies a high. The clockwise swing of the winds draws in cold air from the north on the east side of the anticyclone and warm air from the south on its west side. If the center of the high is passing north of us, the wind will shift from north to east as the barometer rises, and from east to south as it falls again. The thermometer will change in the opposite direction from the barometer.

INTERPRETING WEATHER MAPS

Using the information that we have just covered, we can study the weather map issued by our local weather-forecasting station and get a good idea of the weather in store for the next twenty-four hours.

Figures 1–35 through 1–38 show sam-

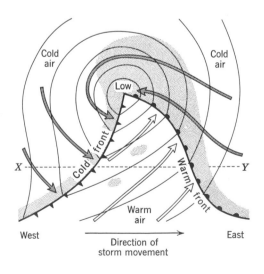

Figure 1–33.   *Detail of a well-developed cyclone.*

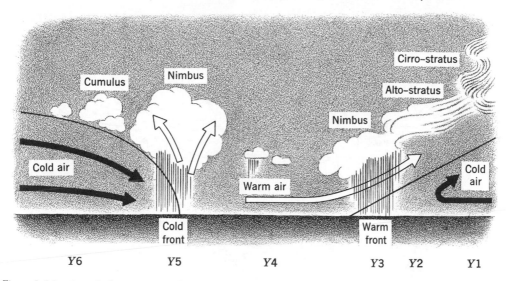

Figure 1–34. *A vertical cross section along the line X-Y of the cyclone shown in Figure 1–33. (After Trewartha.)*

ple weather maps. Figure 1–35 is a typical summer map. The lows and highs are not extreme and are widely spaced. Figures 1–36, 1–37, and 1–38 are for three successive days in winter. They show greater extremes in pressure and more closely spaced lows and highs. By examining them closely we can follow the paths of each disturbance. Figure 1–39 shows the most frequent paths taken by winter cyclones in the United States. From this it is easy to see why long periods of good weather are common in the southwest and most unusual in the northeast.

As we saw, most particularly in Figure

Table 1-4

STATION	WIND DIRECTION	TYPE OF CLOUDS	TEMPERATURE	PRESSURE	PRECIPITATION
Y1	E	Cirrus changing to cirrostratus	Cool	High	None
Y2	NE	Altostratus changing to nimbus	Slightly warmer	Dropping	Just beginning
Y3	N changing to NW	Nimbus	Increasing sharply	Dropping	Heavy
Y4	W changing to SW	Partly cloudy	Warm	Dropping	Scattered showers
Y5	SW changing to NW	Nimbus	Decreasing sharply	Rising sharply	Heavy for a short time
Y6	NW	Cumulus changing to clearing	Cool	Increasing	None

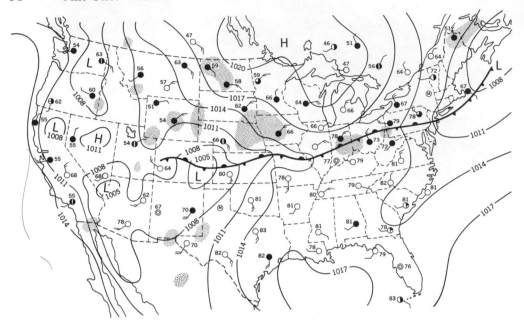

Figure 1–35.   Weather map for a typical summer day. Note the small differences in pressure between the highs and lows. (Data from U.S. Weather Bureau.)

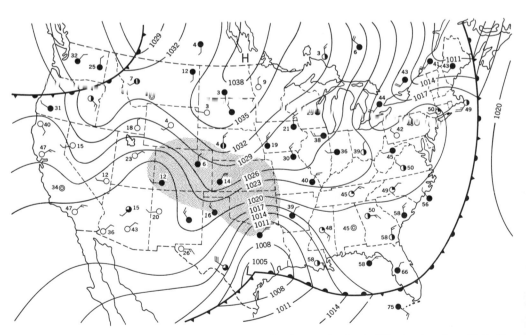

Figure 1–36.   A storm is born in Texas. Figures 1–37 and 1–38 record it for the following two days. (Data from the U.S. Weather Bureau.)

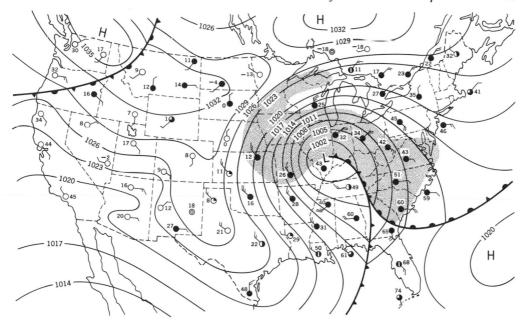

Figure 1–37.   Twenty-four hours after the situation shown in Figure 1–36, the storm has moved nearly a thousand miles to the northeast and has developed rapidly. (Data from the U.S. Weather Bureau.)

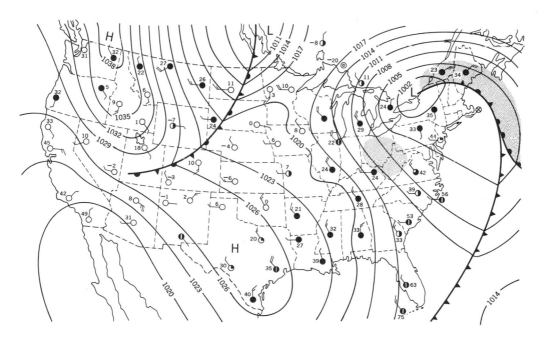

Figure 1–38.   After another twenty-four hours the storm has moved over New England and is starting to break up. (Data from the U.S. Weather Bureau.)

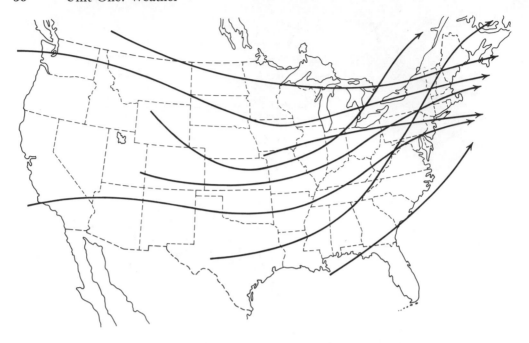

Figure 1–39.   The most frequent paths taken by winter cyclones in the United States. (After Trewartha.)

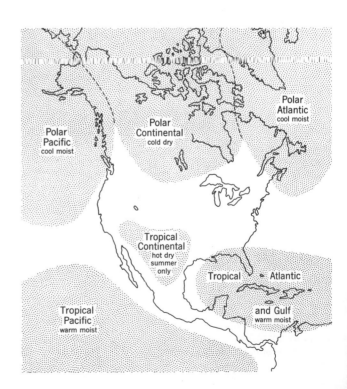

Figure 1–40. The principal air masses that determine the weather over the continental United States. (After Trewartha.)

1–34, at position Y1 the air high above the ground was warm and moist, while that close to the surface was cold and dry. The importance of radiosondes is that they locate these high masses of air that give warning of weather which is still a day or so away.

PERMANENT AIR MASSES

As weather data have accumulated, we have learned that a few large masses of air are relatively stationary and consistent in composition (Figure 1–40). Our storms come from the interaction of these masses. When a region has unusual weather for a number of weeks at a time, we find that one of these masses of air has moved beyond its usual boundaries. A knowledge of how and why these move will be valuable for long-range weather prediction, but our understanding of these factors is yet not sufficiently advanced to be of much help to the layman.

JET STREAMS

One of the factors related to the movements of large air masses is the so-called jet streams. The investigation of these started so recently that only a brief report can be given. The term "jet streams" refers to relatively high velocity winds that blow always in a west to east direction at an altitude of from 10,000 to 40,000 feet. They may be as much as 300 miles in width and blow with speeds up to 300 miles per hour. Their course lies to the north in the summer and at a latitude of about 30° in the winter. They will meander (north and south) much as a river does, and when a loop is cut off, a whirlpool of either warm or cold air is left isolated far from its point of origin. When the jet streams are displaced from their normal path for any great length of time

then periods of "unusual" weather are experienced. The study of this phenomenon is so new that we do not know why it occurs nor how to predict its behavior with accuracy.

SUMMARY

1. A warm front is the line between a mass of cold air and an advancing mass of warm air.
2. A cold front is the line between a mass of warm air and an advancing mass of cold air.
3. An occluded front is the line between two masses of cold air which have met and pinched off the contact between a mass of warm air and the ground.
4. A typical well-developed cyclone is characterized by a low-pressure area of ascending air, with a counterclockwise whirlpool of winds blowing in toward it, a warm front extending southeast and a cold front extending southwest from its center, precipitation east of the warm front and west of the cold front, and a sequence of clouds that starts with cirrus at the eastern edge and drops to lower altitudes near the warm front, with cumulus clouds following the clear-up shower at the cold front.
5. A typical anticyclone is characterized by a high-pressure area of descending air that moves out from the center in a system of winds rotating in a clockwise direction.
6. Summer highs and lows are usually spaced far apart, with only moderate differences in pressure between them.
7. In winter, the lows and highs show greater extremes in pressure and they are spaced closer together.
8. A few large masses of air surrounding our continent are relatively stationary and consistent in composition over long periods of time. The position of these masses with respect to each other is a major factor in determining our weather.
9. There are high altitude, high velocity, west-east winds known as jet streams. They have an important but little understood influence on the weather.

QUESTIONS AND EXERCISES

1. Copy the chart shown in Figure 1–33.
2. Draw a north-south line through the center of the low-pressure area in the chart made in Problem 1, and make a sketch of a vertical section along this line.
3. Choose five representative points along the north-south line drawn in Problem 2, and describe the weather conditions at each point.
4. Assume that the center of an anticyclone passes about 200 miles north of you. Describe the sequence of weather conditions that you would observe.
5. What is the sequence of clouds that accompanies a cyclone?
6. Does the rain accompanying a cyclone come from the air that is already in it or from the air that is drawn in as it proceeds?
7. What stage in the life of a cyclone is indicated by an occluded front?
8. What are the principal differences between a typical summer and winter weather map?
9. If a radiosonde were sent up from position Y2 in Figure 1–34, what sort of a record of temperature and humidity would it send back as it ascends?
10. Explain a long period of unusual weather that you have had this year in terms of an extraordinary location of some of the principal air masses shown in Figure 1–40.
11. The jet streams have important effects on air travel between San Francisco and Tokyo. Explain what some of these effects would be.

Chapter 9

Miscellaneous

Weather Conditions

FIGURE 1–41 shows the annual distribution of rainfall over the United States. For many agricultural purposes the distribution throughout the months of the year is extremely important. Figure 1–42 shows how different the pattern is for various parts of the country. No absolute significance can be attached to the figures on the vertical axes; the significant part of these curves is their shape.

TYPES OF ANNUAL
DISTRIBUTION OF RAINFALL

The Pacific Coast gets most of its rain in the winter months. During the summer little or none falls in California, a few inches are expected in Oregon, and about 10 inches is normal for Seattle, Washington. The polar front retreats northward in the summer, so that any storms enter the country at its northwest corner. The Rocky mountain region has a low total rainfall with a slight minimum during the summer. The plains region has its maximum rainfall in the spring and summer. Most of this results from local ascending air currents heated by the ground. The Gulf States have a coastal climate; the hottest time of year lags behind the season, and their maximum rainfall occurs in late summer and early fall. As New England is the funnel through which

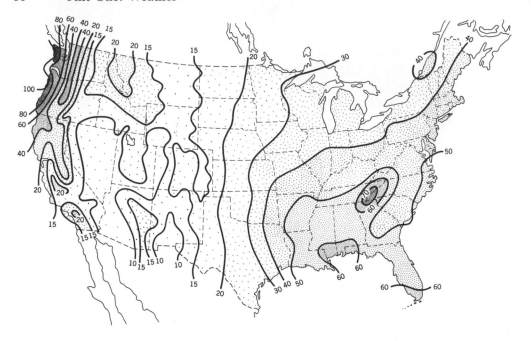

Figure 1–41.   The annual distribution of rainfall over the United States.

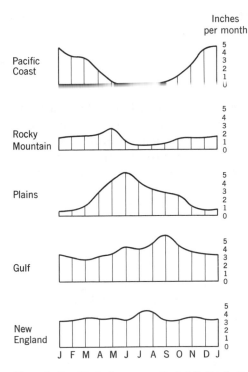

Figure 1–42.   Typical patterns of rainfall distribution throughout the year.

most of our storms leave the country, its rainfall is evenly distributed over the year.

CLOUDS AS BLANKETS

We have mentioned several times that the earth receives energy from the sun by radiation. However, the process is not one-way, with the earth receiving energy and giving none out. One of the fundamental laws of radiation states that every object in the universe is radiating energy to every other object at a rate which depends upon its temperature. The earth also radiates to the sun, but since the earth is cooler, it receives more than it gives. We have all noticed that clear nights are colder than cloudy ones. At night the earth is giving off more energy than it is receiving. Clouds act like a blanket and hold in this energy, so that the earth does not cool off as fast as it does when the sky is clear.

FOG AND FROST

When a cloud is resting on the ground it is called fog. Along our West Coast the term "high fog" is applied to a cloud that is within a thousand feet or so of ground level. Fog occurs most frequently near large masses of water such as the Pacific Ocean, the Gulf of Mexico, the Atlantic Ocean, and the Great Lakes. Warm, moist air will condense into fog if it is blown from the land over cold water, or from the warm ocean over the colder land mass. Where hills hem in a saucer-like area, air that has been cooled by radiation will flow downhill and collect at the lowest point. If the cooling reduces the temperature below the dew point, a radiation fog results. This is usually thick, and it sticks close to the ground until the morning sun evaporates it. If the air is dry and the cooling carries it below the freezing point, a frost results. Frost is always heavier in the bottom of valleys than on their sloping sides. In southern Cali-fornia and Florida frosts are rare, but they do occur. It is of the greatest importance that the weather bureau warn the citrus farmers when a frost is to be expected, so that they can protect their crops with orchard heaters.

THUNDERSTORMS

Thunderstorms are most frequent in the southeastern part of this country, and they occur with less frequency farther north and west (Figure 1–43). Since they are so dangerous to aviation, they are being studied intensively. An updraft in warm, moist air is needed for the formation of a thunderstorm. Its development may be outlined in three stages. In stage 1 (Figure 1–44) a strong updraft of air turns a cumulus cloud into a towering cumulonimbus one. Air is drawn in from the sides as well as through the base. The air rises rapidly, attaining a speed greater than 35 miles per hour. As

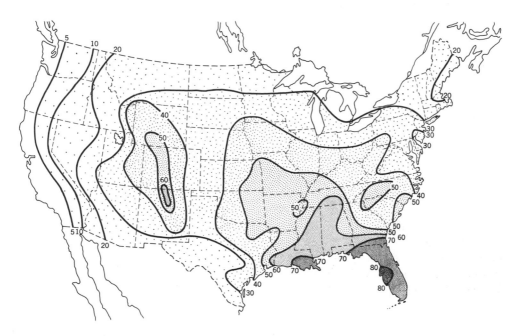

Figure 1–43.   The annual distribution of thunderstorms over the United States.

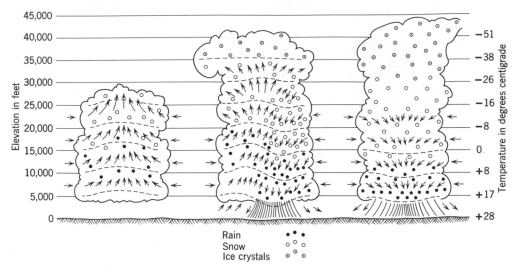

Figure 1–44.   *Three stages in the life of a thunderstorm. (Redrawn from* Scientific American.*)*

the cloud reaches a height of 20,000 to 25,000 feet, the precipitation of rain and snow is heavy (Figure 1–25). This precipitation falls near the leading edge of the storm and carries a stream of cold air with it. With the formation of the downdraft, the second stage in the thunderstorm has been reached. Much rain reaches the earth, but some is swept back up by the ascending currents. It becomes mixed with snow, freezes into hail, and descends again. After a few round trips the hailstones are large enough to fall to earth. As several such circulating cells will be found in any one thunderstorm, the pattern of rainfall is spotty. What falls is usually of short duration, and adjacent towns may get very different amounts.

Lightning results from the difference in electric charge between the drops of water that fall and the fine mist that breaks off them and stays in the cloud. It consists of a huge spark between regions of opposite charge. The heating effect of this spark makes the air expand with explosive violence. By checking the interval between the time you see the lightning and hear the thunder, you can tell how far off the lightning struck. Remember that sound travels a mile in about 5 seconds. As the thunderhead reaches 40,000 or even 50,000 feet, the fall of rain is so great that the updraft is blocked and the third, or dissipating, stage is reached.

SUMMARY

1. The United States may be divided into five regions which have characteristic distributions of annual rainfall.
2. Every object in the universe is radiating energy to every other object at a rate which depends upon its temperature.
3. The earth cools off at night because it is radiating more energy than it is receiving.
4. A cloudy night is warmer than a clear one because the clouds are warmed by radiation from the earth and reradiate energy to it.
5. Fog is a cloud resting on the ground or close to it.
6. A thunderstorm contains several separate cells of violently turbulent air. Warm, moist

air is swept up until its moisture condenses; these drops circulate up and down several times till they fall as rain or hail; and finally the heavy precipitation dissipates the storm.

7. Lightning results from the difference in electric charge between the drops of water that fall rapidly and the fine mist that breaks off them and falls slowly or not at all.

8. Thunder is the noise produced when the stroke of lightning heats the air very rapidly.

QUESTIONS AND EXERCISES

1. Why is the Rocky mountain region low in total rainfall?

2. How would you expect the total annual rainfall to change as you go north from Louisiana to Iowa?

3. Obtain the average annual rainfall data for your locality and plot it on a graph like the ones in Figure 1–42.

4. Plot the rainfall data for last year as you did in Problem 3. The chances are good that there will be important differences between the two graphs.

5. Why is there less danger of frost when the humidity is high than when it is low?

6. Can you have thunder without lightning?

7. How does the formation of rain aid the updraft in a thunderstorm?

8. What is responsible for the "roll" of distant thunder?

9. What would be some of the dangers of flying an airplane through a thunderstorm?

10. What are the different kinds of conditions that produce a fog?

Unit Two

Photography and Wave Motion

Chapter 1

The Camera and Lens Action

WHEN we take good snapshots with our cameras, we have made use of many important scientific principles. We are going to study these principles carefully, and when we have finished, we will be taking better pictures and we will have a more thorough understanding of light, color, and sound.

THE CAMERA

From the cutaway view of a simple camera (Figure 2–1) we can see the working parts, which consist of the light stop D, the lens L, the shutter S, and the film F. While changing the film in a camera, take the back off and hold the cam-era up to the light. Experiment with changing the exposure time and the f opening. Contrast the ordinary camera with an even simpler type, the pinhole camera (Figure 2–2), which has no lens, and in which the light stop can be no larger than $\frac{1}{250}$ inch in diameter or the image will appear blurred. With it an exposure time of many minutes is needed to get a picture on the light-sensitive film. A study of the behavior of light will help explain how the modern camera developed from the pinhole camera into the remarkably sensitive and versatile instrument that it is today.

The list of a few of the extreme conditions under which photographs are taken would include the camera that is used to

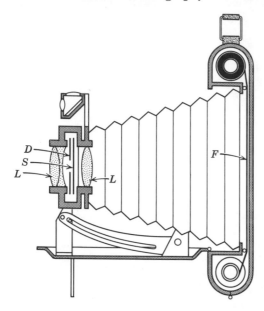

Figure 2-1.   Cutaway view of a camera. Between the two compound lenses, L and L, are the diaphragm, D, and the shutter, S.

study the flight of bullets, and which requires less than 1/100,000 second for exposure; the camera used by astronomers, which needs an exposure of many hours to record the faint light from distant galaxies; the camera which includes many thousands of square miles on a single

negative as it takes pictures from high-flying rockets; the camera attached to an electron microscope, which enables us to see objects one millionth of an inch long; the X-ray camera, which takes pictures through several inches of steel; and the infrared-sensitive camera, which takes pictures through several miles of haze.

REFLECTION

Our experience with mirrors and still pools tells us that smooth surfaces reflect light with little distortion. On an upright mirror place a piece of tape at a height exactly half the distance from the floor to your eyes. No matter how far you stand from the mirror, the tape will cut out the reflection of your feet. This situation is diagramed in Figure 2-3. The light ray which strikes the mirror from your feet is called the incident ray, and the angle it makes with a line perpendicular to the mirror is called the angle of incidence (angle i in Figure 2-3). The angle between this perpendicular and the ray reflected to your eye is called the angle of reflection (angle r in Figure 2-3). In this example, from the similar triangles involved, you can see that the angle of

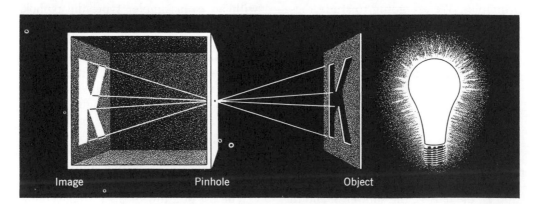

Figure 2-2.   Showing how an image is formed by a pinhole camera.

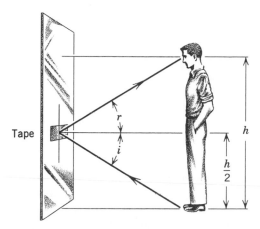

Figure 2–3. Illustrating the law of reflection.

incidence equals the angle of reflection. A number of similar experiments will provide convincing evidence that this is a general rule. For reflection from a flat surface, the angle of incidence equals the angle of reflection. This law of reflection holds for curved surfaces as well as for flat ones. Here the angles are measured between the path that the light takes and the perpendicular to the line tangent to the curve at the point where the light strikes it. Through the use of properly curved reflectors, all the reflected light from a bulb can be directed into the narrow beam of a searchlight or an automobile headlight (Figure 2–4) or the absurd effects of the hall of mirrors in a fun house can be achieved. If a well-defined reflection is to be avoided, a number of small, irregular surfaces will break up the reflection as in the case of velvet cloth and face powder.

The percentage of incident light reflected from even the best mirror is less than is generally supposed, and that reflected from what appears to be a completely transparent pane of window glass is much more than one usually realizes. Eighty per cent reflection is considered

good for a mirror. The mirror of the two-hundred-inch telescope at Mt. Palomar has been surfaced with a special aluminum coating to give about 90% reflection. The annoying glare from the windshield of an approaching car when you are driving with the sun at your back is an indication that much of the light falling on a pane of glass is reflected. It is important to bear this in mind when taking pictures indoors by daylight. A snapshot is hard to get under these conditions because much of the outdoor light is reflected and does not pass through the window.

A technique has been developed for treating the surface of glass so that reflection is almost eliminated. Such "coated lenses" transmit the light that would have been reflected. They are useful in cameras, telescopes, binoculars, and meters (Figure 2–5). The problem of avoiding glare is a very real one for architects designing storewindows, for museum directors in lighting pictures, etc.

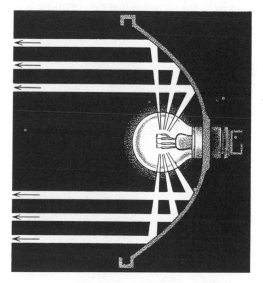

Figure 2–4. The reflector of an automobile head-light sends out a beam of parallel rays of light.

Figure 2–5.   *The left half of the glass front of this meter has been "coated" to cut down on reflection. (General Electric Co.)*

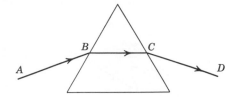

Figure 2–7.   The path of a ray of light through a prism.

REFRACTION

The statement is frequently made that light travels in straight lines. This is true only under ideal conditions. Certainly, as light travels through the eye to the retina, the light is bent, and it is this bending that we are now going to study. We can easily

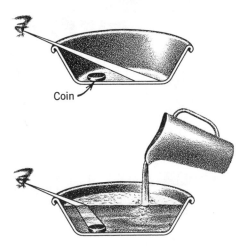

Figure 2–6.   An experiment illustrating the refraction of light.

experiment with seeing around a corner by placing a coin in the bottom of a pan, standing far enough away so that the coin is just hidden by the rim of the pan, and having someone fill the pan with water. The coin appears to rise into view. If the water is siphoned out of the pan, the coin will sink out of sight again. Figure 2–6 shows the path that the light takes. A magnifying or "burning" glass forms a small image of the sun. If a glass 2 inches in diameter is used and a 1-inch circle of black paper is pasted over the center of it, an image will still be formed, and it is obvious that the straight path of the light from the sun to the image has been blocked off.

If a narrow beam of light falls on a prism as in Figure 2–7, it will take the path *ABCD*. It will be bent at *B* as it passes from air to glass, and at *C* as it passes from the glass out into the air again. This bending of light as it passes from one substance to another is called refraction. In Figure 2–8, the line *BX* has been drawn perpendicular to the face of the prism at *B*. If the light had not been bent as it entered the glass it would have gone to *C'*, but, instead, it follows the path *BC*. Here it is bent toward the perpendicular, *BX*. In Figure 2–9, the line *Y'CY* is perpendicular to the face of the prism at *C*. In passing from glass to air, the light does not travel the straight line *BCD'* but is bent at *C* and goes to *D*. This time it is bent away from the perpendicular. Figure 2–10 shows the path

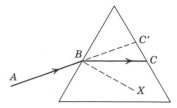

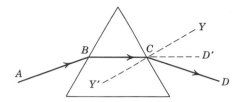

Figure 2–8. Refraction of a beam of light as it passes from air to glass at B.

Figure 2–9. Refraction of a beam of light as it passes from glass to air at C.

of a beam of light when it enters a tank of water at *B*, is reflected from a submerged mirror at *P*, and leaves the water at *C*. The beam is bent toward the perpendicular as it enters the water at *B*, at the mirror the angle of incidence *BPP′* equals the angle of reflection *P′PC*, and the beam is bent away from the perpendicular as it leaves the water at *C*.

To understand the reason for the change in direction of a beam of light when it passes from one medium into another, consider a car traveling along a paved road which has sandy shoulders. If one of the front wheels goes off the pavement and into the sandy soil, the whole car tends to turn off the road. The one wheel

in the sand travels more slowly than the others on the pavement, and the car swings around. Similarly, the bending of the path of light as it passes from one medium into another is due to its change in speed. Figure 2–11 shows a beam of light traveling in air and water. If we think of it as coming into the water from the air, the part of the beam which strikes the water first is slowed down, and the part in the air continues on its original path until it, too, strikes the water, and then, after the bending, or refraction at the surface, the beam proceeds in the new medium with its direction altered. In changing direction, the light is bent toward the perpendicular to the air-water

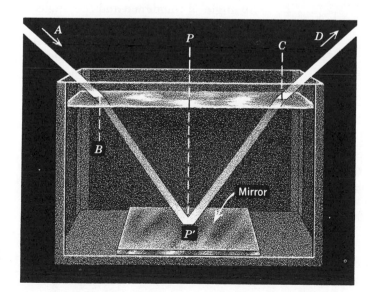

Figure 2–10. Refraction and reflection. The beam of light is refracted at B, reflected at P, and again refracted at C.

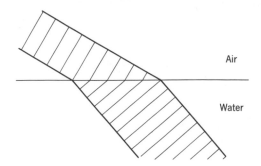

Figure 2–11. Refraction explained as a change in speed on passing from one medium into another. The waves travel faster in air than they do in water.

surface. If we consider that the beam of light is traveling upward into the air, the line of travel is bent away from the perpendicular to the surface.

INDEX OF REFRACTION

The speed with which light travels through a medium (water, for instance) is not affected by the angle at which it enters that medium. For any pair of substances, such as air and water, the ratio of the speed of light in the two is a constant. This is known as Snell's law, and it may be stated

$$\frac{\text{speed of light in air}}{\text{speed of light in water}} = K$$

$$= \frac{\text{sine of angle of incidence}}{\text{sine of angle of refraction}}$$

In this equation K is called the index of refraction of water with respect to air. The comparison is usually made against a vacuum. The speed of light in air is slightly less than it is in a vacuum so the index of refraction of air is slightly greater than one. This results in the light from the sun at sunrise and sunset being bent down over the horizon so that we see the sun

before it has actually risen and after it has set (Figure 2–12).

There is no simple way to predict the value of the index of refraction for a substance, but with two samples of the same substance, the one with the greater density will have the greater index of refraction. Density is defined as the mass of a certain volume (usually 1 cc) of a substance. For instance, water has a density of 1, and glass a density of about 2.5 g per cc. The density of air is only a little more than 0.001 g per cc. As we saw earlier, this varies considerably with temperature and pressure, so that it is almost impossible to find even two adjoining cubic feet of air that have exactly the same density. As the density of air changes, so does the index of refraction, and light passing through it is constantly zigzagging back and forth. The twinkling of stars and of distant lights serves to illustrate this point.

In Figure 2–9, the angle BCY' is called the angle of incidence and the angle DCY the angle of refraction. When light passes from glass into air, the angle of refraction is always greater than the angle of incidence. Therefore, as both the angle of incidence and the angle of refraction are increased, the angle of refraction will reach a right angle first, and the emerging light will just graze the surface of the prism. If the angle of incidence is made even greater, the light will not get out at all; it will be reflected at the glass-air surface and return into the prism. This situation is called total internal reflection. When the angle of refraction is a right angle, the angle of incidence is called the critical angle. For water, the critical angle is about 48½°. A fish, or a submerged swimmer, as he looks above him, can see out of the water at an angle of 48½° from the perpendicular. If he looks at a greater angle, he sees the bot-

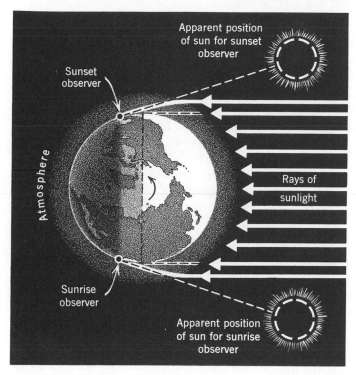

Apparent position
of sun for sunset
observer

Sunset
observer

Atmosphere

Rays of
sunlight

Sunrise
observer

Apparent position
of sun for sunrise
observer

*Figure 2–12.   When the sun is
near the horizon, refraction by
the atmosphere makes it appear
higher than it really is.*

tom of the pond reflected at the under surface of the water. This total internal reflection is more efficient than the reflection given by a mirror.

For the experiment with the critical angle of water described above we can write the equation for the index of refraction as

$$\frac{\text{sine angle ray in air}}{\text{sine angle ray in water}} = K$$

At the critical angle, the angle of the ray in air is 90°, and the sine 90° = 1, so $K = 1$/sine angle ray in water or sine angle of ray in water = $1/K$. We can obtain the index of refraction of water from the fact that the critical angle is 48.5°. The sine of 48.5° = 0.749, $K = 1/0.749 = 1.335$. The index of refraction for ordinary crown glass is 1.515. The critical angle for a ray emerging from

glass into air can be obtained from sine angle ray in glass = $1/K = 1/1.515 = 0.660$. The angle is $41 + °$.

LENS ACTION

We have all experimented at some time with a "burning glass," and have observed that its burning action is most effective at a certain distance. There is one distance at which the light from the sun is concentrated into the smallest area. The plane in which the lens converges the sun's rays (F in Figure 2–13) is called the focal plane. The distance from the center of the lens to the focal plane is the focal length of the lens. (This term will be defined in a different way later on.) In any optical system the direction of the rays can always be reversed,

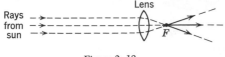

Figure 2–13.

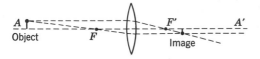

Figure 2–14.

so if we place a tiny source of light at *F*, a beam of parallel rays will emerge from the lens to the left. It is obvious that we could just as well have had the sun's rays coming from the right and we would have located another focal point on the left.

Some of the following discussion will involve drawing the formation of an image by a lens, so let us study the rules for doing this. An image is formed when essentially all the rays that go from any one point on the object through the lens converge at a unique point on the other side. In Figure 2–14, the line *AA'* is the horizontal axis of a thin convex lens. From the top of the object, draw a line parallel to the axis. The ray following this line is bent as it enters the lens and again as it leaves the lens, so that it passes through the focal point *F'*. Draw another line from the top of the object through the focal point *F*. If the ray following this line strikes the lens, it will be refracted twice and will emerge parallel to the axis. These two rays will cross at some point. Another image locating line that can be drawn is the essentially straight line from the point through the center of the lens. For an ideal lens, all rays from the top of the object that pass through the lens will converge at this same point. If an image screen is placed here there will appear a sharp image of the top of the object. A similar construction can be carried through for any other point on the object and the position of the image located.

If the object is placed closer to the lens, the construction in Figure 2–15 shows that the image will be formed farther away from the lens than it was in Figure 2–14 and it will be larger. If the camera is of the type that can be adjusted for the distance of the object we are photographing, we will notice that the lens moves away from the film for objects that are near.

Examination of Figures 2–15 and 2–14 shows that as the object distance increases the image distance decreases and the image is found closer and closer to the focal point. At some considerable object distance, the distance between the image and the focal point will be too small to measure. Any increase in object distance will produce no observable difference in image distance. This leads us to a definition of the focal length that is rather clumsy to phrase but which has a great advantage of being operational. The focal length of a lens is the distance between the lens and the image, when the object distance is so great that increasing it makes no measurable change in the image distance.

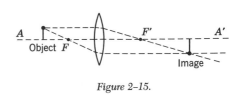

Figure 2–15.

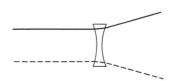

Figure 2–16.   A concave lens diverges the rays passing through it.

A lens may be ground so that it is thick at the edges and thin in the middle (concave). This kind of lens diverges the rays that pass through it (Figure 2–16). Many irregular shapes of lenses have been worked out for special purposes.

APPLICATIONS TO CAMERAS, TELESCOPES, ETC.

By means of suitable combinations of lenses we can extend our ability to see objects. For those that are very small we use a microscope, and for those that are distant and faint, a telescope. A simplified diagram of the lens system of a microscope is shown in Figure 2–17. Since the image is 100 to 1000 times the diameter of the object, a very strong light must be used.

In the astronomical telescope, we are interested in enlarging the image when viewing members of the solar system, but even more important is the gathering of as much light as possible from faint stars.

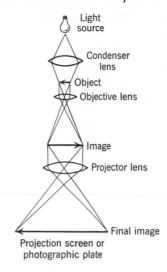

Figure 2–17. Schematic drawing of optical microscope. (Taken from College Physics *by C. E. Mendenhall, A. S. Eve, D. A. Keys, and R. M. Sutton. D. C. Heath and Co.)*

The refracting telescope has a large lens to gather and focus the light, and a small eyepiece to magnify the image (Figure 2–18). The area and hence the light-gathering power, of the objective of a tele-

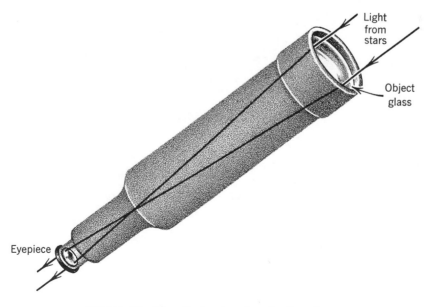

Figure 2–18.   The optical system of a refracting telescope.

Figure 2–19.   Forty-inch refracting telescope at the Yerkes Observatory. (Yerkes Observatory.)

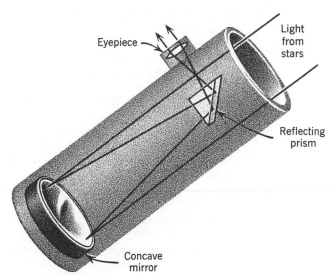

Eyepiece

Light from stars

Reflecting prism

Concave mirror

Figure 2–20.   The optical system of a reflecting telescope.

scope is proportional to the square of the diameter. The large forty-inch lens of the Yerkes Observatory telescope (Figure 2–19) intercepts about 45,000 times as much light as the lens of the average human eye.

A concave mirror ground to the shape of a parabola in cross section will bring the parallel rays of light from a star to focus at a point. By placing a small reflecting prism in front of the mirror, the light

can be turned aside for study (Figure 2–20). The reflecting telescope is popular with those who enjoy astronomy as a hobby, and it is the type used in all the larger telescopes in observatories.

Prism binoculars use two reflecting prisms between each lens (Figure 2–21). This shortens the distance between the lenses so that the binoculars are much easier to carry and hold steady than an old-fashioned spyglass.

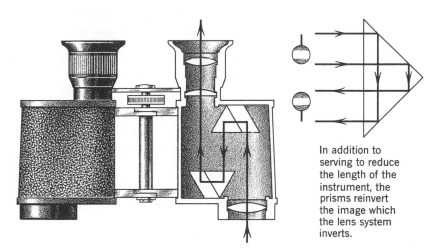

In addition to serving to reduce the length of the instrument, the prisms reinvert the image which the lens system inverts.

Figure 2–21.   The optical system of prism binoculars.

SUMMARY

1. The working parts of the camera are the lens, light stop or iris diaphragm, shutter, and film.
2. The law of reflection states that the angle of reflection equals the angle of incidence.
3. Refraction is the bending of a beam of light as it passes from one medium into another.
4. Law of refraction: the index of refraction for a substance =

$$K = \frac{\text{speed of light in a vacuum}}{\text{speed of light in substance}} =$$

$$\frac{\text{sine of angle of incidence}}{\text{sine of angle of refraction}}$$

5. The critical angle for a substance is the angle of incidence of an emerging ray of light which gives an angle of refraction of 90°.
6. Density is mass per unit volume.
7. For a lens that has an index of refraction greater than the surrounding medium (glass in air), a convex lens is converging and a concave lens is diverging. If the lens has an index of refraction less than the surrounding medium, the reverse is true.
8. For a converging lens, the greater the object distance, the less is the image distance.
9. The focal length of a lens is the image distance when the object distance is so great that any increase in it makes no measurable change in the image distance.
10. The optical system of a microscope is designed primarily to furnish an enlarged image, and of a telescope to gather and concentrate light.

QUESTIONS AND EXERCISES

1. What is the minimum length of a vertical mirror that would be needed by a person 5 feet 10 inches tall to see himself from head to toe?
2. Examine the difference between the construction of velvet and satin and show how this explains the fact that one is dull and the other is shiny.
3. Explain how a spherical fish bowl filled with water can start a fire.
4. Look outside through a pane of window glass and move your head back and forth. Notice how the scene is distorted. What causes this?
5. The index of refraction for water is less than that for glass and greater than that for air. Would the focal length of a convex glass lens be greater in air or in water?
6. Why does a microscope need a particularly bright source of illumination?
7. What are some of the advantages of a reflecting over a refracting type of telescope?
8. If 80% transmission is obtained each time light passes from air into glass and from glass into air, what per cent of light that strikes the simple refracting telescope (Figure 2–18) would reach the observer's eye?
9. As you look at a stone on the bottom of a stream, does it appear closer or farther away than it actually is? Make a sketch of the situation that explains your answer.
10. What is the weight of a cylinder of glass that has a diameter of 10 cm and a height of 5 cm?
11. What is the least distance between the object and the image formed by a convex lens?
12. At what distance from a convex lens is an object located when the object and the image are the same size?
13. In a pinhole camera, how does the height of the image compare with the height of the object?
14. On a photographic negative, the image of a person is just 1 inch high. If the person is actually 6 feet tall and he stood 12 feet from the camera, what focal length was used?

Chapter 2

Light Intensity

Whent taking a picture, we must consider the brightness of the light reflected from the subject. The same setting of a camera will not give a satisfactory pi_ture of both a brightly lighted beach scene and a family group on the porch with an overcast sky. When a reading light is being used, it is not only the brightness of the bulb but also its distance from the written word that is important.

MEASURING INTENSITY

The common unit for measuring intensity of illumination is the foot-candle. By carefully defining the composition, method of manufacture, and rate of burning of the standard candle, a reasonably reproducible unit is obtained. In actual practice we use incandescent bulbs that have been calibrated in terms of the standard candle. Our modern incandescent bulbs give off an amount of light that is roughly proportional to the power consumed (a 100-watt bulb is about four times as bright as a 25-watt bulb), so rating by watts rather than by the amount of illumination is satisfactory in this case. This kind of bulb is very inefficient as a light source because it wastes a great deal of the electrical energy in heating up the filament to incandescence. Fluorescent bulbs, which operate at a low temperature, give much more illumination per watt than do the incandescent types.

In order to see how the illumination decreases with increasing distance from the source, picture a standard candle burning at the center of a transparent sphere with a radius of 1 foot, and outside that, another sphere with a radius of 2 feet. All the light passing through the first sphere will strike the second. Recalling that the area of a sphere is $4\pi r^2$, we can see that the area of two spheres stand in the ratio of the squares of their radii. The same amount of light is falling on both these spheres, but the larger one has four times the area of the smaller; hence, each square inch of the smaller one has four times as much light striking it as does each square inch of the larger (Figure 2–22). This may be generalized as $I \propto 1/d^2$ or $I_1/I_2 = d_2^2/d_1^2$. The intensity, I, is inversely proportional to the square of the distance, d. This is illustrated in Figure 2–23.

The problems involved in taking a photograph under various lighting conditions will be taken up later (page 83). In view of the importance of adequate lighting to health and efficiency, a lighting survey of a home or college could be an interesting study. A light meter based on the photovoltaic effect (page 147) and calibrated to read in foot-candles can usually be borrowed from a local light and power company.

As a rough approximation, 60- and 100-watt frosted tungsten-filament bulbs give about 1 foot-candle per watt without reflectors. With a light-colored lamp-shade, a 100-watt bulb gives a satisfactory intensity for ordinary reading (20 to 50 foot-candles in Table 2–1) at a distance of 3 feet.

f VALUE OF LENSES

The f-value adjustment of a camera regulates the size of the opening (aperture or stop) near the lens. By using a large opening on a dull day and a small one on a bright day, the same amount of light will fall on the film in each case. The f value is defined as the distance from the lens to the film divided by the diameter of the aperture. Since the distance from the lens to the film usually

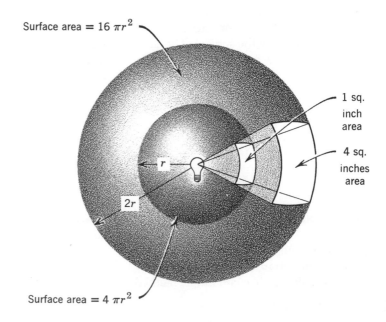

Surface area = $16\,\pi r^2$

1 sq. inch area

4 sq. inches area

r

$2r$

Surface area = $4\,\pi r^2$

Figure 2–22. The same amount of light that falls on 1 square inch of the sphere with a radius r is spread out over 4 square inches of the sphere with a radius 2r.

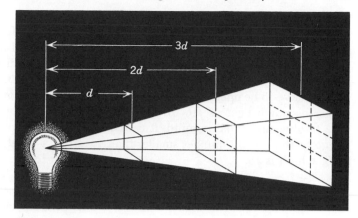

Figure 2-23. An illustration of the law that the intensity of light varies inversely with the square of the distance.

Table 2-1° Conservative Foot-Candle Recommendations on a National Basis of Characteristics of the Visual Task and Requirements of Performance

100 foot-candles or more. For very severe and prolonged tasks such as fine needlework, fine engraving, fine penwork, fine assembly, sewing on dark goods, and discrimination of fine details of low contrast, as in inspection.

50 to 100 foot-candles. For severe and prolonged tasks, such as proofreading, drafting, difficult reading, watch repairing, fine machine work, and average sewing and other needlework.

20 to 50 foot-candles. For moderately critical and prolonged tasks, such as clerical work, ordinary reading, common benchwork, and average sewing and other needlework on light goods.

10 to 20 foot-candles. For moderate and prolonged tasks of office and factory and, when not prolonged, ordinary reading and sewing on light goods.

5 to 10 foot-candles. For visually controlled work in which seeing is important, but more or less interrupted or casual and does not involve discrimination of fine details of low contrasts.

0 to 5 foot-candles. The danger zone for severe visual tasks, and for quick and certain seeing. Satisfactory for perceiving larger objects and for casual seeing.

° Luckiesh and Moss, *The Science of Seeing*, p. 345, Table LVIII. New York, D. Van Nostrand Co., 1937.

does not change significantly (with changing focus), the f value is inversely proportional to the diameter of the aperture, $f \times 1/d$. The larger the f value, the smaller the opening. If the lens opening is ½ inch across and the lens is 4 inches from the film, the f value $= 4 \div ½ = 8$. If the stop is cut down to ¼ inch, the f value $= 4 \div ¼ = 16$.

The light stop is a circular opening so its area (and I, the intensity of light striking the film) is proportional to the square of the diameter, $I \propto d^2$. Thus we can write $I \propto 1/f^2$ of $f \propto 1/\sqrt{I}$.

It is convenient to be able to calculate the f value that will provide twice the light intensity of any given opening. To do this we write the relationship given above as $f_2/f_1 = \sqrt{I_1/I_2}$ or $f_2 = f_1\sqrt{I_1/I_2}$. Since we want $I_2 = 2I_1$, $f_2 = f_1\sqrt{1/2}$ or $f_2 = 0.7f_1$. The f value that corresponds to twice as much light as $f8$ is $0.7 \times f8 = f5.6$. Fortunately, the f value scale on cameras has been standardized into a set of numbers, each one of which represents approximately twice as much light as the next smaller one. The scale runs like this: 45, 32, 22, 16, 11, 8, 5.6, 4, 2.8, 2. Very few cameras cover the full range, but it is important to memorize the part of the sequence that is on yours. As an example, assume that your camera was set for a regular snapshot under fairly good lighting conditions, such as 1/25 second and *f*16. If you suddenly had occasion to take an action picture, you would want to change the shutter speed to ⅟₁₀₀ second. To get a proper exposure the light stop would have to be opened up to let in four times as much light as *f*16. If you have the *f*-value scale well in mind, it is easy to go to the second number smaller than *f*16, which is *f*8.

CHANGING APERTURE AND
DEPTH OF FOCUS

Referring to Figure 2–14, you can see that, as the rays of light from any one point on the object converge and then diverge again, they form two cone-shaped bundles with their points together. If we cut across these cones parallel to the lens we will have a nearly circular image, except at the focal plane where it is a point. If a camera is not focused correctly,

so that the film is either in front of or behind the focal plane, then the image on the film will be a conglomeration of overlapping circular images. This circle over which the image is spread is called the "circle of confusion." If the diameter of the circle of confusion is less than 0.1 mm, we are not able to distinguish it from a point, and the picture appears to be in focus. If it is any larger than that, the picture looks fuzzy. This is the reason for the statement that the opening in a pinhole camera should be no larger than 1/250 inch (page 67).

Since objects at different distances form images at different distances back of the lens, it is clear that the object at only one distance from the lens can be in perfect focus on the film of your camera. The circle of confusion for objects immediately in front of and behind the one you are focusing on will be so small that they will appear to be in focus. The smaller the light stop you are using, the

Figure 2–24.   Picture taken with small aperture (f 32) and a long exposure (1 sec.). Notice that all the objects are in sharp focus (great depth of focus). (Robert John Wright, photographer.)

Figure 2–25. Picture taken with large aperture (f 5.6) and short exposure (1/50 sec.). Notice that the region of sharp focus is very shallow. Only one box (the second from the right) is in good focus. (Robert John Wright, photographer.)

narrower will be this cone of converging images, and the greater will be the range of objects that appear to be in focus. The distance from the nearest object which seems to be in clear focus to the farthest one which is also in good focus is called the depth of focus. A good depth of focus can be obtained with small f openings like $f16$, 22, and 32; but with large openings life $f4$ and an object close to the lens, the depth of focus may be only an inch or two (Figures 2–24 and 2–25).

CHOOSING THE PROPER EXPOSURE CONDITIONS

An exposure meter is practically a necessity if frequent failures with a camera are to be avoided. The eye adjusts to give satisfactory vision with such a wide range of light conditions that the impression of how bright it is may be very inac-

curate. An exposure meter is a light meter (page 80) that is graduated to read in units that correspond to the shutter speed and lens opening of the camera (Figure 2–26). The meter is adjusted for the type of film being used, and it then gives a choice of several shutter speeds and f openings. For example, from a certain meter reading there will be a choice of $f5.6$ and $\frac{1}{100}$ second, $f8$ and $\frac{1}{50}$ second, or $f11$ and $\frac{1}{25}$ second. They will all allow the same amount of light to fall on the film.

Which one of the above combinations of f values and shutter speeds is the one to choose? It is generally considered good technique to have as great a depth of focus as possible. To be sure, it is a matter of taste, but in current practice the photographer does not deliberately have part of his picture out of focus. This means that he uses the smallest light stop (the largest f number) that the conditions

Figure 2–26.   Photographic exposure meter. (Weston Electrical Instrument Corp.)

will permit. Therefore, he chooses the slowest shutter speed that will stop the action in his picture and then uses the f opening that is appropriate. For ordinary snapshots, a shutter speed of ⅟₂₅ second is about right. For pictures of children, or of anything in motion, ⅟₁₀₀ second is needed, and for some rapidly moving subjects an even faster shutter speed may be necessary.

SUMMARY

1. A foot-candle is the intensity of the light 1 foot from a standard candle.
2. Variation of light intensity with distance:

$$1 \propto 1/d^2 \qquad \text{or} \qquad I_1/I_2 = d_2{}^2/d_1{}^2$$

3. f value of lenses:

$$f \text{ value} = \frac{\text{distance from lens to image}}{\text{diameter of lens opening}}$$

4. The circle of confusion is the circular area on the image screen covered by the image of any one point on the object.
5. The depth of focus is the distance from the nearest object which appears to be in good focus in a picture to the farthest one which also appears to be in good focus.

QUESTIONS AND EXERCISES

1. A light meter gives a reading of 20 foot-candles at a distance of 5 feet from a light. What would the reading be at a distance of 3 feet?
2. Calculate the f value of a camera lens which has an aperture of ⅜ inch and which is 4 inches from the film.
3. What size aperture for the lens in problem 2 would have an f value of 8?
4. Does an f opening at 5.6 let through more or less light than one of f8? How much?
5. What exposure time should be used with f4 if f8 takes ⅟₂₅ second?
6. Make a survey of the lighting conditions in your home or college and see how they compare with the recommendations presented.
7. If the illumination 3 feet from a bulb is 20 foot-candles, what would it be 10 feet from the same bulb?
8. There are two lights 10 feet apart, and one light is twice as bright as the other. At what point between them would the illumination from the two be equal?
9. If f8 and ⅟₁₀₀ second give the correct exposure, what f value is correct for ⅟₂₅ second?
10. By actual measurement check the minimum f value of your camera. Be careful not to scratch the lens.
11. When two light sources are placed side by side, one is twice as bright as the other. If the dimmer one is located 10 feet from you, how far away would the brighter one have to be placed for them to show the same reading on a light meter?

Chapter 3

The Eye and Waves

THERE are many striking similarities between the structure of the eye and that of the camera. This is not too surprising, since they have similar functions.

PHYSICS OF THE EYE

Structure of the Eye

The principal parts of the human eye are shown in Figure 2–27. Light passes through the cornea, C, and the pupil, P, which is the dark circular opening inside the iris, I. The lens, L, converges the rays so that they form an image on the retina, R, at the back of the eye. The light energy striking the retina sends a nerve impulse along the optic nerve, O, to the brain, where the image is interpreted. The space A is filled with a watery fluid, and V with a gelatin-like material that helps the eyeball maintain its shape.

The light stop of a camera is called an iris diaphragm because it looks and acts like the iris of the eye. It is an interesting experience to look carefully at your iris in a mirror as you shine a flashlight directly into your eye. As the iris can only contract and expand enough to change the area of the opening about ten times, it is not particularly effective as a light-intensity regulator.

The normal human lens is plastic, in contrast to the rigid glass lens of a cam-

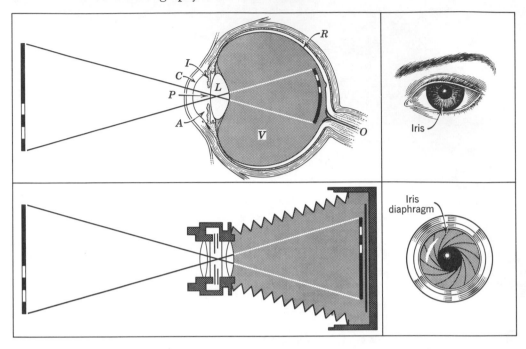

Figure 2–27.   A comparison between the eye and the camera. (Redrawn from Scientific American.*)*

era. The camera focuses by changing the distance between the lens and the film. The eye can accommodate to a slight extent this way, but it does so principally by changing the shape of the lens. A thin lens of slight curvature is used for seeing at a distance; the shape changes to a thick, more nearly spherical one for seeing objects close up.

The retina is covered with light-sensitive rods and cones, which change the light energy into nerve impulses. The chemical changes brought about by light on a film (latent image) last indefinitely, but on the retina they disappear after about 0.1 second. The rods enable us to judge light intensity, and they are sensitive over an extremely wide range of illumination. The cones give us color vision, and they do not respond to low intensities. This is why we cannot distinguish colors very well by moonlight.

Binocular Vision

There are two simple experiments you can perform to illustrate the way you judge distances by binocular vision. Hold a paper match-cover edge on at arm's length, and observe that you can see one side of it with your right eye and the other side with your left eye. Then have a friend focus on his finger as he moves it from arm's length up to his nose, and see how his two eyes move. To the extent that you see different pictures with each eye, and from the muscular tension of converging your two eyes more on near objects than on far ones, you have a binocular way of judging distances. You can test how much you depend on binocular vision by closing one eye and trying to put the cap on a fountain pen when it is held about a foot from your face.

Figure 2-28.   A chart for testing for astigmatism.

Optical Defects of the Eye

We can consider only a few of the many things which may go wrong with the eye. If the surface of the cornea is not spherical, then there is astigmatism. In Figure 2-28 all the lines appear of equal intensity to a normal eye, but to a person with astigmatism some will appear darker than others.

The normal eye reads print most easily at a distance of about ten inches. If anyone needs to hold the page much closer than this, he is nearsighted. The lens of the eye is focusing the image in front of the retina. This fault is corrected by using a lens which is diverging—thick at the edges and thin in the center (Figure 2-29). Those whose most comfortable reading distance is much greater than ten inches are farsighted—the image is falling back of the retina, and glasses with converging lenses are needed (Figure 2-30). The area where the optic nerve fibers join to form the optic nerve (Figure 2-27) is not supplied with rods or cones, hence it is a "blind spot." Fortunately, this area is off to one side of the eye, so that each eye sees what is being missed by the blind spot on the other one.

Visual Illusions

We should not forget that in the seeing process the brain plays as important a part as the eye. Our eyes may be entirely normal and yet we may be fooled by what we see. This subject is far too large to cover here, but a few illustrations may be well worth while.

In Figure 2-31, the trees are actually the same size, but the one to the right appears to be much larger. In Figure 2-32, what appears to be a spiral is made up of a number of concentric circles. The two areas in Figure 2-33 are the same; in fact, one may be exactly superimposed on the other. The apparent difference in size of the full moon near the horizon and high in the sky has been shown by photography to be entirely an illusion. Figures 2-34 and 2-35 show how stubbornly the brain insists that the room is normal when the appearance of the two individuals shows that the ceiling

Figure 2-29.   The shape of concave lens used in eyeglasses.

Figure 2-30.   The shape of convex lens in eyeglasses.

Figure 2–31.   An optical illusion due to perspective. The three trees are the same height.

Figure 2–32.   An optical illusion consisting of a series of concentric circles. (After Luckiesch.)

must be farther from the floor on the right than on the left.

BEHAVIOR OF WAVES

Characteristics of Waves

The question, "What is light?" is frequently asked and is almost as frequently answered. To a scientist, such a question is meaningless. Scientists have made the progress that can be credited to them by rephrasing the above question to read, "How does light behave?" They study such completely abstract things as waves and such real things as water waves; and when they find a certain amount of similarity between the behavior of light and of the water waves they can say that, to a certain extent, light has the characteristics of a wave motion. There are many ways in which light has a wave-like behavior, and many in which it behaves very differently, and so it would be most

misleading to say that light "is" a wave or a wave-like phenomenon. Gertrude Stein uttered a profound philosophical truth when she wrote, "A rose is a rose is a rose." A wave is a wave is a wave, and light is light is light. Light is not a wave, although the two do have some properties in common. We shall find it profitable to study waves in general and sound waves in particular before examining the wave-like behavior of light.

Certain terms that are used in describing waves are illustrated in Figure 2–36.

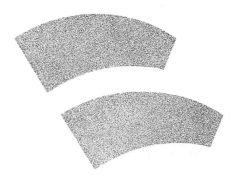

Figure 2–33.   An optical illusion of areas. The two areas are the same size and shape.

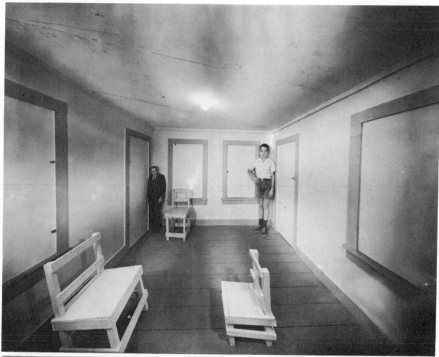

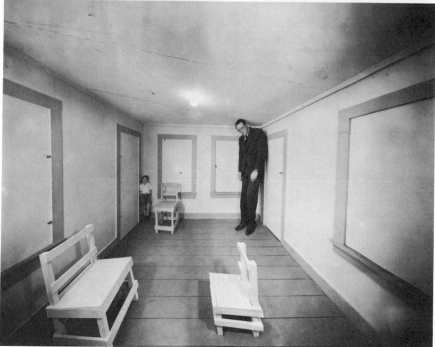

Figure 2–34 and 2–35.   Two views of a room constructed to produce a visual illusion. The room obviously cannot be rectangular at the back end but our eyes refuse to believe this. (Courtesy Life © Time.)

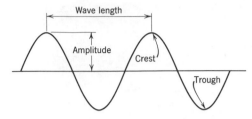

Figure 2–36.   An illustration of terms used in describing wave motion.

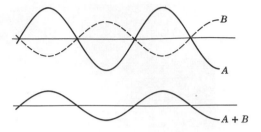

Figure 2–38.   Destructive interference of two waves.

Representing a wave by the familiar sine curve, the high points are called crests, and the low points troughs. The distance from any part of a wave to the corresponding part of the next wave is called the wave length, and half the difference in height between the crest and the trough is called the amplitude.

In talking about how waves travel, it is easier if we think in terms of something tangible, like a water wave. If a stone is dropped into quiet water, the waves can be seen traveling out from the spot where the stone struck. Waves have a speed, and, as they strike the shore, a certain number hit every minute. The number of waves arriving per unit of time is called their frequency. The length of time between the arrival of one crest and the next is called the period. If 5

crests strike the shore in 1 minute, the frequency is 5 per minute and the period is ⅕ minute. Or, stated as an equation, Period = 1/Frequency.

As you **watch the water** wave roll toward the shore, **you know that** the water disturbed by **the stone is** not traveling from it to the shore; only the wave motion travels, while the water remains pretty much where it was. Or, better still, when you wiggle one end of a clothesline, whose other end is tied to a post, the waves travel along the line as the line moves up and down. We get the impression that the stripes on a rotating barber pole are moving up. In order to set up a **wave motion there must be some sort of** a vibrating source and something, a medium of some kind, to pass the vibrations along. If the particles of the medium move back and forth in the direction the wave is traveling, the wave motion is called longitudinal. If the particles of the medium move perpendicular to the direc-

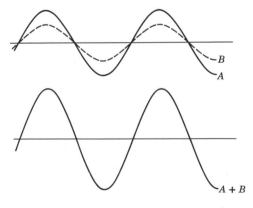

Figure   2–37.   Constructive   interference   of   two waves.

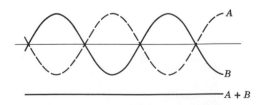

Figure 2–39.   Destructive interference of two waves. When the waves have the same wavelength and amplitude and are exactly out of phase, the result is that no wave motion is observed.

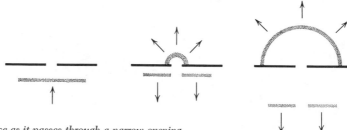

Figure 2–40.   Diffraction of a wave as it passes through a narrow opening.

tion of the wave, the wave motion is called transverse. Very seldom is an actual wave purely one or the other. Any one drop of water will rise with the crest of the wave and travel forward with it, then drop down into the trough and move back to meet the next crest, so that it follows a roughly circular path.

When two waves arrive at the same place at the same time, their interaction is called interference. When a crest of one meets a crest of the other, and a trough meets a trough, the result is that the two add together to make a high crest and a deep trough (Figure 2–37). This situation is called constructive interference or reinforcement. When a crest combines with a trough, they add together to produce a very small wave (Figure 2–38). This combining is referred to as destructive interference; when the crest and trough are the same size they exactly cancel each other so that two waves combine to give no wave at all (Figure 2–39).

Reflection, Diffraction, and Refraction of Waves

The reflection of waves of all kinds is such a familiar phenomenon that we do not need to spend time on that, but diffraction may need some explaining. When a wave passes through a narrow opening, the opening behaves like the source of a new wave, which proceeds outward in a semicircle. Figure 2–40 shows a wave front as it approaches and passes through a narrow opening. Diffraction is the name applied to this spreading out of a wave motion as part of it passes through a narrow opening or around a corner.

When part of a wave front changes speed, it also changes direction. This change in direction with change in speed is called refraction. As you would expect, the slow part of the wave lags behind, the faster-moving part speeds ahead, and the whole wave bends, so that it moves into the region where it travels more slowly. As waves roll up onto a gently sloping beach they are refracted, so that they approach parallel to the shore, regardless of their angle to it in deep water (Figure 2–41).

SUMMARY

1. The parts of the eye are the cornea, pupil, lens, retina, rods, cones, and optic nerve.
2. Binocular vision helps us judge distances by the tension of the eye muscles and the differences in the images seen by the two eyes.
3. Optical defects of the eye include astigmatism, nearsightedness, and farsightedness.
4. Beware of visual illusions; don't believe all you see. What you see clearly may be misinterpreted by your mind.
5. A wavelength is the distance from one crest of a wave to the next one.

Figure 2–41.   Refraction of waves as they approach the shore. (Aerial photograph by Clyde Sunderland, Oakland, Calif.)

6. Amplitude is half the difference in height between a crest and an adjacent trough.

7. Frequency is the number of waves passing a given point per unit time.

8. The period is the interval of time between the passage of two successive crests of a series of waves.

9. In a longitudinal wave the motion of the particles is back and forth in the direction of travel of the wave.

10. In a transverse wave the motion of the particles is perpendicular to the direction of travel of the wave.

11. Interference is the interaction of two or more waves.

12. Diffraction is the spreading out of a wave motion as it passes through a narrow opening or around a corner.

QUESTIONS AND EXERCISES

1. Compare the eye and the camera for similarities and differences.

2. What is the ratio of the aperture areas of a camera with an opening of $f\,5.6$ and of $f\,22$?

3. Examine carefully a pair of pictures that are to be used together in a stereoscope. Describe the differences between them.

4. Using a piece of graph paper, draw: (a) a series of sine waves with a wavelength of 2 inches and an amplitude of ½ inch; (b) a series of sine waves with a wavelength of 3 inches and an amplitude of ½ inch; (c) the wave that would result from the interference of (a) and (b).

5. Do water waves travel faster in deep or in shallow water?

6. If waves roll up on the shore once every 12 seconds, what is their frequency? What is their period?

7. Bring to class examples of optical illusions not mentioned in the text.

8. Which one of the optical defects of the eye would probably result from a slight imperfection in the curvature of the cornea?

9. What type of wave motion is illustrated by a rotating barber pole? by a column of marching soldiers?

10. Point out one difference between the phenomena of reflection and refraction and one similarity.

11. Devise a way to locate your own blind spot in each eye.

Chapter 4

Sound

STRIKE a tuning fork, and then suspend a pith ball so that it barely touches one of the tines (Figure 2–42). This experiment will convince you that the fork is vibrating even though it is moving so rapidly that you cannot see the motion. Sound always has a vibrating source. This vibrating source may be a bell that has been struck by the clapper, a string that has been bowed, plucked, or struck, a column of air in an organ pipe, a reed in a clarinet, etc.

VIBRATION AND MEDIUM

There must be a medium to carry the vibrations. If a noisy alarm clock or a ringing bell is suspended in a bell jar which can be evacuated, the sound will grow fainter and fainter as the air is pumped out. The medium can just as well be a liquid or a solid. Try holding your head under water while someone holding two stones under the water hits them together. The "clicking" sound will be surprisingly loud. The childhood "telephone" made from two empty tin cans with a wire stretched tightly between them shows how effectively a solid will carry sound.

Sound takes time to travel, as you know well enough from hearing echoes. It is clear by now that sound has several of the properties of a wave motion, and we shall explore several more. The previ-

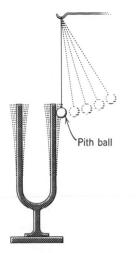

Figure 2–42. *A pith ball used to detect the vibration of a tuning fork.*

the properties of a wave motion. And so, by observing that sound has certain properties of waves, we can draw on the extensive knowledge of waves to help us study sound.

When a tuning fork is vibrating, the tines move out—knocking the air molecules away—then move back together, giving the air molecules a chance to bounce back toward the fork (Figure 2–43). The back-and-forth motion of the air particles is transmitted outward from the source in a longitudinal type of wave motion.

ous paragraphs illustrate a technique that has been very fruitful in the hands of scientists. The mathematically trained scientist notices many similarities between the properties of waves as an abstract mathematical study and those of the real waves in water. The field of mathematics developed more rapidly than the experimental sciences, so that much more was known about abstract waves than about water waves. The mathematicians could suggest things to look for in any phenomena that were suspected of having

FREQUENCY AND SPEED

The range of frequencies that the human ear can hear runs from about 16 per second to 20,000 per second or somewhat higher. Vibrations above the range that can be heard by human ears are called ultrasonic. Many animals, such as bats, dogs, and insects, can hear sounds well above 20,000 per second. Extremely high frequencies of several hundred thousand per second have curious and damaging effects. They churn up oil-and-water mixtures into a stable emulsion, and they may kill bacteria, for instance.

When an ordinary calling card is made

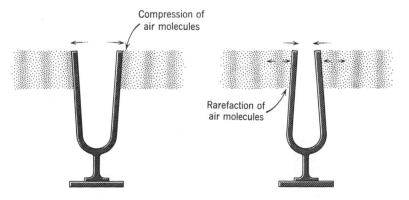

Figure 2–43. *Sound waves consist of a longitudinal-type wave motion of air molecules.*

to vibrate by being held against a rotating toothed wheel, a clear musical note is heard. If the wheel is speeded up, the note is of a higher pitch. A difference in pitch involves a difference in frequency of vibration. When an orchestra is tuning up, the note usually sounded is A above middle C. This note has a frequency of 440 vibrations per second, and middle C is 261.6.

The speed of sound in air varies with the temperature, but it is close to 1100 feet per second (750 miles per hour) under normal conditions. The speed is less at lower temperatures (for example, at higher altitudes). The speed of sound in air represents the speed at which the air molecules can pass on a disturbance to their neighbors. As the speed of an airplane approaches the speed of sound, the air molecules tend more and more to pile up in front of the leading edge of the wing instead of flowing smoothly around it. At this speed the propeller is no longer able to knock the air molecules aside fast enough to give the plane a forward velocity. The word "supersonic" refers to speeds greater than the speed of sound. For nearsonic and supersonic speeds a new wing design is necessary and a different type of propulsion (jet or rocket, etc.) is required. Ernst Mach, the Austrian physicist, worked out the theoretical implications of this situation, and we now use the term Mach number to represent the ratio of a plane's speed to the speed of sound.

Since feet/seconds $\times$ seconds = feet, the wavelength can be obtained by multiplying the speed by the period, or by dividing the speed by the frequency:

wavelength = speed $\times$ period
wavelength = speed/frequency
speed = wavelength $\times$ frequency

The third of these equations may be the easiest one to "see." If a string is vibrating 20 times per second, and if the first crest travels so fast that it is 55 feet away when the second one starts out, then the first crest will be 1100 feet away after 20 vibrations. It will have traveled 1100 feet in 1 second, which is one way of expressing the speed. The lowest note on a standard piano keyboard has a wavelength of about 49 feet. A above middle C has a wavelength of

$$1100 \frac{\text{feet}}{\text{seconds}} \times \frac{1}{440/\text{seconds}} = 2.5 \text{ feet}$$

The A which is three octaves above the standard A has a frequency of 3520 per second, and its wavelength is therefore 0.312 foot = 3.82 inches.

REFLECTION

Echoes not only show us that sound takes time to travel but also that it can be reflected. There are many famous whispering galleries where reflection concentrates sound waves so that a whisper can be heard at a great distance. When an architect designs an auditorium or a radio studio he must be careful to avoid large, flat, hard surfaces that will focus the sound waves or let them bounce back and forth (reverberate) for a long time. A reverberation time of about 1 second is considered the most desirable. Soft drapes and acoustical tile, which has many small holes to break up the sound waves, are effective in controlling echoes.

A very successful method for measuring the depth of the ocean depends on sending out sound impulses and timing the return of the echo from the bottom. A continuous record can be kept which is of great aid in navigation and which has revealed interesting facts about mountain ranges reaching nearly to the surface in the middle of the Atlantic Ocean.

Sonic depth finding is used by petroleum geologists to locate strata which might contain oil (Figure 2–44).

A blind person will tap a cane and listen for the echo to warn him of obstacles in his path. An extremely refined version of this technique of navigation (echolocation) is used by bats. While flying, they send out high-pitched ultrasonic squeaks which start at a frequency of 80,000 and drop to 40,000 vibrations per second, and which last for 0.001

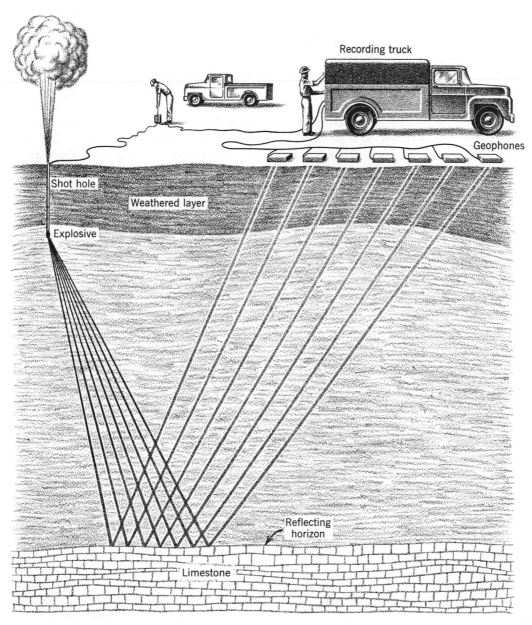

Figure 2–44. *Exploring for oil by observing the reflection of underground sound waves.*

second. The echo from an object as close as twelve inches gives them sufficient warning, so that they fly very successfully in pitch-dark caves, and catch insects at twilight.

INTENSITY

In sound waves a change of amplitude is heard as a change in loudness. Our unit for measuring sound intensity is the decibel. The scale of decibels is set up so that 0 represents the threshold of hearing, 120 the threshold of feeling, and a sound that differs by 10 decibels from another is 1 power of 10 times louder or fainter. In Table 2–2 the noise from an average radio (70 decibels) is 10 times as loud as that from a noisy office (60 decibels), and it is 100 times as loud as the average restaurant (50 decibels).

The whole range of hearing varies by 120 decibels, which is a difference in loudness of 10^{12}, or a million million.

Table 2–2 °

SOUND	LEVEL, db
Threshold of hearing	0
Whisper	15
Rustle of leaves in gentle breeze	20
Purring cat	25
Turning page of newspaper	30
Quiet home or private office	40
Average restaurant	50
Noisy office or store	60
Average radio	70
Street noise, large city	75
Truck, unmuffled	80
Noisy factory	85
Newspaper pressroom	90
Noisiest spot at Niagara Falls	95
Inside subway car	100
Loud thunder	110
Threshold of feeling	120

° L. W. Taylor, *Physics, The Pioneer Science,* Houghton Mifflin Co., New York, 1941.

The ear has the greatest range of sensitivity of any of our sense organs.

Interference of sound waves is responsible for the effect of beats. If we listen to the sound from two tuning forks which have exactly the same frequency, we will hear a steady tone; but if one fork is vibrating a little faster than the other, the two sets of waves will get out of step at regular intervals. While they are in step, crests and troughs from each arrive at your ear together. When they get exactly out of step, a crest (a compression) from one and a trough (a rarefaction) from the other arrive together and cancel each other (Figure 2–45), so that the sound dies out momentarily. This rising and falling of the intensity of the note is called beats. Each note on a piano is sounded by three strings, and on a mandolin by two. These strings must be very well tuned or the beats will spoil the tone.

The fact that we can "hear around a corner" is largely due to diffraction (Figure 2–46); otherwise, diffraction is not of much importance in the study of sound. Similarly, refraction is not commonly observed, although the familiar fact that sound carries unusually well over water is partly due to refraction. With a layer of cool air close to the water and a warmer one above it, some of the sound energy is refracted by the warm air and comes back to the surface (Figure 2–47).

DOPPLER EFFECT

The abrupt change in pitch of the note from a passing automobile horn or locomotive whistle is an example of the Doppler effect. Another example is observed when you are riding in a train and you whip past the warning bell at a railroad crossing. Just as you pass it, the pitch of the bell drops, and the faster the train is traveling, the greater is the change in pitch.

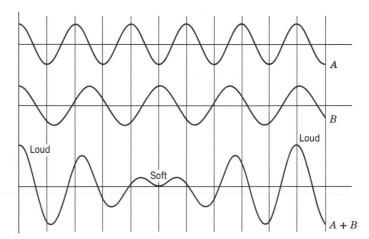

Figure 2–45. *The formation of beats by the interference of sound waves of nearly the same wavelength.*

If you are listening to a steady note of 500 vibrations per second, the actual number of crests and troughs reaching your ear each second depends on whether you are remaining at the same distance from the source of the sound, retreating from it, or approaching it. When you are approaching the source of the sound, more than 500 vibrations reach your ear each second, and the faster you approach, the greater is the apparent increase in pitch. It is only when you and the source of the sound remain at a constant distance that you hear the true pitch. As you travel past the crossing, the bell appears to drop in pitch and the locomotive whistle to remain constant. To the person waiting at the crossing, the bell

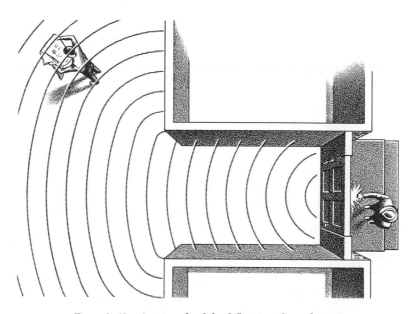

Figure 2–46. *An example of the diffraction of sound waves.*

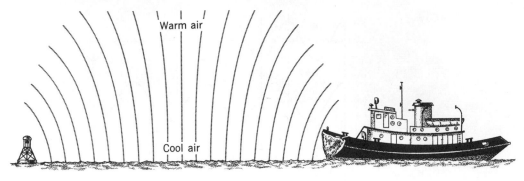

Figure 2–47.   An example of the refraction of sound waves.

continues to give out the same note but the locomotive whistle drops in pitch as it goes by.

As you will discover later, the Doppler effect is used to calculate some important relative motions so we will treat it quantitatively. Consider the case in which the source of the sound is stationary, the frequency of the sound emitted is fs, and the observer is approaching the source with a velocity V_0 feet per second (Figure 2–48). What is the frequency f_0 that

Figure 2–48.

the observer hears? If the observer remained at O_1, then fs vibrations would reach him in 1 second. But he moves through the distance O_1O_2 feet in 1 second so the number of vibrations that reaches him is fs plus the number in V_o feet. This number is

$$\frac{V_0}{\lambda} \text{ or } fs \; \frac{V_0}{V}$$

where V is the speed of sound. The frequency that he hears is

$$f_0 = fs + fs \frac{V_0}{V} = fs\left(1 + \frac{V_0}{V}\right)$$

If the observer is moving away from the source of the sound the observed frequency will be

$$f_0 = fs\left(1 - \frac{V_0}{V}\right)$$

RESONANCE

If two steel bars (xylophone bars, for instance) are tuned to the same note and one of them is struck the other will be set into vibration. This phenomenon is called resonance. The pressure waves striking the second bar are weak, but they are timed to the natural period of vibration of the bar and it responds to them. This isolated example is only one of many in which an absorber will pick up energy of the frequency to which it is tuned.

SUMMARY

1. Sound requires a vibrating source and a medium to carry it.
2. Sound waves behave like a longitudinal type of wave motion.
3. The speed of sound waves is about 1100 feet per second in air.
4. Sound waves show reflection, refraction, diffraction, and interference.

5. The frequency of sound waves is called pitch.
6. "Supersonic" refers to either motion of a velocity greater than that of sound, or sound waves of a frequency above that audible to human ears.
7. Amplitude in sound waves is called loudness.
8. Sound intensity is measured in decibels.
9. The Doppler effect is the apparent change in wavelength (or frequency) when the source of a wave motion is moving relative to the observer.
10. In the Doppler effect, the observed frequency,

$$f_0 = fs\left(1 \pm \frac{V_0}{V}\right)$$

QUESTIONS AND EXERCISES

1. What type of wave motion is a sound wave?
2. Calculate the wavelength of the note of middle C.
3. Calculate the frequency of the lowest note on the piano.
4. How far would you have to stand from a cliff for the echo of your shout to take 4 seconds to reach you?
5. An unmuffled truck is how many times noisier than a quiet home?
6. How fast would you have to approach the source of a steady sound to have it appear to be twice the frequency that it really is?
7. A man fires a bullet (speed = ½ mile per second) and hits a metal target ¼ mile away. How long after firing the shot does he hear the hit?
8. Use two tuning forks that give out the same note, and listen to them sounding together. Then wrap a rubber band several times around one tine and sound them together again. Notice the beats.
9. How far from a cliff are you standing if you hear the echo 5 seconds after you shout?
10. What is the advantage to the bat of having the pitch of its squeak change in frequency from start to finish?

Chapter 5

The Physical Basis of Music

WE HAVE considered such properties of sound waves as amplitude, frequency, and wavelength, but none of these explains how it is that you can tell the difference between middle C when played on a saxophone and on a violin. The amplitude and frequency can be the same, but there is no question as to which you are listening to. The difference must be in the shape of the wave between one crest and the next.

FUNDAMENTALS AND OVERTONES

Experiments with vibrating strings show that, other characteristics being the same, the shorter the vibrating section of the string, the higher is the frequency.

The vibrations of a string may be not only a simple swinging up and down of the middle section with the ends at rest; the middle also may be stationary with each half vibrating; or the string may vibrate in three, four, or several segments (Figures 2–49 and 2–50). The string on a musical instrument goes through a complicated combination of all these possibilities and consequently gives out a number of different notes. The simple vibration of the whole string determines what we call the "note" that is being played, middle C, for instance. This is called the fundamental. The other notes that accompany it are called overtones. The overtones have frequencies which are 2, 3, 4, etc., times that of the fundamental. The relative loudness of these differ-

Figure 2–49. Photograph of a string vibrating as a whole. (Photograph by Professor D. C. Miller.)

ent overtones determines the quality or timbre of the tone coming from the instrument. Not only string instruments, but also wind and percussion instruments, have combinations of overtones that characterize them. Figure 2–51 shows a graphical representation of notes from various instruments. The tuning fork is the only one that gives a pure fundamental without overtones.

INTERVALS

The earliest music probably consisted of singing in a monotone, with changes in tempo and loudness to give variety. As soon as two different notes were used, the problem of harmony and discord was introduced. The ratio of the frequencies of two notes is known as the interval between them. For A_3 ($f = 220$) and

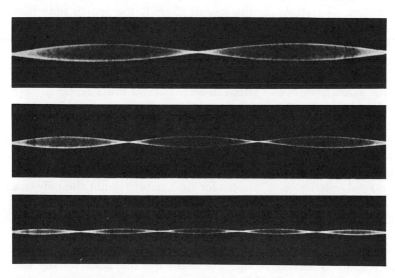

Figure 2–50. Photograph of a string vibrating in two, three, and five parts. (Photograph by Professor D. C. Miller.)

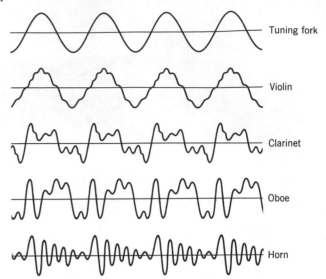

Tuning fork

Violin

Clarinet

Oboe

Horn

Figure 2–51. Shapes of the waves form from different instruments. All these have the same wavelength. The tuning fork is the only one without overtones. (From Classical and Modern Physics, *by E. H. White, D. Van Nostrand Co.)*

A_4 ($f = 440$), the interval is $440/220 = 2/1$. It is customary to write the fraction so that it is greater than 1. The only limit to the number of intervals possible is the ability of the human ear to distinguish tones. From this almost indefinitely large number of possible intervals, only a few have been used. The decision whether to use an interval is an entirely subjective one. There is nothing in the structure of our ears or nervous systems that makes a given pair of notes sound pleasant or unpleasant, but it is undoubtedly true that we prefer some combinations to others, and that the preferred combinations are not the same from one society to another, or from one century to another in the same society.

At this particular time in our society it is generally considered that a harmonious combination is obtained from any two tones for which the interval can be expressed by the whole numbers from 1 to 6. Less than two centuries ago the intervals 5/4 and 6/5 were felt to be discordant, and it appears that it will not be long before we will accept such intervals as 8/7 and 9/8 as pleasant. The notes G and A have an interval of 9/8, for in-

stance. The deplorable structure of our present musical scale will be explained in the next section, and you will see that it is responsible for much of the lack of harmony in some contemporary music.

The term interval has another use in the field of music, and this should be explained briefly. The interval called a fourth is obtained from the combination F/C (the higher note is written first). In the key of C, F is the fourth note that we strike, if we start with C as the first note. The combination G/D would also be a fourth. G/C is a fifth, and C/C is an octave. *The term interval will not be used in this sense in this chapter.*

THE MUSICAL SCALE

Our present musical scale of twelve notes for each octave is not the only one in use, but it would take us too far afield to study the others. Using the intervals mentioned in the previous section, the musical scale of twelve notes was built up, the notes for the scale in any one key having the following intervals: 9/8, 10/9, 16/15, 9/8, 10/9, 9/8, 16/15. For the octave starting with A = 220, this would work out A = 220, B = 247.5, C♯ = 275, D = 293.3, E = 300, F♯ = 366.7, G♯ = 412.5, A = 440. If you move up a note and start the scale with B = 247.5, the next note is C♯ = 278.4 (247.5 × 9/8). Already we have two different frequencies for C♯. Students of music who have taken their scale for granted will be interested to see the variety of frequencies represented by the same note in Table 2–3. This was obtained by starting with A, B, A♯, and C, and multiplying by the intervals given above.

It is obvious that we have here a chaotic situation in which an instrument tuned to one key could not be played in any other. This was exactly the situation two hundred and fifty years ago. Numerous ways out of the difficulty were suggested, and the one popularized by J. S. Bach (1685–1750) was the one finally adopted. It is not known who originally proposed the so-called "equal-tempered" scale but it stands as one of the most important examples of compromise in the history of Western civilization. In this scale the octave is built up of twelve notes, and the intervals for successive notes are equal. The frequency of any one note is obtained from that of the next lower one by multiplying by the factor of the twelfth root of 2, or 1.059.

The final column in Table 2–3 shows the frequencies of the notes on the equal-tempered scale. A careful comparison of this column with the others will show compromises of greater than 1%. Such discrepancies are readily observed by the trained ear. However, we are living in a period of active musical experimentation, and it may be that a more satisfactory solution for this problem will be devised.

SUMMARY

1. A fundamental tone is the note of lowest pitch that any sounding body can emit.
2. Overtones are any tones except the fundamental that a sounding body can emit.
3. Timbre is the quality of the note from a sounding body as determined from the overtones.
4. An interval is the ratio of the frequencies of two notes.
5. The intervals of the notes on the absolute scale are 9/8, 10/9, 16/15, 9/8, 10/9, 9/8, 16/15.
6. The intervals for all the notes on the equal-tempered scale are 1.059.

QUESTIONS AND EXERCISES

1. In the equal-tempered scale is the interval A/G actually 9/8?
2. Are the overtones of a certain note always higher in pitch than the fundamental?
3. In the equal-tempered scale, all the intervals are equal. Does this mean that it is the differences or the ratios between adjacent notes that are always equal?
4. Start with C♯ = 275, and calculate the frequencies for D♯, F, F♯, G♯, A♯, and C; compare your values with those in Table 2–3.
5. In the key of C, the interval E/C should be 5/4. Use decimal fractions and calculate how close it is to this in the true tone scale (C = 261) and in the equal-tempered scale.

Table 2–3

KEY	A=220	B=247.5	A♯=232	C=261	EQUAL-TEMPERED SCALE
A	220				220
A♯			232		233.1
B	247.5	247.5			246.9
C				261	261.6
C♯	275	278.4			277.4
D	293.3		290	293.6	293.7
D♯		309.4	309.3		311.1
E	330	330		326.3	329.6
F			348	348	349.2
F♯	366.7	371.2			370
G			386.7	391.5	392
G♯	412.5	412.5			415.3
A	440		435	435	440
A♯		464	464		466.2
B		495		489.4	493.9

Chapter 6

Light as a Wave Motion

S INCE we have studied certain aspects of the behavior of light, and
since we have explored wave motion even
more carefully, let us now see to what extent we can explain the facts about light in
terms of its acting like a wave motion.

REFLECTION, DIFFRACTION, AND REFRACTION

In reflection, the parallel is complete.
The angle of incidence equals the angle
of reflection in both cases. Waves and
light can be focused or diffused by
reflection, etc.

Figure 2–52 showing diffraction bands
was made by passing a beam of light

through a narrow slit. A series of dark
and light bands is observed on either side
of the central one.

Figure 2–53 is an analysis of what is
happening to the beams of light passing
through slits a and b. The distances ao
and bo are equal, but bp is longer than
ap by the distance bc. If light behaves
like a wave motion, then waves leaving
a and b will travel the same distance to
o and will always arrive in step; there
will be constructive interference (a bright
line) at o. At some distance above o there
will be a place p where the wave from b
has to travel a half wavelength farther
than the wave from a, so that they will
arrive out of phase, and there will be
destructive interference and a dark line.

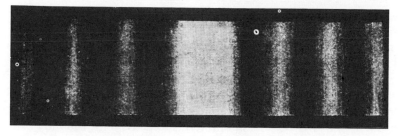

Figure 2–52. *Diffraction bands produced by light passing through a narrow slit. The wide central band is directly in front of the slit, the others are off to the sides. (General College Physics, by Randall, William, and Colby; Harper and Brothers.)*

The distance *bc* is half the wavelength of the light under these conditions. It was through this type of experiment that Thomas Young, in 1803, demonstrated the wave nature of light and showed that the different colors of the spectrum have different wavelengths. We can see in Figure 2–53 that, if *bd* is 1 wavelength, *q* will be a bright line. The longer the wavelength, the greater will be the distance from *o*, the central bright line, to *q*, the nearest bright line on either side of it.

A diffraction grating is made by ruling a number of closely spaced lines on a piece of glass through which light is transmitted or on a piece of polished metal from which it is reflected. These gratings have from 1000 to 25,000 lines per inch. Studying the diffraction of a beam of sunlight, we find that we get a spectrum of colors ranging from violet through blue, green, yellow, and orange to red. The violet is nearest the central bright spot, and the red is farthest away (diffracted through the greatest angle). If any small section of this spectrum is passed through a second grating, it is not broken up further, and so we see that the white light from the sun is actually a mixture of all the colors of the spectrum and that they differ from each other in wavelength. The red has the longest wavelength, the yellow an intermediate one, and the violet the shortest. These

wavelengths are measured in angstrom units (1 A $= 10^{-10}$ meter) or in millimicrons (1 mμ $= 10^{-9}$ meter). Visible light ranges in wavelength from 4000 to 8000 A, or 400 to 800 mμ. There are about 64,000 wavelengths of violet light in an inch.

The speed of light is one of the important constants of nature and is given the symbol *c*. $c = 3 \times 10^{10}$ cm per sec. From the relationship $c = \lambda \times f$ we can calculate the approximate frequencies in the range of visible light. These frequencies vary from 3.75 to 7.5×10^{14} vibrations per second.

On page 70 we studied refraction of light and on page 91 the refraction of waves in general. Here, again, we find that light has a wave-like behavior. A

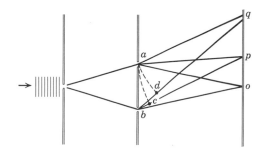

Figure 2–53. *Diffraction of monochromatic light. Bright spots appear at o and q, and a dark spot at p; bc is a half wavelength of the light, and bd is a whole wavelength.*

prism not only bends a beam of light but also spreads it out into a spectrum. As a wave passes from one medium into another, it is refracted toward the perpendicular if it travels more slowly in the second medium. The greater the change in speed, the greater is the change in direction, and so we see that, in passing through glass, violet light is slowed down more than red.

There seems to be no question about the fact that light in many ways resembles a wave motion. Many philosophers and scientists from Aristotle on have held this point of view. Later on we shall come to several experiments with light and other parts of the electromagnetic spectrum that are best explained in terms of light's behaving like a stream of particles. Newton (1642–1727) considered both theories carefully, and he decided that rays of light consisted of small bodies, or corpuscles. He thought that as these corpuscles approached a prism they were speeded up by attraction, and therefore had their direction changed. Actually, light is slowed down as it enters glass from air, but it was not possible, in Newton's day, to measure these speeds. His point of view was generally accepted until Thomas Young performed his experiments with diffraction. These brought the wave theory back into popularity, and only recently have we come to realize the awkward fact that both ways of looking at the behavior of light are valid.

THE COMPLETE ELECTROMAGNETIC SPECTRUM

As we look carefully at the brilliant spectrum from the sun, we see that at both ends the colors fade rather rapidly, but there is not a sharp line to mark the end. Could it be that there is "light" coming from the sun that we are unable to see? It is obvious that special methods of trying to detect this type of light will be necessary.

When sunlight is passed through a prism made of quartz, and the resulting spectrum is photographed, we find that the photographic plate is darkened all along the visible spectrum and for a considerable distance beyond the violet. In sunlight there must be rays that we cannot see, that have a shorter wavelength than the violet light. These unseen rays are ultraviolet. If we place a thermometer beyond the red end of this same spectrum we notice that it shows an increase in temperature, indicating an invisible infrared region in the sun's radiation. The infrared and ultraviolet rays are the same type of radiation as the visible light; they differ from it only in wavelength.

The invisible parts of the spectrum must be detected by many special means; when they are detected, we find an amazingly extensive spectrum of vibrations similar in nature to light.

Curiously enough, the two ends and the middle of the complete spectrum have been the most difficult to work with. Near the end of longest wavelength we have the ordinary amplitude-modulated radio waves with a wavelength of many miles. Special, short-wave radio broadcasting uses wavelengths down to about 100 feet, and also in this range are the wavelengths used for induction heating. Large metal castings can be heat-treated or roasts of beef can be cooked in a few minutes by radiations of these wavelengths. Television and frequency-modulated radios operate on wavelengths of a few feet. Radar detectors send and receive waves a few inches in length, and we are learning to use shorter and shorter waves in this region.

The region around 1 mm, or 10,000,000 A, has turned out to be exceedingly difficult to work with. From a wavelength of 1,000,000 A to 10,000 A is the infrared region, which is used principally for

Figure 2–54. Scene photographed by visible light. (Eastman Kodak Co.)

Figure 2–55. Same scene photographed on film sensitive to infrared light. (Eastman Kodak Co.)

radiant heating and, at the shorter end, for photographing through haze and smoke (Figures 2–54 and 2–55). The visible spectrum lies in the range 8000 to 4000 A. Between 4000 and 100 A is the ultraviolet region. Here are the wavelengths that tan the skin, increase the amount of vitamin D in milk, and kill bacteria (Figure 2–56). X-rays have a wavelength from 100 A to 0.1 A, and are particularly useful because of their penetrating power. Photographs taken through the human body locate broken bones and other internal disorders (Figure 2–57), and industrial products like steel castings and propellers can be examined for hid-

Figure 2–56.   Blood donations are processed in an atmosphere kept sterile by the long, slender ultraviolet lamps near the ceiling. (Lamp Division, Westinghouse Electric Corp.)

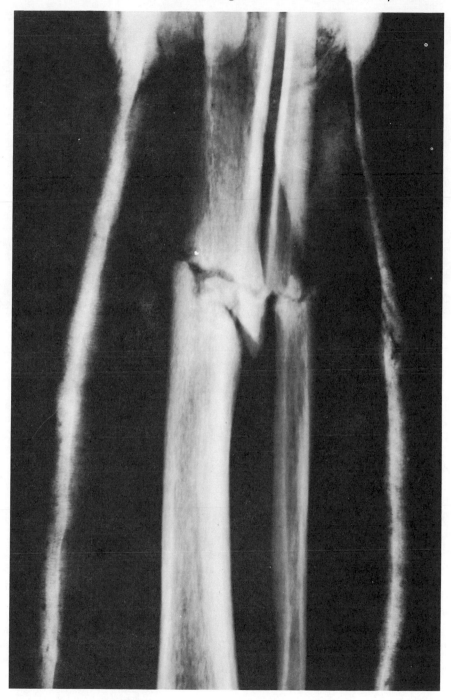

Figure 2–57.   An X-ray picture of a broken arm. (General Electric Co., X-ray Department.)

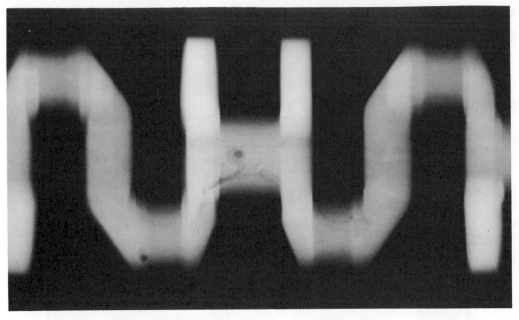

Figure 2–58.   An X-ray photograph of an automobile crankshaft, showing a flaw in the casting. (General Electric Co., X-ray Department.)

den flaws (Figure 2–58). Another important use of X-rays is in treating cancer. Overlapping the shorter X-rays and going down to 0.001 A are the gamma rays, which are the extremely penetrating and damaging radiation from atomic-bomb explosions.

Of even shorter wavelength and greater penetrating power than gamma rays are cosmic rays. Of their origin or behavior we may say only, on the basis of our present knowledge, that they come from outside the earth, can penetrate many feet of lead, and when they make one of their rare "hits" on a chromosome cell they may bring about a hereditary change that contributes to evolution.

SUMMARY

1. Light and waves follow the same laws of reflection, diffraction, and refraction.

2. The spectral colors differ in wavelength.
3. Visible light is only a small part of a wide spectrum of vibrations of a similar nature.
4. The complete electromagnetic spectrum includes (starting at the long wavelength end) radio waves of various kinds, infrared, visible, ultraviolet, X-rays, gamma rays, and cosmic rays.

QUESTIONS AND EXERCISES

1. In Figure 2–53 what other distance is equal to cp?
2. In the newspaper, look up the frequency of your favorite radio station. Calculate the wavelength on which it broadcasts. This "carrier frequency" will be explained in Unit Three.
3. What are some of the uses of the part of the electromagnetic spectrum with wavelengths longer than visible light?
4. Why do we get a tan at high altitudes faster than at sea level?

5. What parts of the complete electromagnetic spectrum affect a photographic plate?
6. Hold two fingers close together and look through the crack at a bright light. This is an easy way to observe a diffraction spectrum.
7. Would a narrow band of green light be bent by refraction as it passes through a prism, or by diffraction as it passes through a diffraction grating?

8. In an experimental determination of the index of refraction of a substance, would you get different results for different colors of light?
9. In Figure 2–53 how would the distance *o-p* be changed if *a* and *b* were closer together?
10. Why is it important to limit your exposure to X-rays to the extent that is medically necessary?

Chapter 7

Color

WHY DO LEAVES look green instead of white? Do they emit a light of their own which is green? Of course not, but how do we know? Try looking at the shiny reflection from the surface of a cobalt-blue glass. The light which merely bounces off the surface cannot have had any colors removed, and these colors all show up in the reflection. The transmitted light, however, is mostly blue. Through such a glass a red book appears to be black.

COLOR BY SUBTRACTION

The color of practically everything we see by daylight is obtained from the color of sunlight after certain wavelengths have been removed or reduced in intensity. When the white light from a projection lamp (or the sun) is passed through a prism, it is spread out into a spectrum. When colored filters are placed in the path of the light, various parts of the spectrum are cut out. What we would call the "color" of the filter is actually the sum of all the colors it transmits. By subtracting certain colors and transmitting others, the filter appears to be colored. A white surface, or a shiny surface of any color, reflects all the colors evenly. Light penetrates a short distance into a green blotter; the blotter absorbs the red and blue ends of the spectrum and reflects the green part of it. By way of contrast, a magenta dye absorbs the central part of the visible spectrum and transmits the red and blue extremes. Our eyes do not analyze colors into their parts the way a prism does. In the experiment with the red book and the blue glass, the dye in the cover of the book absorbs all but the red end of the spectrum, and this is reflected. This red light is absorbed by the blue glass so that no light from the book reaches our eyes, and we judge it to be black. When one filter absorbs exactly that part of the spectrum which is transmitted by another, the colors of the two filters are said to be complementary. By subtraction, complementary colors give black.

COLOR BY ADDITION

Color by subtraction, as described in the previous section, can also be thought of as color by addition, in that the color we see is made up of the sum of several colors. We have a somewhat altered situation when we use several sources of different-colored lights, as is the custom in stage lighting. Many different-colored bulbs are used in the battery of footlights to accent the color of shadows. If we examine the color prints in a magazine with a magnifying glass, we will see that each colored area is made up of tiny dots of a few different colors (probably three), with different proportions of each giving the over-all impression of several different colors.

The difference between color by subtraction and color by addition is illustrated in painting by the usual technique of mixing pigments on the palette, and by that of Seurat, who placed tiny dots of pigment close together. Look at a Seurat painting at close range and see the confusing mixture of small spots of color; then step back several feet and the individual spots will appear to fuse into areas of solid color that have an unusual brilliance. When the pigments are mixed on the palette,

each one subtracts certain wavelengths, so that the mixture is duller than any of the colors that went into making it up.

If two spotlights are focused on the same screen, and filters of complementary colors are placed in front of them, the whole spectrum will be present on the lighted spot, and it will appear white. Complementary colors by addition give white.

SPARK SPECTRA AND THE SPECTROSCOPE

When the light from a neon advertising sign is passed through a prism or a diffraction grating, we find that the spectrum consists of a number of bright lines with relatively long dark spaces between them. Such an apparatus, set up to measure the wavelengths of the different bright lines, is called a spectroscope, or spectrometer. An electric spark is used to excite different elements, and the spectra obtained are peculiar to the element. Sodium has a rather simple spectrum, with two prominent lines close together in the yellow; nitrogen, on the other hand, has many lines spaced across the spectrum. The spectroscope is an important tool of the astronomer (see page 246), and in the unit on the solar system we shall consider some of the information it gives us about the sun and stars. The colors seen in the northern lights are essentially this same phenomenon. Electrically charged particles from the sun enter the earth's atmosphere near the magnetic poles and excite a glow in the gases of the upper atmosphere.

FLUORESCENCE

We have found that an object may be colored because it absorbs some of the wavelengths from the light that strikes it and reflects others, or it may be colored because it takes the energy from an electric spark and radiates it as visible light. There are a few substances that can absorb visible or ultraviolet light and radiate it as light of a longer wavelength. This behavior is called fluorescence. The rather startling advertising billboards that seem to glow on an overcast day and the teenager socks that can be seen for blocks are examples of fluorescence.

Several important minerals fluoresce with a characteristic color when struck by ultraviolet light or X-rays. This property is used in prospecting. Fluorescent lamps consist of glass tubes coated on the inside with a mixture of fluorescent minerals. A mercury arc in the tube provides the ultraviolet light that makes the coating glow with a visible light. The color of the light given off by these tubes can be varied over a wide range by the use of different minerals, and the decorative possibilities here have barely been touched upon. Fluorescent minerals are finding another use on the screens of television sets.

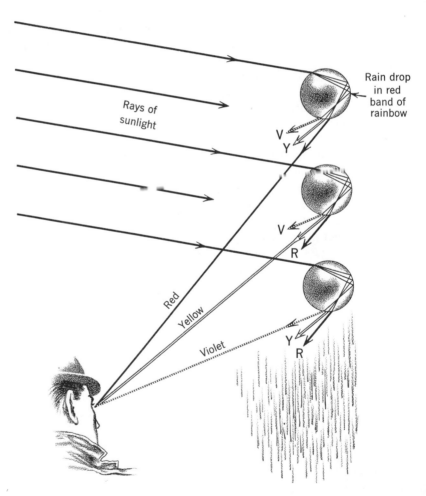

Figure 2–59.   The formation of the primary rainbow.

When a doctor "fluoroscopes" someone, he places a fluorescent screen in
front of the person and an X-ray tube
behind him so that the shadows cast by
the bones and organs of the person's
body can be examined. Since neither the
one being fluoroscoped nor the doctor
can stand exposure to X-rays for many
minutes, it is more usual to take a picture
which can be studied carefully.

SOME APPLICATIONS OF COLOR

There are innumerable situations in
which an understanding of color will
help us know more about what is going
on around us; we can discuss relatively
few of them here.

We have certainly observed the changing color of the sun as it sinks toward
the horizon. At noon it is a blinding yel-
low-white; at sunset we can look directly
at it and its color has changed to red.
The color of the sky during the day is
blue, which would suggest that the blue
end of the spectrum is scattered out
of the sunlight. The nearer the sun gets
to the horizon, the more of the earth's
atmosphere it must travel through, and
the greater is the amount of the blue
light that is scattered. The light that sur-
vives this long journey through the atmosphere has lost nearly all the short visible
wavelengths and consists almost entirely
of those in the long (red) end of the
spectrum.

A brilliant rainbow is one of the most
spectacular sights in nature. Remember
that to see a rainbow we must stand with
our backs to the sun and that colors
range through the spectrum from red on
the top and outside to violet on the inside
of the arc.

As the sunlight enters a raindrop it is
refracted, internally reflected at the back,
and refracted a second time as it leaves

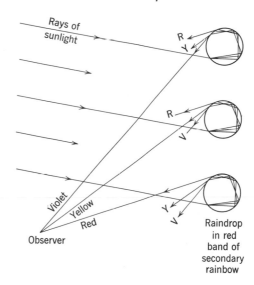

Figure 2–60.   The formation of a secondary rainbow.

near the bottom (Figure 2–59). Since the
violet end of the spectrum is bent through
a greater angle than the red in both these
refractions, as we look higher we see the
red light coming from some drops. The
yellow, green, and blue coming from
these same drops pass over our heads,
and we must look at the drops a little
lower to see these colors.

The secondary rainbow is outside the
primary one; the colors appear in the reverse order, and it is always fainter than
the primary one. By studying Figure 2–60
we can see why this is so.

Since the index of refraction of a certain kind of glass is different for different
colors, we would expect that a lens would
bring the red and the blue light to a focus
at different points. There is always a color
fringe around the image formed by a
simple lens. This behavior of lenses is
called chromatic aberration, and it is
usually a nuisance. It can be corrected
by making use of the fact that some types
of glass give a greater spread (dispersion) to
the colors than other types. If a slightly diverging lens made of glass with a high

dispersing power is placed behind a converging lens made of glass having a low dispersing power, then both the red and the blue rays can be brought to a focus at the same place. The image will be farther back of the lens than it would be for a simple converging lens, but it does not suffer from chromatic aberration. All good camera and binocular lenses are made this way (Figure 2–1).

SUMMARY

1. Color by subtraction is the partial or complete removal of certain wavelengths of incident light during reflection or transmission.
2. Color by addition is the adding together of light of two or more different wavelengths to produce a combination color.
3. A spark spectrum is the light given out by a substance when it receives energy from an electric spark. This type of spectrum consists of a number of narrow lines.
4. Fluorescence is light which is given out by a substance as a result of the absorption of energy or light of a different wavelength. Fluorescence stops immediately after the exciting rays are cut off; in phosphorescence, the glow continues for some time afterward.
5. The particles of the atmosphere scatter the blue end of the spectrum more effectively than the red end.
6. A rainbow is the result of a combination of refraction and internal reflection of sunlight in raindrops.
7. Chromatic aberration occurs when a simple lens focuses the blue light from an object closer to the lens than the red light. A lens corrected for chromatic aberration is said to be achromatic.

QUESTIONS AND EXERCISES

1. What color is the complement to magenta?
2. Are the colors we see around us in life mostly due to color by addition, by subtraction, or a combination of the two?
3. Explain in detail how the use of many different-colored bulbs in theatre footlights produces colored shadows on the stage and, at the same time, the impression of white light on the actors.
4. How could a spectroscope be used to identify the elements present in a mixture of gases?
5. What sources of color have been mentioned which do not have their origin in sunlight?
6. If we had no atmosphere, what would be the color of the sky?
7. Why can't we see the stars in the daytime?
8. Under what conditions could we see a rainbow as a complete circle?
9. Make a sketch showing what an achromatic lens looks like.
10. Suggest two ways of detecting ultraviolet light.

Chapter 8

Motion Pictures

and Polarized Light

PHOTOGRAPHY is much more than a hobby; it is one of our most important means of entertainment, an art form, an aid in education and job training, and a scientific tool. Motion pictures are widely used in all these ways. You may have noticed and been puzzled by the appearance of carriage wheels in the movies. Usually they seem to be rolling forward or backward with no relation to the actual motion of the vehicle. An examination of this problem will help you understand how movies are made and projected.

CAMERA AND PROJECTOR

A movie camera takes a picture with such a fast shutter speed that there is usually little or no blurring of the image. The film is stationary while the shutter is open. While the shutter is closed a new frame of film moves into place, the motion of the film stops for another picture to be taken, etc.

Moving pictures are normally filmed at a speed of twenty-four frames per second. After a reel has been exposed, it is developed, fixed, and washed, and contact prints are made. In this case, the positive print is printed on a transparent celluloid base because it is going to be projected and not viewed by reflected light.

A motion-picture projector is constructed much like a camera with a bright light behind the film (Figure 2–61). The film is motionless while the shutter is open; the shutter closes while the frames are being shifted. Of course, there is no motion in any one picture, and the original subject was moving while the shutter of the camera was closed, so what is projected is a series of stills that differ from each other by a slight extent. The image of each picture persists on our retina (page 86) during the brief time the shutter of the projector is closed. We interpret the series of overlapping images as one of smooth motion.

Getting back to the appearance of the carriage wheel, consider one with four spokes for convenience. If the wheel makes a quarter revolution during the

time the shutter is closed, every picture will show the spokes in the same position and the wheel will seem to be stationary. If the wheel makes a little less than a quarter (or a half, etc.) revolution while the camera shutter is closed, each picture will show it a little behind the position of the last one, so that it appears to be revolving slowly backward. At other speeds it will look as though it is going slowly forward or moving rapidly.

THE MOVIE PROJECTOR AS A TIME MACHINE

A movie camera can be used as a time microscope to enlarge an interval of time which is too short to examine carefully; or, as when binoculars are used to minimize rather than magnify, a long interval of time can be condensed so that it can be studied more effectively. By running the camera fast, so that it takes ninety-six pictures a second, and projecting the film at twenty-four frames per second, action which took place in fifteen seconds is slowed down so that it takes a minute to project. Athletic coaches find this "slow-motion" technique very handy. When we want to study the germination of seeds, the growth of a fern, or the opening of a flower, the subject is photographed on a new frame every five minutes, or even every half hour, and the resulting film is projected at the normal rate. This compresses this action of many hours into a few minutes and is referred to as "time-lapse" photography. For special industrial problems, lights have been developed that flash brilliantly for a millionth of a second at intervals of one hundred thousandth of a second, the film rolls through the camera continuously, and rapid motion can be studied with precision (Figure 2–62).

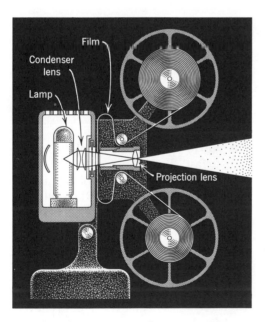

Figure 2–61.   A motion-picture projector.

Figure 2–62.   Rapid action caught by technique of high-speed photography. (Harold E. Edgerton.)

POLARIZED LIGHT

The sciences have been extremely fortunate in that the definitions in these fields are usually operational. In an operational definition a term is defined in words that tell you how to measure or observe it. Contrast the definition of the index of refraction (page 72), which is given in terms of angles that can be measured, with the following one taken from a dictionary: "*free.* (Political.) Having, conferring, or characterized by political liberty; not subject to despotic or arbitrary rule." Just think how that use of that word is open to a variety of interpretations, how many groups of people would disagree about their own and the others' freedom.

In regard to polarized light, we will

soon come to a definition that is couched in terms of how it is observed, rather than in terms of what we think is happening. As we learn more about it, our definition will not need changing. If you place a single dot on a piece of paper and look at it through a crystal of Iceland spar, you will see two dots, one of which rotates around the other as the crystal is rotated. If you observe the two dots through a second crystal of Iceland spar, you will find that one or the other dot can be made to disappear by rotating the second crystal in a horizontal plane. The two crystals can be interchanged and the behavior is the same.

It is obvious that the light emerging from the first crystal is different from that entering it. Each of the two dots that you see consists of a beam of light which is said to be polarized. Looking through the second crystal, you can ro-

tate it so that one of these polarized beams is cut out and the other comes through. By rotating the second crystal through 90° you can cut out the first ray and let through the second. The word polar implies that the beam is different in one direction than it is in another. In order to judge whether a certain source of light is polarized, you need a crystal of Iceland spar or some material that behaves like it. If this can be rotated in the plane perpendicular to the path of the beam of light to produce a change in intensity of the light, then the light is polarized.

The most suitable explanation for this situation seems to be the conception of light as a wave motion. If we picture a beam of light as consisting of a large number of waves, like waves in a vibrating string, which vibrate in many different planes, and polarized light as consist-

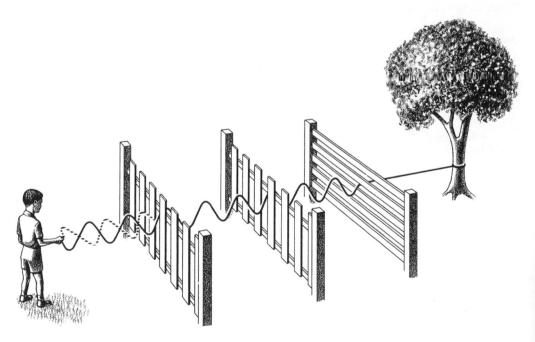

Figure 2–63.   An analogy to show why polarized waves are transmitted through a filter held in one position and blocked when the filter is held at right angles to that position. (After Polaroid Corp.)

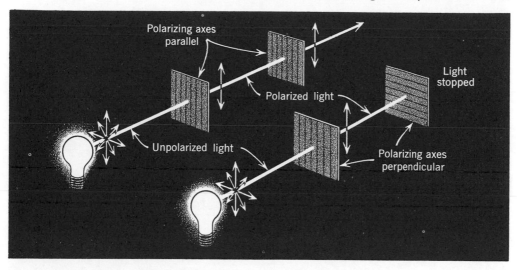

Figure 2–64.   The action of polarizing filters on light.

ing of waves which vibrate in only one plane, then this situation makes sense. Imagine a clothesline tied to a tree and passed through three sections of picket fence (Figure 2–63). If the line is vibrated in several different planes, only the waves in a vertical plane will pass through the first fence. The waves approaching the second fence are polarized. The fact that they pass through the second fence does not tell us that they are polarized, but when the third fence stops them we know that they are polarized, and they must have been vertically polarized to have gone through the second fence. Figure 2–64 applies this picture to light. Few human eyes can observe the difference between unpolarized and polarized light.

There are many substances that will polarize light. The only one developed, so far, that can be made in large thin sheets is Polaroid. This was developed by E. H. Land while he was an undergraduate at Harvard University. There are many interesting applications of polarized light that have been opened up by the production of Polaroid. Since a pair of Polaroid disks will not transmit light when their polarizing axes are crossed (Figure 2–65), they can be used to control the intensity of light. Reflection partially polarizes light, so that glare can be cut out with Polaroid glasses. These are particularly useful at the beach and for driving. A polaroid filter placed over a camera lens will cut out the glare from a brightly lighted scene and show more detail (Figures 2–66 and 2–67).

The sunlight scattered by the particles of the earth's atmosphere is partially polarized, the effect being most pronounced in a direction at right angles to the sun. There are a few people who can detect polarized light with the unaided eye. Experiments with bees indicate that they can detect it accurately and that it serves to guide them in their flight.

If a solution of sugar in water is placed between a pair of crossed Polaroid disks light will be transmitted through the system. The disk closer to your eye can be turned clockwise and the transmitted light is again cut out. The sugar solution

Figure 2–65.   Two Polaroid disks do not transmit light when their polarizing axes are crossed. (Polaroid Corp.)

is said to be optically active and to twist the plane of polarization of the light to the right. Optical activity is a property possessed by some solids, liquids, solutions, and gases. A study of optical activity has furnished some valuable clues to the structure of molecules and these will be studied in Unit Four.

SUMMARY

1. The ordinary motion-picture camera takes a series of pictures on a long roll of film which moves past the lens in a series of jerks. The shutter is open when the film is stationary and closed when the film is moving.

Figure 2-66.   Picture taken without Polaroid filter. Note glare. (Polaroid Corp.)

Figure 2-67.   Same picture taken with Polaroid filter. Most of the glare has been eliminated. (Polaroid Corp.)

2. Motion-picture positive film (print) has a transparent base.
3. The motion-picture projector works like a camera, except that there is a light source behind the film.
4. Slow-motion pictures are taken at a faster rate than normal and are projected at the usual rate. This technique is used for studying rapid motion.
5. Time lapse pictures are taken at long intervals and are projected at the normal rate. This technique is used for studying motion that is too slow to observe otherwise.
6. There are certain transparent substances (referred to as the analyzer) that will reduce the intensity of the transmitted light when they are rotated in a plane perpendicular to a beam of a certain type of incident light. When this happens the incident light is said to be polarized.
7. A substance (solid, liquid, or gas) is said to be optically active if it exhibits the following behavior: the analyzer is set for minimum transmission of a beam of polarized light; the substance in question is placed in the beam; the light transmitted by the analyzer increases in intensity.
8. Unpolarized light may be polarized by transmission through a polarizing medium, by reflection, and by other special techniques.
9. A polarizing medium, such as Polaroid, may be used to control light intensity and glare, to study optical activity, and for many other purposes.

QUESTIONS AND EXERCISES

1. What are the two most important factors in determining that motion pictures should be filmed and projected at a speed of twenty-four frames per second?
2. How long does any one image persist on the retina?
3. In the very highest-speed rapid photography, the film does not stop while the picture is being taken. Why is the image not blurred?
4. If, as you view a movie of a moving carriage wheel, it appears to be stationary, what does this tell you about how fast it is rotating?
5. By looking through one lens of a pair of Polaroid sun glasses and rotating it as you look at a source of light, you can judge whether the light is polarized. Examine light reflected from shiny surfaces, various parts of the sky, the moon, and dots seen through a crystal of Iceland spar.
6. How would the use of a Polaroid filter over your camera lens affect exposure time?
7. In what way would a Polaroid filter help in taking a picture of white clouds and a bright-blue sky?
8. When threading film in a movie projector, why is it important to leave a substantial loop of film on either side of the film gate?
9. Which of the two types of wave motion is indicated by the fact that light can be polarized?
10. Devise a simple experiment to determine whether your own eyes can detect polarized light.

Unit Three

Electricity and Magnetism

Chapter 1

Static Electricity

ELECTRIC MOTORS start our cars and run our tools and washing machines; all long-distance communication depends on electricity; the majesty of lightning and the crackle of cat's fur are two extremes of the same thing—a spark of electricity. Two of the three basic particles of atomic structure bear electric charges. We shall study some of the laws of this subject that reaches into so many aspects of our lives.

There are many examples of static electricity that can be noticed on dry days. On a clear, cold day the air indoors is almost sure to be dry. Hair follows the comb; the cat's fur crackles when it is stroked; we get shocks from metal objects or other persons after scuffing our feet on carpets; rayon or nylon slips or shirts, as they are taken off, cling to the body.

THE INTERACTION OF CHARGES

Phenomena similar to the above ones have intrigued mankind for well over two thousand years, yet it was not until two hundred years ago that someone worked out a reasonable explanation. With a few well-planned experiments, this explanation will become apparent to you in a few minutes.

We shall use two rods, one of hard rubber and one of glass; two pieces of

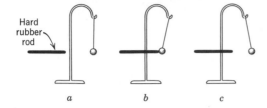

Hard
rubber
rod

a   b   c

Figure 3–1.   Behavior of a pith ball near a charged rod.

material, one of cat's fur and one of silk; and two pith balls suspended on silk threads. First touch one of the pith balls with your finger, then rub the hard-rubber rod with cat's fur and bring the rod close to the pith ball. The ball will jump toward the rod, cling to it for a second or so, and then spring away from it (Figure 3–1). As we follow the ball with the rod, it keeps swinging away. Now repeat the above experiment with the glass rod, the silk cloth, and the other pith ball. The results will be exactly the same. We say that we have charged the pith balls with electricity.

Now let us perform three more experiments which will give us further insight into the behavior of electricity. Charge each of the two pith balls with the hard-rubber rod rubbed with cat's fur, then bring them close together. Figure 3–2 shows how they will repel each other. Repeat the experiment, charging the two balls with the glass rod rubbed with silk. Again the balls repel each other. Finally, charge one pith ball with the hard-rubber rod rubbed with cat's fur and the other

ball with the glass rod rubbed with silk. When the two balls are brought close together they swing toward each other (Figure 3–3) and touch.

Whatever we may decide later about electric charges, it is reasonable to assume that the two pith balls charged by the hard-rubber and cat's-fur technique received the same kind of charge. That experiment indicates that like charges repel each other. The experiment in which the pith balls were charged with the glass rod and silk technique supports this conclusion. When the two balls charged by the two different techniques are brought close and show attraction, we are forced to the conclusion that there are at least two different kinds of electricity. Like charges repel in each case, but unlike charges attract each other. The names negative and positive have been given to these two kinds of electricity, and they are the only kinds discovered so far. The name negative is applied by definition to the kind of electricity left on the surface of a hard-rubber rod after it has been rubbed with cat's fur. This is the basic definition in the field of electricity.

As we shall see in the unit on atomic structure, we now think that all matter is composed of three fundamental types of particles, which are called electrons, protons, and neutrons. The electrons bear a single negative charge; the protons, a single positive charge; and the neutrons have no electric charge. The protons and

Figure 3–2.   Behavior of two pith balls when charged alike.

Figure 3–3.   Behavior of two pith balls when they carry opposite charges.

neutrons constitute the mass and the structural unity of any substance, and the electrons are relatively free to wander through matter and to be transferred from one substance to another.

INDUCTION

After one more experiment we can start talking about these effects in terms of the motion of electrons. Use a blunt, cigar-shaped, metal cylinder, as in Figures 3–4a and b, with negatively charged pith balls hung near the ends as indicators. The + − charges at either end of the cylinder indicate that it is electrically neutral and that the charges are evenly distributed. In Figure 3–4b a negatively charged rod, R, has been brought up near the left end of the cylinder. The left pith ball swings toward the cylinder, and the right one swings away from it, indicating that the left end of the cylinder is charged positively and the right end is charged negatively. The excess electrons on the rod have repelled the free-moving electrons on the cylinder, so that they are crowded toward the far end. When the charged rod is removed from the vicinity of the cylinder the two pith balls will again hang vertically, showing that the charge on the cylinder is again distributed uniformly. This temporary separation of charges is called induction.

In the process of charging the pith balls as described on page 130, the cat's fur and the hard-rubber rod each had approximately the same number of electrons as protons. The rubbing transferred some electrons from the fur to the rod, and we represent these extra electrons by (−) around the rod, as in Figure 3–4b. The pith ball was touched to neutralize any excess charge which it may have had from a previous experiment. When the rod was brought near the pith ball, induc-

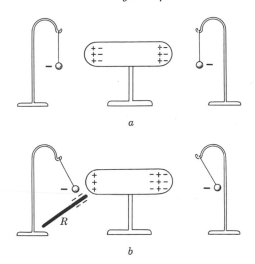

Figure 3–4. Part a shows a neutral metal cylinder with charges evenly distributed. Part b shows these charges separated by induction. Pith balls on stands show up this separation of charges.

tion forced electrons to the far side and the excess protons were attracted to the electrons on the rod. This made the ball swing toward the rod and cling to it. Some electrons then flowed from the rod to the ball, and the ball soon had more electrons than protons. It was now charged negatively as a whole and was repelled by the rod, which was still left with a negative charge.

CONDUCTORS, SEMICONDUCTORS, AND INSULATORS

If experiments of the above type are carried out with metal rods, or if the pith ball is suspended by a metal thread, no charge can be detected. Electrons flow along some substances much more easily than along others. Substances along which electrons flow easily are called conductors. Metals are good conductors, and copper is one of the very best. Substances along which electrons do not flow readily are called insulators. Glass, rubber, dry thread, and paper are examples of insulators. The human body is a moderately poor conductor, but it is good enough to conduct a charge from the earth to any charged body that is touched. You are sufficiently well insulated to acquire a fair charge by scuffing your feet on the carpet on a dry day. You might plan and carry out an experiment to test whether this charge is positive or negative.

Certain elements, particularly silicon and germanium, have conducting properties intermediate between those of metals and insulators. They are called semiconductors. A moderately high voltage will send only a small current through them. With metals there are many electrons free to move when a voltage is applied to the two ends of a conductor. The electrons in an insulator are so tightly bound that it takes a very high voltage to move even a few of them.

The conductance of semiconductors can be controlled by the inclusion of small amounts of impurities. If arsenic is introduced, extra electrons are added to the crystal structure and a so-called n or negative type semiconductor is obtained. When boron is the added impurity, there

are then extra holes in the crystal structure into which electrons can move from nearby silicon atoms. When an electron moves, a hole is left behind, so that the electrons and holes move in opposite directions. This kind of a semiconductor is referred to as a p or positive type. The conductance of both the n and the p types is higher than that of pure silicon and can be regulated by the amount of impurity introduced.

THE GOLD-LEAF ELECTROSCOPE

Another sensitive instrument that can be used to detect an electric charge is a gold-leaf electroscope. This device consists of two strips of gold leaf attached to a metal rod and enclosed in a box with glass sides to protect the fragile gold leaf from air currents. The metal rod projects through an insulator in the top of the box, and the strips of gold leaf hang vertically beside each other (Figure 3–5). When a positively charged rod is brought close to the knob on top of the rod, some of the electrons are drawn up from the gold leaf. Both leaves are left charged positively, and so they repel each other and diverge (Figure 3–5). When a negatively charged rod is brought near the knob, the electrons on the knob are driven down to the gold leaves, which thereby acquire a negative charge and again diverge. Thus, an uncharged electroscope detects the presence of a charge but not its sign.

If the positively charged rod is touched to the knob of the electroscope and then withdrawn, some electrons will jump from the knob over to the rod and the electroscope will be left with more protons than electrons. It will be charged, and the leaves will remain diverged. If a negatively charged rod is brought near the knob of this positively charged electroscope, the leaves will approach each

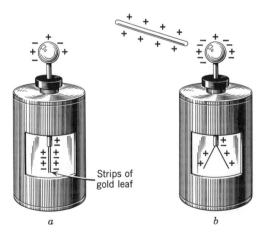

Figure 3–5. *Gold-leaf electroscope used to detect charge on rod.*

Strips of gold leaf

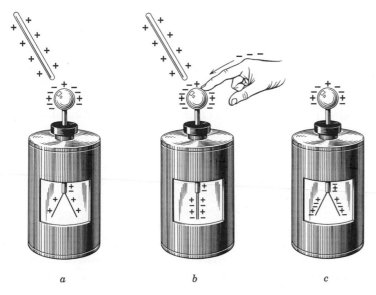

Figure 3–6. Charging an electroscope by induction. In part b, electrons move from the hand to the knob so that the leaves receive a charge opposite to that on the rod.

other. Why? The approach of a positively charged rod will make the leaves diverge farther. A charged electroscope can be used to indicate the sign of the charge on a body.

An electroscope can be charged by induction, as indicated in Figure 3–6. Notice that the rod does not touch the knob and that the charge acquired by the electroscope is the opposite of the one on the rod.

If there are charges in the air surrounding a charged electroscope, they will be attracted to the leaves and neutralize them. This kind of device has been most useful in studying X-rays and radioactivity, and it will be discussed again in the unit on atomic structure.

CONDENSERS

An insulated metal plate can be charged by contact with a charged rod (Figure 3–7). After a certain number of electrons have been transferred from the rod, the ones on the tip of the rod are repelled as much by those already on the plate as by those behind them on the rod. We can say that the plate has been filled to its capacity with electrons. A similar situation would hold if the rod were positive and electrons were being removed from the plate. Now let another plate (the left one in Figure 3–7), which is connected by a wire to the ground (notice the symbol), be brought up close to the first one.

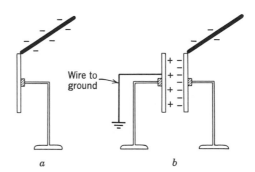

Figure 3–7. Condenser action. The proximity of a grounded plate at b makes it possible to transfer more electrons from the rod to the insulated plate.

There is a force of repulsion between the electrons on the two plates, and those on the left-hand plate can move through the wire to the ground. They will do so, and that plate is left with a positive charge. The positive charge partially neutralizes the negative charge on the other plate so that now a negatively charged rod can transfer more electrons to it. Its capacity has been increased by the proximity of the grounded plate. Such a combination of parallel plates is called a condenser. The symbol for a condenser is ——————||—————— or —————⊏▭⊐————— . One of the plates of a condenser does not have to be connected to the ground, but both should be made of material that is a good conductor, so that the electrons can distribute themselves over the surface readily.

One form of condenser which is convenient for lecture demonstration and laboratory work is the Leyden jar (Figure 3–8). A large glass jar has a metal lining inside and outside. With the outside lining grounded a very high charge can be put on the inside lining, and a juicy spark can be drawn from it. You should be extremely careful in handling a charged Leyden jar.

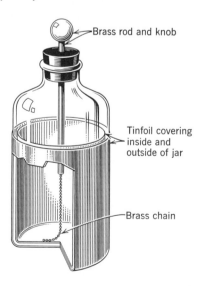

Figure 3–8. Diagram of a Leyden jar condenser.

Brass rod and knob

Tinfoil covering inside and outside of jar

Brass chain

USING METALS TO OBTAIN AN ELECTRIC CHARGE

We have learned that different non-conductors have different tendencies to hold on to electrons. Cat's fur will give up electrons to hard rubber and to glass. Glass will give electrons up to silk, and silk will give them up to hard rubber. Arranging them in increasing order of their tendency to hold on to electrons, we would have cat's fur, glass, silk, and hard rubber.

Metals also have different tendencies to hold on to electrons. This is best illustrated by the following type of experiment. Drop a strip of zinc into a solution of copper sulfate and a strip of copper into a solution of zinc sulfate. The strip of metallic copper will remain unchanged for days. The zinc will be covered with a dark deposit, and after a few hours the blue color of the copper sulfate solution will fade. By the end of twenty-four hours the zinc strip will have disintegrated, leaving a dark, reddish-brown deposit, and the solution will be clear.

In the solution of the metal salts, the metals are in the form of atoms that have lost two electrons. (Atomic structure is described in Unit Four.) These charged particles are called ions. The zinc and copper ions can be represented as $zinc^{2+}$ and $copper^{2+}$. In the metal strips the atoms of zinc and copper are neutral—they have the same number of electrons and protons, and they can be represented as $zinc^{2\mp}$ and $copper^{2\mp}$.

Both the disappearance of the blue color typical of copper ions in solution and the formation of the reddish-brown deposit indicate that $copper^{2+}$ ions have taken on electrons and have been deposited as $copper^{2\mp}$. This explanation is strengthened by the fact that the zinc strip dissolved. The $zinc^{2\mp}$ gave up electrons and went into solution as $zinc^{2+}$. In the competition for electrons the copper

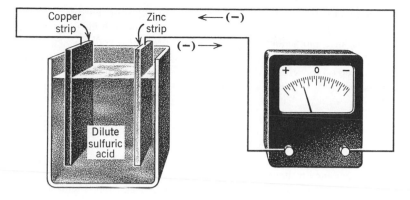

Figure 3–9.   A meter is used to show the direction of flow of the electrons in the circuit.

was able to take them away from the zinc. In the experiment in which the copper strip was placed in the zinc sulfate solution there was no change. The zinc ions were not able to take electrons away from the copper atoms. From this observation we can conclude that, in the competition for electrons, copper will win out over zinc.

Copper and zinc strips can be placed in the same solution of very dilute sulfuric acid and connected to a meter that indicates which way the electrons are flowing through the wire (Figure 3–9). In this case the zinc is going into solution and giving up electrons to the wire. They pass through the meter and go over to the strip of copper.

This experiment will show you which way the needle swings for a known direction of the flow of the electrons. Now you can compare different pairs of metals and arrange them in a series with the one having the greatest tendency to give up electrons at the top and the one having the strongest tendency to hold on to electrons at the bottom. An example of a list of metals arranged in such a series is: potassium, calcium, sodium, magnesium, aluminum, zinc, iron, tin, hydrogen, copper, silver, gold.

In the setup illustrated in Figure 3–9, the electrons will continue to flow through the wire so long as there is any zinc left to dissolve. We will have a current of electricity instead of just a temporary charge put on a rubber rod or Leyden jar. The discovery of current electricity was made in 1800, and it introduced a whole new era in the study of electricity.

SUMMARY

1. Electrons are fundamental units of atomic structure that bear a single electric charge.
2. The electrons are mobile, but the other two fundamental units, protons and neutrons, are relatively fixed.
3. Any two different substances have different tendencies to hold onto electrons.
4. Negative electricity is the kind of electric charge left on the surface of a hard-rubber rod that has been rubbed with cat's fur.
5. Like electric charges repel each other.
6. Unlike electric charges attract each other.
7. Induction is the displacement of electrons by the force of a nearby electric charge.
8. All degrees of resistance to the flow of electrons through materials may be observed, and these materials are divided roughly into conductors, semiconductors, and insulators.
9. Small amounts of certain elements are added to pure semiconductors to give either an *n* or a *p* type.
10. A gold-leaf electroscope is charged with the same kind of electricity as the charging

rod by contact and with the opposite kind by induction.

11. A condenser is an arrangement of metal plates such that the number of electrons that can be stored on (or withdrawn from) one is increased by the presence of the other.

12. The elements have been arranged in an electromotive series that lists them in the increasing order of their tendency to hold onto electrons. Those listed first (at the top) have the least tendency to hold onto electrons. They have a tendency to give up electrons to those listed below them and to go into solution as positively charged ions.

QUESTIONS AND EXERCISES

1. Describe, in terms of the motion of the electrons, the process of charging a pith ball positively.

2. In the experiment with induction illustrated in Figure 3–4, what would have been the position of the pith balls if the rod had been touched to the cylinder and then removed?

3. In the experiment with induction illustrated in Figure 3–4, what would have been the position of the pith balls if, when the rod was near the cylinder, the operator had briefly touched the right-hand end of the cylinder with his finger and had then withdrawn the rod?

4. Describe in detail an experiment that you could perform at home to test the sign of the charge you acquire by scuffing your feet on the carpet.

5. Pith balls and gold leaf are used in studying static electricity because they are so light. Why is this quality important?

6. Describe the behavior of an uncharged pith ball when a Lucite plastic rod which has been rubbed with wool is brought near it.

7. In the experiment illustrated in Figure 3–9, the pointer on the meter is shown swinging to the left. Which way would it swing if, for the zinc strip, there was substituted one of aluminum? Iron? Silver?

8. As in Problem 7, which way would the pointer swing if, instead of the copper strip, there was substituted one of aluminum? Tin? Silver?

9. What is the sign of the charge left on a gold-leaf electroscope that has been charged by induction by means of a glass rod rubbed with silk?

10. If you bring a negatively charged rod near an electroscope that has divergent leaves and if the leaves are spread apart even farther, what is the sign of the charge on the electroscope?

Chapter 2

The Development of Our

Ideas About Electricity

THALES (640–560 B.C.) was the first to record an observation of static electricity; he noticed that after amber had been rubbed with cloth it would pick up small pieces of straw and lint. Not until 1600 were there any significant new discoveries in the field of electricity. William Gilbert, the physician to Queen Elizabeth, prepared a list of substances that he could charge by friction and another list of those that he could not charge. From the Greek word for amber, "elektron," he coined the word electricity.

In 1650 Otto von Guericke described his experiments using a large ball of sulfur which was rotated on an axle (Figure 3–10). He could give the ball a charge by holding his hands against it as it turned.

Many other experimenters used this same technique to study static electricity.

In 1735 Du Fay came to the conclusion that there must be two types of charge, resinous and vitreous, and that like charges repel each other and unlike charges attract each other. The Leyden jar was discovered in 1745. This was the first condenser, and it furnished a means for storing large amounts of charge. With this more potent source of electricity many new discoveries were made.

In 1747 Benjamin Franklin suggested that we did not need to assume that there were two different kinds of electricity. He argued that a neutral body had just its normal amount of electricity, and when the body was charged we had either

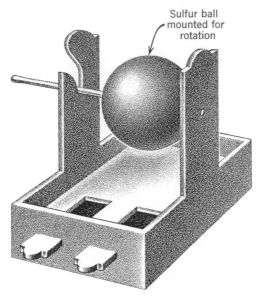

Sulfur ball mounted for rotation

Figure 3–10.   Von Guericke's electrostatic machine.

have combined his terms with the theory of Du Fay.

In 1752 Franklin carried out his famous experiment with the kite (Figure 3–11). The report of this experiment caused much excitement in Europe, and many scientists repeated it. Lightning, which had been looked on with superstitious awe, was now understood to be no more than a large-scale spark. With his practical turn of mind, Franklin invented the lightning rod, and this represents the first practical application of the knowledge of electricity to everyday life.

The large charges available from a Leyden jar had made many an experimenter jump. A systematic study of the muscular effects of electricity was made during the last half of the eighteenth century. When the exposed nerve of a frog's leg was touched with even a small charge the leg twitched. If the leg muscle was removed and stretched on a board, a shock would make it contract. This similarity between the behavior of the

given it more or taken some away. This led to his suggestion that we use the terms plus and minus to describe how a body was charged. As you can see, we

Figure 3–11.   Franklin proving that lightning is a form of electricity. (Photo courtesy Museum of Science and Industry, Chicago.)

muscle in a live frog and a dead one added fuel to the philosophical controversy over the nature of life and death.

In 1780 Galvani, the Italian physician, was carrying out some experiments with frogs' legs. A static machine was in the same room. One of his assistants noticed that there was a muscular contraction if a frog's leg was touched with a metal scalpel at the same time that a spark was drawn from the static machine. There was no metallic connection between the machine and the frog's leg. It was not realized at the time, but this was actually a radio-broadcasting and receiving experiment of sorts.

Although the observation was accidental, Galvani was quick to see that it was important, and he followed it up with detailed experiments. He reached the erroneous conclusion that the source of the electricity was in the frog's nerve and that the metal scalpels were significant only as conductors. He came tantalizingly close to the truth when he observed that the muscle twitched when two points of the nerve were touched by the ends of two different metal rods that were crossed.

It remained for Volta, in 1800, to realize that the source of the electricity was in the two different metals and that the frog was only a detector. Working on this hypothesis he built up a "pile" of disks of silver, zinc, and moist cardboard. When he combined several layers in that order he was able to draw a large spark from the two ends. This was the first battery (Figure 3–12). He discovered that the more disks he had in his pile the more vigorous was the effect, and that it would give a continuous current. The previous static machines had to be recharged after each spark.

The battery opened up even more exciting possibilities than had the Leyden jar. Sir Humphry Davy (1778–1829) discovered that a spark could be obtained between two pieces of charcoal. This furnished a steady, brilliant light and was used to make the first projection lantern. Later it was used in street lamps. The introduction of street lights had a considerable effect in cutting down petty crimes in big cities.

By the use of the steady current available from a battery it was soon discovered that molten salts could be decomposed, and that certain materials dissolved in water would deposit at the electrodes as the current passed through the solution. The forcing of a current through a salt or a solution is called electrolysis; it is the reverse of the action in a battery. At least one of the two different kinds of plates in a battery is used up as it generates electricity. In electrolysis something is deposited at at least one of the two electrodes.

When an electric current is passed through a solution of sodium hydroxide (caustic soda), oxygen is released at one electrode and hydrogen at the other. This is one important commercial method for making pure hydrogen. Plated silver is made by depositing a thin coat of silver from solution onto a steel electrode shaped like a spoon, fork, etc. Chromium, copper, many other metals, and rubber can be electroplated this way. The aluminum industry uses tremendous quantities of electricity in obtaining the metal from its ore by electrolysis.

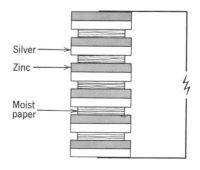

Figure 3–12.   Volta's battery.

SUMMARY

1. Some facts in the field of static electricity were observed by the early Greeks.
2. Gilbert coined the word electricity, and he found that some substances would hold a charge (insulators) and others would not (conductors).
3. Von Guericke made the first machine for generating static electricity.
4. Du Fay suggested that there must be two different types of electricity.
5. The first condenser, in the form of the Leyden jar, made it possible to accumulate much larger charges than had been available before.
6. Franklin contributed the terms positive and negative electricity, although he thought there was only one kind.
7. Franklin demonstrated that lightning is only a large-scale example of the common electric spark.
8. Galvani discovered that different metals have different tendencies to hold on to electrons. He misinterpreted his results and did not realize the significance of his discovery.
9. Volta correctly interpreted Galvani's experiments and constructed the first electric battery. This made possible a continuous current of electricity for the first time.
10. Current electricity soon led to practical applications like street lights, electrolysis of solutions, and electroplating.

QUESTIONS AND EXERCISES

1. Gilbert experimented with metals, among other substances. How would he have classified them?
2. Name five different nations whose scientists contributed to our understanding of electricity.
3. In Volta's battery, as illustrated in Figure 3–12, which way are the electrons traveling in the wire outside the battery?
4. Give an example of a scientist who was working with an incorrect theory but who obtained valuable information. There are many such instances in the history of science.
5. Why is an insulator, like glass, used to separate the two metal plates of a Leyden jar?

Chapter 3

Electrical Measurement

and Circuits

THERE are various adjustments possible on a static machine (Figure 3–13) that can change the type of spark. With the condensers in use and the sparking knobs an inch or more apart the sparks come every second or so; they are bright and make a loud crack. With the condensers disconnected and the knobs less than half an inch apart the sparks are very frequent, but they are hard to see and make little noise. Clearly two different quantities are involved; one is the amount of electricity flowing in each spark, and the other is the distance it will jump, or the drive behind it.

ELECTRICAL UNITS

An analogy may be helpful in this situation. If a turbine or water wheel is being turned by water falling on it, the rate at which work can be done depends on both the height through which the water falls (the head, or pressure) and the rate of flow of the water in gallons per second. In electricity, the quantity that measures drive or pressure, is the volt. The quantity that corresponds to amount (gallons) is coulombs and the rate of flow is measured in amperes. When electrons are being pushed through a wire there is

Wide spark gap

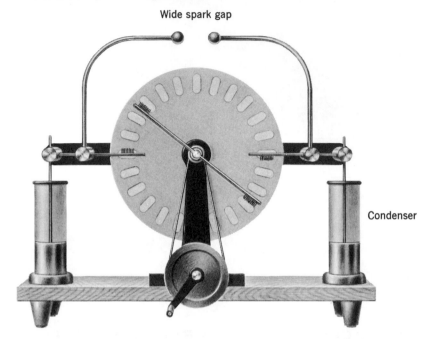

Condenser

Figure 3–13.   Diagram of a static machine.

always a resistance to this current. The unit of resistance is called the ohm. Finally, the unit of electric power is the watt. There is no need to go into the precise definition of any of these quantities, but we shall be concerned with relationships between them.

LAWS OF CURRENT AND POWER

In the chapter on static electricity we got a qualitative description of the interaction of charges. To study these quantita-

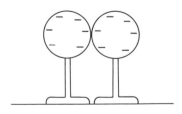

Figure 3–14.

tively we need to devise a technique for isolating known amounts of charge. This can be done with two insulated spheres that are as nearly identical as possible, When they are in contact and are charged from a hard-rubber rod (Figure 3–14) the extra electrons will distribute themselves evenly over the surfaces, and, when separated, the two spheres will have the same charge. It is only necessary to know that the charges are equal, their absolute value is not important for the following experiments.

To compare the forces between electrically charged bodies, we will have to operate on a horizontal plane so that the force of gravity does not complicate the results. Figure 3–15 shows a torsion balance that consists of a light insulating bar suspended by a fine thread and with a negatively charged knob on one end. The wheel at the top can be rotated to bring the bar to any desired position. By applying a series of known forces to the rod and rotating the wheel to return the bar to its original position, the scale at the top can be calibrated to measure the applied force.

Figure 3–15 shows the two charged spheres placed at a distance, d, from the charged knob. In placing the spheres and the knob at different distances, it is found that the force is inversely proportional to the square of the distance $F \propto '/d^2$. The charge on the spheres and on the knob can be halved repeatedly by the technique described above. Repeating the experiment with the distance kept constant and the charges (Q on the spheres, q on the knob) varying, shows that the force is proportional to the product of the charges $F \propto Q \times q$. These two expressions can be combined into Coulomb's law $F \propto Q \times q/d^2$ or $F = k(Q \times q/d^2)$. The force could be measured in newtons, the quantity, of charge in coulombs, and the distance in meters. In the above description it was implied that the experiment was carried out in the air. It could be carried out in a vacuum or with the whole apparatus immersed in some liquid. In different

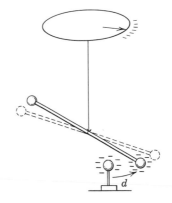

Figure 3–15.

environments the relationships remain the same but the magnitude of the force is different.

In order to illustrate further experiments in this field we shall need some symbols. A few common ones are illustrated and defined in Table 3–1.

Using a setup like the one illustrated in Figure 3–16, we can study the current (amperes) that a constant voltage will drive through a resistance that can be varied. On the reasonable assumption

Table 3–1 Electrical Symbols

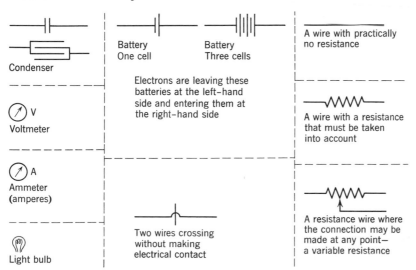

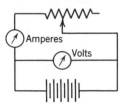

Figure 3–16.   Diagram of apparatus used to study Ohm's law.

that the resistance of the wire is directly proportional to the length of it used in the circuit, it is found that the current (I) is inversely proportional to the resistance (R). $I \propto /R$. By using fixed resistance and different numbers of batteries or cells, it is found that the current is directly proportional to the voltage $I \propto E$. Ohm's law I (amperes) = E (volts)/R (ohms) combines these two statements into one equation.

As the power that can be obtained from a turbine depends upon both the head and the rate of flow, so electric power depends on the voltage and the current. Watts = volts × amperes = volts × coulombs per second. Household appliances are rated according to the power they consume in watts. Light bulbs usually run from 25 to 300 watts, an electric mixer may use 70 watts and an iron 575. One thousand watts is called 1 kilowatt, abbreviated kw. An electric stove may use 2.5 kw. We pay for electricity by the kilowatt-hour, and the rates vary considerably, depending on how much you use and what part of the country you live in. If you use an average value of four cents per kwhr you can figure the cost of operating several of the above appliances for one hour. Ten 100-watt bulbs burning for one hour will use one kwhr of electricity.

TYPES OF CIRCUITS

Two different types of Christmas-tree lights are now on the market. One of them, the old-fashioned kind, has eight small bulbs with a single wire running from one socket to the next and with both ends meeting at the same plug. When one of these bulbs burns out or becomes loose in its socket the whole string goes out. The wiring of this type is illustrated in Figure 3–17. The other kind of light has a male plug at one end, a female plug at the other, two wires going to each socket and larger bulbs. This is illustrated in Figure 3–18. In the first type the current passes through each light in turn, and if the circuit is broken at any one point no current can flow. This is called a series circuit. In the second, part of the current is diverted to pass through each bulb, so that the rest stay on when any one or several of them are not connected. This is called a parallel circuit.

Figure 3–19 is a sketch and a diagram of two dry cells connected in series (*a*) and in parallel (*b*). These batteries give a potential of about 1.5 volts each. Dry cells are constructed so that the outside terminal is negative, that is, electrons enter the circuit from it. When they are connected in series they furnish a voltage that is the sum of the two, or 3.0 volts. When they are connected in parallel the voltage is no greater than that from one

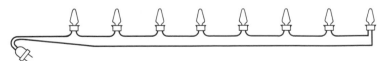

Figure 3–17.   Bulbs connected in series.

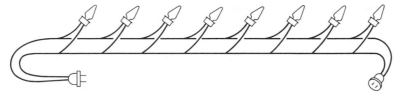

Figure 3–18.   Bulbs connected in parallel.

cell. The series connection is like two irrigation pumps, one of which takes water from a river and pumps it up fifty feet into a reservoir and the other pumps it from the reservoir into a ditch fifty feet higher. The flow of water is the same as from one pump, but the level reach is twice as high. The parallel connection is like the same two pumps taking water from the river and pumping it into the reservoir. The volume of flow would be twice as great but the height is no greater than one pump can supply.

There are two common ways in which electricity is supplied. The most frequently used system is 60-cycle alternating current (AC), wherein the electrons

in the wires move first in one direction and then in the other, 60 times each second. They swing back and forth like a pendulum without ever getting anywhere. In direct current (DC) they flow along the wires like a current of water. Throughout almost the whole of the United States current is furnished at either 120 or 240 volts AC. Most home-generated current is 25 or 60 volts DC, and some cities use this voltage.

Now we can tackle some practical problems of electricity in your homes. Since the lights and base plugs in your homes are wired in parallel, you can use any one or all of them at once. Although the insulated copper wires that carry

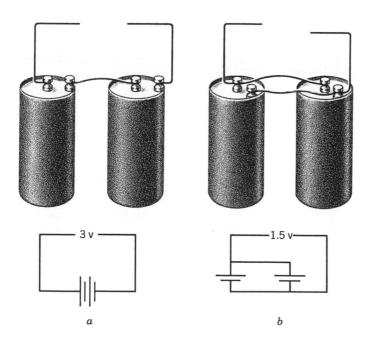

Figure 3–19.   Batteries connected in series, a, and in parallel, b.

current to the lights and plugs have a very low resistance, they do have some. This frictional resistance to the flow of electricity results in the wires' warming up when they are being used. The electricians who wired your house used a wire heavy enough to carry all the current that would normally be used. But if a short circuit develops or you connect too many appliances at one time, then there is danger of the wires' overheating and setting fire to the house. To guard against this a fuse is placed in the line. A fuse contains a short piece of metal which will melt and break the circuit if more than a predetermined amount of current flows through it. Fuses are rated according to the maximum number of amperes that they will carry. Most household fuses will carry from 15 to 30 amperes.

How many 600-watt waffle irons can you safely connect on the same line when it has a 20-ampere fuse? Practically everything electrical in your house uses 120 volts except the stove, which uses 240 volts; so, using the relationship watts = amperes × volts, you can figure the amperes flowing through one waffle iron. Amperes = watts per volts = 600 watts per 120 volts = 5 amperes. Therefore, four such waffle irons would be the max-

imum that you could use on one circuit, and that would be crowding it.

Sometimes the label on household appliances lists amperes instead of watts. How much would it cost to run a washing machine for 1 hour if it draws 6 amperes? Watts = 6 amperes × 120 volts = 720 watts = 0.72 kw. At 4 cents per kwhr this would come to 0.72 kw × 1 hour × 4 cents per kwhr = \$0.0288.

What is the resistance of the wires in an electric toaster that is rated at 500 watts? Here it is best to work the problem through in units first; in fact, it is always wise to do so to see whether the problem can be simplified. Since $I = E/R$, then $R = E/I$. E is 120 volts, but we do not know I. $I =$ watts/E. Substituting this in the previous equation, we get $R = E^2/$watts. We do not need to figure I separately. $R = \overline{120}^2$ volts$^2/$ 500 watts = 28.8 ohms.

ADDITIONAL SOURCES OF POTENTIAL

Batteries and generators (to be discussed later) furnish most of our electric power but there are several other sources of electric potential that are interesting and important for special reasons.

If a semicircular piece of iron and one of copper are put together to form a ring (Figure 3–20), there is a tendency for electrons to move from iron to copper at both junctions. Some electrons do flow across the junctions, but the copper is given such a high negative charge that the current soon stops. Since the voltage is the same at both junctions, the two opposing pressures balance each other and no continuous current can flow around the circle. If anything can be done to alter the voltage at only one of the junctions, then the balance will be thrown off and a current can flow around the circle. In Figure 3–20 the voltage at the

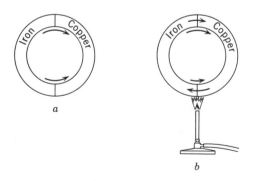

Figure 3–20.   Both copper-iron junctions are at the same temperature in a, and no current flows. In b one junction is warmer than the other, and current can flow around the ring.

lower junction has been weakened by the heat applied (symbolized by the shorter arrow over the junction). At the cold junction electrons move from the iron to the copper, and at the hot junction they are pushed from the copper to the iron. A current flows around the circle, and the magnitude of the current is a measure of the difference in temperature between the two junctions. A sensitive meter can be put into the circuit and calibrated to read directly in degrees. This kind of thermometer, called a thermocouple, is useful for measuring the extremely high temperatures encountered in furnaces and ceramic kilns and the extremely small amounts of energy received from distant stars (page 246).

A peculiar electrical effect is observed in certain crystals, such as quartz and Rochelle salt. If one of these crystals is compressed a difference in potential will develop between two faces. Conversely, if a difference of potential is applied to two faces, the crystal will expand or contract. Thus, it can be set vibrating by a rapidly alternating current. Each crystal has a characteristic frequency of vibration that is determined by its thickness. Crystals that behave like this are said to be piezoelectric.

Light has three important effects on the electrical behavior of certain substances. In the effect called photoconductivity, the electrical resistance of selenium and several metallic sulfides is lowered when light strikes them. The change in resistance is approximately proportional to the intensity of the light. This effect could obviously be used to construct a light meter. It has been used in this way, but the effect mentioned in the next paragraph is a more convenient one.

In the photovoltaic effect a continuous current will flow around a circuit between two substances when one junction is illuminated. This action is analagous to

that of the thermocouple. The modern exposure meter used in photography is constructed on this principle (Figure 2–26). The current generated is small, but a sensitive galvanometer will record it or it can be used to operate a relay (Figure 3–45). When a steady light is focussed on one of these light-sensitive cells anything coming between the two interrupts the current. Many uses for such "photoelectric eyes" have been devised. They open doors as you approach, ring burglar alarms, count or inspect objects on a conveyor belt, etc.

When light strikes certain metals (such as cesium) in a vacuum it knocks electrons out of the surface layer. By connecting the negative pole of a battery to the metal film and placing a positively charged collector near the film a continuous current will flow through the circuit as long as it is illuminated. This photoelectric cell (Figure 3–21) can do the sort of job handled by the photoelectric eye mentioned above, and it has found use in sound movies and television.

Behavior similar to that of cesium in a photoelectric cell is shown by crystals of cadmium sulfide. Light of X-ray wavelengths will liberate swarms of electrons from these crystals. They are the most sensitive detectors of X-rays and are find-

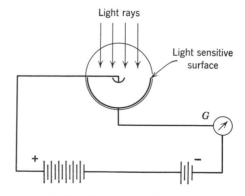

Figure 3–21. *Diagram of a photoelectric cell.*

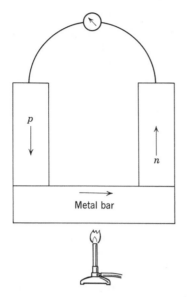

Figure 3-22. The arrows indicate the direction of flow of the electrons when the bar is heated.

ing use where X-rays are used to inspect large opaque objects.

When semiconductors of the n and p types (page 132) are heated they behave differently. The electrons tend to accumulate at the cold end of the n type and at the hot end of the p type. When the two ends of these are joined by a heated metal bar, a current will flow as illustrated in Figure 3-22. There is only a fraction of a volt of potential difference developed by a single pair, but with many

such junctions linked in series a practical source of power is available.

In the paragraphs above we saw how heat can be used to generate an electric current. If electricity is driven through the circuit illustrated in Figure 3-23 the connecting bar is either heated or cooled, depending on the direction of electron flow. A gas flame, for instance, can be made to cool a refrigerator with no moving parts or circulating gas.

Semiconductors can be used to convert the energy of light, as well as that of heat, into electricity. When an n type and a p type are brought into contact they are each electrically neutral at the beginning (Figure 3-24a). Do not be confused by their names. The letter n is to indicate that there are more electrons (negative) than can be bound in the crystal lattice but the crystal as a whole is electrically neutral. After a very short time some electrons will have diffused from n to p and some holes from p to n (Figure 3-24b). The result of this is that the p layer has a negative charge and the n layer a positive one. Diffusion is stopped by this potential difference.

Picture an n type layer about the dimensions of a razor blade with an extremely thin p layer on top of it as illustrated in Figure 3-25. Light coming from above is partly absorbed in the p layer and the rest in the n layer. The energy of the light is used to pull an electron out of the crystal structure and create a

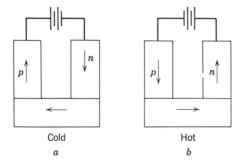

Figure 3-23.

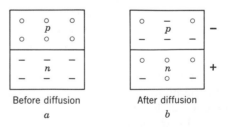

Figure 3-24.

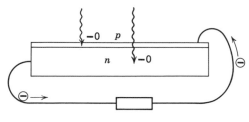

Figure 3–25.

separated electron-hole pair. The electrons move downward toward the positively charged *n* layer, pass out through the wire, are used somehow in the outside circuit and return to the *p* layer. This is why the device is called a solar battery. The holes from each pair travel from the *n* to the *p* layer. This kind of battery is extremely light in weight and keeps working as long as it is in sunlight so it has been particularly useful to furnish the power needs of orbiting satellites.

SUMMARY

1. The unit for measuring the driving force or pressure of an electric current is the volt (E).
2. The unit for measuring the amount of electric charge is the coulomb (Q).
3. The unit for measuring the rate of flow of electric current, Q/t, is the ampere (I).
4. The unit for measuring resistance to the flow of an electric current is the ohm (R).
5. The unit for measuring electric power is the watt.
6. Coulomb's law is

$$F = k\frac{Q \times q}{d^2}$$

7. Ohm's law is $I = E/R$
8. Watts $= E \times I$
9. A series connection in an electrical circuit is an arrangement of parts in which all the current passing through one also passes through the others.
10. A parallel connection in an electrical circuit is an arrangement of parts in which the current divides, some going through one part and some through another.
11. For resistances in series $R = R_1 + R_2 +$ etc.
12. For sources of potential in series $E = E_1 + E_2 =$ etc.
13. For sources of potential in parallel, when $E_1 = E_2$, then $E = E_1 = E_2$.
14. There is a large number of sources of electric potential that have been discovered and exploited for practical uses.

QUESTIONS AND EXERCISES

Note to students: Unless stated otherwise, all numerical problems in electricity assume 120-volt AC.

1. Rearrange the equation $I = E/R$ to read $E = ?$ And $R = ?$
2. Using the proper symbols, draw a circuit showing a two-cell battery that is driving electrons, first through a fixed resistance and then through a light bulb connected in series with it.
3. Is the fuse placed in parallel or in series with its circuit in the house?
4. How many amperes will flow through a toaster rated at 500 watts (see note above)?
5. What is the resistance of the wires in an electric iron that draws 1 ampere of current?
6. With electric power costing 4 cents per kwhr, how much would it cost to use the iron in Problem 5 for 2 hours?
7. List several ways for obtaining a current of electricity.
8. How could you use two photoelectric cells to measure the speed of an automobile?
9. How does increasing the temperature affect the tendency of electrons to flow from iron to copper?
10. What voltage would be obtained from five dry cells connected in series? In parallel?
11. Draw a diagram showing how a gas flame and suitable semiconductors could be combined to cool a refrigerator.

Chapter 4

Magnetism

THE COMPASS and the magnetic knife holder are familiar examples of the phenomenon of magnetism. Although magnetism has been observed and studied for many centuries, we are still learning new facts about it, and our understanding of it is by no means complete. Considering the complexity of the subject, it is surprising that a few well-chosen experiments will reveal so much about the basic nature of magnetism.

EXPERIMENTS WITH MAGNETISM

For our experiments with magnetism we shall need only a few simple pieces of apparatus. When we use a bar magnet and some steel tacks, we find that we can pick up a string of tacks with either end, but not very many along the middle of the bar. You can show that the magnetic attraction operates through a piece of paper or glass. Another very illuminating experiment is to place a magnet under a sheet of glass, sprinkle iron filings on the glass, and tap it gently. The iron filings are lined up in a typical pattern around the magnet. Each small sliver is lined up the way a small compass needle would point in this same position. Two or more magnets can be arranged under the glass and the resulting pattern of iron filings studied. These patterns seem more real to us than the entirely imaginary concept of a magnetic field of force that we say exists around a magnet.

If one bar magnet is suspended in the

middle by a string and another bar magnet is brought near either end, we find that the ends either attract or repel each other. Bar magnets are usually stamped *N* on one end and *S* on the other. The ends with the same letter repel each other, but the *N* end of one attracts the *S* end of another. Magnetic attraction and repulsion are thus similar to attraction and repulsion in static electricity.

In passing, it would be well to observe that there are also striking differences between the phenomena of electricity and magnetism. In magnetism we do not need to be careful to insulate our magnets. The bar can as well be suspended by a flexible wire as by a string. We observe strong magnetism in only a very few substances, such as iron, steel, special alloys, and a mineral called magnetite. When two magnetic poles are touched together, the magnetism does not jump across from one to the other so that they both end up nonmagnetic. Positive and negative charges of electricity exist separately from each other, but magnetic poles always occur in pairs.

When a bar magnet is floated on a cork in a dish of water you will see that it orients itself so that one end points north and the other end south. A compass needle is a lightweight magnet mounted on a pivot so that it can turn readily. If a compass is held on its side in a north-south direction, the needle does not lie horizontally; the north-pointing end dips down at a steep angle (Figure 3–26).

EARLY KNOWLEDGE OF MAGNETISM

A knowledge of magnetism seems to have been arrived at independently in several parts of the world. We have records from China, India, and Greece, all of which date back more than 2000 years. Thales, who experimented with static

Figure 3–26.   A magnetic dip needle.

electricity, also knew about magnetism. In the Arabian Nights is a story of a magnetic island that pulled the nails out of the planks of ships, whereupon the ships fell to pieces and the dismayed sailors were dumped into the sea. The mariner's compass was in use in Europe before A.D. 1200. It soon became apparent that the compass did not point to the north geographic pole. Or, more precisely, the compass did not point north as determined from the North Star. In Europe it pointed several degrees west of north.

On his first trip across the Atlantic Columbus discovered that this variation, which is called magnetic declination, decreased as he proceeded. It soon reached zero, and from then on the compass pointed east of north. This unexpected behavior of the compass nearly demoralized his superstitious crew, and it must have bothered Columbus himself. Later explorers recorded and mapped the magnetic declination all over the globe. Figure 3–27 shows a magnetic map of the United States. As you can see, the effect is considerable. Compasses in the states of Washington and Maine stand at half a right angle to each other. The north magnetic pole is northwest of Hudson Bay in Canada and considerably south of the north geographic pole. It shifts its

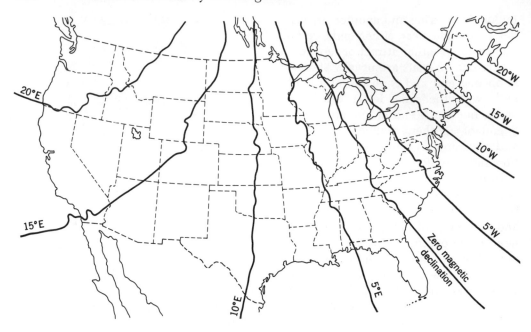

Figure 3–27.   Lines of equal magnetic declination in the United States.

position slowly through the centuries, for reasons which are not understood.

William Gilbert, another scientist whom we met in connection with electricity, carried out extensive investigations with

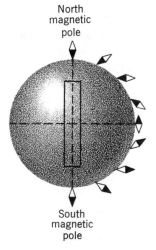

Figure 3–28.   Gilbert's model to demonstrate that the earth behaves like a big magnet.

magnetism. One of his most important contributions to science was his use of a small-scale model to illustrate the behavior of nature. This is a commonplace technique today, but Gilbert seems to have been the first person to employ it consciously. He constructed a globe with a bar magnet inside to represent the behavior of the earth as a magnet. By putting his magnet in just the right position he could show magnetic declination and inclination by means of small compass needles moved over the surface of the globe (Figure 3–28). Kepler tried to utilize Gilbert's ideas in explaining the motion of the planets around the sun.

Although the earth behaves as though it had a huge bar magnet buried deep in its interior, we know that this is not the explanation of the earth's magnetism. The iron-nickel core must be far too hot to be strongly magnetic (see later on in this chapter). Almost certainly there are eddy currents in the semifluid core of the earth (page 304) and this core is moving relative to the solid outer layer. If there are electrically charged particles in the core, their motion would constitute an electric current that would set up a magnetic field. This is the most generally accepted theory of the origin of the earth's magnetic field and it leads one to expect the observed wanderings of the magnetic poles.

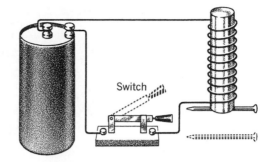

Figure 3–29.   Model of an electromagnet.

THE MEETING OF TWO STREAMS

Thales and Gilbert were only two of a host of experimenters who worked with both electricity and magnetism. It was long suspected that the two had something in common, but the connection was not made until 1819. In that year Hans Christian Oersted (1777–1851) casually tried the experiment of holding a wire that carried a current of electricity directly over and parallel to a compass needle. This took place immediately after a lecture to his class; to the astonishment of students and teacher, the needle swung around at right angles to the wire. He reversed the electric current and the needle swung in the opposite direction. This was something new under the sun— a force (the electric current) was showing an effect at right angles to its line of motion. The communication of this discovery touched off a regular chain reaction of experiments which soon established most of our basic laws of electromagnetism. Oersted had discovered that a wire carrying a current of electricity is surrounded by a magnetic field.

It occurred to Michael Faraday (1791–1867) that the inverse effect should be observable. He tried thrusting a bar magnet into a coil of wire, hoping to observe a current induced into the coil. His instruments for detecting the current were not sensitive enough, and it was not until 1831 that he succeeded in observing the phenomenon of magnetism generating electricity. If the magnet is held stationary in or near the coil no current is generated, but when the magnet is in motion there is a current.

One of the earliest applications of Oersted's discovery was the electromagnet. A coil of insulated wire was wrapped around an iron bar and a direct current was sent through the wire (Figure 3–29). This produces a magnetic field that can be turned on or off at will; consequently, pieces of iron that are large or awkward to handle can be moved about with ease (Figure 3–30).

THEORY OF MAGNETISM

Before exploring some of the practical applications of the new discoveries about electricity and magnetism, let us sort out some of the facts that will help us understand what happens when a bar of iron is magnetized.

The black oxide of iron, magnetite, was the earliest known magnetic substance. It was discovered that rods of iron could be made magnetic by stroking them with magnetite and by hammering them while they were held with one end pointing north. You will find that few objects made

Figure 3–30.   A large industrial electromagnet. (General Electric Co.)

of iron or steel around the laboratory do not affect a compass needle. It was observed that, when a chunk of magnetite was broken in two, both pieces were magnets. If a magnetized bar of iron is sawed into a number of small pieces, each one will be a small magnet (Figure 3–31).

A bar of iron can be more or less strongly magnetized. To observe this, find out how close a magnet must be brought

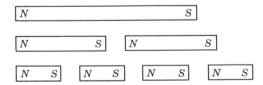

Figure 3–31.   When a long magnet is sawed into short pieces, each piece is a small magnet.

to a certain compass needle to deflect it through 10° (Figure 3–32). Make the same measurement using the same compass and a different bar magnet. You will find that the various magnets available differ considerably in their strength. There is a maximum amount to which any given bar can be magnetized. When a highly magnetized bar is heated and then cooled, or dropped on the floor several times (do not try this without permission), it loses much of its magnetic strength.

The facts mentioned in the previous two paragraphs give us enough to go on to construct a simple theory of magnetism. Let us suppose that a bar of iron is made up of a great number of small particles, each of which is a small magnet. Before the bar is magnetized, these tiny individual magnets are arranged in a random fashion; consequently, there is no appre-

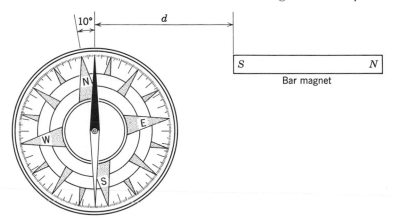

Figure 3–32. *The strength of various bar magnets may be compared by this type of experiment.*

ciable resultant magnetic field (Figure 3–33*a*). The kinetic theory tells us that these particles are being jostled around constantly. If the bar is stroked with a piece of magnetite or hammered while it is held in line with the earth's magnetic field, several of these individual magnets will be lined up so that they work together. The bar will be magnetized weakly (Figure 3–33*b*). When substantially all of them are so lined up, the bar will be as strong a magnet as it can be (Figure 3–33*c*). Heating the magnet or dropping it will tend to break up this regular pattern and weaken the magnetism.

The "small individual magnets" referred to above are called magnetic domains, and they consist of microscopically small aggregations of iron atoms. In each unit the magnetic fields of the individual atoms are all lined up to form a saturated magnet, but, in an unmagnetized bar, the domains are arranged in a random fashion as indicated in Figure 3–33*a*. Thus, with a rather simple theory, we can organize these many facts about magnetism.

Many special alloys have been found that can be made into even stronger magnets than bars of iron or steel. Magnets are now made by letting a hot bar cool in a strong electric field. One possible deduction from our theory of magnetism and the kinetic theory is that a rapidly alternating electric field should swing the small individual magnets around so rapidly that the temperature of the bar would be increased. This technique has been developed to the point where a large bar of steel can be heated red hot.

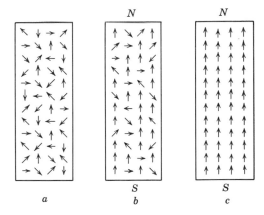

Figure 3–33. *An explanation of how a bar of iron can be nonmagnetic, a, partially magnetized, b, and completely magnetized, c.*

SUMMARY

1. There are two kinds of magnetic poles, which are called north and south.
2. Like magnetic poles repel and unlike poles attract each other.
3. Although many substances possess magnetism, only magnetite, iron, and a few alloys show this property strongly.
4. The earth acts like a huge magnet. The north and south poles of the earth's magnetic field do not quite coincide with the geographic poles.
5. The early knowledge of the magnetic properties of magnetite was widely spread over Europe and Asia. The mariner's compass was in use before A.D. 1200.
6. Gilbert investigated magnetism as well as electricity.
7. Magnetic declination is the angle at any place on the earth between true north and magnetic north.
8. Magnetic inclination is the angle at any place on the earth between the horizontal and the position of a dip-needle compass.
9. Oersted discovered the fact that an electric current is surrounded by a magnetic field at right angles to the direction of flow of the current.
10. Faraday discovered that a changing magnetic field could generate an electric current.
11. When a magnet is broken in two, each piece is a complete magnet. Magnetic poles always occur in pairs.
12. Magnetism seems to depend upon the orientation of the particles of a substance. Any mechanical disturbance which tends to make this arrangement more random weakens the magnetism.

QUESTIONS AND EXERCISES

1. If you had an unlabeled magnet, how could you find out which pole was north and which south?
2. From Figure 3–27, determine the magnetic declination in your locality. Check this with the value given on a geological survey map of your district.
3. Why is it unlikely that the Norsemen used a compass in their explorations of Iceland, Greenland, and Labrador?
4. Will a steady electric current produce a magnetic field? Will a steady magnetic field produce a current of electricity?
5. Take a soft iron bar and increase its magnetic strength by one of the techniques suggested.
6. Use a diagram to explain the fact that a magnetized bar can be cut into several small pieces, each one of which is a magnet. (Combine the features of Figures 3–31 and 3–33).
7. Mention several ways in which the facts observed in the field of magnetism support the kinetic-molecular theory of matter.
8. Give one good reason why the connection between electricity and magnetism was not discovered until after 1800.
9. Explain why a magnet will attract only something that can be magnetized.
10. At approximately what part of the globe would a magnetic dip needle remain horizontal?
11. Explain how deposits of naturally magnetic minerals could be studied for clues concerning the location of the magnetic poles in previous geological eras.

Chapter 5

Electricity and

Magnetism at Work

BOTH ELECTRICITY and magnetism have many uses as separate phenomena, but the great convenience available from the combined effect has made electromagnetism one of our most widespread sources of power.

THE INDUCTION EFFECT

Although Faraday failed to detect the current generated by pushing a magnet into a coil of wire, he finally did succeed when he used an electromagnet. His apparatus was similar to that sketched in Figure 3–34. A current is induced in the right-hand coil at the moment that the key either makes or breaks the circuit on

the left, but no current is flowing through the right-hand coil when that in the left-hand coil is running steadily. When the key is first pressed down, the magnetic field in the left-hand coil builds up from zero to its normal value. It holds this steady value while the current flows, and when the key is released it drops again to zero. Thus, it is a changing magnetic field that induces a current in another coil.

In the experiment described above it is observed that if the induced current is positive when the switch is closed it is negative when it is opened and vice versa. Let us look into this directional effect more closely.

Oersted's discovery of the magnetic

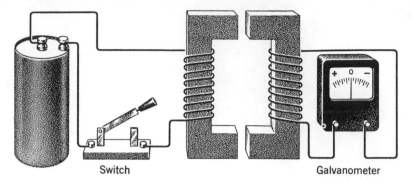

Switch   Galvanometer

Figure 3–34.   Apparatus for demonstrating an induced current.

field produced by a current of electricity (page 153) is illustrated in Figure 3–35. If you curl your left hand around a conducting wire with your thumb pointing in the direction the electrons are traveling, your fingers will indicate the direction of the north-pointing pole of a compass needle.

In Figure 3–35, when the switch is closed electrons will spiral upward in a clockwise direction, and the lower end of the [-shaped bar will be magnetized as a north pole. As the strength of this magnet increases it will begin to line up the magnetic domains in the bar across from it so that the south pole will be at the bottom. The build up of this magnetic field will drive the electrons down the

spiral winding and into the left-hand side of the galvanometer. When the current from the battery has been running for a small fraction of a second the magnetization of both bars will remain constant and the galvanometer needle will return to zero. The direction of the induced current is reversed when the magnetic field collapses after the current is turned off.

Experiments were carried out with various numbers of turns of wire in the two coils. The coil through which the current is driven is called the primary, and the coil in which the current is induced is called the secondary. It was found that the ratio of the primary to the secondary voltage was the same as the

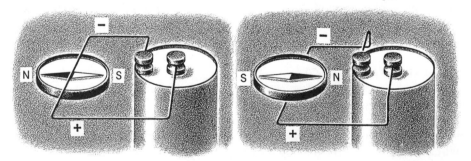

Figure 3–35.   Oersted's experiment. A compass needle tends to swing into a position at right angles to a wire carrying a current. (Redrawn from Fundamentals of Physical Science, *Third Edition, by K. Krauskopf, McGraw-Hill Book Co., 1959.)*

ratio of the number of turns of wire in the two coils. This gives us a device for transforming voltage from any given level to a more convenient one, and it is appropriately named a transformer. If a transformer steps up the voltage there must be a corresponding decrease in amperage to keep the power output the same as the input. Actually, a transformer is not 100% efficient, and there is a slight power loss.

ELECTRIC HEATERS

As electrons move through a wire under the pressure of the applied voltage, the frictional resistance of the particles of the wire generates heat. Or, to put it another way, the myriad blows from the moving electrons speed up the motion of the atoms in the wire. The power consumed, expressed in watts, is: watts = volts $\times$ amperes = $E \times I$. From Ohm's law we have: $E = I \times R$, so watts = $I \times R \times I = I^2 \times R$. The power loss from heat for any given resistance is proportional to the square of the current. Alloys with a conveniently high resistance can be made into wires, and these are used to heat toasters, ovens, waffle irons, etc.

The usual electric-light globe is fitted with a fine tungsten wire. This wire has a very high melting point ($3370°C$) and offers so much resistance that the current heats it white hot. The white-hot wire gives off a good light, but a large fraction of the energy used is wasted as heat.

The lines carrying electric current from the generating stations to our homes have a certain resistance. Because many of these lines are hundreds of miles long it is important to keep the heat loss of transmission as low as possible. Since the power transmitted is proportional to

$E \times I$, and the power loss from heat is I^2R, it is desirable to keep the current (I) as low as possible. This means that we must transmit current at a very high voltage. As an extremely high voltage in our homes would be dangerous, it is cut down from the many thousands of volts used in the distributing system to 120 volts when it enters our homes. Since a transformer requires a changing magnetic field, the current we use is not a steady, direct current but it alternates at the rate of 60 cycles per second.

MOTORS AND GENERATORS

By the proper timing of the approach of a bar magnet, we can keep a compass needle spinning. How can we use this to make a motor? When the north pole of the magnet is brought near the north pole of the compass, the compass starts swinging. When the south pole comes around, it is attracted by the north pole of the magnet, and the swing stops. Instead of a compass needle we can use a coil of wire around an iron bar for our rotating magnet and run an alternating current through it. If the rotating bar, which is called an armature, keeps time with the alternations of the current, there will always be a north pole at the top end of the armature and a south pole at the bottom end. Thus, there will always be a force of repulsion between the armature and the fixed magnet, which is called the field. Once a motor of this type is started running it cannot possibly get out of step with the alternations of the driving current, and it is this kind that is used for driving electric clocks (Figure 3–36).

It is desirable to be able to control the speed of a motor and also to have a more powerful motor than can be obtained by means of permanent magnets. Using alter-

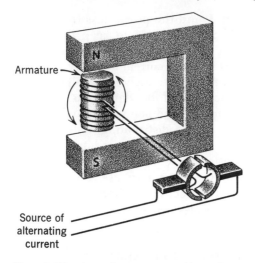

Figure 3–36.   A synchronous motor. Alternating current enters the armature through a commutator and the field is a permanent magnet.

nating current, the connection to the armature is made through a commutator (Figure 3–37). The commutator consists of two semicircles which are connected to the two ends of the armature coil and

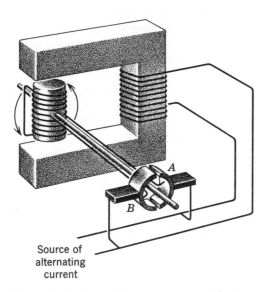

Figure 3–37.   Alternating-current motor with armature and field connected in parallel.

which turn with the armature. They have sliding connections (brushes) with the source of current. As the armature turns, first one and then the other arc of the commutator touches the sliding contact at A. If the current is entering at A and leaving through B, it goes through the coil first in one direction and then in the opposite one as the armature turns. With this arrangement the end of the armature that is up is always magnetized in the same direction (always a north pole, for instance), no matter how fast the armature is turning. The greater the voltage used, the greater is the force of repulsion and the faster the motor turns. More power can be obtained from such a motor when the field and the armature are wired in parallel.

We have seen how a current driven through a coil in a magnetic field will force the coil to move at right angles to this field. If the coil is forced by mechanical means to move across a magnetic field, will the electrons in the wire of the coil receive a thrust? Faraday had discovered that the answer was "yes." An electric generator is just like a motor except that the armature is turned by waterpower, a steam engine, a gasoline motor, etc., and an electric current is pushed out through the line (Figure 3–38). When the current is drawn off through the usual commutator, it is direct current; if a slip ring is used, alternating current is obtained.

It would be hard to imagine what our life would be like without the many electric motors we depend on each day. A single modern airplane has over two hundred electric motors to control various operations. The people of the United States annually use more than 250 billion kwhr of electricity, much of which goes for running electric motors.

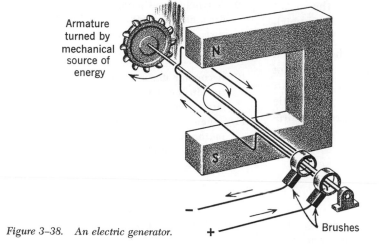

Figure 3–38. An electric generator.

ION PROPULSION

The force of repulsion between an electrostatic field on a space ship and metal ions that are generated on the ship is not great, but there are practical considerations that suggest this as the most likely means of propulsion for long journeys into space. Such an ion propulsion rocket along with an adequate fuel supply is both lightweight and small.

A diagram illustrating the operation of such an ion engine is shown in Figure 3–39. Cesium is used as a fuel because it is readily vaporized and gives up an electron easily to form Cs^+. Tungsten is used as the ionization grid because it has a strong tendency to attract electrons from the vaporized cesium. The cesium ions pass through a strongly positive electrostatic field. The interaction between the ions and the field gives each an accelera-

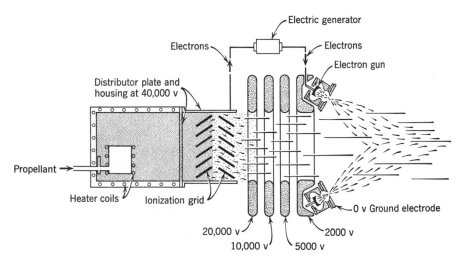

Figure 3–39. Simplified diagram of ion rocket.

tion—the ions to the right and the rocket to the left. An electric generator which acts just like a high voltage battery removes the electrons from the tungsten and expels them to the right. Because of the small mass of the electrons, this part of the operation produces very little thrust, but it is essential in order to prevent the rocket from acquiring a high negative charge.

SUMMARY

1. A transformer is a device consisting of two coils of wire insulated from each other. The one through which the current is driven is called the primary, and the one in which a current is induced is called the secondary.
2. In a transformer

$$\frac{\text{voltage in primary}}{\text{voltage in secondary}} =$$

$$\frac{\text{number of turns of wire in primary}}{\text{number of turns of wire in secondary}}$$

and

$$\frac{\text{voltage in primary}}{\text{voltage in secondary}} =$$

$$\frac{\text{amperes in secondary}}{\text{amperes in primary}}$$

3. A conductor is heated up as an electric current passes through it.
4. This heating effect is used to make electric toasters, blankets, light bulbs, stoves, etc.
5. The power loss from the heating of a conductor is watts $= I^2 R$.
6. Because of this power loss, electricity is transmitted at as high a voltage and as low an amperage as possible.
7. An armature is the rotating coil of an electric motor or generator.
8. A field is the stationary coil of an electric motor or generator.
9. A synchronous motor uses a fixed magnet for a field and 60-cycle AC on the armature. With this arrangement its speed is strictly controlled by the rate of alternation of the current.
10. A commutator is a connection to an armature in the shape of two semicircles insulated from each other.
11. A generator is similar in construction to a motor. Mechanical power turns the armature, and an electric current is generated in the coil.

QUESTIONS AND EXERCISES

1. How much power is used from a 120-volt line by a resistance of 12 ohms? from a 240-volt line by a resistance of 48 ohms?
2. Why is it the general practice to use alternating rather than direct current?
3. What would be an undesirable result if our AC operated at 20 instead of 60 cycles per second?
4. If a coil carrying 60-cycle AC were held near the north pole of a compass needle would the needle be deflected?
5. How many turns would there be in the secondary coil of a transformer that has 120-volt AC running through one hundred turns in the primary and which delivers 24 volts from the secondary?
6. If 3 amperes are flowing through the secondary circuit of the transformer in Problem 5, what is the current flowing in the primary?
7. In the experiment illustrated in Figure 3–34, if the needle swings to the left when the key is first pressed down, which way will it swing when the key is let up?
8. What is the resistance of the tungsten wire in a 300-watt light bulb?
9. Why does an electric motor heat up when it is running?
10. List the parts of an electric motor.

Chapter 6

Communication I

IN USING electricity to carry messages we must have some way of modifying or modulating the current at the sending end of the circuit, and the modulated current must have some way of making a signal at the receiving end.

TELEGRAPH AND TELEPHONE

One of the simplest signal circuits is the one used to ring a doorbell (Figure 3–40). When you put your finger on the bell push, the circuit is completed so that the battery can send a current and magnetize M. The iron bar, A, is drawn over to M, and the clapper hits the bell. While this happens, the circuit is broken at B, so that the clapper bar springs back, makes a new contact, and again sounds the bell. These circuits are now operated through a step-down transformer from the regular house current.

The telegraph, invented by Samuel Morse in 1837, has a circuit similar to the house bell except that it does not have a current interrupter. The sender can hold down the sounding bar at the receiving end for any length of time he wishes and can spell out his message in short and long pulses called dots and dashes. There is no return wire to complete the circuit; only one wire is used, and the current returns through the earth.

Figure 3–41 shows a simple telegraph circuit. In the example shown, a is send-

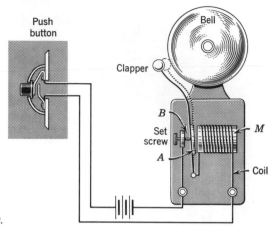

Figure 3–40.   *Diagram of a doorbell circuit.*

ing to *b*. The key at *b* must be held down mechanically so that the circuit can be completed at will by the key at *a*. In the circuit used here, both sounders would click in rhythm with the key.

A telephone operates much like a telegraph. Here the problem is to find a way to modulate the current so that it follows the frequencies of the human voice. Alexander Graham Bell (1847–1922) invented the first successful telephone, and Thomas Edison (1847–1931) improved it with his carbon-granule transmitter. Figure 3–42 shows a diagram of a telephone circuit, and Figure 3–43 is a diagram of a modern instrument. The transmitter is like a pillbox full of small pieces of coke put in series in the circuit. Any pressure on the lid of the box squeezes the carbon

granules closer together and increases the current that is flowing (Figure 3–44). This changing pressure is provided by the sound waves of your voice. The current, which has been modulated by your voice, operates an electromagnet in the receiver. The electromagnet controls the vibrations of a steel membrane in the earpiece. As the membrane vibrates it sends out sound waves to your ear. This simple arrangement can reproduce with surprising fidelity the complicated vibrations of the human voice.

AMPLIFIERS AND RECTIFIERS

A way had to be found to amplify the signals, in order to send messages over any great distance. The basic problem of amplification is an extremely important one. We need some way to make a small current control a large one. An analogy is provided by a single policeman controlling the heavy traffic at a busy intersection.

Morse used a relay for his purposes. A relay (Figure 3–45) is an electromagnetic switch which controls a second circuit. A feeble current on the incoming signal can pull the switch over and send out a

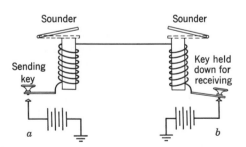

Figure 3–41.   *Diagram of a telegraph circuit.*

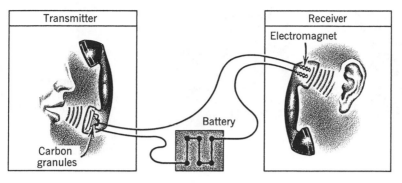

Figure 3–42. A telephone circuit.

signal from a very high-powered battery. With relays placed at suitable intervals along the line, telegraph messages were soon sent across the country. A simple relay cannot act fast enough to follow the vibrations of the human voice. Telephoning over long distances had to await the invention of the vacuum-tube amplifier.

The common radio tube is an example of the vacuum-tube amplifier. This was developed by De Forest in 1906 from an observation made by Edison in 1883. Edison had sealed an electrode into the side of an electric-light globe. When the electrode was charged positively a current of electrons flowed from the hot filament across the evacuated space to the electrode. Electrons were literally boiling off the hot wire, and this vapor of electrons was attracted by the oppositely charged electrode. When the electrode was charged negatively no current flowed to it from the filament.

The Edison effect was developed by Fleming into a vacuum-tube rectifier. The symbols inside the circle of Figure 3–46 represent the elements actually inside a highly evacuated glass tube. F stands for the filament which is heated by the battery. A variable resistance (not shown) may be used to control the temperature of the filament. P represents a metal plate which is sometimes a complete cylinder around the filament. We are going to consider the current along the wire C when a source of alternating current is connected to points A and B. When A is negative and B positive, electrons will flow from F to P and down through C. When A is positive and B negative, the current through C will stop,

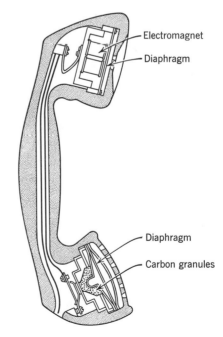

Figure 3–43. Details of a telephone mouthpiece and receiver.

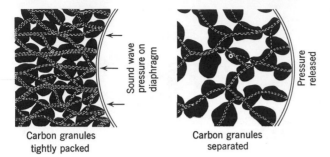

Sound wave pressure on diaphragm

Carbon granules tightly packed

Pressure released

Carbon granules separated

Figure 3–44.   Detail of a carbon-granule transmitter. The electric current (dotted lines) through the carbon granules varies as the granules are squeezed more or less tightly together by the diaphragm in front of your mouth.

because electrons cannot boil off of the cold plate *P.* An alternating current attached to *A* and *B* will produce an intermittent direct (in one direction only) current through the wire *C.* A device which changes an alternating current into a direct current is called a rectifier.

De Forest had the inspiration to try putting a third element between the other two in this tube. He put a wire mesh, which he called a grid, between the filament and plate in an effort to control the current flowing to the plate. The symbols representing such a tube are shown in Figure 3–47. In operation, *F* is always negative and *P* positive. De Forest found that with *G* strongly negative the current to the plate was stopped. The current rose as *G* became less negative, and it was high with *G* slightly positive. A small variation in the voltage applied to *G* makes a considerable variation in the current flowing to *P.* It is this magnifying

or amplifying, effect of the grid voltage which makes it one of the most useful inventions ever made. Amplifications of a hundred thousand fold can be made in one tube. When the output (plate current) of one tube is used to operate the grid of a second tube, and this in turn feeds into a third tube, etc., the amplification achieved is fantastic.

The connections to a vacuum-tube amplifier are shown in Figure 3–48. Low-intensity signals come in to the step-up transformer, *A.* The battery, *B* (the *B* battery of a radio set), heats the filament, *F.* The variations in voltage from the secondary of the transformer are led to the grid, *G,* where they control the current to the plate, *P.* The plate is kept at a high positive potential by the battery, *C* (the *C* battery of a radio set). The pulsating direct current from *P* passes through a step-up transformer, *D,* and high-intensity signals are sent out. The usual

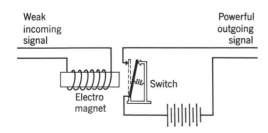

Weak incoming signal

Powerful outgoing signal

Electro magnet

Switch

Figure 3–45.   A relay suitable for use in a telegraph circuit.

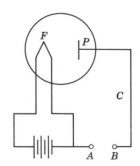

F

P

C

A   *B*

Figure 3–46.   Diagram of a vacuum-tube rectifier.

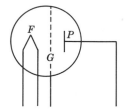

Figure 3–47.   A vacuum-tube amplifier.

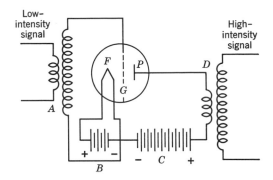

Figure 3–48.   A circuit using a vacuum-tube amplifier. Low-intensity signals coming in at the left are amplified and sent out at the right.

radio is operated on household alternating current and has no batteries. Vacuum-tube rectifiers take their place. Further details about the operation of a radio will be discussed in a later chapter.

A new type of rectifier and amplifier, called a transistor, was developed in 1948. A transistor exactly parallels the action of a vacuum tube and has many advantages over it.

Semiconductors of the *n* and *p* type (page 132) are combined as shown in Figure 3–49. Since there are extra electrons in the *n*-type and extra places for them (holes) in the *p*-type, electrons will flow much more readily across the boundary in the *n* to *p* direction than in the *p* to *n* direction. It can be seen in Figure 3–49 that the one-cell battery is driving electrons around the circuit in the preferred direction (from *n* to *p*). The three-celled battery, on the other hand, is able to push only a tiny current from *p* to *n*.

The slice of *p*-type germanium is so thin that some of the electrons moving in the left-hand circuit pass through it and become involved in the right-hand circuit. The result of this is that the modulations

of the low voltage circuit on the left add electrons to the high voltage circuit on the right and an amplified signal emerges. With the resistance of the *p-n* direction being so high, few electrons are moving that way and the addition of a few from the other circuit has a relatively large effect.

Since a vacuum tube has a filament which has to be heated red hot, its power requirements are much greater than those of a transistor, and its useful life is much shorter. With the modern tendency to make apparatus as small as possible, the problem of dissipating heat from even a tiny vacuum tube has been a limiting factor in design. A transistor can be made considerably smaller than a vacuum tube, and there is practically no heat loss to contend with. These advantages, and the practically indefinitely long useful life of a transistor, will revolutionize the building of long-distance telephone lines, electronic

Figure 3–49.   A transistor. Signals coming in from the left are amplified and sent out on the right.

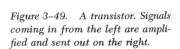

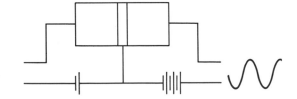

calculators, hearing aids, etc. This tiny device has already found many useful applications.

RECORDERS

Edison also had a hand in developing the phonograph. Basically, the phonograph consists of a lever, one end of which fits into a long groove and the other end is attached to a diaphragm. If the groove has the shape of one of the sound waves pictured in Figure 2–35 and it is drawn past the lever, the other end will vibrate the diaphragm so that it gives out a musical note. Since the fundamental and all the overtones will be present, a reproduction of the original note will be obtained. Now, reverse the process and start out with a straight groove cut in rather soft material. Draw it past the lever as sound waves strike the diaphragm. The vibrations of the diaphragm will make the lever vibrate back and forth so that it shapes the groove into a reproduction of the sound wave.

The playing and making of phonograph records are essentially as simple as the preceding description implies. You can hold the corner of a playing card on a rotating record and get a fair reproduction of the sound. This simple lever system has certain mechanical defects that spoil the quality of the tone. The more rapid vibrations of the overtones are lost. To obtain higher fidelity in recording, a piezoelectric crystal is used. This crystal translates the vibrations of the diaphragm (microphone) into an electric current. After being amplified, this current controls the needle that is cutting a groove in the wax of the master record. Since the parts of an electrical system can be light in weight (low inertia) they can respond to the low-amplitude vibrations of the higher overtones, and much better

reproduction can be obtained. The same system, a crystal pickup, is used to play the records.

We hear much of wire and tape recorders these days. They are used for recording interviews and radio programs and for teaching foreign languages. The same piece of wire or tape can be used indefinitely, the message being erased when it is no longer needed, or a full-length symphony can be recorded and stored on a small spool. The heart of these instruments is an electromagnet which varies the intensity of magnetization of a steel wire or a tape carrying a coating of magnetite. The electromagnet is actuated by the modulated current coming from a microphone. As the strip of wire or tape runs between the poles of the magnet it is more or less highly magnetized by the changing strength of the magnet.

To reproduce the message, the strip is passed through a coil in which it induces a varying current that corresponds to the original one. This current operates a loudspeaker either through a piezoelectric crystal or an electromagnet like the one used in a telephone earpiece.

SUMMARY

1. In a telegraph circuit the sending key is a switch controlling the current through an electromagnet at the receiving end. When the current is flowing a metal bar is drawn to the electromagnet, making an audible click.
2. In a telephone circuit the compressions and rarefactions of sound waves vary the resistance and, hence, the current flowing through a carbon-granule transmitter. The modulated current flows through an electromagnet and vibrates a steel diaphragm in the earpiece at the receiving end.
3. A relay consists of an electromagnet which operates a switch in a second circuit. In this way a weak current can control a strong one and messages can be amplified.

4. In the Edison effect electrons will boil off a heated filament placed in a vacuum.

5. A triode vacuum tube contains (a) a filament from which electrons evaporate when it is heated; (b) a plate charged positively, and to which the electrons from the filament flow; and (c) a grid placed between the filament and the plate, which controls the current to the plate by relatively small changes in voltage.

6. A diode containing only a filament and a plate can be used to rectify alternating current.

7. A triode is used to detect radio-frequency waves and to amplify feeble currents.

8. Transistors are made from *n* and *p* type semiconductors. They perform the same tasks as do vacuum tubes.

9. In making a phonograph record a needle cuts a sinuous groove in a wax disk. The needle is part of a lever arm that is actuated by the vibrations of sound waves. When the record is played the process is reversed. The moving groove actuates the needle, whereby the vibrations are relayed to a loud-speaker. In electrical recording and transcription a piezoelectric crystal is used in the circuit.

10. In making a wire or tape recording the variation in magnetization of a steel wire or a tape carrying magnetite is controlled by sound waves striking the microphone. When the wire or tape is run through a coil it induces a modulated current which, in turn, controls the vibrations of a loud-speaker.

QUESTIONS AND EXERCISES

1. When a doorbell is rung, where in the circuit could you observe a rapid sparking? Where could you put a condenser in the circuit to cut down the sparking?

2. What would be different about the telegraph circuit in Figure 3–41 if *b* were sending to *a*?

3. At what point might a piezoelectric crystal be used in a telephone circuit?

4. Using the correct symbols, sketch a vacuum-tube rectifier, including a variable resistance to control the filament current.

5. In what way is a triode superior to a relay as an amplifier?

6. In a triode, which pole of the *C* battery is connected to the plate?

7. In England, a triode is called a valve. What part of the triode corresponds to the gate of a valve?

8. What would go wrong with a triode if you used a *C* battery that gave less volts than the *B* battery?

9. Look at a phonograph record with a strong magnifying glass and notice the shape of the grooves.

10. Describe the electrical parts of a record player that uses a crystal pickup.

11. Draw a transistor amplifier similar to the one in Figure 3–49 but consisting of a *p-n-p* sandwich. Be careful to get the battery connections in correctly.

Chapter 7

Communication II

W~HEN AN~ electron is at rest it repels other electrons and attracts positive charges, and so we say that it is surrounded by an electric field. When the electron moves it is surrounded by a magnetic as well as by an electric field. These combined fields are spoken of as an electromagnetic field. They can exert force at a distance.

RADIO

Figure 3–50 shows a static machine, S, connected to a heavy wire rectangle, A, containing a narrow spark gap. On a separate insulated base is a similar heavy wire rectangle, B, with the movable rod, R, forming the side across from the spark gap. If the static machine is operated so that sparks jump across the gap of A, and the rod R is moved back and forth, a position will be found at which sparks jump across the gap at B in time with those at A.

This experiment is similar to one in which a stone is dropped near a cork floating on a still pond. The waves moving out from where the stone hit the water will make the cork bob up and down. By analogy, we say that the electromagnetic waves traveling out from the moving electrons of the spark at A make the electrons of B move back and forth across the gap. There is also a similarity to the experiment with the vibrating bars described in the chapter on sound (page 100). The second bar would pick up the energy of the sound wave only if it had the same natural frequency of vibration as the first bar (the two bars had to be tuned to the same note). By moving the rod *R* (Figure 3–50) back and forth we tuned the circuit *B* and found a position where *A* and *B* had the same period of electric vibration. From this type of experiment there developed the point of view that electromagnetic waves were generated at *A* and were detected at *B*.

With water and sound waves something tangible is vibrating; there is a medium to transmit the energy. With electromagnetic waves no medium can be found. The term aether (or ether) was invented to apply to the medium, but since there is absolutely no evidence to indicate its existence, we have reluctantly abandoned the idea. We have to imagine waves traveling through space with nothing there to vibrate. Or we can look at the matter somewhat differently and assume that the energy travels in the form of particles, like bullets, which also have all the properties of a wave motion, such as wavelength and frequency.

In 1865 James Clerk Maxwell had predicted the existence of electromagnetic waves and had suggested that waves with properties similar to light could be generated electrically. He said that light constituted only a small fraction of the many wavelengths possible. The experiment described in Figure 3–50 was performed in 1888 by Hertz. Following the lead of Maxwell's theory he found that these waves showed reflection, refraction, and interference. In 1896 Marconi succeeded in applying Hertz's technique to the problem of sending a message through space.

The inadequate details above merely touch some of the high spots leading to

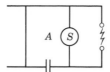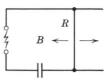

Figure 3–50. A primitive radio sender and detector. A static machine, S, sends sparks across the gap of A. With R in the correct position, a faint spark may be seen to jump across the gap of B.

the development of radio communication. They do, however, suggest how completely dependent we are upon the interaction of the minds of many men from many countries for scientific progress. Contributions from the United States, England, France, Germany, Russia, and Italy were fitted together in a sequence that depended upon free exchange of ideas and upon freedom for the experimenters to work on the problems that seemed significant to them. At no point along the line was the driving force the idea of making a radio.

A modern radio-sending station operates on a fixed frequency or carrier wave of very long wavelength and high frequency. This carrier wave is generated by a piezoelectric crystal which vibrates at about 550 to 1600 kilocycles per second. The amplitude of the carrier wave is modulated by the sound wave striking the microphone so that an amplitude-modulated (AM) wave is broadcast (Figure 3–51). The electrical characteristics of a radio receiver are modified by tuning it to the characteristic frequency of the sending station. Notice that the numbers on the radio dial range from 550 to 1600. The amplitude-modulated wave is detected and amplified by tubes like the one in Figure 3–48. The current from these tubes controls your loudspeaker.

Instead of having the sound waves that strike the microphone modulate the am-

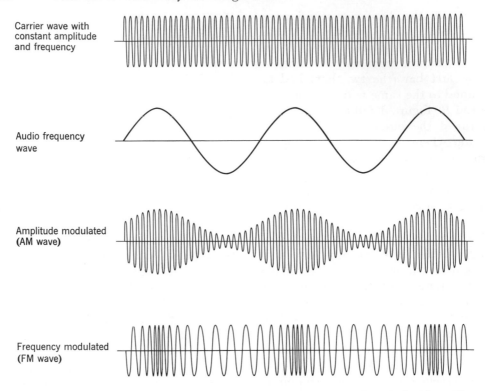

Carrier wave with
constant amplitude
and frequency

Audio frequency
wave

Amplitude modulated
(AM wave)

Frequency modulated
(FM wave)

Figure 3–51.   A radio station broadcasts a carrier wave with a frequency much too high to hear. The sound waves entering the microphone modulate this carrier wave either in amplitude (AM) or in frequency (FM).

plitude of the carrier wave, they can be made to modulate its frequency (Figure 3–51). This gives us frequency modulation, or FM radio. One of the principal advantages of FM over AM is that static is not detected and does not interfere with FM reception. Another is that FM stations can transmit more of the higher frequencies of the characteristic overtones without interfering with each other. Two AM stations operating on neighboring channels (nearly the same carrier frequency) must cut out the higher overtones to avoid overlapping and interference.

One of the surprising facts about radio transmission is that signals will carry around the curve of the earth. Since the signals travel in straight lines like light, those going up into the air must be refracted back to earth. In fact they must bounce back and forth between the earth and the upper atmosphere several times in traveling thousands of miles. The existence of such a refracting layer in the atmosphere was predicted by Kennelly and Heaviside, and it is named in their honor. Apparently, radiation from the sun splits the particles of the air into charged ions that refract radio waves to give total internal reflection for the frequencies used in AM broadcasting (Figure 3–52). Since the higher-frequency waves used in FM broadcasting, television, and radar are not refracted satisfactorily, their reception is limited to a radius of a hundred miles or so from the sending station.

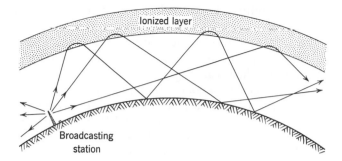

Figure 3-52. The Kennelly-Heaviside layer of ionized gases refracts AM radio waves so that they can be transmitted around the curving earth.

CATHODE-RAY OSCILLOGRAPH

In the Fleming diode rectifier (page 165) electrons boil off the hot filament and travel to the positively charged plate. If the plate is perforated there will be a beam of electrons streaming through the hole and traveling in a straight line beyond it. This is a convenient way of obtaining the beam of electrons used in a cathode-ray oscilloscope. The beam next passes between two condenser plates that are in a vertical plane and then between two that are in a horizontal plane, and finally it strikes a fluorescent screen at the end of the tube (Figure 3-53). With no charge on either set of condensers, a single bright spot is observed on the screen. If a 60-cycle alternating current is applied to the first set of condensers, the beam will sweep back and forth in a straight, horizontal line as it is attracted to first one and then the other of the two plates. The alternations of the current and the sweeping of the oscillograph beam back and forth might be compared to the swinging of a pendulum.

If the deflecting voltage on the condenser built up relatively slowly and then dropped rapidly we could compare the action to the motion of a pile driver. The luminous spot on the screen would still

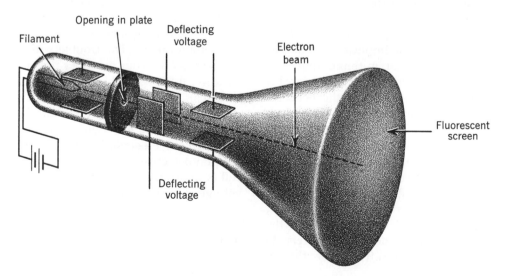

Figure 3-53. Diagram of a cathode-ray oscillograph.

be describing a horizontal line, but it would travel slowly across the field in one direction and would then return very rapidly to the starting point. This type of motion is called scanning.

The second set of condenser plates, the ones in the horizontal plane, can deflect the beam in a vertical direction. With the beam scanning horizontally, an alternating voltage on the vertical deflectors will make the spot snake its way across the field. As the beam moves steadily from left to right, for instance, it is deflected upward and then down below the center line so that its path is like a sine-wave curve.

The cathode-ray oscilloscope can be used to study sound waves by leading the current from a microphone to the condensers, which deflect vertically. The variations in air pressure of the sound are translated into variations in electric current, which affect the path of the scanning beam so that we can see and photograph them. The pictures showing the difference in shape of the sound waves from different instruments were taken this way.

Any signal that can be translated into an electric current can be studied by this technique. In navigation by radar a short-wavelength radio impulse is sent out from a directional antenna that also serves as a detector. If the radio signal is reflected from something, the echo returns to the antenna and is led to an oscillograph. The original signal shows up as a peak, and the echo appears beside it as a small "pip." The distance between the two is a measure of how far away the reflecting object is. Ships can avoid each other in a foggy harbor; airplanes can tell how high above the ground they are; and a radar screen to detect hostile aircraft can be thrown around a continent.

We have yet to send a manned rocket to the moon, but we have shot a radar signal to the moon and recorded the echo. The short-wavelength, high-frequency radar waves penetrated the Kennelly-Heaviside layer, sped to the moon, bounced off its surface, and returned to earth in less than three seconds.

TELEVISION

Television combines several of the problems of movies and radio. A scene must be recorded, transmitted, and projected, and this sequence must be repeated thirty times a second to give the illusion of smooth motion. In the television "camera" (Figure 3–54) there is no film. The scene is focused on a screen which is a fine-grained honeycomb of photoelectric cells. Such a screen is comparable to the mosaic of rods and cones on the retina of the human eye (page 86). The variations in light intensity of the image build up variations in voltage on these cells. A scanning beam of electrons sweeps across the cells very much as the eye scans a page of a book. It moves steadily across, rapidly back and down a row, and across again until it has covered the whole screen. (The trouble with this analogy is that your eye does not move steadily; it proceeds by a series of jerky motions). A complete scanning of the screen constitutes one picture, and thirty pictures a second are transmitted.

When the electron beam hits one of the photoelectric cells the voltage on the cell is neutralized, and it is this drop in voltage which is used to modulate the outgoing radio-frequency signal. The modulated signal is detected and amplified by the receiving set and used to control the intensity of its scanning beam. The scanning beam in the tube of the set

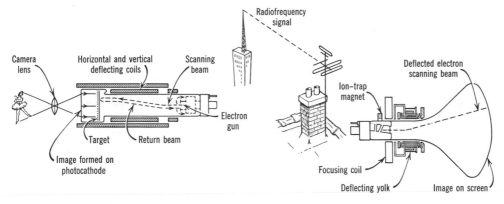

Figure 3–54. A television camera (left) and picture tube (right).

travels from side to side, starting at the top and adding line after line until the picture is completed. A bright spot on the original image produces a high intensity of the scanning beam, and so there is a corresponding bright spot on the screen. The picture is actually drawn before your eyes, but it happens so fast that it appears to be instantaneous.

Since 525 horizontal lines are drawn for each picture and each line has 420 bright or dark spots, the picture is made up of over 200,000 elements. Electronic engineers have a reputation for accomplishing the fabulous, but they still have room for considerable improvement in the quality of television pictures. Their headaches have been tripled by the attempts to perfect color television. Here each final picture is made up of three: one red, one green, and one blue, and they are fused together (color by addition).

SUMMARY

1. A moving electron generates an electric and a magnetic field (electromagnetic waves) that travels out from it through space with the speed of light.

2. Electromagnetic waves can be detected by a properly tuned receiver.

3. Electromagnetic waves show the usual properties of waves, such as wavelength, speed, reflection, refraction, and diffraction, but they do not require a medium for transmission.

4. Maxwell predicted electromagnetic waves and said that light was this kind of vibration.

5. Hertz was the first to demonstrate the existence of long-wavelength electromagnetic waves (radio waves).

6. Marconi developed the technique of sending and receiving radio waves to such a point that they were practical for communication.

7. Radio stations send out a carrier wave of fixed frequency and modulated amplitude (AM), or of fixed amplitude and modulated frequency (FM).

8. Radio waves are detected and amplified by triode vacuum tubes.

9. The Kennelly-Heaviside layer is a region of ionized gas molecules in the upper atmosphere that refracts AM frequency radio waves in such a way that they can be sent completely around the earth.

10. Since the higher frequencies used for FM, television, radar, etc., are not refracted by the Kennelly-Heaviside layer, their reception is limited to straight-line distances from the transmitting station.

11. In a cathode-ray oscillograph, a beam of electrons strikes a fluorescent screen after

passing between two sets of condensers at right angles to each other.

12. By having the potential on one set of condensers build up slowly and break down rapidly, a luminous horizontal line is drawn in one direction across the screen. This process is called scanning.

13. Variations in the potential of the other set of condenser plates give the scanning beam a vertical motion, so that it follows a curved path across the screen. A study of the path reveals information about the current reaching the second set of condensers.

14. Sound waves and any other signal that can be translated into an electric current can be studied with a cathode-ray oscillograph.

15. In echo location by radar, the time for return of a reflected radio wave measures the distance to the reflecting object.

16. In television the image is recorded on a screen consisting of a mosaic of tiny photoelectric cells. They are scanned by a beam of electrons that neutralizes their charge. The drop in potential of each cell modulates the radio-frequency signal going out at the time. The modulated signal controls the intensity of a scanning beam in the receiving set.

17. Thirty times a second the whole scene is sent out and portrayed on the receiving screen. The completed picture is composed of 525 lines with 420 spots of varying brightness in each line.

QUESTIONS AND EXERCISES

1. How fast do radio waves travel?

2. What is the wavelength of a carrier wave with a frequency of 550 kilocycles per second?

3. Is the speed of AM radio waves in the Kennelly-Heaviside layer greater or less than in un-ionized air?

4. In a cathode-ray oscillograph tube, if the scanning voltage were placed on the horizontal pair of deflecting plates, what would appear on the screen?

5. Electromagnetic force acts at a distance without the need of a medium. What other force like this have we studied?

6. The following scientists were citizens of what countries: Maxwell, Hertz, Marconi, De Forest, Fleming?

7. Describe the motion of a scanning beam.

8. How long did it take the radar signal to travel from the earth to the moon and back?

9. How many lines are drawn by the scanning beam of a television tube each second?

10. In what way is the picture on a television screen similar to a colored magazine picture? Why is it a mistake to sit close to a large television screen?

11. The Doppler effect is not noticeable on your car radio. How fast would a car have to be moving toward the broadcasting tower for the pitch of the music to be raised by 1%?

Chapter 8

Electricity and Your Car

UNDER THE HOOD of a car there is a complete electric power plant. The services that use electricity include the lights, self-starter, horn, and ignition system, and possibly a radio, fan, and motors to raise and lower the top and the windows. When the car motor is running it operates a generator to supply the current for these devices, and there is a battery to furnish current when the car is not running.

LIGHTS, HORN, ETC.

In the battery a series of chemical reactions furnishes a current of electricity as described in Chapter 1 of this unit, in the section on "Using Metals to Obtain an Electric Charge." Although the particular reactions need not concern you here, you should know a few things about them. They are reversible; that is, after the materials have been pretty well used up (discharged) an electric current can be driven backward through the battery to regenerate the substances. This is called charging a battery. Since the density of the liquid in a fully charged battery is higher than that in a discharged one, the condition of a battery can be checked with a hydrometer. The liquid in a well-charged battery freezes at a much lower temperature than that in a discharged battery, and so it is important to keep track of this in cold weather. It is also

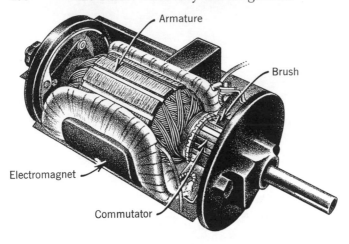

Armature

Brush

Electromagnet

Commutator

Figure 3–55. An automobile generator. (From Electricity and Wheels, *by General Motors Corp.)*

important to keep track of the liquid level and replace any distilled water that evaporates. The battery furnishes current at a pressure of 12 volts, which is not very high, but it can supply it so fast (about 100 amperes) that you can get a most uncomfortable spark by placing a metal tool across the two terminals.

The generator (Figure 3–55) is driven by the engine when it is running; it supplies all the current needed and recharges the battery. The battery is designed to

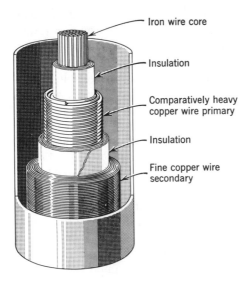

Iron wire core

Insulation

Comparatively heavy copper wire primary

Insulation

Fine copper wire secondary

Figure 3–56. Diagram of an ignition coil.

operate for short periods, such as starting the car, and any long-term drain on it will wear it out rapidly.

The lights, horn, blowers, etc., of an automobile are not particularly different from those in use elsewhere. The parabolic reflector for the headlights was described on page 69. There are two filaments in the headlight bulbs. For country driving the lower, brighter one is used to send a horizontal beam far out ahead, and for city driving and passing the upper filament sends a beam which strikes the road close to the car and avoids serious glare in the eyes of the approaching driver. Only one wire passes to each of the above mentioned electrical devices, the frame of the car being used to return the electrons to the battery and generator.

The self-starter is a powerful electric motor which turns the engine over until it can operate on its own power. A motor strong enough to do this job properly would be almost as large as the engine itself, but since it operates for such a short time, a smaller motor can be overloaded temporarily without burning out. C. F. Kettering had used this line of reasoning in building an electrically operated cash register, and he fooled the

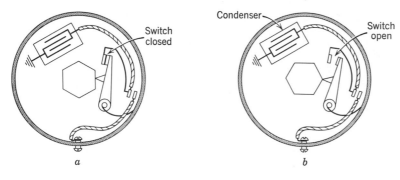

Figure 3–57. *Diagram of a circuit breaker. (Redrawn from* Electricity and Wheels, *by General Motors Corp.)*

scoffing experts in the automobile industry by developing the first successful self-starter in 1912.

THE IGNITION SYSTEM

In the ignition system of a car sufficient voltage must be provided to make a spark jump across the gap of the spark plugs and this current must be directed to the right spark plug at the right time. The 12 volts from the battery must be stepped up to about 10,000 volts at the spark plugs. A transformer is the obvious solution to the problem, but a current interrupter of some sort must be provided because the battery delivers a steady, direct current. The transformer used is called an ignition coil (Figure 3–56). This coil has a hundred or more windings of comparatively thick copper wire for a primary, and many thousands of turns of fine wire on the secondary. The current interrupter is called a circuit breaker, and one for a six-cylinder car is illustrated in Figure 3–57. As the hexagon turns, its points push back the switch and stop the current (*b*). When a side comes across from the switch it closes and the current flows (*a*). Notice that there is a condenser in the circuit. It serves as a reservoir for the current to surge into when

the circuit is being broken. This not only cuts down on excessive sparking in the circuit breaker but it also provides a greater flow of current when the switch is closed. The current flows from the battery, through the primary of the ignition coil, through the circuit breaker, and back to the battery.

When a momentary current flows through the primary, a high-voltage current is induced into the secondary and it flows to the distributor (Figure 3–58). The distributor is easy to recognize under the hood because it is the center of the spiderweb of wires leading to each spark plug. In it is a rotating arm which acts as a switch to send the current from the ignition coil to each of the spark plugs in turn. The distributor is mounted on top of the circuit breaker, and, since the same

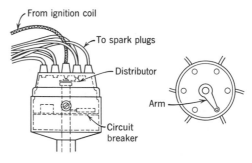

Figure 3–58. *An automobile distributor.*

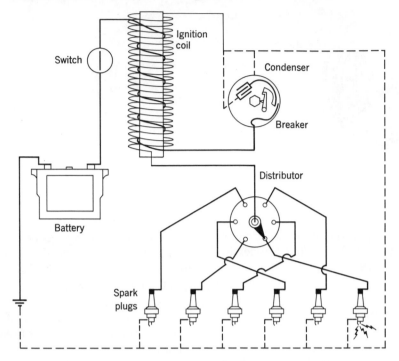

Figure 3–59.   The ignition system of an automobile. (Redrawn from Electricity and Wheels, *by General Motors Corp.)*

rod turns the hexagon of the circuit breaker and the arm of the distributor, they keep in perfect time. This whole system is put together as shown in Figure 3–59.

SUMMARY

1. Since the chemical reactions that furnish an electric current from a storage battery are reversible, a battery that has run down can be recharged.
2. The generator supplies all the current needed and also recharges the battery when the motor is running.
3. Kettering developed the self-starter by designing a small electric motor that could be overloaded for the short time necessary to get the engine started.
4. The ignition coil is a step-up transformer that changes the 12 volts from the battery into about 10,000 volts at the spark plugs.
5. The circuit breaker is a switch that interrupts the direct current from the battery to give the changing magnetic field necessary for the operation of a transformer.
6. The distributor is integrated with the circuit breaker so that the pulses of high-voltage current are directed to the proper spark plug at the right time.

QUESTIONS AND EXERCISES

1. Would the float in a hydrometer used to test a fully charged automobile battery float high in the liquid or sink low with only a little of the stem showing?
2. What is the purpose of the ignition coil? the circuit breaker? the distributor?
3. Why can very fine wire be used in the sec-

ondary of the ignition coil, whereas comparatively heavy wire is needed for the primary?

4. Look under the hood of a car and see how many of the parts of the ignition system you can recognize.

5. Current runs through the starting motor of a car at the rate of about 80 amperes, and the generator produces it at about 7 amperes. If you take half a minute to start your car, how long will the engine have to run before the battery is recharged?

Chapter 9

Be Careful

EVERY YEAR many people are killed through carelessness or ignorance of the dangers of electricity. We have so many potentially dangerous contacts with electrical devices every day that we all should know what precautions to take.

There is no simple rule about the number of volts that can be handled safely. Four dry cells connected in series will deliver 6 volts, and the shock from them would not hurt a kitten; but the difference in potential across the two terminals of an automobile battery is only 12 volts, and a shock from it can be an unpleasant experience. A spark at 100,000 volts from a static machine is a rude surprise but not dangerous, yet contact with the 120 volts of the usual home wiring system has been fatal to many a person.

As a general rule, avoid contact with any wire that might be carrying electricity. If you are repairing any electrical gadget be sure that its plug is pulled out, and turn off a lamp when you are replacing a burned-out bulb. It is well to have a neon test lamp handy to be sure whether a circuit is "live" or "dead." When a fuse blows out, something is wrong—probably an overloaded circuit or a short circuit—so find and fix the trouble before replacing the fuse. Never put a coin underneath a fuse. This is comparable to tying down the safety valve on a steam boiler.

Electrical devices are supposed to be insulated perfectly, but they rarely are. If your hands are dry you will seldom get a shock from a toaster or radio, etc.,

182

but it is not unusual to notice a warning tingling when your hands are wet. When you are really well connected (electrically) to the ground, as when your feet are wet, your hand is on a faucet, or you are in the bathtub, you should avoid touching any electric switch, bulb, radio, etc. You may get away with such foolish practices several times, but it takes only one good shock to kill you and several people are killed every year by just these kinds of careless actions.

An electric current through your muscles makes them contract, and if it flows through your heart muscle the muscle may tighten up and not be able to relax again. Lacking any other way of testing a wire in a crisis, you may touch it lightly with the back of your fingers. If you get a shock the finger muscles will contract and pull your hand away from the wire. The shock from a live wire touching the front of your fingers makes your hand contract around the wire and hold it with a grip that will not relax.

"Cause of the fire—defective wiring." This is the verdict all too frequently after a fire that has left families homeless and has even sacrificed lives. Frayed insulation or kinked extension cords will allow a small current to leak away. This current heats up a rug until it bursts into flame, and the rest of the story depends on luck and the efficiency of the fire department. Cords should be replaced at the first sign of wear. Plan for numerous wall outlets rather than for one or two that are stuffed with multiple plugs and many long extension cords. When a home is left unoccupied for any length of time it is wise to pull out all extension cords and disconnect all radios, refrigerators, etc.

We have replaced human slaves by electrons, and a little understanding and care will keep them in their proper place as servants.

Chapter 10

A Pause to Take Our Bearings

Before we go any further in our specific study of science it is time we examined the ways that scientists work. It is important to do this because there are many decisions that we need to make that can be approached by the same techniques used on problems in science: a home owner has to evaluate conflicting claims before making purchases; a voter is faced with problems of school bonds, sanitation, zoning, etc.; medical authorities point out how impending antivivisection legislation would hamstring medical research; and the question of effective control of atomic energy continues to plague mankind. The operations used by scientists have been so amazingly effective that it is high time they were used more widely.

The field of intellectual activity in which there has been the most substantial progress in the past 2000 years is the field of science. Progress implies more than trying something new and different. It implies a structural unity, with the old being continuously tested so that some is discarded and some serves as a foundation for the new growth. Certainly there is no evidence for any significant change in man's brain during this period. His progress has been in his organization of his knowledge and in his techniques for acquiring new and more reliable information.

THE SCIENTIFIC PROCESS

The so-called scientific process is a method of attacking problems that has an entirely general application. The name is perhaps unfortunate, because it implies that it is to be used only by scientists. It is a genuine tragedy that this process has not been used more widely. There seems to be no lack of ingenuity in the human race for thinking up clever explanations. What is needed is a technique for examining this multitude of guesses and revealing their faults. Contrary to popular opinion, the scientific process does not reveal the truth; its greatest virtue is that it serves as a touchstone for identifying that which is false.

Lucretius thought that we saw by means of a series of dart-like particles emitted from our eyes, which bounced off things we looked at and returned to our eyes—a sort of visual radar. Newton considered that light consisted of tiny particles, which he called corpuscles, and Huygens argued for a wave-like nature of light. We now see justification for both these latter points of view but not that of Lucretius. Later we shall see that the Babylonians, the Egyptians, the Greeks, Ptolemy, Copernicus, and Kepler, all had different ideas about the structure of the solar system. It is not so much a question of which idea is right, because none was entirely correct in all details. We want to know which theories are way off the track and what are the imperfections in those that are partly right. By this procedure of elimination we can build, piece by piece, a picture that comes ever closer to the thing it represents.

To a certain extent the scientific process can be analyzed. It may be considered to consist of the four steps of (1) observation, (2) generalization, (3) deduction, and (4) examination. Let us look at these in order. The first step is the collection of information either by simple observation or by planned experiment. Sometimes this step is taken completely in the dark, but more often than not the experimenter already has a hunch which guides him in planning his experiments. The original hunch frequently is wrong; in fact, it usually is, but it forms a basis for action and can be revised as the experimenter goes along. Dalton's ideas about atoms were extremely naïve. We now know that his theory was wrong in several particulars and incomplete in many others, but it started a fruitful line of inquiry and brought together many apparently unrelated facts. The studies on the behavior of gases made by Boyle, Charles, and Gay-Lussac are a good example of a deliberate attempt to obtain an orderly body of information.

When we are faced with a number of related facts we always try to simplify the situation. We pick out the things that are similar and emphasize them. This thought process is generalization. Possibly the most significant part of the process is that we ignore differences. The classification of clouds into a few categories is a case in point. This is the step in the scientific process that is called induction. The kinetic-molecular theory of gases gives an over-all picture of the nature of gases and explains much of their behavior. In the next three units we shall encounter many theories that generalize such subjects as the behavior of the elements and of the stars. Creative imagination can play an important role in induction. There are many different generalizations possible from any given set of observations. It is not particularly difficult to think up a slight modification of the theory that is popular at the moment, but it takes an unusual mind to break through the current trend and to propose something radically new. Planck's quantum theory and Einstein's theory of the equivalence of mass and energy are examples of a fresh approach.

The larger the number and variety of experiments on which a generalization is based, the more likely it is to be accurate. One must be careful to avoid jumping to conclusions from insufficient data, and it pays to be critical and to ask to see the supporting data when someone propounds a theory. If you are the kind of person who insists on examining the data behind generally accepted theories, the ones that "everybody knows are true," then you are already applying the skepticism characteristic of the scientific process. Do not expect to be generally admired for your skepticism. Many people do not like having to examine cherished beliefs.

The first two steps described above are common practice in all fields of learning. Collecting data (observation) appeals to most of us, and thinking up explanations for why things are as they are (induction) is good exercise for the imagination. Some people are more gifted at it than others, but we all practice it more often than we realize. The third and fourth steps, however, give the scientific process its peculiar strength. They involve a conscious effort to undermine and demolish the brain children created in the second step.

The third step is usually called deduction. If the new generalization is correct, certain conclusions must follow. Maxwell pointed out that if light is an electromagnetic type of wave motion, then it should be possible to generate waves like light electrically. Later, Hertz succeeded in producing and studying these waves that we now call radio waves. The scientific process always involves a consistent follow-up of deduction so that even a theory that is completely wrong may be the basis for progress, even for its own correction. A striking example of this is the story of the discovery of radioactivity by Bequerel, which will be told later on.

The fourth step, examination, follows inevitably. The deductions—predictions—are checked. If they turn out to be correct, the investigator beams happily and feels that his brain child has a promising future. Since the predictions almost inevitably fall short of being completely correct, the theory is reviewed carefully to see where it needs to be modified. Deductions from the caloric theory of the nature of heat were not consistent with the facts observed by Rumford, so he suggested a radical revision of the theory. Newton's corpuscular theory of light explained reflection and refraction but not diffraction. The theory had to be modified to include the idea of a wave-like behavior. Kepler's theories of planetary motion furnish an excellent example of the growth of a theory as it was repeatedly subjected to the test of deduction and examination. As we shall see in the next unit, Mendeleef's periodic classification of the elements was not taken seriously until some of his daring predictions about elements yet to be discovered were verified. To have any scientific standing, a theory must make predictions that are capable of being tested.

The terms generalization, hypothesis, theory and law, as used above, mean much the same thing; they differ in degree. A generalization covers relatively few particulars; if it is more sweeping, but not yet carefully checked, it is called a hypothesis. After a large number of deductions from a hypothesis have been checked and found to be correct, the hypothesis advances to the status of a theory. The distinction between these two is not always observed, and the word theory is used frequently for either one. After a theory has become well established and generally accepted it may be called a law. The law of gravity and the gas laws are examples.

A law (and a theory) is not a statement of how things must behave, it is a brief statement, in general terms, that describes the way things do behave. A good theory outlines the results obtained from a large number of experiments and is revised whenever new evidence shows that it is somewhat inaccurate here or inconsistent there. To overthrow a theory completely requires the construction of an entirely new picture that is consistent with all the old evidence and that provides deductions differing from those of the old theory. If, when the new deductions are checked, they are found to fit in with the facts, the old theory will gradually be discarded in favor of the new one. The death of an outmoded theory is seldom rapid, because there are always persons who would rather try to patch it up than to go over to a different point of view. The corpuscular theory of light advanced by Newton died a slow death even though all the facts known by, say, 1820, were better explained by Huygens' wave theory. After a theory (such as the atomic theory) has been refined over the period of a century, it is extremely improbable that something completely new and different will replace it.

Notice the use of the expression "extremely improbable." Science is not the field of certainties that so many people seem to think. It is a field of probabilities, of suspended judgments, and it requires a willingness to let the evidence decide the case. A scientist realizes that any theory he may propose is not the final word; he tests it to find out how nearly right it is, not to prove that it is right. Einstein, who was so eminently successful in proposing revolutionary theories, once remarked "No amount of experimenting can prove me right. One experiment can prove me wrong."

INFORMATION

In such a course as this you can learn something of the techniques that science has found so successful; you can learn something about the world around you; and you can develop your own critical thinking so that it will be more effective.

The weather, light, color, sound, electricity, and magnetism offer experiences that touch you frequently. We will soon come to a consideration of our ideas about the behavior of atoms and molecules, the planets and stars, and the story of the earth. An attempt has been made to balance a basic understanding with practical appreciation of how familiar things work. New things and new ideas not yet dreamed of will come during your lifetime, and it is hoped that many of these will be extensions of material covered here, so that you will be able to follow these new developments as they come along. Certainly life is richer to the extent that you are alert to the physical world around you.

CRITICAL THINKING

A third objective in this course is to develop effective critical thinking. Many courses that you take will contribute to this important part of your education, but it will be worthwhile to examine some of the ways that a study of physical science helps.

Logic can help you reach valid conclusions only when you start from correct assumptions. Make it a habit to start from verifiable facts as a basis for your opinions. In this book a consistent effort has been made to show the factual evidence on which the theories are based. Some theories have been presented that rest on meager experimental evidence, and you will do well to view these with more than the usual amount of skepticism. Two examples of this are the theory of the origin of rain which lead to cloud seeding and the theories that explain the recent ice ages. The point in presenting these was to make you aware of the fact that science is a living, imperfect, human activity. It thrives on informed criticism.

Words have a chameleon-like quality of changing their meanings; but there is little chance of confusion when a definition, even though it is expressed in words, is based on a description of how one observes or measures the thing being defined. This way of defining terms is called operational definition, and by consistently using it, scientists have reduced the amount of misunderstanding in their conversation and writing.

One of the greatest contributions you can make to your own clarity of thinking is to realize that you think in words. The words you use for expressing an idea are symbols, like a map, of the part of the world around you. The words are not the things they stand for, just as the paper map is not the actual countryside through which you are traveling. To the extent that your map is accurate, your thinking can be accurate. Any details that are fuzzy or actually wrong in your word picture will lead you astray in your thinking, just as you may get lost on a trip if your map is inaccurate. So long as electricity and magnetism were thought to be separate and unconnected phenomena no such thing as a modern electric generator was possible. No order or predictability was possible on the basis of the geological theory that each formation and fossil was a special act of creation. With a better understanding of the nature of geological change, it became possible to trace veins of ore, prospect more successfully for petroleum, and design buildings that were more resistant to earthquakes.

The great importance of this point makes it worth our while to consider a few more examples. Notice how the statement, "Now, let's look at both sides of the question," limits the discussion to two sides. There may be many different aspects that are important, but because of the way the statement was phrased, there is the danger that only two will be brought out. A statement such as, "The planets must obey the law of gravitation," is misleading in the implication that there is something compulsive about the law. A natural law is no more than a description, and it is useful to the extent that it is accurate. Another example is the dismay felt by a scientist when he is asked if he believes in the theory of relativity, or of evolution, for instance. He is accused of hedging unless he gives a yes-or-no answer, yet either one is misleading. The word "believe" implies an unquestioning acceptance, and a scientist can give no more than a provisional acceptance to any theory. You may have noticed that the word "true" has been avoided in this textbook. There is a real difference between saying, "This is the true explanation," and "This is the most nearly correct explanation that we have obtained so far." The first statement discourages further inquiry; the second suggests the need for it.

The subject of critical thinking is far too broad to be covered fully here, but it is hoped that this chapter will help you to see some of the ways in which this course may contribute to your growth. Try consciously to start your thinking from operational definitions expressed in words that symbolize the things they stand for as accurately as possible. When you reach conclusions (hypotheses or theories), make deductions from them and test them to see whether they hold up. Do not hide or defend your mistakes; acknowledge them and learn from them.

Unit Four

Atoms in Action

Chapter 1

The Language of Chemistry

A s ONE becomes well acquainted with a number of scientists, it is clear that one characteristic they have in common is curiosity. This is often a general reaction—they are intrigued by much of what goes on in this world. They are interested in the stars, the weather, the seashore, rock, birds, flowers, behavior, etc. And in addition, this curiosity is not satisfied to stop at the superficial level where differences are most obvious. The scientist tends to look into the situation more closely in order to see connections and similarities. In many areas of study, such as astronomy, biology, and geology, the explanations have now reached the point where they are being given more and more in terms of the behavior of atoms and molecules. We have studied the evidence for the existence of these small units, now it is time to learn more about their interaction.

FORMULAS AND EQUATIONS

When natural gas is burned in air we can readily observe the color of the flame and the heat released. With the appropriate apparatus it can be shown that water and carbon dioxide are also formed. A more sophisticated study would show even more details of the process.

We can concentrate on only a few aspects and consider just the molecules that are affected. Nitrogen, which is the main constituent of air, can be ignored in our description because it does not change. We will leave out the flame, and, for the moment, ignore the heat effect. Using the shorthand language of chemistry we will write our description as follows: $CH_4 + 2O_2 = CO_2 + 2H_2O$. This compact description raises a host of problems for the uninitiated.

Instead of the common every-day name natural gas, the symbol CH_4 has been used. One might guess that O stands for oxygen, but why write a big 2 in front of it and a small 2 at the lower right-hand corner?

The symbols of chemistry are the result of many generations of experience and they have been refined until they are extremely effective and efficient tools for communication. The names of the elements are represented by one or two letter symbols. A list of these is presented in the Table of Atomic Weights (see inside back cover). The symbols for a molecule are grouped together and if there is more than one atom of a certain element in the molecule, the subscript number shows that. Natural gas, or methane, consists of one atom of carbon and four of hydrogen —five atoms in all. The function of the 2 in O_2 should be clear by now. The other 2, in $2O_2$ and again in $2H_2O$, has a different function. It is put there either as a bookkeeping device to show that all the atoms are accounted for on both sides of the equation, or it represents an actual measurement and means that 2 molecules of oxygen reacted for every one of methane and that, under these conditions,

one molecule of carbon dioxide and two molecules of water were formed. This is represented pictorially in Figure 4–1.

This is all very well to say, but how do we know these details? The answer is not a brief one and will be developed in this unit. We will be concerned with atoms in action, their interaction with each other, their dynamic internal structure, and their tendency to change when left alone.

Since the formula for a molecule such as H_2O represents a certain number of atoms, it must also represent a certain weight. The weight of a single molecule of water is about 3×10^{-23} grams, which is an inconveniently small number to work with. It would be simpler to take some small whole number, assign it as the atomic weight of some element, and to experimentally determine the weights of all the other elements in comparison with this. Many such bases for comparison have been proposed.

Using the atomic weight of oxygen as 16.000 was the international standard for a long time. This has recently been supplanted by $C = 12.000$. The reasons for this change and a more precise statement of the previous sentence will be given later in this unit. When the weights of all of the atoms in a molecule are added up, the resulting figure is called the molecular weight. In round numbers the molecular weight of methane is $12 + 4 = 16$.

The implications of the equation for the oxidation of methane can now be extended. $CH_4 + 2O_2 = CO_2 + 2H_2O$ tells us that 16 grams of methane will

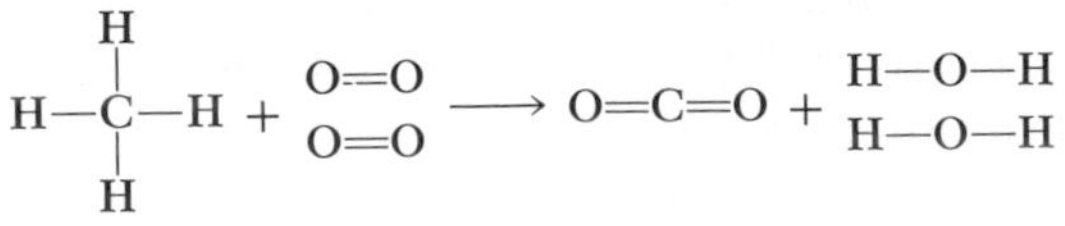

Figure 4–1.

react with 64 grams of oxygen to form 44 grams of carbon dioxide and 36 grams of water. It is easy to see that this quantitative weight relationship is useful when you want to know how much raw material you will need to get a desired amount of product, for instance. In order to obtain 44 grams of carbon dioxide you will need to burn 16 grams of methane. If you burn 10 grams of methane, how much carbon dioxide will be formed?

$$\frac{x}{10} = \frac{44}{16}$$

$$x = \frac{440}{16} = 27.5 \text{ grams}$$

So far we have failed to take into account the heat of combustion. When one molecular weight of methane (16 grams) is burned as indicated by our equation, 211,000 calories of heat are liberated. The equation can now be written $CH_4 + 2O_2 = CO_2 + 2H_2O + 211,000$ calories. All chemical reactions involve an energy change. This is not usually included in the equation for the reaction and we shall mention it only when it is pertinent to the discussion. The amount of heat liberated by the combustion of 16 grams of methane is sufficient to evaporate over 363 grams of water at the boiling point. When a certain amount of energy is needed, this equation enables us to calculate how much fuel will be required.

TYPICAL COMPOUNDS

This section will be largely descriptive and will make no attempt at being inclusive. We will discuss a few of the more common examples chosen from the thousands of types of compounds that are known.

Almost all of the elements combine readily with oxygen. Carbon dioxide, CO_2, and water, H_2O, were encountered earlier in this unit. Sand is impure SiO_2, lime is CaO and Al_2O_3 is the oxide of aluminum found in clay.

There is a large group of compounds that have the common property of tasting sour and turning litmus test paper pink. They are called acids and when they dissolve in water they furnish a hydrogen ion, H^+ (called a proton), to the solution. All charged particles will move in an electric field and are called ions—from the Greek word for go. Much commercial vinegar is a 5% solution of acetic acid, CH_3COOH, in water. Lactic acid is in sour milk. Some commercially important acids are HCl, hydrochloric acid, HNO_3, nitric acid, H_2SO_4, sulfuric acid, and H_3PO_4, phosphoric acid.

At this point you might well wonder why acetic acid was not written as $H_4C_2O_2$. The reason for this will be developed later but in the meantime we shall encounter other molecular formulas where it is important to show this additional detail of molecular architecture.

There is an important group of compounds that taste bitter, turn litmus paper blue, and react with hydrogen ions to remove them from solution; these are called bases. One of these is the gas, ammonia, NH_3. It dissolves in water to form NH_4OH which is familiar as household ammonia. Two other bases that are common in the household are $NaHCO_3$ and Na_2CO_3. You know the first of these (sodium bicarbonate) as baking soda and the second (sodium carbonate) as washing soda. When CaO reacts with water it forms $Ca(OH)_2$ slaked lime or calcium hydroxide. NaOH, sodium hydroxide is an important base in industry. The alkaloids, such as nicotine and strychnine, are bases.

The reaction between HCl and NaOH produces water and NaCl, or table salt.

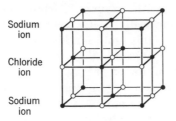

Sodium ion

Chloride ion

Sodium ion

Figure 4–2.   Model of salt (NaCl) crystal; simple cubic crystal. (Redrawn from Introduction to Atomic and Nuclear Physics, *Third Edition, by O. Oldenberg, McGraw-Hill Book Co., 1961.)*

The cubic crystals of salt (Figure 4–2) consist, not of sodium and chlorine atoms, but of Na^+ and Cl^- ions. This is true of all salts, the crystals as a whole are electrically neutral but they are made up of ions. In the NaCl crystal each Na^+ is surrounded by 6 Cl^- and each Cl^- is, in turn, surrounded by 6 Na^+. One cannot say that any particular positive ion is associated with any particular negative ion. It would be inappropriate to use the term molecule of sodium chloride in this connection.

When we say that sodium chloride has a molecular weight of 58.45 we are saying that, in sodium chloride, the Na^+ and Cl^- are present in the ratio of 1:1 and that the sum of the weight of 1 Na^+ and 1 Cl^- is 58.45 on the atomic weight scale.

A substance may fall into more than one of the classifications used in this chapter. For instance, $NaHCO_3$ and Na_2CO_3 are salts as well as bases.

When the blue crystals of copper sulfate are heated carefully, water is driven off and a white powder is left behind. The formula for the white powder is $CuSO_4$. For every molecular weight of this formed from the blue crystals we can obtain 5 molecular weights of water, so we write the formula for the hydrated copper sulfate as $CuSO_4 \cdot 5H_2O$. The clear crystals of washing soda are $Na_2CO_3 \cdot$

$10H_2O$. The minerals in many rocks have water of crystallization that is released at fairly high temperatures. This is the source of the great amounts of steam that accompany volcanic eruptions.

If the finely powdered $CuSO_4$ is left exposed to humid air it will slowly react with water and turn to $CuSO_4 \cdot 5H_2O$. Sometimes salts will pick up an indefinite amount of water from the air. Table salt becomes sticky in very humid weather and $CaCl_2$ will absorb water until it dissolves in the pool of liquid.

Carbon is unique among the elements in that large numbers of carbon atoms can join together to form straight chains, branched chains and rings. These complex structures are found in petroleum, coal tar, and living cells. Only a few simple examples will be given in Table 4–1.

The molecular weight of cyclohexane is $6 \times 12 + 12 \times 1 = 84$. In living systems we encounter molecules of almost incredible size and complexity. The molecular weight of cellulose is in the hundreds of thousands and proteins range from several thousand to a few million.

SOLUBILITY AND PRECIPITATION

If a crystal of sodium chloride is dropped into a flask of water the crystal will slowly disappear. You say the salt dissolved and formed a solution of salt in water. The solution contains many water molecules and relatively few sodium and chloride ions. Now let us carry out this experiment under more precisely specified conditions. Using 100 ml of water and holding the temperature at 0°C, add 30 grams of NaCl. After a while most of the salt will have dissolved. If we could observe what is happening at the surface of any one crystal (Figure 4–3), we would see that individual $Na^+ + Cl^-$ ions were

Table 4-1

Methane	CH_4	
n-Butane	C_4H_{10}	
Isobutane	C_4H_{10}	
Cyclohexane	C_6H_{12}	
Ethyl alcohol	C_2H_5OH	
Acetic acid	CH_3COOH	
Chloroform	$CHCl_3$	

migrating away from the crystal face and other ions were moving toward it. There is a net loss of salt to the solution and the dissolving process continues slowly. Then if we add another 10 grams of salt we will find some of the solid left even after many hours. The rates of solution and of precipitation have reached a dynamic equilibrium. The solution is said to be saturated with sodium chloride, and the amount of salt that has dissolved (35.7 grams) is the solubility of sodium chloride at this temperature.

The above experiment is similar in many respects to the one in which the saturated vapor pressure for water was measured (page 24). If the solubility experiment is repeated at 100° a value of 39.12 grams will be found for the solubility. (It should be noted that such a slight change of solubility with temperature is rather unusual). As the hot, satu-

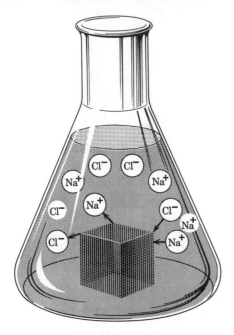

Figure 4–3.

rated solution in contact with excess salt is allowed to cool, the rate of precipitation is slightly greater than the rate of solution. When the temperature of 0°C is reached, it will be found that, again, 35.7 grams of salt remains dissolved.

Now we are going to examine a solubility experiment in which there are four different ions. This will be carried out at 0°C. At this temperature the solubility of $NaNO_3$ is 73 grams, of $AgNO_3$ is 122 grams, and of AgCl is 0.00008 grams per 100 ml of water. Again we will set up a flask containing 100 grams of water and we will pour 1 gram of NaCl into one side and 1 gram of $AgNO_3$ into the other. These will dissolve to form the four ions Na^+, Cl^-, Ag^+, and NO_3^-. These ions will bump into each other and form the four possible compounds NaCl, $NaNO_3$, AgCl, and $AgNO_3$. Each of these will dissolve at its peculiar rate. It is obvious that no appreciable amount of NaCl, $NaNO_3$, or $AgNO_3$ will accumulate, but

that most of the Ag^+ will be removed from the solution as AgCl.

This preferential precipitation of the least soluble compound from a mixture is a crucial factor in the formation of certain geological deposits. A considerable amount of our table salt is obtained by letting sea water evaporate in open ponds until the NaCl deposits and leaves the many other ions in solution.

The observed range of solubilities of different salts is truly amazing and not at all well understood. There are several substances that are miscible with water in all proportions and some that are so insoluble that we cannot measure the small amounts present in a saturated solution.

SUMMARY

1. When writing the chemical formula for a molecule, the letter symbols stand for one atom of an element and the subscripts designate the number of those atoms in the molecule.
2. A chemical reaction may be formulated to indicate the raw materials and the products.
3. A chemical equation is a formulation that is balanced. Every atom that is found on one side of the equation is accounted for on the other side.
4. The symbol for an element also stands for a certain weight of that element, usually an atomic weight in grams.
5. All chemical reactions involve an energy change.
6. A few examples of various types of compounds were presented.
7. A saturated solution of a solid in a liquid involves a dynamic equilibrium between the dissolved material (solute) and the precipitate.

QUESTIONS AND EXERCISES

1. Explain in detail each of the symbols in the formulation: Na_2CO_3 + HCl NaCl + H_2O + CO_2. Write it as a balanced equation.

2. Calculate the molecular weights of SiO_2, Al_2O_3, $CuSO_4 \cdot 5H_2O$, ethyl alcohol.
3. How much phosphorus would it take to make 1 gram molecular weight of phosphoric acid? To make 65 grams of the acid?
4. Using Table 4–1 as a guide, draw a reasonable structural formula for the compound C_3H_8O.
5. In the experiment described in the text involving the precipitation of $AgCl$, which ion would have the highest concentration in grams per 100 ml?

Chapter 2

Valence and

the Periodic Table

I N THIS chapter many formulas will be presented. From these we can draw some generalizations about the ways in which different elements combine to form molecules, and one of the most important organizing principles in the whole field of science, the periodic table, will be studied.

After examining Table 4–2 carefully, decide what you would expect for the formula for space (1), hydrogen iodide. Similarly in space (2) should go the formula for magnesium chloride, (3) aluminum bromide, (4) silane, (5) phosphine, (6) calcium sulfide, and (7) carbon tetraiodide. In column 10 what are the values for the x and y subscripts for each of the four compounds?

VALENCE

If you multiply these examples by many hundred similar ones it becomes clear that elements have a definite capacity to combine with each other and that a number can be assigned to each element indicating what this capacity is. This number is called the valence of the element, and originally the valence was thought of as something like a hook sticking out from the atom. This concept has been modified beyond recognition and it is still the center of active research.

The simplest whole number that we can start with is to assume that hydrogen has a valence of 1. Since all of the elements in column 1 combine with hydrogen in

Table 4-2

1	2	3	4	5
NaF	HF	BeO	BeCl$_2$	AlF$_3$
NaCl	HCl	MgO	(2) Mg$_x$Cl$_y$	AlCl$_3$
NaBr	HBr	CaO	CaCl$_2$	(3) Al$_x$Br$_y$
NaI	(1) H$_x$I$_y$	SrO	SrCl$_2$	AlI$_3$

6	7	8	9	10
CO$_2$	NCl$_3$	H$_2$O	CF$_4$	(Al$_x$O$_y$)
SiO$_2$	PCl$_3$	H$_2$S	CCl$_4$	(Si$_x$Cl$_y$)
CH$_4$	NH$_3$	CaO	CBr$_4$	(Mg$_x$H$_y$)
(4) Si$_x$H$_y$	(5) P$_x$H$_y$	(6) Ca$_x$S$_y$	(7) C$_x$I$_y$	(Na$_x$S$_y$)

the ratio of 1:1, all of them also have a valence of 1. The formula for water is H$_2$O, so we assign a valence of 2 to oxygen. All of the elements in column 3 plus sulfur are seen to have a valence of 2. This leads to the formulas for the chlorides shown in column 4. Aluminum, nitrogen, and phosphorus are seen to have a valence of 3, and carbon and silicon a valence of 4.

Look back at the formulas in Table 4–1 and you will observe that all of the elements found there have the valences just worked out. The = between the carbon and oxygen in acetic acid indicates that the 2 valences of oxygen combine with 2 of the 4 valences of carbon.

A word of caution is in order here—not all elements combine with each other. No such compound as Na$_4$C is known, for instance. The valences tell us the ratios of the elements to expect in the event that they do combine with each other.

MULTIPLE VALENCES

In certain cases two elements will form more than one combination with each other. Carbon dioxide, CO$_2$, and carbon monoxide, CO, are a case in point. FeO and Fe$_2$O$_3$ are both common oxides of iron. We are forced to revise our simple picture of valence.

The concept of valence can be treated at many different levels, and in this general text we will stop at a fairly simple and incomplete one. The valence of an element is a small whole number that refers to its tendency to combine with other elements. The basis of comparison is hydrogen with a valence of one. Some elements exhibit only one valence, others may have two or more.

In CO$_2$ the proportion of oxygen to carbon is greater than it is in CO. Carbon in CO$_2$ is said to be more highly oxidized. The term that is the opposite of oxidized is reduced. In CO the carbon is more reduced than in CO$_2$. What is the situation in FeO and Fe$_2$O$_3$? Later in this unit the definition of these terms will be extended.

MOLECULAR ARCHITECTURE

From the results of chemical analysis we can deduce the formulas for molecules, but this tells us nothing about the way the atoms are assembled in space. Many different houses can be made from the same pile of building materials. The following discussion will be limited to the structure of a few compounds of carbon, but it will serve to illustrate the tremendous importance of circumstantial evidence in science.

The term optical activity was defined earlier (page 124). In terms of their behavior toward plane polarized light, there are three forms of lactic acid known. There is the d form that twists the plane of polarized light to the right, the l form that twists it to the left, and a form that is optically inactive. The activity of the d and the l forms are exactly equal in magnitude but opposite in direction. All of the chemical behavior of lactic acid is consistent with the formula

$$CH_3CHOHCOOH \quad \text{or} \quad H-\overset{\overset{\displaystyle H}{|}}{\underset{\underset{\displaystyle H}{|}}{C}}-\overset{\overset{\displaystyle OH}{|}}{\underset{\underset{\displaystyle H}{|}}{C}}-C\overset{\displaystyle O}{\underset{\displaystyle O_{\diagdown H}}{}}$$

There is nothing in this formula to suggest the existence of three forms with different optical behavior. By 1870 there were a few hundred compounds known that were optically active and many that showed no activity. Van't Hoff of Germany and Le Bel of France almost simultaneously proposed a theory to account for this.

Their lines of thought can be summa-rized as follows. Only in the optically active compounds do you find a carbon atom with four different groups attached to it. The fact that a compound is optically active suggests that the molecule is asymmetric. If four groups around a carbon, such as

$$a-\overset{\overset{\displaystyle b}{|}}{\underset{\underset{\displaystyle d}{|}}{C}}-c$$

are located at the corners of a tetrahedron, as in Figure 4–4, the result is a structure that is asymmetric—its mirror image cannot be superimposed on it. The relationship is like that of a right and left hand glove. If any two of the groups are the same, as in

$$a-\overset{\overset{\displaystyle a}{|}}{\underset{\underset{\displaystyle c}{|}}{C}}-b$$

the two models can be superimposed. Working with ball and stick models is a good way to convince yourself of this.

Van't Hoff and Le Bel suggested that the valence bonds of carbon must point towards the corners of a tetrahedron. This would explain the known cases of optical activity and those of optically inactive molecules. To return to lactic

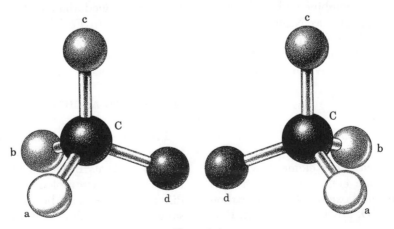

Figure 4–4.

acid, the four different groups would be CH_3-, $H-$, $HO-$, and $-COOH$. The third, inactive form, would result from a mixture of equal parts of the d and l forms. According to this theory, propionic acid, CH_3CH_2COOH, should be optically inactive, and this is the case.

This theory was immediately successful in explaining the known cases of optical activity and the new ones that were discovered. Ways were developed to separate the d and l forms from an inactive mixture. The actual shapes of the molecules have turned out to be extremely important factors in determining their behavior. No one has yet been able literally to see a molecule, but we have complete confidence in the reality of this tetrahedral model of the carbon atom. We are able to explain such diverse things as the octane number of a gasoline and the protective action of a vaccine in terms of molecular architecture.

MENDELEEF'S PERIODIC TABLE

During the first half of the nineteenth century there was rapid progress in the discovery of new elements, the determination of atomic weights, and the preparation of new compounds. The fuzzy thinking of the alchemists had given way to the quantitative approach of the modern scientist. After about sixty elements had been discovered a new problem became important. Was there any pattern to the behavior of the elements?

Although there appeared to be no broad generalizations that could be made, certain small scale similarities were obvious. There was a group of low density, soft metals that all had a valence of 1 and whose oxides reacted with water to form strong bases. These were lithium, sodium, potassium, rubidium, and cesium, and they were grouped together under the name alkali metals. There was a group

called the halogen family that had a valence of 1 and reacted with the alkali metals to form salts and with hydrogen to form strong acids. Examination of Table 4–2 will show other elements that are similar in the types and formulas of the compounds they form.

Several attempts at a larger ordering met with little success until Mendeleef proposed a scheme based on a periodic variation in chemical and physical properties of the elements when they are arranged in the order of their atomic weights.

Let us follow his reasoning for the first several elements. If we place them in the order of increasing atomic weight on a horizontal line, we have

H Li Be B C N O F

The next one known at that time (1871) was sodium. As mentioned earlier this element is strikingly like lithium. Its valence is the same and its chemical and physical properties are more like those of lithium than any other element encountered so far. Let us start a new line with Na under Li. By the same reasoning we can build up a second horizontal line with each element resembling the one above it

H Li Be B C N O F
   Na Mg Al Si P S Cl

The element with atomic weight next higher than chlorine was potassium. This fits naturally under sodium and calcium goes below magnesium. The next element was titanium. It has a valence of four and in many ways resembles carbon and silicon. Definitely it did not belong under aluminum. Mendeleef rose to the occasion, placed titanium under silicon, and left a blank space for an element yet to be discovered. This happened in several other places in his table. For some of these unknown elements he was able to predict their chemical and physical properties from a study of the elements surrounding them.

Mendeleef's guiding principle was that the chemical and physical properties of the elements are a periodic function of their atomic weight. When the elements are arranged in a calendar-like chart they show a smooth change in properties horizontally with a return at regular intervals to repeat the changes.

Now let us take a closer look at some of the features of his periodic table. A more recent form, with many elements added is shown in the Periodic Table (see inside back cover). Hydrogen is given a unique position. It is fairly common to observe the first member of a series to be atypical and this did not throw Mendeleef off his stride. The fact that there are blank squares shows the strength of his ideas. A good theory not only correlates, it also predicts the unknown. You will notice that tellurium with an atomic weight of 127.6 is placed before iodine, atomic weight 126.9. Mendeleef placed them in that order because their chemical properties required it and he stated that there must be some mistake in the figures for those atomic weights. In this statement he was wrong, and it was about seventy years later that an explanation for this and two other such anomolies was found. The whole column of elements He, Ne, Ar, Kr, Xe, Rn was unknown in 1871, so, of course, he left no room for them. When they were discovered several years later they were found to be chemically inert, valence 0, and each one fitted neatly between a halogen and an alkali metal right down the chart.

This organizing principle of Mendeleef's is one of the most helpful theories in the whole of science. It enables us to predict the properties of an element from a general knowledge of how properties change from one part of the table to another. For several years after his table was published he was not taken seriously because his statements were so improbable. It was not until several of his predictions were found to be accurate that Mendeleef received the acceptance and praise that were due him.

SUMMARY

1. The valence of an element is a small whole number that refers to its tendency to combine with another element. The basis of comparison is hydrogen with a valence of 1.
2. Some elements exhibit more than one valence.
3. The four valence bonds of carbon are normally as far apart from each other as possible. This means that they point out towards the corners of a regular tetrahedron.
4. If there are four different groups attached to a carbon atom, the molecule is asymmetric and optical activity may result.
5. Mendeleef organized the elements into a calendar-like chart based on the principle that the chemical and physical properties of the elements are a periodic function of their atomic weights.

QUESTIONS AND EXERCISES

1. Write the correct formulas for: C_xS_y, Na_xO_y, Mg_xN_y, Fe_xCl_y (2).
2. Locate the asymmetric carbon atoms in each of the following: $CH_3CHClCH_2CH_3$, $CH_3CH_2CH(CH_3)CH_2CH_3$, $CH_3COCH_2CHClCH_3$.
3. What is the average of the values for the atomic weights of chlorine and iodine? By how much does this differ from the atomic weight of bromine?
4. How many elements are now known?
5. Look up the following elements in the periodic table and write the formulas for their oxides and chlorides: cesium, radium, tin.
6. What type of semiconductor would you expect if indium was the impurity added to silicon? If antimony was added?

Chapter 3

Inside the Atom

DURING the first three-quarters of the nineteenth century the atomic theory was placed on a firm foundation. By 1875 is was generally accepted that atoms and molecules were the fundamental units of chemical change, and the actual spatial arrangement of the atoms was worked out for many molecules. Since no one ever had seen (and probably no one ever will see) any of these simpler molecules, the theory was a most impressive triumph. The nonscientist may well be disturbed by this situation. How can we be so sure of something that we cannot actually see? One place that we can get an answer to that question is in a modern police station. The criminologist is constantly putting together bits of evidence into a consistent picture that describes how a crime was committed and who did it. For example, the gun is identified by comparing the scratches on a test bullet and the fatal one. The victim's shirt is analyzed for gunpowder to determine how far away the shot was fired. Fingerprints are identified. Analysis of the suspect's pocketknife shows traces of copper from cutting the telephone wires. A hair caught by a splinter of the window frame matches the suspect's. The cumulative evidence is overwhelming. The detective was not there at the time, but he can describe the crime in detail. The evidence for the theory of the atomic structure of matter is also overwhelming. It will undoubtedly be modified and improved, but that it will be completely discarded is most unlikely.

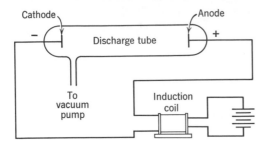

Figure 4–5. Diagram of vacuum discharge tube for studying cathode rays.

CATHODE RAYS

The last quarter of the nineteenth century saw the accumulation of evidence indicating that these basic particles called atoms were, in their turn, made up of smaller units. One of the major problems of the present century has been to work out the architecture of the atom. What are these more basic units, and how are they put together?

If we use a discharge tube connected to a vacuum pump and an induction coil (a step-up transformer) (Figure 4–5), we can watch the change in the nature of the spark between the electrodes as the pressure is lowered. No spark passes at atmospheric pressure. As the pressure drops, a feeble spark shoots the length of the tube; soon the whole tube glows; and finally a series of luminous zones can be seen. The electrode through which electrons are entering the tube is called the cathode and the positively charged electrode is called the anode. Investigations of this low-pressure discharge were made possible by H. Geissler, a German glass blower, who developed a technique for sealing metal wires through glass and who improved the vacuum pump about 1854. Edison's electric-light bulbs were also dependent on this technical advance. Other shapes of vacuum discharge tubes are shown in Figure 4–6. In part *a* of Figure 4–6 the cross casts a sharp shadow on the glass opposite the cathode. This phenomenon showed that something was

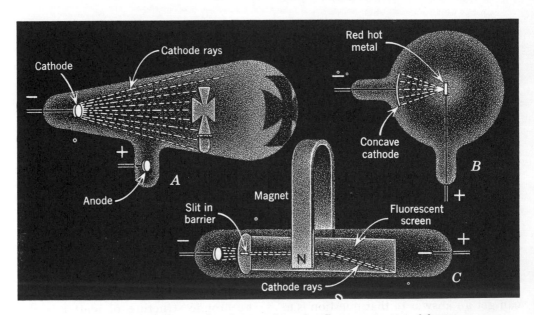

Figure 4–6. Cathode-ray tubes of various forms that illustrate properties of the rays.

coming off the cathode and traveling through the tube to the glass wall. For lack of a better name, this something was called a cathode ray.

William Crookes, an English physicist, made a thorough study of cathode rays about 1880. He showed that they could be focused on a piece of metal in the tube to heat it red hot (Figure 4–6b), that they made the glass of the tube and certain minerals in the tube fluoresce, that metal objects in their path cast sharp shadows, and that when passed between the poles of a magnet (Figure 4–6c) they were deflected in the same direction as a wire carrying a current of negative electricity. From these observations he concluded that cathode rays were a stream of negatively charged particles.

THE ELECTRON

Quantitative studies by J. J. Thomson in 1897, using a combination of electric and magnetic fields, demonstrated that all the negative charges obtained from cathode rays, by thermal means, and by the photoelectric effect, had the same ratio of charge (e) to mass (m). In 1911 Millikan perfected his oil-drop apparatus for measuring the elementary unit of charge, and it was determined that the mass of these negative particles was about ½₀₀₀ of that of a hydrogen atom. A hydrogen atom weighs 1.673×10^{-24} gram and an electron 9.106×10^{-28} gram. Dividing the second by the first gives the ratio $1/1838$.

In his oil-drop experiment Millikan used a microscope and a stopwatch to measure the rate of fall and rise of a tiny oil drop between the two plates of a condenser. With no charge on the plates the drop would fall at a steady speed.

From this measured rate of fall the mass of the drop could be calculated. Millikan found that the drops were usually charged so that they could be made to rise away from the lower plate when it was given a charge of the same sign. When the charge on the plate is held constant the rate at which the drop rises is a measure of the charge on the drop. Millikan observed that the charge on his drops would change now and then, but that it was always by jumps of a certain minimum size. He interpreted this to mean that there was a smallest unit, an "atom" of electricity. Sometimes the drops picked up two or three units of charge at a time, but it never picked up less than a whole one. This was our first proof that electricity comes in particles of a certain-size charge. Thomson had obtained an average value for the ratio of charge to mass, but Millikan could watch individual charges hopping on and off his oil drops. It was as though Gulliver had landed in a modern Lilliput where the inhabitants were so small that he could not see them. He could, however, see their trains. Every time a train started up from a station on its run he picked it up and weighed it and then put it back again. He found that the difference in weights from one station to the next was always some multiple of 0.1 milligram. Sometimes the difference in weight was 0.3, sometimes 0.4, 0.1, 0.2, 0.5, etc., milligram. He concluded that there were passengers getting on and off the train and that they weighed 0.1 milligram each.

No matter what the means of obtaining them, no matter what the residual gas in the cathode-ray tube, these negatively charged particles were always the same and they were far lighter than the lightest atom known. Here, then, was an even more basic building unit, and it was called the electron.

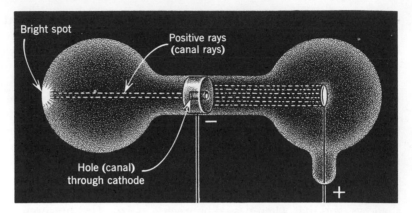

Figure 4–7. *A tube that demonstrates positive rays. Some positively charged parti-cles strike the cathode, others pass through the hole and strike the wall of the bulb on the left.*

THE PROTON

It was natural that a search would be made for positively charged particles in vacuum discharge tubes. Using a perforated cathode (Figure 4–7) Goldstein observed these particles, and they were called positive rays. They were found to have masses of the order of magnitude of the atoms of the gases used in the tubes. The lightest positively charged particle which exists for more than a small fraction of a second is the hydrogen ion, which is called a proton. We now have two of the basic units of atomic structure.

X-RAYS

Several scientists working with cathode-ray tubes had been bothered by the fact that packages of photographic film were fogged after being left near the tubes. This was merely a nuisance until Roentgen, in 1895, looked into the reason for it. He discovered that it was not cathode rays penetrating the glass but a new type of radiation originating from the spot being struck by the cathode rays. This radiation had the remarkable ability of penetrating paper, wood, and even thin sheets of metal. Since it was not bent by

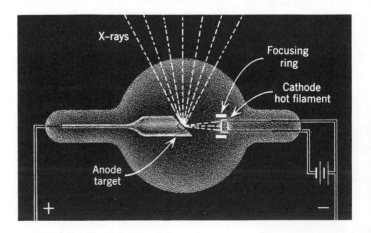

Figure 4–8. *Diagram of a modern X-ray tube.*

electric or magnetic fields and could be made to take pictures, it was thought to be a type of light. To call attention to the unknown nature of these rays, Roentgen called them X-rays (Figure 4–8). They were soon used by doctors to help in setting bones and for studying internal disorders. Their discovery created a tremendous sensation, and one London shop even went so far as to advertise X-ray-proof underwear for modest Victorian women. In 1912 the diffraction spectrum of X-rays was successfully measured and their wavelengths determined to be of the order of magnitude of 0.1 to 100 A.

SUMMARY

1. A spark will travel long distances through a gas that is at a very low pressure.
2. This spark consists of charged particles which travel in straight lines away from the electrodes. The particles leaving the cathode are called cathode rays, and those traveling in a direction from the anode toward the cathode are called positive rays.
3. Crookes showed that cathode rays traveled in straight lines, that they could make materials fluoresce, and that they were negatively charged.
4. Thomson showed that the average value of e/m was the same for negatively charged particles from several different sources. These particles were called electrons.
5. Millikan demonstrated that electricity was atomic in nature, that is, that there was a smallest unit of charge.
6. Using the value for e, the charge of an electron, its mass m is calculated to be 1/1838 of that of a hydrogen atom.
7. The lightest known stable, positively charged particle is a hydrogen ion. It is called a proton.
8. Roentgen discovered that when cathode rays strike a solid it becomes the source of a type of short-wavelength electromagnetic radiation.
9. He called this type of radiation X-rays and found that they were extremely penetrating.

QUESTIONS AND EXERCISES

1. Back of the discovery of the electron as a particle lies the work of Newton, Boyle, Volta, Oersted, Faraday, and Geissler, to mention only a few. Point out one relevant discovery made by each of these men.
2. What are some of the properties of cathode rays?
3. Why were cathode rays not thought to be a type of electromagnetic vibration like light?
4. What is the actual weight in grams of an oxygen atom?
5. How many oxygen atoms are there in 16 grams of oxygen? This number is known as Avogadro's number.
6. How does our first definition of "atom" stand up in the light of what was learned in this chapter?
7. What would be the effect of a magnetic field on positive rays?
8. What is the most convincing evidence that X-rays are a type of electromagnetic vibration?
9. Where do X-rays originate in a modern X-ray tube?
10. List five properties of X-rays.

Chapter 4

Radioactivity

ROENTGEN had noticed that his X-rays originated from the fluorescent spot where the cathode rays struck the end of the tube. A French physicist, Becquerel, was interested in fluorescence and decided to see whether fluorescent minerals in general emitted X-rays. He wrapped a photographic plate with black paper, attached a crystal of fluorescent uranium salt to the outside of the package, and exposed it to sunlight. When he developed the plate it showed a black spot under the crystal. Further experiments showed that the radiation from the crystal could pass through thin sheets of metal. One day he put away some of these packages that were all made up for an experiment but which had not been exposed because of cloudy weather. He developed them the next day, expecting to find only a faint image, but he discovered an unusually dark image. Apparently, exposure to sunlight had nothing to do with the results, and the effect was not connected with fluorescence. As so often happens, a false hypothesis, when followed through carefully, led to an important discovery.

QUANTITATIVE MEASUREMENTS AGAIN

A brilliant young scientist, Marie Curie, was in Paris at the time looking about for a subject for her thesis for the doctor's degree. She decided on a quantitative study of this new phenomenon discovered by Becquerel, and she soon named it radioactivity. After discovering that the intensity of the radiation was proportional to the amount of uranium present, she went on to investigate all the known elements for signs of radioactivity. Only one other element, thorium, showed any measurable amount. Then she tried a variety of minerals. Pitchblende, which is a complex mineral containing uranium, showed a greater activity than either pure uranium or thorium. Since she had already studied all known elements, she felt sure that pitchblende must contain a new one that was more highly radioactive than any so far studied. With the help of her husband, Pierre, who had investigated piezoelectricity, she worked four years under abominable conditions, breaking down a ton of pitchblende. They finally isolated two new radioactive elements, to which they gave the names polonium and radium. The following year, 1903, they shared the Nobel Prize in physics with Becquerel.

THE PROPERTIES OF RADIOACTIVITY

Mme. Curie in France and Ernest Rutherford in England were among the leaders of the scientists studying the nature of the radiation from radioactive elements. Their findings may be summarized as follows:

1. Elements emit radiation spontaneously. The rate is not affected by heat, light, pressure, chemical combination, or any other force brought to bear on the material.
2. Radium and some other radioactive elements glow in the dark.
3. Radioactive disintegration is accompanied by the evolution of heat. One gram of radium emits 132 calories per hour. This was a startling discovery

which, at the time, seemed to be inconsistent with the law of the conservation of energy. Although the amount of energy from 1 gram of radium is not great, that which results from all the radioactive material in the earth's crust may well be enough to explain volcanic activity.

4. The radiation affects a photographic plate and brings about other chemical changes.
5. Among the chemical changes observed was the destruction of living tissue. Cancerous tissue is more susceptible to damage than normal tissue, but continued exposure to radiation will start a cancerous growth. Obtaining increasing amounts of radium for the treatment of cancer was one of the life-long projects of Mme. Curie. She and Pierre published their technique for isolating radium without patenting it or asking for any royalties.
6. When the radiation from radium is studied as indicated in Figure 4–9, it turns out that the beam is split into three parts by an electric field. One part is deflected slightly toward the negative electrode (alpha rays); a

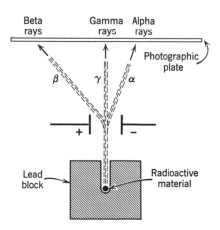

Figure 4–9. The radiation from radioactive material is split into three parts when it passes through an electric field.

second part is deflected more strongly toward the positive electrode (beta rays); and a third part passes unbent through the field (gamma rays). These three parts were called rays because they were investigated by their action on a photographic plate. Later research showed that the alpha rays were positively charged helium ions, and so they are more properly called alpha particles. The beta rays turned out to be the same as electrons, and the gamma rays are a type of electromagnetic vibration with a wavelength like that of shortwave X-rays.

7. The radiation ionizes air. It knocks electrons out of the molecules of oxygen and nitrogen, leaving positively charged ions. These ions were first observed by their action in discharging an electroscope. Later, two instruments for observing the ionization of air were developed into powerful tools for studying radioactivity. They are the Wilson cloud chamber and the Geiger counter.

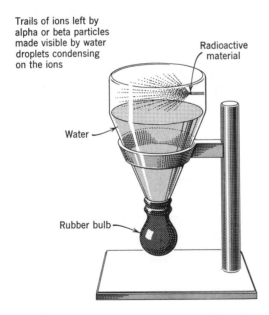

Trails of ions left by alpha or beta particles made visible by water droplets condensing on the ions

Radioactive material

Water

Rubber bulb

Figure 4–10.   Diagram of a Wilson cloud chamber.

THE WILSON CLOUD CHAMBER

A Wilson cloud chamber is an artificial fog-making device (Figure 4–10). A small volume of air is trapped above water or alcohol that is dyed black. When the rubber bulk at the bottom is squeezed the water compresses the air. Releasing the bulb allows the air to expand rapidly. This quick expansion cools the air below the dew point, and a fog forms. After the apparatus has been worked a few times all the dust particles present are used up, and the fog has no nuclei on which to form. If, during an expansion, an alpha or beta particle dashes through the chamber, leaving in its wake a trail of ions, these serve as condensation nuclei. There will be a visible track of water droplets to betray the path of the radiation. Although we cannot see the actual particles, we can see and photograph their paths just as surely as we can see and photograph ski tracks across the snow.

When the cloud chamber is placed in a strong magnetic field the paths of charged particles are curved. From the appearance of the track and its radius of curvature the mass and charge of the ionizing particle can be determined. Much of the information that will be presented henceforth has been obtained from photographs of tracks in a Wilson cloud chamber.

THE GEIGER COUNTER

A Geiger counter (more precisely, a Geiger-Mueller counter) detects ionizing radiation by means of its electrical effects. The basic idea of such a counter is shown in Figure 4–11. In this figure, A is a glass tube containing two electrodes across which is applied a difference in voltage by battery B. C is a counter which flashes a light or makes an audible click when a pulse of current flows through it. When a low voltage is applied to the electrodes and an ionizing radiation forms an ion pair between them, the two ions will move in opposite directions and reach the electrodes. A single, very small pulse of current will flow. If the applied voltage is high enough, the ions, particularly the negative ion (electron), will be moving fast enough to start a cascade of ionization, and a single pair will result in a fairly large current flowing around the circuit. This is much easier to detect. Care must be taken to keep the applied voltage below that which will make a spark jump from one electrode to the other. A Geiger counter operates in the cascade voltage range (about 1000 volts). It has proved to be another invaluable tool in the field of radioactivity.

SUMMARY

1. Becquerel inadvertently discovered radioactivity in an attempt to show a connection between fluorescence and the production of X-rays.
2. Mme. Curie demonstrated that there were some minerals which had a more intense radioactivity than any known element. This fact indicated that the minerals contained an unknown and very active element.
3. Working on this theory, Pierre and Marie Curie isolated polonium and radium.
4. Radioactive elements show certain peculiarities of behavior, such as: (a) they emit radiation spontaneously; (b) heat is evolved during radioactive disintegration; (c) their radiation affects a photographic plate and brings about other chemical changes; (d) their radiation destroys living tissue, acting more rapidly on cancerous than on normal tissue; (e) their radiation consists of alpha particles, electrons, and gamma rays; and (f) their radiation ionizes air.
5. In a Wilson cloud chamber droplets of fog form on the ions produced by ionizing radiation, making the path of the radiation visible and subject to study.

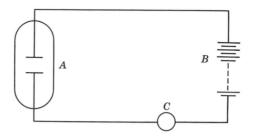

Figure 4–11.   Diagram of a Geiger-Mueller counter.

6. When a cloud chamber is placed in a magnetic field the charge and mass of the radiation may be determined.
7. A Geiger-Mueller counter detects and counts ionizing radiation as it passes between the plates of a condenser.

QUESTIONS AND EXERCISES

1. Name four accidental scientific discoveries that we have studied so far.
2. Neither Marie Curie nor Ernest Rutherford was born in the country in which his or her scientific work was done. Where did each come from?
3. Show how an electroscope could be used to study radioactivity.
4. List some similarities and some differences between X-rays and the radiation from radium.
5. What is the meaning of a zigzag track in a Wilson cloud chamber?
6. Why are alpha-particle tracks straighter than electron tracks in a Wilson cloud chamber?
7. Are ions always formed in pairs (one positively charged and the other negatively charged) in a Geiger counter?
8. What is the advantage of applying 1000 volts instead of 100 volts across a Geiger counter?
9. Why must the window on a Geiger counter be very thin? It is so thin that it is extremely fragile, so treat it carefully.
10. If a Geiger counter is operated on 120 volts AC, what kind of a vacuum tube must be in the circuit?

Chapter 5

The Solar System Atoms

L ET US now get back to atomic structure and see what the study of radio-activity contributed to it. From the next few paragraphs it will be obvious that the first effect was to spread confusion into a nice, orderly picture.

EXPLODING ATOMS

When an atom of radium explodes it expels an alpha particle and a gamma ray, and an atom of radon gas is left behind. The radon gas is radioactive in its turn (it is radon, not radium, that is ordinarily used in radium therapy). It expels an alpha particle and a gamma ray and turns into radium A. Radium A is also radioactive, and a series of changes follows that ends with inactive lead.

Each of these different radioactive elements has its own peculiar rate of decay. A given sample of radium is half gone at the end of 1600 years; this period is called its half-life. The half-life of radon is 4 days, and that of uranium is over 4 billion years. In a vast majority of disintegrations either an alpha or a beta particle is shot out of the atom during the disintegration. We have no way of predicting when a particular atom is going to explode. It is like trying to predict which kernal of corn in a pan is going to be the next one to pop.

This fascinating field soon attracted a large number of workers and they discovered nearly thirty radioactive elements whose atomic weights ranged between the weights of lead and uranium, and which were related by some extremely perplexing changes. In reading the following there is no need to remember the names of the elements or the parenthetical numbers after them (their atomic weights), but the point can be made only by using specific instances. Thorium (232) → alpha particle + mesothorium (228) → beta particle + mesothorium II (228) → beta particle + radiothorium (228). Thorium and radiothorium are chemically the same element, yet they have different atomic weights; mesothorium I and II are chemically different elements, yet they have the same atomic weight. With the discovery of these bewildering relationships, the whole basis for the organization of the periodic table (the arrangement of the elements in the increasing order of their atomic weights) began to crumble. Several more examples of this same sort turned up, and confusion gave way to chaos. It was found that the series of disintegrations that started with uranium 238 ended with lead 206. The series starting with protoactinium 231 ended with lead 207, and that starting with thorium 232 ended with lead 208.

The English physicist Soddy stepped into the breach with a term to clarify this situation. He suggested that we apply the word isotope (meaning same place) to those forms of an element that had different atomic weights. Lead 206, 207, and 208 are all isotopes of the element lead. He further suggested that, since we know the length of time required for a given amount of lead 206 to accumulate from the disintegration of a sample of uranium, we could measure the amount present in a uranium ore and calculate how long it had been disintegrating. The resulting figure would give a measure of the age of the earth's crust. Several such

measurements have been made, and the results average close to 3 billion years. This is considered to be the most accurate way to estimate the age of the earth.

ATOMIC NUMBER

In an X-ray tube the cathode rays are focused on a metal plate called the target (Figure 4–8). The X-rays are given off by the target. In 1913 Moseley measured the wavelength of the X-rays obtained when he used a number of different metals as targets. He found that each element had a characteristic wavelength and that the wavelengths decreased regularly as he went up through the periodic table. He could then put all the elements in a definite order depending on the characteristic wavelengths of their X-ray spectra. On the basis of hydrogen as number 1, each element could be given an atomic number. The atomic number of an element is a more fundamental property than its atomic weight. In three cases, potassium and argon, cobalt and nickel, and tellurium and iodine, the periodic table has elements in the reverse order of their atomic weights because their chemical properties require it. Determination of the atomic numbers of these six elements confirmed the sequence in which they had been placed by their chemical properties. Since the atomic numbers of all the elements from 1 to 100 have been determined and no blank spaces remain, we feel sure that no new elements will be discovered between any of the known ones.

THE ATOMIC NUCLEUS

One final experiment performed by Rutherford in 1911 led to a picture of atomic structure that helped clear up the confusion caused by radioactivity. He studied the scattering of alpha particles that were shot through thin sheets of metal. A high percentage of the particles passed through the metal foil undeflected, indicating that what we think of as solid matter is largely empty space. Of those few particles that were bent out of a straight path, an unexpectedly large proportion were bent through as much as a right angle, and some were even reversed in direction. Alpha particles are helium ions with a mass of four units and a positive charge of two units. This wide-angle scattering of a few alpha particles was interpreted as meaning that the atoms of the metal were mostly empty space with a small central kernel that had a high positive charge. Enough electrons to balance the positive charge and make the whole atom neutral needed to be scattered around the empty space outside this positively charged nucleus, as the kernel was called. The electrons are so light that they would have a negligible effect in scattering the alpha particles.

SPARK SPECTRA

In the previous unit we described the spectrometer and spark spectra. You will remember that spark spectra are characterized by a limited number of narrow lines. The pattern of these is unique for each element. In 1900 Planck showed that light as it was being emitted or absorbed had to be thought of as occurring in particles, or quanta. His argument was similar to that of Millikan, who showed that electricity came in unit packages. Planck found that the energy (E) of a light quantum could be calculated from the frequency (f) by the equation $E = hf$, where h is a universal constant now called Planck's constant. Neither Planck nor anyone since has suggested

an easy way to think of a wave as consisting of particles or of a particle that behaves like a wave.

From the measured wavelengths of the lines in a spark spectrum we can use the relationship $f = c/\lambda$, where c = speed of light and λ = the wavelength, to obtain the frequency. The energy associated with each bright line can be calculated from Planck's equation.

PUTTING THE PIECES TOGETHER

In 1913 Niels Bohr proposed an atomic model that incorporated the various facts presented in this chapter. He suggested that the nucleus of an atom was a heavy central sphere that contained the same number of protons as the atomic number of the element. Around the nucleus were electrons revolving in orbits much as the planets revolve around the sun. The size of the outermost orbit is what we call the size of the atom. Rutherford's experiments showed that the diameter of the nucleus is about 1/10,000 the diameter of the atom.

From the spark spectra data he calculated the sizes of the electron orbits. Since the electron and the nucleus are of opposite charge, energy must be supplied to an electron to move it away from the nucleus, and the electron will release energy when it approaches the nucleus. Bohr assumed that the spark provided energy to move the electrons in the gas atoms away from the nucleus and when they fell back toward it they gave off energy in the form of the light seen in the spectrum. The energy associated with any particular line in the spectrum represents the difference in energy that the electron has at two different distances from the nucleus.

Since the spark spectra are made up of a few bright lines, this analysis suggests the surprising idea that there are only a restricted number of orbits that the electrons can occupy. A picture of the atom emerges that bears a superficial resemblance to the structure of the solar system. When an electron drops from an outer orbit to one nearer the nucleus it gives off energy that we see as one of the bright lines that is typical of the spectrum of the element.

Let us take some specific examples and account for the particles involved. Hydrogen would have 1 proton in the nucleus and 1 electron revolving around it. Helium would have 2 protons and 2 electrons. The electrons contribute less than 0.1% of the weight of an atom, and, since helium has an atomic weight of 4, how do we account for the other 2 units? The third fundamental atomic particle, the neutron, was not discovered until 1932, but it should be mentioned here to avoid useless confusion. The neutron has essentially the same mass as a proton, but as it is electrically neutral it contributes 1 unit of mass and no charge to the atom. A helium nucleus contains 2 protons and 2 neutrons, and 2 electrons revolve around it.

We now have an explanation for isotopes. The atomic number of an element is the same as the number of protons in the nucleus and the number of electrons outside it. The rest of the atomic weight is made up of neutrons in the nucleus. For lead 206, 207, and 208 the atomic number is 82. Lead 206 is made up from 82 electrons, 82 protons, and 124 neutrons. The nucleus of lead 207 contains 125 neutrons, and that of lead 208, 126 neutrons. Later we shall have a few occasions to refer to isotopes by their symbols, and this is done in a shorthand fashion as follows: the symbol for lead is Pb (Latin plumbum); its atomic number is 82; and the isotope with an atomic weight of 206 is written $_{82}Pb^{206}$.

Bohr's theory of the atom with its definite electrons revolving in definite orbits around the nucleus is a clear-cut, intellectually satisfying picture that is, unfortunately, a little too good to be true. One of the essential points about an acceptable scientific theory is that there be some way to test its validity. And one of the necessary difficulties with any such definite theory about the detailed structure of the atom is that we have no particles lighter than the electron to use to check it. If we try to locate the electrons by studying the scattering of other electrons in the same way that Rutherford studied the nucleus, we knock our quarry completely out of their orbits. It is like hunting rabbits with a cannon. We might kill some, but we would not know where along the path of the shell they had been when they were hit. So, strictly speaking, we are reduced to vague terms such as the probability distribution of electrons, etc. With this reservation, the Bohr atom is an extremely helpful model.

THE NEUTRON

Since the neutron was not discovered until several years later, Bohr suggested that in addition to protons in the nucleus there were proton-electron pairs. The probable existence of a neutral particle with the mass of a proton was forecasted several times, and in 1932 Chadwick showed that some very puzzling results obtained by Bothe and Becher and by Irène Joliot-Curie (Mme. and Pierre Curie's daughter) and F. Joliot could be explained by assuming that such a particle was formed in their experiments. Neutrons are very difficult to detect because of their lack of electric charge. Since they pass through gases without ionizing them, the usual cloud chambers and counters do not detect them. If a neutron is given off after the collision of two atomic nuclei, the fact can be deduced from a study of the recoil paths of the nuclei in a cloud chamber. Chadwick bombarded boron (B) with alpha particles (He) and obtained nitrogen (N) and a neutron (n).

$$_5B^{11} + _2He^4 \rightarrow _7N^{14} + _0n^1$$

The fine structure of the nucleus is only just beginning to emerge. At present it, too, seems to have a layer-like structure. This early interpretation is a natural extension of our picture of the outer structure of the atom, and it may be far from correct.

Let us turn back and follow through the radioactive changes described on page 213. When $_{90}Th^{232}$ loses an alpha particle ($_2He^4$), it loses 2 protons and 2 neutrons. This results in a nucleus that has an atomic number 2 units lower and an atomic weight 4 units lower. This is mesothorium I with an atomic number of 88 and an atomic weight of 228. Look up in the modern version of the periodic table given inside the back cover and find the name we now use for this element. In the next radioactive change, mesothorium I loses an electron from the nucleus. This process involves a neutron changing into a proton which stays in the nucleus and an electron which is shot out of it. The resulting atom would not change its atomic weight, but its atomic number would gain by 1 unit to give mesothorium II (atomic weight 228, atomic number 89). Mesothorium II gives off an electron and returns to an element with an atomic number of 90 and an atomic weight of 228. That is why radiothorium is chemically like thorium but has a different atomic weight. We now have a clearer idea of what is meant by the word element. All the atoms of a given element have the same atomic number. The atomic weight of the element represents the average atomic weights of all the isotopes

taken in the proportion in which they occur in nature.

As stated earlier (page 192) $O = 16.0000$ was the basis for comparison in the table of atomic weights. After the discovery of the existence of isotopes it was found that there were three isotopes of oxygen $_8O^{16}$, $_8O^{17}$, and $_8O^{18}$ and that there were measurable differences in the proportion of these from different sources. It is crucial to have a single, unvarying standard of comparison so the new one recently adopted is the isotope of carbon $_6C^{12} = 12.0000$. The changes in atomic weights that result from the adoption of this standard are so slight that we do not need to be concerned with them.

ELECTRONIC STRUCTURE AND SOME PROBLEMS IN CHEMISTRY

A broad interpretation of chemical behavior in terms of the electronic structure of the different elements is beyond the scope of this book. We can, however, examine a few examples that have already been discussed.

The production of positive ions in a gaseous discharge tube (page 206) comes about when cathode rays (rapidly moving electrons) hit one or more of the outermost electrons in a gaseous molecule. These electrons are knocked completely out of the atom, leaving it with a net positive charge.

The metal ions in salts, Na^+, Cu^{2+}, etc., have the number of protons corresponding to their atomic number, but they have lost one or more of their normal number of electrons. The chloride ion (Cl^-) has 17 protons in its nucleus and 18 outside electrons.

Two oxides of iron were mentioned earlier, FeO and Fe_2O_3. The valence of iron in these is 2 and 3 respectively. It is obvious that ferric oxide (Fe_2O_3) is more highly oxidized than is ferrous oxide. In

$FeCl_2$ and $FeCl_3$ iron again has the valences of 2 and 3. These formulas could be written in more detail as Fe^{2+} $(Cl^-)_2$ and Fe^{3+} $(Cl^-)_3$. It is convenient to extend the concept of oxidation and reduction to include cases where electrons are lost (oxidation) and gained (reduction).

In the electrodeposition of a metal, an electric current is passed through a solution of salt. The metal ions (always positively charged) pick up electrons at the cathode and plate out as neutral atoms. This is an example of reduction. When metallic copper reacted with zinc ions (Zn^{2+}) to form Cu^{2+} and zinc, the copper was oxidized and the zinc reduced.

SUMMARY

1. Half-life is the length of time required for half a given sample of a radioactive element to disintegrate.
2. The study of a number of radioactive-decay series revealed that two different elements could have the same atomic weight and that two different samples of the same element might have different atomic weights.
3. Soddy proposed the name isotope for those forms of the same element which have different atomic weights.
4. He also pointed out that we could analyze the disintegration products of uranium in natural ores and thus estimate the age of the earth's crust. By this method it is calculated to be about 3 billion years old.
5. Moseley discovered that the wavelength of X-rays depended upon the element used as a target material in the X-ray tube.
6. When the elements are arranged in the order of their characteristic X-ray spectra, this order turns out to be almost the same as that in the periodic table.
7. Numbering the elements in this order gives each its atomic number.
8. Rutherford studied the scattering of alpha particles and discovered that most of the

space inside an atom is empty and that most of the mass of an atom is concentrated in a small, positively charged nucleus.
9. Chadwick demonstrated the existence of neutrons as electrically neutral particles with the mass of a proton.
10. Bohr developed the solar-system theory of the structure of the atom. A slightly modified outline of this theory includes the idea of a small nucleus containing the same number of protons as the atomic number of the element. Also in the nucleus are neutrons. The sum of the number of protons and neutrons is the same as the atomic weight of the isotope being considered. Revolving in orbits outside the nucleus are the same number of electrons as the atomic number of the element.
11. Isotopes of the same element differ in the number of neutrons in the nucleus. The isotopes of an element are chemically and physically similar, but they are not identical in their behavior.
12. Since we have no experimental way of determining with precision both the position and the velocity of the electrons in their orbits, our picture of atomic structure is necessarily vague in this respect.
13. Oxidation is a chemical change in which an element loses one or more electrons.
14. Reduction is a chemical change in which an element gains one or more electrons.

QUESTIONS AND EXERCISES

1. In a sample of radon weighing 1 gram how many atoms will disintegrate in 4 days? Avogadro's number (Chapter 3, Problem 5) is the number of atoms in an atomic weight.
2. Describe the make-up of $_3Li^7$.
3. How many neutrons are in the isotope of oxygen $_8O^{18}$?
4. Using the proper symbols, write the series of changes from $_{90}Th^{232}$ to $_{90}Th^{228}$. Use $-e^0$ for the electron.
5. Which of the three fundamental particles discussed has the least effect on the chemical properties of an atom?

6. If atoms are largely empty space why do they not interpenetrate?

7. How much of 1 gram of radon would be left after 12 days?

8. How has the meaning of the word element changed through the years?

9. Of the characteristic X-rays from cobalt and nickel, which has the greater wavelength?

10. What percentage of the diameter of the solar system is the diameter of the sun? Compare this figure with that of the atom and its nucleus.

Chapter 6

hf = E = mc² and

Some Consequences

THE YEARS around 1900 were very disconcerting for the older physicists. A century of progress had developed a picture of a universe made up of stable, dependable atoms and molecules that obeyed Newton's laws of motion. Light and other forms of electromagnetic energy were in a separate mental compartment and were satisfactorily wave-like in behavior. The laws of the conservation of mass and the conservation of energy were two separate, experimentally well-established pillars to build on.

AN INTELLECTUAL REVOLUTION

The discovery of radioactivity showed that atoms were not immutable. Not

only did they change, they changed spontaneously. In 1900 Plancks quantum theory blurred the distinction between waves and particles. Einstein, in 1905, derived the relationship that $E = mc^2$, where m is the mass of a particle and c is the velocity of light. It had been known for centuries that neither mass nor energy is ever observed alone. A particle of a certain mass has a certain energy. They are always associated. But Einstein went beyond this. He said that the terms mass and energy are just two ways of expressing the same thing. We concentrate our attention on the mass of an atom at rest and on the energy of a quantum of light (a photon).

Einstein's famous equation enables us to calculate the amount of energy that could be obtained if an atom at rest were changed completely to energy. This law does not contradict either the law of the conservation of mass or the law of the conservation of energy. It links them together into a single, more general statement.

Consequently, the decade from 1895 to 1905 saw the introduction of some most upsetting ideas. The transmutation of one element into another, which had been the will-o'-the-wisp of the medieval alchemist, was found to occur spontaneously; an intellectual hyphen was added to give the new words "wave-particle" and "mass-energy." Needless to say, these revolutionary ideas were considered by many to be subversive at the time, and they were not accepted without a struggle.

THE ELECTRON MICROSCOPE

In 1923 de Broglie calculated what the wavelength of an electron would be if it did show wave-like behavior. The experiments suggested by this calculation were carried out in 1927 in two different laboratories, and the theory was confirmed. By the use of thin sheets of crystalline metal for a diffraction grating, the wavelength of a beam of electrons was measured. The wavelength turned out to be 1.65 A, and this measurement immediately suggested a new type of microscope.

By merely examining the appearance of the ocean waves that pass by a rowboat you might not realize that the boat was there. But a large ocean liner disturbs the waves passing it enough to cast a shadow. In order to be seen, an object must be larger than the wavelength of light used to examine it. Since violet light has a wavelength of about 4000 A, we cannot see objects smaller than about 10,000 A (1 micron) with a light microscope. Tiny ripples on a pond would be distorted by the rowboat mentioned above, and, correspondingly, objects only 100 A or so across should be visible when viewed by a beam of electrons. Furthermore, an electromagnetic field will act

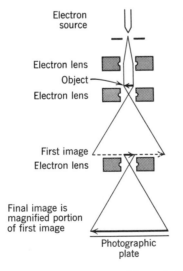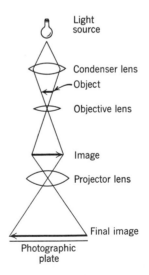

Figure 4–12.   A comparison of the optical systems of an electron microscope and a light microscope.

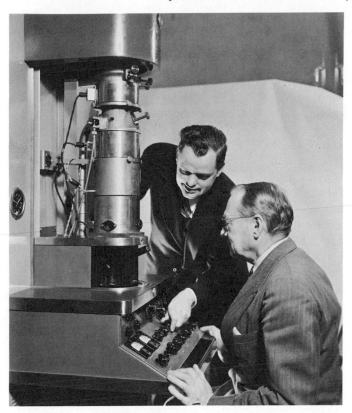

Figure 4–13. The RCA electron microscope shown with its inventors, Dr. V. K. Zworykin and Dr. James Hillier. (Radio Corp. of America.)

like a lens for a stream of electrons; it will focus them. In a short time after 1927 an electron microscope with all its parts analogous to a light microscope was developed (Figure 4–12). A picture of one is shown in Figure 4–13, and Figure 4–14 shows a picture of a virus which would be no larger than a tiny dot under a light microscope. In industry and in medical research the electron microscope has been a most valuable tool. You may well ask why gamma rays or short X-rays are not used in a microscope since they have the same wavelength as electrons. They would be used if we could find a satisfactory way to focus them. Ordinary lenses do not work. Electrons, on the other hand, are easily focused by electromagnetic fields.

ADDITIONAL SUBATOMIC PARTICLES

In addition to the proton, neutron, and electron, other subatomic particles have been discovered. Since they have yet to be fitted into our picture of atomic structure they will receive only scant mention here, but you may hear more about them in science articles in the future. In 1932 Anderson obtained a cloud-chamber picture of a positron. This is a particle with the mass of an electron and a single positive charge. In confirmation of Einstein's theory of the equivalence of energy and mass, pictures have been obtained (Figure 4–15) showing the energy of a cosmic ray turning into an electron and a positron. As may be seen, the paths curve in opposite directions in the magnetic field of the cloud chamber. Just as this pair is formed from a high energy photon, so, when a positron and an electron collide, they disappear as discrete particles and their mass is observed in the energy of the resulting photon. For this reason each is called the anti-particle of the other. They have the same mass, are opposite in some characteristic (in this case, the sign of their charge) and are annihilated on collision.

In 1935 Yukawa postulated the existence of a particle intermediate in mass between an electron and a proton. It was given the name meson, and before long an embarrassing variety of these strange particles was discovered. There are the neutrino with a zero rest mass, and several kinds of mesons and a few hyperons with masses even greater than that of a proton. All of these subatomic particles have their corresponding anti-

particle and there are certain regularities in mass, but it may be some time before they are assimilated into a broad theory.

SUMMARY

1. Planck demonstrated the particle-like nature of light and developed the relationship $E = hf$.
2. Einstein derived the equation $E = mc^2$, relating mass and energy.
3. Using the above relationships, de Broglie calculated that electrons should have a wavelength of the order of magnitude of 1.65 A.
4. An electron microscope was constructed using electromagnetic fields to focus the beam of electrons. This instrument has proved very useful for photographing large molecules, viruses, etc.
5. Some of the subatomic particles that have been studied but that are not included in

Figure 4–14. An electron microscope photograph of influenza virus particles (the big spheres) at a magnification of about 79,000 diameters. (Radio Corp. of America and R. C. Williams and R. W. Wyckoff.)

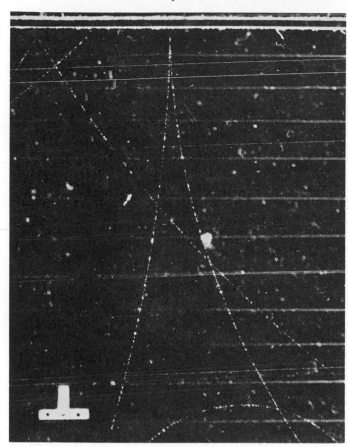

Figure 4–15. A cloud-chamber photograph, showing the production of an electron-positron pair. At the top center of the picture a cosmic ray (not visible) struck the lead plate and turned into an electron and a positron which shot off with opposite curvatures in the magnetic field of the cloud chamber. (Dr. W. M. Powell, Radiation Laboratory, University of California.)

our picture of atomic structure are: the positron, with a single positive charge and the mass of an electron; the neutrino, with no charge and a mass much less than that of an electron; and several kinds of mesons with positive, negative, or zero charges, and masses ranging between those of an electron and a proton.

Chapter 7

Atomic Energy

and Nuclear Changes

WHEN THEY used Einstein's equation relating mass and energy, $E = mc^2$, scientists and science-fiction writers did some figuring and came up with rather astonishing claims. A pound of coal turned completely into energy would supply as much energy as 1,500,000 tons of coal burned in the usual way. If the energy given off during natural radioactive changes came from a loss in mass, it could be shown that only a minute fraction of the total mass was being turned into energy. Would it be possible to prepare artificially radioactive substances and thus increase the energy available?

ARTIFICIAL RADIOACTIVITY

The first step in this direction was taken by Irène Joliot-Curie and F. Joliot in 1934. They bombarded boron with alpha particles and obtained a radioactive isotope of nitrogen and a neutron:

$$_5B^{10} + _2He^4 \rightarrow _7N^{13} + _0n^1$$

The nitrogen was separated and identified and found to be radioactive, decaying into carbon and a positron

$$_7N^{13} \rightarrow _6C^{13} + e^+$$

On the basis of this development many new artificially radioactive elements were prepared by bombardment. This technique, however, does not bring us any nearer the goal of getting useful energy from the nucleus. In the bombardment with alpha particles the percentage of successful hits is extremely small. Much more energy is consumed in getting the products than is obtained from them.

THE CYCLOTRON AND
OTHER ACCELERATORS

This inefficiency from an energy point of view is particularly true of the cyclotrons, synchrotrons, betatrons, bevatrons, etc., that are sprouting up in the physics departments of universities all over the country. All of them are glorified versions of the vacuum discharge tube in that they accelerate positive or negative particles in an evacuated space. They use electric and magnetic fields to accelerate and control the stream of particles. To express the energy which the accelerated particles attain in these atom smashers, the term mev (million electron-volts) is used. One mev is the energy that an electron has after being accelerated from rest by a potential difference of 1 million volts. The bevatron is so named because it accelerates particles so that they have an energy of more than a billion electron-volts.

The cyclotron, invented by Lawrence in 1931, gives a positively charged particle a series of small pushes that builds up its speed to a high value. The acceleration is accomplished in a relatively small area by using a vertical magnetic field to keep the particles moving in a circular path between pushes (Figure 4–16). Remember that a charged particle is deflected at right angles to the direction of a magnetic

field. The cyclotron has been called an atomic merry-go-round, but it may be compared more aptly to a discus thrower. The particles spiral outward from the center and are finally thrown free of the machine to travel in a straight path to the target. The energy used to operate the cyclotron and the other machines is many thousands of times greater than that obtainable from the radioactive products. These are quite impractical as sources of energy, but they are extremely valuable as research tools for studying atomic nuclei.

NUCLEAR FISSION

All the radioactive disintegrations that we have encountered so far involved the loss of a small particle (electron, positron, or alpha particle) and energy in the form of gamma rays, and the remaining atom always had an atomic number within two units of the starting material. In 1939 two German scientists, Meitner and Hahn, observed a peculiar kind of nuclear disintegration. When an isotope of uranium, $_{92}U^{235}$, was bombarded with neutrons, elements with an atomic number of around 45, several neutrons, and an unusually large amount of energy were obtained. This was something entirely different from previous experience. The nucleus was being split wide open; a larger amount of energy than usual was being liberated; and several particles (neutrons) like the one that started the process were resulting from it. This new type of disintegration is called a fission reaction, a cleavage of the nucleus (Figure 4–17).

Uranium 235 is a relatively rare isotope, constituting less than 1% of natural uranium, which is mostly uranium 238. If a

Figure 4–16.   *Cyclotron at the Radiation Laboratory, University of California. The chamber in which the particles are accelerated is in the middle of the picture, immediately above the stairs on the foreground. (Radiation Laboratory, University of California.)*

small amount of pure uranium 235 is prepared and a neutron strikes it to produce a single fission, the chance that the resulting neutrons will, in turn, make any effective hits is small. With small amounts of fissionable material the reaction fails. As more and more uranium 235 is piled together, the chance for the fission reaction to spread from the first atom to the next and then to successive ones increases.

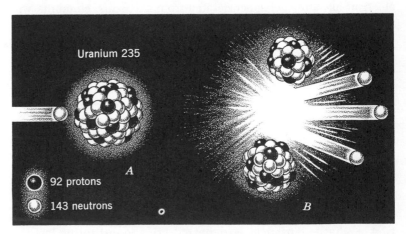

Figure 4–17.   *Details of a single fission reaction. A neutron is striking a uranium 235 nucleus at A. The fission reaction at B produces two medium-sized nuclei, several neutrons, and much energy.*

Finally, a critical size will be accumulated, the neutrons from the first fission will break up more than one additional atom, and the reaction will spread like wild-fire by geometrical progression through the whole mass (Figure 4–18). This spreading of the fission is called a chain reaction, and it takes place only after the critical size has been exceeded. Since there are sufficient stray neutrons around, it takes place inevitably when the critical size is exceeded.

The concept of critical size and chain reaction may be illustrated by the imaginary experiment of firing a bullet into a pile of shotgun shells. If one shell is hit properly it will explode and send out shot which, in their turn, are capable of exploding other shells, and so on. With a small pile of shells, the explosion from a successful hit would probably not set off even one more. As more and more shells are added to the pile the chain of explosions would lengthen. There would hardly be any direction that a shot could travel without exploding another shell. Below the critical size the chain dies out; above it, it grows.

It took scientists all over the world only a short time to appreciate the significance of this discovery by Meitner and Hahn. With a small expenditure of energy a tremendous amount could be realized. Calculations showed that only about 0.1% of the mass of the uranium 235 was being converted into energy, but even this amount is enough so that the material in one atom bomb (about 20 pounds) releases energy equivalent to 20,000 tons of TNT. Atomic energy (more properly, nuclear energy) for constructive and destructive purposes was a distinct possibility.

A word might well be included here about the so-called secret of the atom bomb that the United States was supposed to possess for several years. Once scien-

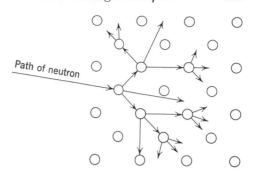

Figure 4–18. A chain reaction which consists of a growing series of fission reactions.

tists knew that such a thing as a fission reaction could occur, the atom bomb was almost inevitable. The reason we got it first was that we had the necessary technical skills to see the job done promptly. Any one of several properly trained groups of scientists throughout the world could have accomplished the task. Because of the unnecessary emphasis on keeping a nonexistent secret, the progress of science has been seriously impeded. By having our own men keep information from each other we have hampered our own development.

THE SEPARATION OF ISOTOPES

The first step in this problem of releasing atomic energy on a large scale was the separation of uranium 235 and 238. The separation of isotopes is a tedious business. They are so nearly alike in all their properties that their separation is a long and costly process. Separation of the isotopes of hydrogen with masses 1 and 2 is the simplest. Ordinary hydrogen consists mostly of $_1H^1$, but it also contains a small amount of $_1H^2$ (sometimes called deuterium or heavy hydrogen). Prolonged electrolysis of water leaves a residue rich in so-called heavy water, which contains oxygen combined

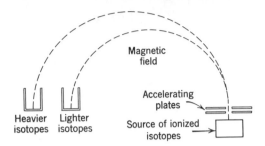

Figure 4–19. *Separating isotopes in a magnetic field.*

with deuterium. This is the usual process for isolating it. If a mixture of isotopes is ionized and shot through a uniform magnetic field, the stream will be bent in circular paths with the heavier isotopes following a wider arc outside the lighter ones (Figure 4–19). From Newton's second law (page 18), $a = f/m$, the acceleration (rate of change in direction in this example) will be inversely proportional to the mass for a constant force, and so the heavier isotopes will not change their direction so rapidly as the lighter ones. This method was very successful at Oak Ridge in separating uranium 235 and 238. In passing through the fine pores of some substance like unglazed porcelain the lighter isotopes of a gas will stream ahead of the heavier ones. This gaseous diffusion process must be repeated hundreds and sometimes thousands of times to achieve a satisfactory separation, but it works well enough to be practical. There are other techniques for separating isotopes, but their usefulness is limited and we do not have space to consider them here.

EXTENDING THE PERIODIC TABLE

Fissionable isotopes are rare, and the possibilities of any large-scale use of atomic energy were severely limited until Seaborg discovered the reaction by which plutonium is produced from uranium 238. This abundant isotope of uranium can capture a neutron and turn into a completely new element, neptunium (Np). Neptunium is radioactive and spontaneously turns into plutonium (Pu).

$$_{92}U^{238} + _0n^1 \rightarrow _{93}Np^{239} + e^-$$
$$_{93}Np^{239} \rightarrow _{94}Pu^{239} + e^-$$

Since plutonium is fissionable, both the isotopes of uranium can be used to liberate atomic energy. The Hanford, Washington, plant of the Atomic Energy Commission is producing plutonium. After his success in making these two new transuranium elements, Seaborg and his coworkers made the next four. Their names and atomic numbers are: americium (95), curium (96), berkelium (97), and californium (98). One could hazard a guess that Seaborg, after noticing that there were no planets beyond Pluto, came back to earth and remembered that he was working at the state university at Berkeley, California. Seaborg and McMillan shared the Nobel Prize in 1951 for this work. Five more transuranium elements have been made in minute traces. Their names and atomic numbers are einsteinium (99), fermium (100), mendelevium (101), nobelium (102), and lawrencium (103). This completes the actinide sequence of metals. If number 104 is made it should have chemical properties similar to those of hafnium.

SUMMARY

1. The Joliots prepared the first artificially radioactive element.
2. The cyclotron is only one of a number of particle accelerators. In it a magnetic field keeps positively charged ions circling around while a rapidly oscillating electric field keeps accelerating them until they reach a very high velocity. The beams

from these accelerators are valuable for making artificially radioactive elements and for studying atomic structure.

3. Meitner and Hahn first observed nuclear fission.

4. The characteristics of a fission reaction are that a nucleus breaks into two nearly equal parts and both a number of neutrons and a large amount of energy are released.

5. In a chain reaction the neutrons released from the fission of one nucleus bring about the fission of at least one more, which, in its turn, releases neutrons which start further fissions, etc.

6. A chain reaction will die out, maintain itself at a steady rate, or spread with increasing rate depending on the average of the number of new fissions that result from a previous one. If this ratio averages less than 1, the chain dies out; if it is greater than 1, it grows.

7. Critical size is the size of the pile of fissionable material that will keep the chain reaction barely self-sustaining.

8. In the fission of uranium 235 only about 0.1% of the mass involved is converted into energy.

9. Some of the methods used for separating isotopes are: (a) the prolonged electrolysis of water concentrates deuterium in the residue; (b) a beam of charged particles is passed through a magnetic field that separates the particles according to their masses; and (c) repeated diffusion through porous membranes separates a gas into lighter and heavier fractions.

10. Seaborg discovered that the nonfissionable isotope uranium 238 could be turned into a new fissionable element, plutonium.

11. Artificially produced elements have been added to the periodic table. These elements and their atomic numbers are: neptunium (93), plutonium (94), americium (95), curium (96), berkelium (97), californium (98), einsteinium (99), fermium (100), mendelevium (101), nobelium (102), and lawrencium (103).

QUESTIONS AND EXERCISES

1. When atomic energy is the source of power, a tremendous saving is made in the space occupied by the fuel. Name some situations where such a saving would be particularly useful.

2. In what countries did the following teams of scientists do their work: I. and F. Joliot, Meitner and Hahn, Seaborg and McMillan?

3. If a solid piece of metal is used as the target for the particles accelerated by the cyclotron, why are so few hits scored?

4. In what ways does a fission reaction differ from the usual radioactive disintegration?

5. How did the concepts of matter change around 1900?

6. Why is an electron microscope so important in research today?

7. What would determine the practical upper limit to the size of an atom bomb?

8. What would be one of the atoms formed in the fission of uranium?

9. How would the kinetic energy of a proton and an electron compare if both were traveling with the same velocity?

10. Compare the ratio of neutrons to protons in two or three of the elements near the middle of the periodic table with some elements having high atomic number. The result shows why a fission reaction is to be expected only with some of the higher ones.

Chapter 8

Putting Atomic Energy to Work

L ARGE quantities of uranium can be accumulated in a so-called pile if suitable neutron-absorbing material is present to keep the chain reaction from spreading (Figure 4–20). The production and absorption of neutrons can be balanced at any desired level. The energy given off can be used to generate power (Figure 4–21). Since the pile must be shielded with several feet of concrete to retain dangerous radiation, its usefulness is limited by its great size. This direct use of atomic energy for power is most promising for parts of the world where the cost of transporting fuel is high and for installations, such as in ocean vessels, where the usual fuel supply takes up much valuable cargo space.

MAKING AND USING
RADIOACTIVE ISOTOPES

Compared with protons and alpha particles, neutrons penetrate into atomic nuclei rather easily. The product of such a collision frequently is a radioactive isotope. In this way the atomic-energy piles are much more useful than the cyclotron. A sample of material to be treated is placed in the center of the pile, where it is exposed to a terrific bombardment from neutrons. After a suitable length of time it is removed, and the radioactive material is purified and used.

Radioactive isotopes are particularly useful in answering such questions as: In what particular form is an element best

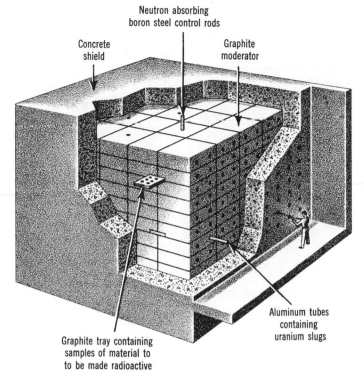

Figure 4–20. *An atomic-energy pile for the production of power and of artificially radioactive isotopes.*

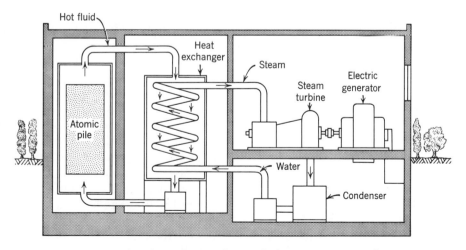

Figure 4–21. *The production of power from an atomic-energy pile.*

supplied as a fertilizer for plants? What is the sequence of compounds formed in photosynthesis? In what way does a particular vitamin or medicine do its job in the body? How far do mosquitoes range from their breeding places? What kind of oil is most effective in cutting down engine wear? Extremely small amounts of radioactivity can be detected by means of a Geiger counter, which can, if necessary, be used on a living plant or animal. Radioactive isotopes are proving to be at least as important a research tool as the microscope. They are usually referred to as tagged atoms in popular articles. The Atomic Energy Commission supervises the preparation and distribution of these isotopes for research purposes.

A particularly useful isotope of carbon is prepared by the reaction

$$_7N^{14} + _0n^1 \rightarrow _6C^{14} + _1H^1$$

Carbon 14 has a half life of 5760 years. It has been used to study the mechanism of photosynthesis and many other important biological reactions. The cells of all living material contain a small fraction of this radioactive isotope of carbon. When the organism dies the amount of carbon 14 begins to decrease and from the amount left in an archaeological specimen we can get an accurate estimate of its age. Objects as old as 40,000 years can be dated by this technique. Radioactive cobalt, which is made by the reaction

$$_{27}Co^{59} + _0n^1 \rightarrow _{27}Co^{60}$$

has practically replaced radium in cancer therapy.

NUCLEAR FUSION

The energy released in a fission reaction comes from a loss in mass when elements of high atomic number break up into elements located near the middle of the periodic table. Calculations show that if the nuclei of elements of low atomic number could be fused together to form heavier elements, there would also be a loss of mass and a release of energy. We have been using an approximate value of 1 for the mass of a proton and of a neutron. To show how energy can be obtained by a fusion reaction we shall have to use the most precise values we can get for these masses. A proton has a mass of 1.00759 units and a neutron one of 1.00899 units. If two of each of these went together to form a helium nucleus we would have the following balance sheet:

$$2 \text{ neutrons} = 2 \times 1.00899 = 2.01798$$
$$2 \text{ protons} = 2 \times 1.00759 = 2.01518$$
$$\text{total mass} = 4.03316$$
$$\text{actual mass of helium nucleus} = 4.00279$$
$$\text{mass loss} = 0.03037$$

The conversion of this mass into energy would release over 1×10^{12} calories, over a million million calories from the fusion reaction producing only 4 grams of helium.

The catch in this process is that four particles have to be brought together, and the positively charged ones would have to be traveling at a terrific speed to overcome their mutual repulsion. The speeds associated with several million degrees centigrade are needed to bring about nuclear fusion.

Calculations have been carried out on several fusion reactions to explore the possibilities of making a super atom bomb. Since the most promising of these involves the isotopes of hydrogen, either $_1H^2$ (deuterium) or $_1H^3$ (tritium), it is usually called the hydrogen, or H, bomb. A fission-reaction bomb would have to be used to give the high temperature required to get the fusion-reaction bomb started. The military advantage of the fusion bomb is that no critical size is involved. With the fission-reaction bomb there is an upper limit to the amount of active material that can be used. The bomb can be made in two parts which are each less than the critical size and which are combined at the time of explosion, or it can be made of a porous structure that is compressed rapidly. Since it is mechanically impractical to try to bring more than two pieces together in the short time required for a bomb to explode, the total fissionable material involved would be less than twice the critical size. With a fusion-reaction bomb there is no theoretical upper limit to its size.

We speak of the "release" of atomic energy as though it were something that was being kept prisoner and we were setting it free. This process does indeed bear a resemblance to the familiar Arabian Nights story in which Sinbad broke the seal on a jar and out burst a jinnee ready to do his will. It seems that we, too, need the wisdom of Solomon to keep this power under control.

THE SUN AS A FURNACE

Geological evidence indicates that the sun has maintained its present high temperature at a remarkably even level for hundreds of millions of years. How can it be so prodigal with its energy for so long? A series of chemical reactions, such as combustion, can offer no satisfactory explanation. There is not enough material in the sun to last for more than a few years if such a process were going on. When radioactivity was discovered it was explored as a possible answer to the riddle of the sun, but it, too, is inadequate.

Several fusion reactions have been examined to see if they can account for the behavior of the stars. The two series of reactions given below account for the known facts very satisfactorily. The first one probably makes the more important contribution to the energy of cool stars like the sun, and the second one is the predominant reaction in hotter stars like Sirius.

In the proton-proton sequence six protons combine to form two helium 3 nuclei which then fuse to one helium 4 (atomic numbers are omitted).

1. $H^1 + H^1 \rightarrow H^2 + e^+ + $ energy
2. $H^2 + H^1 \rightarrow He^3 + $ energy
3. $2He^3 \rightarrow He^4 + 2H^1 + $ energy

This shows the sun in the role of a furnace for which hydrogen is the fuel and helium the ashes. There is enough hydrogen in the sun to keep the process going for another thirty billion years.

Hydrogen is the predominant element in all the stars. Although the process outlined above goes on in all of them, the one described below is thought to be more important in the hotter stars. In this series of reactions the nucleus of a carbon atom acts as a landing field for four successive protons. After all four have gathered there they break off as a helium ion, leaving the carbon nucleus free to repeat the process. The net change is very much like that discussed above. Four hydrogen atoms change into one helium atom with the release of energy.

The cycle of changes, which is summarized in Figure 4–22, takes place in the following six steps: (atomic numbers are omitted):

1. $C^{12} + H^1 \rightarrow N^{13} + $ energy
2. $N^{13} \rightarrow C^{13} + e^+$
3. $C^{13} + H^1 \rightarrow N^{14} + $ energy
4. $N^{14} + H^1 \rightarrow O^{15} + $ energy
5. $O^{15} \rightarrow N^{15} + e^+$
6. $N^{15} + H^1 \rightarrow C^{12} + He^4$

It is to be hoped that all of us who understand the basic ideas of atomic energy will work for a world order in which its constructive possibilities can be realized.

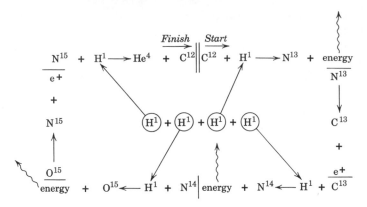

Figure 4–22. One of the fusion-reaction cycles that supplies energy for the sun.

SUMMARY

1. By using neutron absorbers as a control, an atomic-energy pile can be balanced at any desired level of rate of fission.
2. Such a pile can be utilized for the direct production of power. Its usefulness is limited, however, by the thick shielding that is essential as a protection against the intense radiation coming from the pile.
3. The atomic-energy pile is a rich source of neutrons. Neutron bombardment of elements placed in a well in the pile will turn them into radioactive isotopes.
4. A few radioactive isotopes are useful for replacing radium in cancer therapy.
5. A large number of radioactive isotopes have been very useful as research tools in science and in industry.
6. Nuclear fusion is the adding together of two or more light nuclei to form a heavier composite nucleus.
7. For the very lightest elements, mass is converted into energy during a fusion reaction.
8. According to our present knowledge, fusion reactions take place only at temperatures of several million degrees centigrade.
9. The fusion-reaction bomb is referred to as the hydrogen bomb because the most practical fusion reactions studied so far involve isotopes of hydrogen.
10. There is no theoretical upper limit to the size of a fusion-reaction bomb.
11. The explosion of a fission-reaction bomb seems to be the best way to get the temperatures needed for starting the fusion reaction of a hydrogen bomb.
12. The temperature and rate of expenditure of energy of the sun can be explained in terms of a series of nuclear fusion reactions, the net result of which is that 4 protons add successively to a carbon nucleus and then break off as an alpha particle. There is a loss of mass, which is transformed into energy.
13. An understanding of science is becoming an increasingly important part of the equipment of a good citizen.

QUESTIONS AND EXERCISES

1. What is the principal reason that neutrons can penetrate the atomic nucleus more easily than protons or electrons?
2. Devise an experiment using the appropriate radioactive element and a Geiger counter to solve one of the problems mentioned on page 232.
3. What equation is used to calculate the energy to be obtained from a loss in mass? Who developed it, and when?
4. Calculate the amount of energy released when 20 pounds of U 235 undergoes the fission reaction.
5. What is the evidence indicating that the sun has maintained its present high temperature at a remarkably even level for hundreds of millions of years?

6. What practical applications of atomic energy have you heard mentioned that are obviously absurd?

7. What elements are formed during the cycle of changes which is assumed to account for the energy of the sun?

8. As this is being written the first practical atomic power plant is being designed and built. What is this power plant to be used for?

9. What group controls the production and use of fissionable material in the United States?

10. What sort of an international agreement for the control of atomic energy would give you a sense of security? The Baruch Report will give you some ideas on this subject.

Unit Five

The Solar System
and Beyond

Chapter 1

The Solar System

and the Stars

IN STARTING our study of the structure of the solar system it would be well for us to put in order the knowledge of the subject that we have accumulated through everyday experience. Where does the sun rise, and where does it set? Does it always rise in the same place and at the same time? Is there any regularity about these changes? Ask yourself the same series of questions about the moon. How does the moon differ in appearance from time to time? Do we notice the same sort of changes in the sun? Is the Big Dipper always in the same position at ten o'clock at night? How about the Pleiades, Orion, Jupiter, Venus? Any physical model that we construct will have to be consistent with the known facts. You probably know that the earth revolves around the sun, but can you point to any fact that is inconsistent with the idea that the sun revolves around the earth? For many hundreds of years the latter was the accepted idea.

Careful observation over several years would be required to answer all the questions asked in the previous paragraph, and people living in different parts of the country would not give the same answer to every question.

APPARENT MOTION OF THE SUN

North of the Arctic Circle and south of the Antarctic Circle there are many successive days when the sun never rises above the horizon. As we approach the Poles, the length of this dark period increases to a maximum of 6 months each year, and there is a corresponding period during which the sun never sets below the horizon. As seen from the Equator the sun rises 23.5° north of east on June 21 and sets 23.5° north of west; on March 21 and September 23 it rises and sets exactly east and west; and on December 21 it rises and sets 23.5° south of east and west. For a house that faces directly north, the sun will shine in the front windows as it rises in the early summer, and in the back windows as it rises in the early winter. We have seen how the length of "day" can vary from zero to 24 hours near the Poles. At the Equator it is slightly over 12 hours long all through the year.

APPARENT MOTION OF THE MOON

The moon always rises later than it did the previous time. On the average, it is 50½ minutes later each day. When it rises just about sunset it appears to be round, and we call it a "full" moon. When it is visible in the west at sunset it appears to be a delicate crescent, and we call it a "new" moon. If you start observing the moon when it is new and make a point of looking for it the same time each night for two weeks, you will notice on successive nights that it is farther away from the sun (farther east), and larger. At the end of one week it will be to the south and half full, at the end of the second week it will be rising in the east as a full moon. After that, you will have to wait later and later to see it, and it will be changing back to a half moon. Instead of waiting up until late at night to see it in the east, you can see it in the western sky during the morning. At the

end of the third week after the new moon, it will be setting in the west at noon. During the next (fourth) week it will be hard to observe unless you are an early riser. If you have the persistence to get up before sunrise, you will be rewarded by seeing a beautiful crescent old moon floating above the faint glow of dawn in the east. The whole change from new moon to the next new moon takes 29½ days.

APPARENT MOTION OF THE STARS

If you are familiar with any bright star, like Sirius, or an easily recognized constellation, like Orion, or the Pleiades, which are prominent in the winter sky, you can observe that they rise about 4 minutes earlier each night. We can make a star map showing the different constellations and their relationships to each other, but the map must be adjusted for the day of the year and the hour of the day to show which groups of stars are above the horizon. The map will also have to be adjusted for the latitude of the observer. Unless the statements in this unit are otherwise qualified they are intended to refer to the heavens as seen from the middle latitudes of the continental United States. The arrangement of the stars in the sky on any one night of the year will be repeated on the same date of the next year. Most of the stars rise in a general easterly direction and set in a westerly one; but those near the North Star (the Big Dipper, the Little Dipper, Cassiopeia, etc.) swing in a great circle around the North Star and never set below the horizon (Figure 5–1). To observers in the far north there are many constellations that never set, and as far south as New Orleans the handle of the Big Dipper will be seen to drop below the northern horizon. The sun is to the

Figure 5–1. A time-exposure picture of the stars in the vicinity of the North Star. The shutter was left open 1 hour. As the earth rotates on its axis the stars leave arclike trails on the photographic plate. (Yerkes Observatory.)

south of those of us in the United States at noon every day; the moon goes through a complete change of phases approximately every month; and the stars repeat their cycle of motion across the heavens every year.

APPARENT MOTION OF THE PLANETS

In contrast to this regularity of motion of most of the heavenly bodies is the behavior of the five visible planets, Mercury, Venus, Mars, Jupiter, and Saturn. These travel approximately the same path in the sky as the sun and moon. If you watch some of these for several weeks, you will see that they do not appear against the same background of constellations over a long period of time. Some-

times they are farther east and sometimes farther west.

SCALE MODEL OF THE SOLAR SYSTEM

We have now assembled a large number of facts that require an explanation. We should be able to construct some sort of physical model that will demonstrate these relationships. It will be less confusing if we study the picture of the solar system that is now considered to be true rather than taking up the various theories in their historical order.

About 1609 Kepler proposed the currently accepted theory of the structure of the solar system (page 285). He said that the earth and the other planets move around the sun in elliptical paths that are nearly circular. To get an idea of the relative sizes involved, imagine the sun as a ball nearly an inch across and at the end of a football field. The earth would be about the size of a pinpoint and at a distance of 7 feet 11 inches in this model. Jupiter, which is the largest planet, would be represented by a pinhead at a distance of 40 feet. Pluto, the outermost planet, would be a pinpoint at the far end of the field (306 feet). The orbits of the planets lie close to a common plane, and all the planets go around the sun in the same direction. On the same scale, the nearest star would be 384 miles away, and the distances to most of them would be many thousands of miles.

If, at the center of the earth, we should draw a line perpendicular to the plane of the earth's orbit, it would form an angle of 23½° with the axis of rotation of the earth. The axis of rotation (the line joining the North and South Poles) points toward the North Star, and so, as the earth travels around the sun, the angle that this axis of rotation makes with a line to the sun changes from 66½° on June 21 to 113½° on December 21 (Figure 5–2). The parts of the earth closest to the sun on June 21 are those along the Tropic of Cancer (Figure 5–3); on March 21 and September 23, those along the Equator; and on December 21, those along the Tropic of Capricorn.

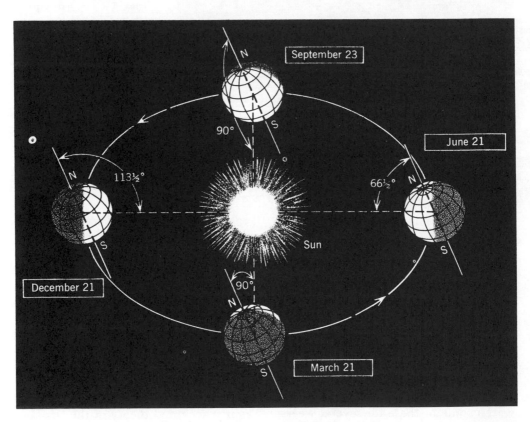

Figure 5–2.   The seasonal changes in angle between the earth's axis of rotation and the line joining the earth and the sun.

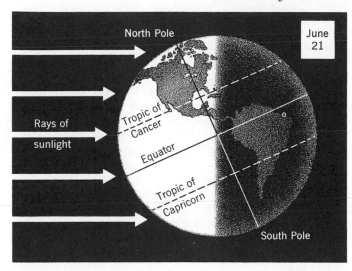

North Pole

June 21

Rays of sunlight

Tropic of Cancer

Equator

Tropic of Capricorn

South Pole

Figure 5–3.   The parts of the earth along the Tropic of Cancer are the ones closest to the sun on June 21. In this region the sun is directly overhead at noon on this date.

In the latitudes of the continental United States, the sun is never directly overhead, and at noon it is directly to the south. From one noon to the next is 24 hours by definition. As you look down on the North Pole the rotating earth is turning in a counterclockwise direction. On its trip around the sun the earth rotates on its axis 366¼ times.

Refer to Figure 5–2, and imagine the stars somewhere beyond the limits of the four sides of the page. You can see that those constellations beyond the bottom of the page would appear overhead at midnight on March 21. In April and May they would set earlier and earlier, and by June 21 they would be low in the western sky at sunset. At midnight on this date we would be looking up toward a different quarter of the heavens—the one to the right of the page. At midnight on September 23 we would be looking in exactly the opposite direction from the one we were looking on March 21, and on December 21 we would see those stars in the fourth quarter of the sky, with the ones we had observed in March rising in the east just before dawn. Those

stars below the page would not be visible from the United States, and those well above it would be toward the north, and the North Star and some of its immediate neighbors would be visible all year long.

SUMMARY

1. The length of time that the sun is above the horizon varies from 6 continuous months at the Poles in summertime to a little over 12 hours each day at the Equator all through the year.
2. The moon goes through its cycle of phases in 29½ days. It rises on an average of 50½ minutes later each day.
3. The stars rise about 4 minutes earlier each night. They repeat their cycle of motion across the sky once a year.
4. The planets follow an irregular but predictable motion in the sky. Their path of motion is always close to that followed by the sun.
5. On a scale model, with the sun represented by a ball 1 inch in diameter, the planets would all be the size of a pinhead or smaller. This entire model would be slightly over 600 feet in diameter.

QUESTIONS AND EXERCISES

1. At the Equator, why does daylight last a little longer than 12 hours instead of exactly 12 hours?

2. If you were a little north of the Arctic Circle, what path would you observe the sun taking during the 24 hours of June 21?

3. On the Tropic of Cancer (latitude 23.5° north) at noon on June 21, what is the angle between a north-south line (meridian) and a line pointing to the sun?

4. As in Question 3, what would the angle be for a place at 24.5° north latitude? 30° north latitude? 40° north latitude?

5. Express the answers to Question 4 in the form of a general equation.

6. What direction would you have to look to see the constellation Orion in April at about 9 P.M.?

7. Take a look at the sky some evening, and sketch the relative positions of the Big Dipper, Little Dipper, and Cassiopeia.

8. What direction from you right now is a constellation which you could see overhead at midnight 6 months ago?

9. What is the greatest number of full moons that could occur in one year?

10. Does a crescent moon ever appear in the eastern sky?

11. Choose some latitude that concerns you and calculate the maximum and minimum length of the noontime shadow of a 10-foot vertical pole. How would an architect make use of such information in planning windows and overhanging roofs?

Chapter 2

The Tools of the Astronomer,

and a Look at the

Sun and the Moon

T HE FIRST phase of any science is descriptive. The early astronomers concerned themselves with observing where each of the stars was at a certain time and with estimating its relative brightness. Despite the apparent multitude of stars, there are only about two thousand which can be seen at one time from any one place on the earth. The position of a star is described by noting its direction, its angular distance above the horizon, and the time of the observation. Long before the days of the telescope, some remarkably accurate observations were made by the Chinese, Polynesians, and Mayans, as well as by people living near the eastern end of the Mediterranean.

TOOLS OF THE ASTRONOMER

Tycho Brahe (1546–1601) used a large-scale quadrant similar to the one in Figure 5–4 and also used a mechanical clock. When Galileo (1564–1642) invented the telescope, he not only increased the accuracy of this type of measurement but also made it possible to study new problems. Details of structure of the sun, moon, and planets could be observed, and the increased light-gathering power of the instrument revealed stars too faint to be seen by the unaided eye. The optical system of a refracting telescope was shown in Figure 2–18. The Yerkes Observatory of the University of Chicago has the largest instrument of this type,

245

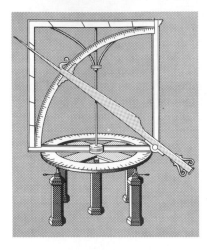

Figure 5–4.   An example of the type of large-scale quadrant in use at the time of Tycho Brahe.

with a forty-inch lens (Figure 2–19). A very large lens absorbs too much of the light that falls upon it and also tends to sag under its own weight, so that the larger telescopes use concave mirrors to gather the light. The optical system of a reflecting telescope is shown in Figure 2–20. The largest telescope of this type, and a real triumph of modern engineer-ing skill, is the two-hundred-inch reflec-tor at Mt. Palomar (Figure 5–5).

Our ability to "see" great distances has been further increased by placing a pho-tographic plate in the focal plane of the telescope. The effect of light on a photo-graphic plate is cumulative, so that expo-sures of many hours will reveal details that would be missed entirely by a look through the eyepiece of the same tele-scope. The temperature of a star can be measured by placing a thermocouple at the focus of the telescope.

Another valuable accessory to the tele-scope is the spectrograph. When the light collected by the telescope is refracted by a prism or diffracted by a grating, the spectrum can be analyzed. From the distribution of energy in the spectrum we can determine the absolute or intrinsic brightness of the star, and we can also tell what elements are present. If the star has a component of motion toward or away from the earth, this will show up as a shift in wave length of the spectrum.

The analysis of the stellar spectrum is carried out either by examining a photo-graph or by placing a photoelectric cell

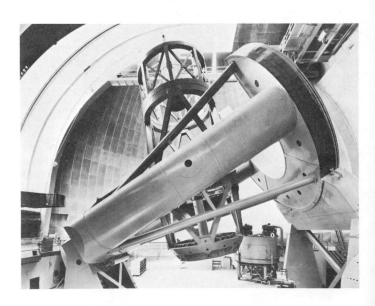

Figure 5–5.   Reflecting tele-scope at Mt. Palomar. The mir-ror is 200 inches in diameter. (Mt. Wilson and Mt. Palomar Observatories.)

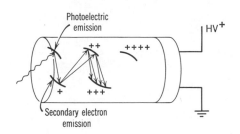

Figure 5–6a. *A photomultiplier tube (Redrawn from* Introduction to Modern Physics, *by C. H. Blanchard, C. R. Burnett, R. G. Stoner, and R. L. Weber, Prentice-Hall, 1958.)*

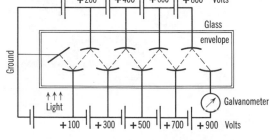

Figure 5–6b. *Schematic diagram of photomultiplier. (Redrawn from* Introduction to Atomic and Nuclear Physics, *Third Edition, by O. Oldenberg, McGraw-Hill Book Co., 1961.)*

directly in the path of the light. When the primary current from a photoelectric cell is amplified in a photomultiplier, the sensitivity is greatly enhanced. This combination is illustrated in Figure 5–6. Electrons released by the photoelectric effect are accelerated toward the first electrode. Each electron striking this electrode liberates more than one electron from it so that an amplified current is accelerated toward the second electrode. Several such amplifications make it possible to measure small differences in light intensity as well as to observe extremely faint images.

The development of radar technology has opened up a whole new field of astronomy. Wave lengths in the centimeter to meter range are observed to come from many parts of the sky. A particularly important band has a wave length of 21 cm. It is due to hydrogen in interstellar space. Because of the long wavelengths involved, radio telescopes (Figure 5–7) must have a very large aperture and, even so, they cannot pinpoint the radiating source with the same precision of one that uses light waves. Besides revealing hitherto unseen features of the sky, radiotelescopes can see through dust clouds and even farther into space than can the two-hundred-inch reflector at Mt. Palomar.

THE SUN

The sun dominates the solar system in many ways. It is more than ten times the diameter of the largest planet; its volume is a thousand times greater than that of all the planets combined; all the planets and comets revolve around the sun, and they all shine by light reflected from it. Energy from the sun makes life possible on earth. All but four planets receive so little of this energy that nearly everything on them is frozen solid.

The sun is a great mass of hot gases with a surface temperature of only about 11,000°F, but an interior temperature which may be as high as 25,000,000°F. From time to time whirlpools of cooler gases appear on the surface of the sun. These may be so large that they can be seen with the naked eye by looking at the sun's reflection in a dish of water. They are called sunspots (Figure 5–8), and by following their progress across the surface of the sun we can observe that the sun rotates on its axis within a period of about 25 days (Table 5–1). There are regularly recurring times of maximum sunspot activity which have been linked with variations in the weather on earth.

Another type of disturbance on the surface of the sun is called solar promi-

Figure 5–7.   *The eighty-four-foot radio telescope of the U.S. Naval Research Laboratory. It is so mounted that it can track any celestial object from horizon to horizon. (Official U.S. Navy photograph.)*

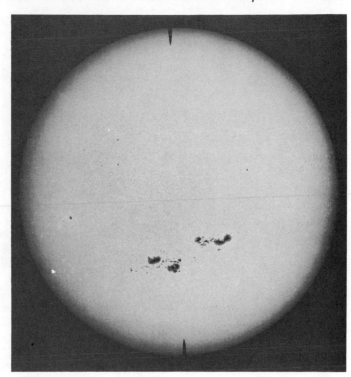

Figure 5–8. Photograph of the sun, showing several large sunspots. (Mt. Wilson and Mt. Palomar Observatories.)

Table 5-1. Data on the Solar System

NAME	MEAN DISTANCE FROM SUN IN MILLIONS OF MILES	EQUATORIAL DIAMETER IN MILES	MASS (EARTH = 1)	PERIOD OF REVOLUTION		PERIOD OF ROTATION	NUM-BER OF MOONS
Sun		864,000	332,000			24.7 days	
Moon		2,160	0.012			27.3 days	
Mercury	36	3,100	0.05	88	days	88 days	0
Venus	67	7,700	0.81	225	days	30(?) days	0
Earth	93	7,927	1.00	365.25	days	1 day	1
Mars	142	4,200	0.11	687	days	24 hr 37 min	2
Jupiter	483	88,700	318	11.9	years	9 hr 55 min	12
Saturn	886	74,100	95	29.5	years	10 hr 14 min	9
Uranus	1783	32,000	14.5	84	years	10 hr 40 min	5
Neptune	2794	31,000	17.2	165	years	15 hr 40 min	2
Pluto	3675	7,000(?)	>1.0	248	years	(?)	(?)

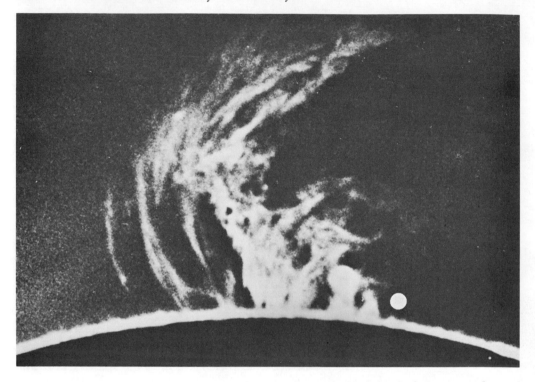

Figure 5–9.   *A large solar prominence 140,000 miles high. Photographed in light of calcium. (Mt. Wilson and Mt. Palomar Observatories.)*

nences. These can best be observed at the edge of the disc of the sun through an instrument called a spectrohelioscope. In one form of this instrument the sun's light is spread into a spectrum by a spectroscope, and a narrow band of that spectrum is viewed through a slit. In this way the light from one bright line of one element can be examined. The picture in Figure 5–9 shows solar prominences photographed by one of the lines from the calcium in the sun. These streamers of hot gases sweep millions of miles out from the sun's surface in a few minutes.

THE MOON

The moon's diameter, 2160 miles, is greater than one-fourth that of the earth

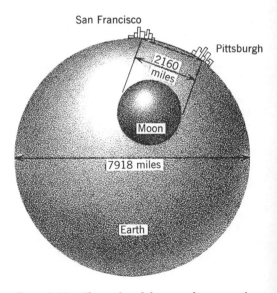

Figure 5–10.   *The earth and the moon drawn to scale.*

(Figure 5–10). No other planet has a satellite so near its own size. In revolving around the earth, the moon always keeps the same side toward us. There is every reason to expect the far side of the moon to look much like the near side, and in fact, the first crude pictures transmitted back from a space rocket tend to confirm this. In Figure 5 11 the moon's orbit around the earth is drawn to scale inside a circle representing the size of the sun. The sun rises and sets on the moon as it does on the earth. There can be no twilight because there is no atmosphere, and at any one spot the sun shines for nearly 2 weeks and then is gone for an equal time.

If the earth's orbit around the sun is

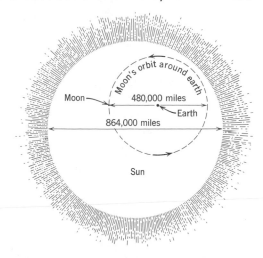

Figure 5–11. A scale drawing showing the moon's orbit around the earth compared with the diameter of the sun.

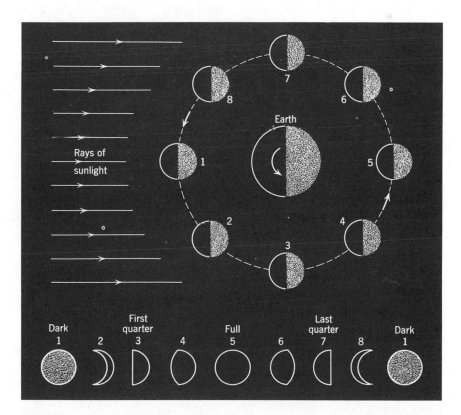

Figure 5–12. The phases of the moon. This shows the position of the moon in relation to the sun and the earth and its appearance as viewed from the earth at approximately 3½-day intervals.

represented by a circle 9 yards in diameter, with a golf ball for the sun at its center, the moon's orbit around the earth would be the size of a nickel. This nickel would tilt slightly as it goes around in the plane of the large circle, making an angle of 5°8′. As the moon travels between the earth and the sun we can see only a small part of the lighted side, and 2 weeks later it is on the side of the earth opposite the sun, so that we are looking at the whole lighted face.

On the date given in the calendar for a new moon, it is too close to the sun to be seen, but a day or so later it appears briefly in the western sky (Figure 5–12) as a thin crescent, which soon follows the sun below the horizon. The next day, the crescent is thicker, the moon is higher in the sky, and it sets later. At this stage, we frequently notice the rest of the circle

of the moon's face shining with a feeble gray light. The source of this light is sunlight which has been reflected first from the earth to the moon and then back again to us. It is understandable that this light is faint when we realize that the earth reflects about 40% and the moon only 7% of the incident light.

Two weeks after the time of the new moon, the moon is rising in the east as the sun sets in the west and we have a full moon shining all through the night. Since the moon travels around the earth in the same direction that the earth rotates on its axis, 24 hours later it will have traveled approximately 1/29 of the way around its monthly circle. The earth will have to keep turning about 45 minutes after the sun has set before we can again see the moon rise in the east. In Figure 5–12 the sun would be located off

Figure 5–13. A part of the surface of the moon, showing the many craters, some of them overlapping. (Mt. Wilson and Mt. Palomar Observatories.)

Figure 5–14.   Crater Lake, Oregon. (Air Force Photograph.)

to the left of the page. A week later, the moon will be high in the southern sky at dawn, appearing half full, and will set at noon. Each following day it will be closer to the sun, until, 29½ days after the previous new moon, it is again between the earth and the sun.

The surface features of the moon can be examined with a good pair of field glasses, and they have been studied, mapped, and named by amateur and professional astronomers ever since the days of Galileo (Figure 5–13). The most conspicuous features are many crater-like formations, which vary in diameter from a few hundred feet to 140 miles. The lack of any atmosphere on the moon has prevented erosion, and some of these walls stand straight up for thousands of feet. Their origin is a mystery, and the only clue we have is their correspondence to similar features on the earth. If they are extinct volcanoes they should resemble Crater Lake in Oregon (Figure 5–14), and if they were made by meteorites plunging into the surface of the moon they should resemble Meteor Crater in Arizona (Figure 5–15). In nearly every respect the craters on the moon fail to resemble volcanic craters, and they bear a striking similarity to Meteor Crater and to impact craters made experimentally by dropping objects onto a layer of dry powder in the laboratory.

SUMMARY

1. Astronomical observation has proceeded from the use of the unaided eye to the use of the telescope, and then the camera, the spectroscope, and other instruments. Each

Figure 5–15. Aerial photograph of Meteor Crater in Arizona. (Photograph by Clyde Fisher, American Museum of Natural History.)

new instrument has provided us with either more detail or more distant vision, or both.

2. The sun's volume and mass are greater than those of all the other members of the solar system combined. Its surface temperature is about 11,000°F, and its interior may be as hot as 25,000,000°F.

3. Sunspots and solar prominences may be observed on the surface of the sun.

4. The moon always keeps the same side toward the earth as it revolves around it.

5. The moon has no atmosphere.

6. At the time of the new and the old moon, the moon is nearly between the earth and the sun. At the time of the full moon the earth is between the moon and the sun.

7. The surface features of the moon can be studied in detail. The craters were probably made by meteors.

QUESTIONS AND EXERCISES

1. Explain how the Doppler effect can be applied to the problem of a star's motion relative to the earth.

2. What must a star's spectrum be like if it is used to tell us what elements are in the star?

3. Explain, on the basis of the structure of your eye, how you can suffer permanent damage to the retina by looking directly at the sun.

4. The symbol on the flag of Turkey shows a star inside the crescent of the moon. Does this represent an unusual situation or an impossible one?

5. Does the sun ever shine on the side of the moon which is facing away from the earth?

6. What would be the relative positions of the earth, moon, and sun, for the moon to appear as a crescent with the tips pointing down toward the horizon?

7. If the moon sets at midnight, what phase is it in?

8. Would we receive more or less than the normal amount of light energy from the sun during a period of maximum sunspot activity?

9. To get an idea of the vast empty spaces in the solar system, figure the distance from the sun to each of the planets on a scale model of 1 inch equals 1 million miles. This was the one used in the model mentioned on page 242.

10. What is the intensity of the sun's light falling on Mars compared to that on earth?

Chapter 3

The Earth

LIGHT traveling from the sun at 186,000 miles per second takes 8 minutes 20 seconds to reach the earth. The earth rotates around an axis, which passes between the north and south geographic poles. Anywhere in the middle latitudes of the northern hemisphere this rotation can be timed by observing the shadow cast by an upright pole. When the shadow points directly north it is local noon, and the time between successive noons is divided by us into 24 hours, each hour into 60 minutes, and each minute into 60 seconds. The second is the primary unit of time and is defined as the 1/86,400th part of a mean solar day. To get the length of time that it takes the earth to travel around the sun, we note the time that the earth is exactly between the sun and a certain star. When this event occurs again, a sidereal year has passed. A year is very close to 365¼ days.

THE SEASONS

From Figure 5–2 it can be seen that on March 21 the light from the sun reaches both the North and the South Poles and that the sun is directly overhead at the Equator. This is one of the equinoxes, when the night and day are of equal length all over the earth. A few days later, the sun shines a little beyond the North Pole, so that it does not set during a 24-hour day, and there is a region near the South Pole that receives no sunlight. On June 21 the whole area north of the Arctic Circle gets 24 hours of sunlight, and people on cruises to Spitzenbergen, Norway, stay up to see the "midnight sun" (Figure 5–3). The whole Antarctic region is now in darkness. For those of us in the northern hemisphere, the nights are short and the days are long; the farther north, the greater is the discrepancy. At the Equator, the nights and days are of equal length throughout the year.

Continuing on to September 23 we reach the other equinox and on December 21 the whole Arctic area is in darkness, the rest of the northern hemisphere has its longest nights and shortest days, and the region south of the Antarctic Circle receives sunlight for 24 hours. As we shall see later, our climate would be very different if the axis of rotation of the earth were perpendicular to the plane of the earth's orbit.

ECLIPSES

From Figure 5–16 it would seem that the moon would cast its shadow on the earth at every new moon, and that it would pass through the shadow of the earth at every full moon. However, the plane of the moon's orbit around the earth is tilted slightly with respect to the plane of the earth's orbit around the sun (page 252), and only twice a month does the moon pass through this plane. When it does this at the time of a new moon, the earth passes through the moon's shadow; and if it is at the time of a full moon, the moon passes through the earth's shadow. Most of the time the shadow of the new moon passes above the North Pole or the South Pole, and on the other side of its orbit the moon slips above or below the earth's shadow.

When the moon's shadow falls on the earth we have an eclipse of the sun (Figures 5–17, 5–18, and 5–19). It is only during the few brief minutes of total eclipse that many problems of interest to astronomers can be studied, and so we now have scientific expeditions going to Brazil, South Africa, or Siberia to observe and record an eclipse. Not too many centuries ago the population was thrown into a panic by the superstitious fear that a dragon was eating up the sun.

The shadow cast by the earth is much larger than the one from the moon, so total eclipses of the moon (Figure 5–17)

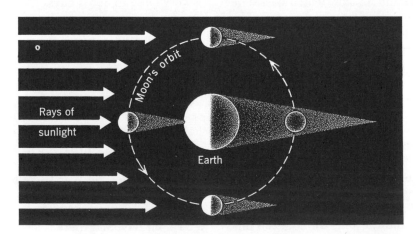

Figure 5–16. An eclipse of the sun and an eclipse of the moon.

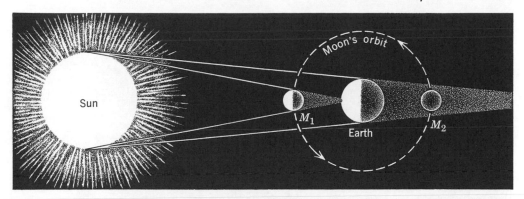

Figure 5–17.   An eclipse of the sun occurs with the moon at M_1. It lasts for a short time and is visible from a small part of the earth. An eclipse of the moon occurs with the moon at M_2. This is visible for a longer time and can be seeen from anywhere on the half of the earth turned toward the moon.

are much more frequent than those of the sun, they last much longer, and of course they can be seen from any part of the earth where the moon is above the horizon.

GRAVITATION

It was while studying the path of the moon around the earth that Sir Isaac Newton (1642–1727) developed his three

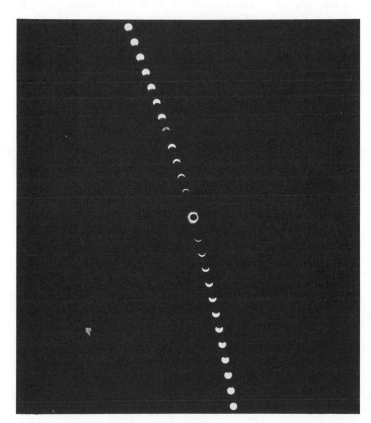

Figure 5–18.   A succession of exposures showing the sun before, during, and after an eclipse. (National Geographic Society.)

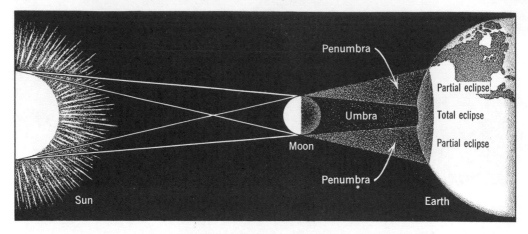

Figure 5–19. Eclipse of the sun.

laws of motion and his law of universal gravitation. The laws of motion were discussed on page 17.

When an apple is hanging on a tree, the earth is pulling down on the apple; applying the third law we know that the apple is pulling up on the earth and that the tree is holding them apart. When the stem finally weakens so that the apple is free to fall toward the earth, the earth is then free to rise toward the apple. Newton had the genius to realize that this might be a familiar example of something that had a far more general application. The moon does not travel in a straight line, it circles around the earth, therefore there must be some force acting on it. In Figure 5–20 the moon does not travel from M_1 to M_3, it constantly falls toward the earth as it travels the path M_1 to M_2. By Newton's time, Kepler had shown that all the planets travel around the sun, so that this idea of an invisible force acting between two bodies in space had an

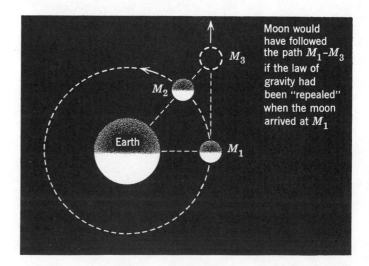

Moon would have followed the path M_1–M_3 if the law of gravity had been "repealed" when the moon arrived at M_1

Figure 5–20. In its orbit around the earth the moon is constantly dropping away from a straight-line path.

entirely general application. Newton stated this in the form: every particle in the universe attracts every other particle with a force that is proportional to the product of the masses of the two particles and inversely proportional to the square of the distance between them, or, put in symbols

$$f \propto \frac{m_1 \times m_2}{d^2}$$

An interesting deduction that can be made from this law is that just as the moon falls toward the earth, so should the earth fall toward the moon. With the earth and the apple the two masses are so different that the motion of the earth is too small to detect. The earth is 82 times heavier than the moon, and the result of their mutual attraction is that they both revolve around a common center. This point is located $\frac{1}{83}$ of the distance along the line joining the centers of the earth and moon, or $\frac{1}{83} \times 240,000$ miles $=$ 2891 miles from the center of the earth. This would be about 1000 miles below the surface of the earth. How could such a deduction be checked?

Imagine yourself in the rather improbable situation of riding on a merry-go-round which is located on a moving train. As you go around you would observe the scenery go by faster when you were facing the locomotive and slower when your back was to it. If our deduction is correct, the earth is not traveling evenly around the sun—as a train would travel on its track, for instance. It is traveling in circles around a point 2891 miles from its own center, and this point is the one that goes around the sun in a smooth curve. This effect would show up as a periodic change in the apparent motion of the sun. The sun does appear to gain and lose, over a period of 29½ days, just the amount that this calculation shows that it should. Here, again, is an example

where deduction from a theory led us to new information, and when this was verified our confidence in the theory was strengthened.

TIDES

To one living near the ocean, keeping track of the tides becomes as much second nature as noticing what time it is. From the scheduled time of departure of ocean liners to plans for swimming or digging clams, the tide must be taken into account. There are times when the difference between high and low tide is only a foot or so, and there are places where the difference is sometimes as much as 40 feet (Figures 5–21*a* and *b*).

On the average, the time between a high tide and the following low tide is 6¼ hours, so that there are usually two high tides and two low tides each day, with corresponding high (and low) tides about an hour later the next day. The difference between the water level at high tide and at low tide passes through a two-week periodic change. When it reaches a maximum (a very high tide followed by a very low tide) we call it a spring tide. A week later, the difference between the two reaches a minimum and we call it a neap tide. After another week, we again have a spring tide. These variations correlate perfectly with the phases of the moon, spring tides coming at the time of the new and full moon, and neap tides when the moon is in the first and third quarter.

Since successive high tides are about 12½ hours apart, there are always two areas of high tides on opposite sides of the earth, with two areas of low tides between them. Let us see how Newton's law of gravitation can be applied to this situation.

Figure 5–21a.   The Bay of Fundy at a high tide. (Geological Survey of Canada.)
Figure 5–21b.   The Bay of Fundy at a low tide, 7 hours later. These two pictures show an extreme example of the differences in tides. (Geological Survey of Canada.)

Imagine three masses, *A*, *B*, and *C*, suspended on elastic cords with their centers a distance *d* apart (Figure 5–22). Now add a large mass, *M*, to one side of this system (Figure 5–23). Masses *A*, *B*, and *C* will be displaced toward *M* by the force of attraction. *C* is closest to *M* and will be displaced more than *B*, and so *C* will be pulled away from *B* and the dis-

tance *BC* will be greater than *d*. Similarly, *B* will be pulled away from *A*, and the distance *BA* will be greater than *d*.

In Figure 5–24, the earth is represented by *B* and the water by *A* and *C*. With the force of attraction of the moon, *M*, acting, the water at *C* is pulled away from the center of the earth and the center of the earth is pulled away from the water

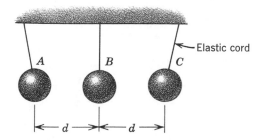

Figure 5-22. An explanation of the formation of tides. The mutual attraction of the masses A, B, and C keeps them at the distances shown.

moon spiral outward from the earth at the rate of 5 feet per century.

Turning to the earth, let us examine the consequences of the gravitational force between the tidal bulges and the moon. The net force would act as a drag on the earth's rotation so that our day would slowly lengthen. The effect is a very small one—the day is lengthening by 1 second in 100,000 years. However, the result will be that the earth will slow down in its rotation until one side always faces the moon. Another interesting outcome of the gradual lengthening of the day is the errors that were made in calculating when and where eclipses took place hundreds of years ago. Eclipses, particularly solar ones, made such a profound impression that we have many definite reports of them for over two thousand years. Over that length of time the accumulated error in our clock (running at the present rate) amounts to more than 3 hours, so we would calculate that these eclipses took place earlier in the day and at a different place from the ones reported in history. When the changing time scale is included in the calculations the estimated and observed times agree closely.

By referring to Table 5-1 you can calculate that the distance from the earth to the sun is 400 times the distance from the earth to the moon, and that the mass of the sun is about 28 million times that of the moon. The tide-raising force of the sun compared with that of the moon is

at *A*, so that two high tides on opposite sides of the earth are formed. Since the tides are a result of the difference in distance between the moon and the water on one hand, and the moon and the center of the earth on the other hand, the force is inversely proportional to the cube of the distance: $F \propto 1/d^3$.

The earth rotates under these bulges of water, so that at any one place there are usually two high tides and two low tides each day. The moon is moving slowly in the same direction that the earth is rotating, and so there is a period of about 6¼ hours between tides, and on successive days the corresponding tides come approximately 1 hour later. Actually, the rapid rotation of the earth carries the tides a little ahead of the moon (Figure 5-25), so that the force of attraction between the moon and this bulge tends to accelerate the moon in its path around the earth. This acceleration is making the

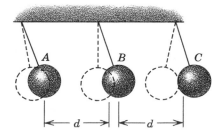

Figure 5-23. The mass M has been added to the system shown in Figure 5-22. C is displaced the most, A the least.

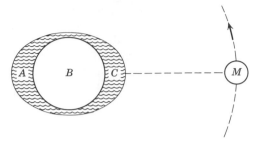

Figure 5–24.   As in Figure 5–23, the water at C is drawn away from the earth, B, and the earth is drawn away from the water, A. The water is drawn toward the moon at C and left behind at A.

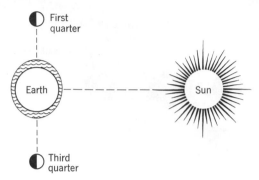

Figure 5–26.   The positions of the moon and the sun at the periods of neap tides.

28,000,000/(400)³ = 0.44. Therefore, tides raised by the sun are about ⁵⁄₁₁ the height of those raised by the moon. When the moon is in the first and third quarter (Figure 5–26), the moon and the sun are competing, so that there is a minimum difference in the tides. When the moon is full or new (Figure 5–27), they are both raising high tides at the same places on the earth and there is a maximum difference in tides. The extremely great differences in tides that are found at certain spots such as the Bay of Fundy and the Bay of Brittany are due principally to the funnel-like shape of the bays.

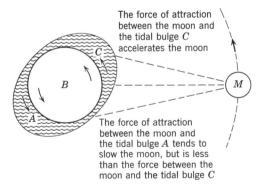

Figure 5–25.   The force of attraction between the moon and the tidal bulges is accelerating the moon as it revolves around the earth and is slowing the rotation of the earth.

In the previous discussion the earth was considered as being a rigid sphere. Of course, this is not literally true, and the earth is deformed by tide-raising forces. These earth tides amount to several inches, but they are difficult to observe because we have no fixed point to compare them with.

SUMMARY

1. Light travels at a speed of 186,000 miles per second.
2. A second is 1/86,400 of a mean solar day.
3. A year is close to 365¼ solar days.
4. The seasons result from the fact that the axis of rotation of the earth is tilted with respect to the plane of its orbit around the sun.
5. When the moon's shadow falls on the earth we have an eclipse of the sun.
6. When the earth's shadow falls on the moon we have an eclipse of the moon.
7. Newton's law of gravitation states that every particle in the universe attracts every other particle with a force that is proportional to the product of the masses of the two particles and inversely proportional to the square of the distance between them.
8. The tides are the result of the differential attraction of the moon for the water and

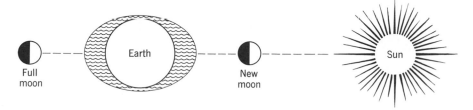

Figure 5–27.   Relative positions of the earth, moon, and sun at the periods of spring tides.

for the earth. The tide raising effect of the sun is ⁵⁄₁₁ of that of the moon.

9. Spring tides occur when the sun and the moon are raising tides at the same place. Neap tides occur when the two lines from the center of the earth to the sun and to the moon form a right angle.

QUESTIONS AND EXERCISES

1. During a total eclipse of the moon we can still see the moon. What is the path of the light that makes this possible?
2. If the distance between the earth and the moon were increased by 200 miles, would the moon have to travel faster or more slowly than it does now to keep in this new orbit?
3. What and where is the international date line, and why is it needed?
4. If you were watching an eclipse of the moon just beginning, would you see the earth's shadow start to cover the side of the moon on your right or on your left?

5. How frequently would you expect to find a 24-hour day with only three tides instead of four?
6. If we succeeded in harnessing the energy of the tide flowing in and out of a large bay, would it make any difference whatever to the period of rotation of the earth?
7. When an astronomer determines that the earth is exactly between the sun and a certain star which is crossing the meridian, what time is it at the observatory?
8. A 1-pound rock and a 10-pound rock are resting side by side on a window sill 16 feet above the ground. How do the forces between the earth and each of the rocks compare? How do the forces necessary to give each rock the same acceleration compare? If they were pushed from the window simultaneously, would they strike the ground at the same time?
9. Is the gravitational force acting between the sun and the moon greater or less than that between the earth and the moon?
10. If the earth always kept the same face to the moon, how would this affect the observation of eclipses?

Chapter 4

The Inner Planets

T HE PLANETS can be divided conveniently into two groups: the inner ones that are small, rotate slowly on their axes, and have densities between 4 and 5.5; and the outer ones that are large, rotate rapidly, and have densities ranging from 0.7 to 2.5.

MERCURY

Mercury is the smallest of the planets and the closest to the sun. It completes its trip around the sun in 88 days, always keeping the same side toward it. Assuming that all the planets rotated on their axes when the solar system was formed, it is to be expected that the powerful

tide-raising force of the sun would have had the greatest effect on its nearest neighbor, Mercury.

One-half of Mercury's surface is blistered with unceasing sunlight, so that the temperature is over 600°F, whereas the other side is forever dark and cold. Mercury has no atmosphere and no satellites.

VENUS

Venus appears brighter to the eye than any other planet or star. Its nearness to both the sun and the earth accounts in part for this, and another factor is the mantle of clouds that completely covers the planet. These clouds reflect 76% of

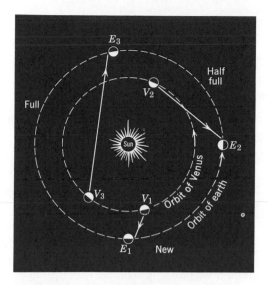

Figure 5–28. An explanation of how we see the phases of Venus.

the sunlight, in contrast to the 7% reflected from the surface of the moon.

This cover of clouds prevents us from seeing the surface of Venus, so that it is difficult to determine how fast it rotates on its axis. Spectroscopic analysis of the atmosphere of Venus shows only carbon dioxide. Water and oxygen, if present, are too scarce to show up. The clouds may well be fine dust particles.

Venus always rises and sets within 3¼ hours of the sun, and for the month before and after it passes between the earth and the sun it can be seen as a crescent (Figure 5–28). It has no satellites.

MARS

Mars is considerably smaller than the earth, has a length of day almost the same as ours, and takes nearly 2 years in its trip around the sun.

Its red color and its brightness make it a familiar object in the sky. Since its orbit lies outside that of the earth, we

never see it as a crescent. It has two small satellites. One of these, Phobos, is of interest because of the speed with which it travels around Mars. Its period of revolution is only 7 hours 39 minutes, so that an observer on Mars would see it rise in the west, go through all its phases and set in the east all in a little over 5 hours. The other satellite, Deimos, revolves nearly as fast as Mars rotates, so that it remains above the horizon for 2½ days and goes through all its phases 2½ times before setting.

Spectroscopic examination of the Martian atmosphere fails to reveal any oxygen or water vapor; if they are present it must be in extremely low concentrations. There are large white areas around the poles that change in size with the seasons as thin caps of polar ice would be expected to do (Figure 5–29). The spectroscope indicates that these almost certainly are ice or hoar frost. There is also a corresponding seasonal change in the appearance of the circumpolar regions suggesting a periodic growth and drying up of vegetation. Most of the surface of Mars is yellow-orange in color and shows no change.

The possibility of the existence of life on another planet has intrigued mankind for centuries. Until interplanetary travel solves the problem, the best we can do is

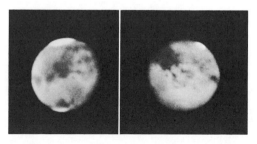

Figure 5–29. Two pictures of Mars showing the change in size of the polar cap. (Lick Observatory Photograph.)

to examine the conditions found on our neighbors in the solar system and compare them with the extreme conditions that living things are known to tolerate. There is nothing about Mars that would make some forms of life as we know it impossible; some of the algae found on earth could exist readily in the conditions of temperature, pressure, and atmospheric composition on the surface of Mars. However, the small amount of water present makes the existence of any higher forms of life extremely improbable.

Ever since Schiaparelli, in 1877, announced the discovery of long straight lines which he called channels, astronomers have studied the surface of Mars, looking for evidence of planned engineering. It is unfortunate that photography is not as useful as direct visual observation for studying fine details in surface features. During the long exposure necessary for a picture, the turbulence of our atmosphere blurs the details that can be seen for a few minutes at a time by the eye. The eye, however, is notoriously liable to subjective error, and no two observers agree on the pattern of channels, or canals, that the Martians are supposed to have built to carry water from the melting polar caps to their parched fields. The evidence for a vegetable-like form of life on Mars is almost conclusive, but beyond that we cannot go.

ASTEROIDS

The asteroids are an unusual group of more than a thousand tiny planetoids traveling in a more or less common orbit between Mars and Jupiter. The largest is 480 miles in diameter, and the smallest located so far is less than a mile across. The reasoning which led to their discovery is an example of the practical value of the scientist's confidence that there is a pattern in nature. When the pattern has been discovered, gaps and irregularities in it suggest something yet to be found.

In 1772 Bode published his "law," which was an approximate description of the distances from the sun to each of the known planets. He showed that the distance from the sun to each planet could be expressed as a multiple of the distance from the sun to the earth, by the following scheme. For the nearest planet, Mercury, the distance is $0.4 + 0 = 0.4$; for the next one, Venus, it is $0.4 + 0.3 = 0.7$; the earth is $0.4 + 2 \times 0.3 = 1.0$; Mars is $0.4 + 2 \times 0.6 = 1.6$; the next one should be $0.4 + 2 \times 1.2 = 2.8$. The number added to 0.4 is always twice the number added for the next-closer planet. Table 5–2 shows the scheme for the planets known by 1800.

With the rather close agreement between the predicted and found values for

Table 5–2

	ADD	APPROXI-MATE DISTANCE	TRUE DISTANCE
Mercury	0.4	0.0	0.4	0.39
Venus	0.4	0.3	0.7	0.72
Earth	0.4	0.6	1.0	1.0
Mars	0.4	1.2	1.6	1.52
(?)	0.4	2.4	2.8	2.8 (Asteroids)
Jupiter	0.4	4.8	5.2	5.2
Saturn	0.4	9.6	10.0	9.54
Uranus	0.4	19.2	19.6	19.2

the known planets, the lack of a planet at the distance 2.8 was not only puzzling, it was irritating. Appropriate portions of the sky were assigned for search to several astronomers. In 1801 the largest of the asteroids was discovered and named Ceres. Others were soon spotted, and modern photographic technique turns up more every year. Some of these are irregular chunks of rock, others seem to be made of ice. It seems probable that they are either a swarm of small fragments that failed to coalesce into a planet or the debris from one that broke up. Some of them travel in extremely eccentric orbits, and these may be what we recover on earth as meteorites.

SUMMARY

1. Mercury is the smallest and the closest to the sun. It always keeps the same face to the sun.
2. Venus is the brightest planet. It is covered with clouds and we do not know its rate of rotation.
3. There is good evidence that there is plant life on Mars.
4. We have not yet detected any oxygen or water vapor in the atmospheres of Venus and Mars.
5. The asteroids, or planetoids, are a swarm of small bodies traveling in orbits that lie in the general area between Mars and

Jupiter. Many hundreds of them have been observed.

QUESTIONS AND EXERCISES

1. How much more strongly does the tide-raising force of the sun act on Mercury than on the earth?
2. As we look at Mercury through a telescope, can we see it go through a series of phases like the moon?
3. If Venus rotated on its axis about as rapidly as the earth, what motion of its clouds would we observe?
4. If Venus always kept the same side toward the sun, what motion of its clouds would we observe?
5. Check the statement that Venus always rises and sets within 3¼ hours of the sun. Draw the two orbits to scale, and measure the greatest possible angle between the lines joining the earth to Venus and the earth to the sun.
6. How does the speed of Mars in its orbit compare with that of the earth? Figure these speeds in terms of miles per minute.
7. What would be the advantages of an astronomical observatory on the moon?
8. Use Bode's law to calculate the approximate distance to the next planet beyond Uranus.
9. Arrange the four inner planets in decreasing order according to size.
10. Phobos revolves around Mars in the same direction that Mars rotates on its axis (like the moon around the earth). How can it be that it rises in the west and sets in the east?

Chapter 5

The Outer Planets

T HE PECULIAR physical characteristics that set apart the outer planets were given on page 264. This interesting situation has not yet been explained, and any theory of the origin of the solar system will have to account for it before the theory can be generally accepted.

JUPITER

Jupiter is the planet that requires the most superlatives in its description. It is the largest of the planets; both its volume and its mass are greater than those of all the other planets combined. It rotates on its axis faster than any other

planet. With its circumference of 270,000 miles and its period of rotation of just less than 10 hours, a spot on its equator is traveling 27 times as fast as one on the earth's equator. This rapid rotation produces a bulge clearly visible in a telescope.

The density of Jupiter is about 1.3 so it can have no more than a tiny rocky core. The great bulk of the planet must consist mostly of hydrogen and helium. Jupiter is so far from the sun that these elements would be liquids, or possibly solids in the deep interior. Jupiter is the source of static-like radio signals.

Another "most" for Jupiter is its number of satellites. Twelve have been discovered so far; four of them can be seen

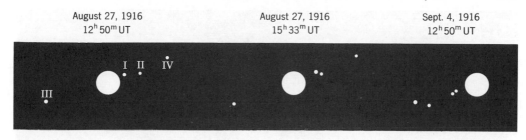

Figure 5–30.   Three photographs showing changes in position of the four brightest satellites of Jupiter. (Yerkes Observatory.)

with a pair of field glasses. They all rotate in the plane of the equator, forming a system which we see edge on, so that we can observe frequent eclipses (Figure 5–30). The four largest satellites were the first heavenly bodies discovered by the telescope. Galileo saw them in 1610.

The larger Jovian satellites have been of extraordinary value to science. They supplied important evidence supporting the Copernican theory of the structure of the solar system, they serve as celestial clocks for navigation, and they gave us the first direct measurement of the speed of light.

In the seventeenth century, navigators had a difficult time telling their longitude. They could set their chronometers by Greenwich time when they left London, and then, as they traveled across the Atlantic, they could observe the clock time when the sun was directly south of them. If this occurred at 1 P.M. they knew that they had traveled ¹⁄₂₄ of the way around the earth, or 15° west of Greenwich. The best clocks were none too good, and when they were subjected to the rolling and pitching of a small vessel they were decidedly erratic. After a voyage of several weeks they were practically worthless for purposes of navigation. The four moons of Jupiter, with their frequent passages behind and in front of

the planet, supplied a set of predictable events that could be used to set mariners' clocks during long voyages.

The astronomers of the Paris Observatory undertook the task of preparing a table showing the eclipses of Jupiter's moons for several years in advance. In 1676, when Roemer checked these calculations with the observed times, he found that they were wrong by as much as 20 minutes at certain times of the year. To a ship's captain this could mean the difference between being a full day's journey from the coast of Brazil or being piled up on the rocks.

Roemer very ingeniously saw that, if the calculations were based on observations made when the earth is at position E, Figure 5–31, and Jupiter at J, and if they were checked when the earth was at E' and Jupiter at J', then the light from Jupiter had to travel the additional distance EE'. If that took 20 minutes, the discrepancy was explained.

More precise measurement shows that the time for light to travel EE', the diameter of the earth's orbit, is 16⅔ minutes, and the distance is 186,000,000 miles. This shows that the speed of light is 186,000,000 miles per 1000 seconds = 186,000 miles per second. Because of its extremely high value, previous efforts to measure the speed of light had failed, and some scientists thought that its ve-

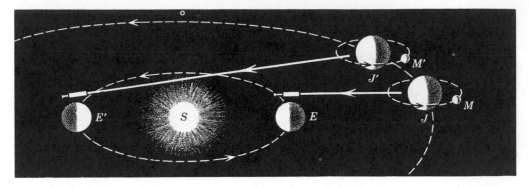

Figure 5–31.   *Roemer's experiment, which determined the speed of light.*

locity was infinite. The solving of a problem in navigation led to an important discovery in science.

SATURN

Saturn, the most distant of the naked-eye planets, is about as bright as Polaris. Its density is less than that of water, so it must consist almost entirely of hydrogen and helium. The breath-taking system of rings makes it one of the most spectacular objects to be seen through a telescope (Figure 5–32). These rings stand out from the planet like the brim of a golden derby hat, starting 7000 miles from its surface and extending 41,000 miles. As one looks at them through a telescope they appear solid. However, bright stars can be seen through them, and the innermost portions are rotating faster than the outer edge. The rings are only about 10 miles thick and are composed of chunks of ice.

As Saturn moves around the sun we see the rings edge on (in 1965) and at a considerable angle (in 1972). Beyond the rings Saturn has nine satellites. One of these, named Titan, is interesting as the only satellite in the solar system that is known to have an atmosphere. It is surrounded by methane.

Figure 5–32.   *Two pictures of Saturn taken at an interval of four years. (Lick Observatory Photograph.)*

URANUS AND NEPTUNE

Uranus is barely visible to the unaided eye, but the fact that it is a planet was not discovered until William Herschel examined it with a telescope in 1781. He thought he noticed a slight disc as he watched it, and after several months of observation it was apparent that Uranus moved among the stars, and its orbit was calculated.

The discovery of Uranus was a well-timed blow at the dangerous practice of arguing by analogy. The great philosopher Hegel had just observed that "just as there are seven openings in the head —the two eyes, two nostrils, two ears, and one mouth—so there must be seven members of the solar system—the sun, Mercury, Venus, Earth, Mars, Jupiter, and Saturn."

Uranus' axis of rotation lies in the plane of its orbit and the four satellites revolve in the plane of its equator. Eclipses, therefore, are possible at only two parts of its orbit.

Neptune is of interest principally because of the way in which it was discovered. When Uranus was first located, Neptune was about a quarter of a circle ahead of it. For the next forty-one years Neptune kept accelerating Uranus, until they passed in 1822, and then it retarded the motion of Uranus. Although the effect was slight, it was well beyond the limits of error of the observations. It was apparent that either Newton's law of gravitation would have to come to the rescue with an explanation of this erratic motion or the law would have to be revised. Newton's law suggested that a planet out beyond Uranus would account for the facts, but calculating its position was no small job when neither its distance from the sun nor its mass was known. Leverrier, in France, and Adams, in England, tackled the problem independently and solved it

nearly simultaneously in 1846. Galle, of the Berlin Observatory, received instructions from Leverrier, turned his telescope to the spot selected, and was the first person to observe Neptune. This was slightly more than two hundred years after the birth of Newton, and it was a remarkable tribute to him. It is also a rather striking example of the international quality of science.

Neptune is intensely cold, without prominent markings, and it has two satellites, one of which revolves in a retrograde direction.

PLUTO

Pluto was discovered in 1930 by the use of a new type of instrument called a blinking comparator. Two different pictures are projected in rapid alternation on a common screen. If they differ at only one point, this point will appear to jump back and forth while everything else remains stationary. This device is ideal for telling whether two documents are identical copies. If pictures of the same section of the heavens are taken on successive days, any planet in the field will appear to move against the background of the far more distant stars. Clyde Tombaugh, working at the Lowell Observatory, used this technique to search for a suspected trans-Neptunian planet and finally located it.

Instead of being much larger than the earth, as the other distant planets are, Pluto turned out to be smaller. Since it is so small and so distant, and shines by reflected light, it is difficult to see with any but the best telescopes. It travels around the sun in an extremely eccentric orbit that cuts inside the orbit of Neptune at its closest approach to the sun and which is inclined 17° from the plane of the earth's orbit. No satellite for Pluto has yet been found.

Are there any planets beyond Pluto? Of course, a positive yes or no answer cannot be given to that question. It is highly improbable that any planets the size of Jupiter could have escaped detection this long, but small ones like Pluto could go undiscovered for many years.

COMETS AND METEORS

Our detailed study of the members of the solar system concludes with a study of comets and meteors. The value of a calm, clearheaded study of natural phenomena is well illustrated by the change in attitude toward comets in the last four hundred years. Large ones are so infrequent and so spectacular when they do appear that they used to be viewed with superstitious fear. They were thought to be the cause of war, pestilence, and revolution. Weird rites were performed to neutralize their power. After Kepler worked out the pattern of behavior of the planets, the orbits of several comets were plotted, and it was found that they also travel in elliptical paths around the sun. These ellipses are usually much more elongated than the orbits of the planets,

so that a comet may pass between Mercury and the sun at one end of its path and swing beyond Pluto at the other end.

The comets, which have a period of a hundred years or so, develop a luminous tail as they approach the sun. This seems to be dust and gas which are blown out of the body of the comet by the pressure of light from the sun. As the comet swings around the sun, the tail flies out like a pennant on the lee side (Figure 5–33); this material is never regained by the comet. Comets that have small orbits and visit the sun frequently do not develop tails, or they may have lost all the fine-grained material that goes into making one.

The main body of a comet, although brilliant, is nearly transparent and must be made up of a swarm of small particles of assorted sizes—probably pebbles, dust, and even individual molecules. Mutual attraction keeps these together fairly well. Some comets keep their identity for centuries. For example, Halley's comet has been recorded every 75 years since 87 B.C. (Figure 5–34). Others have shown up regularly for a while and have then disappeared.

When the earth passes through the orbit of a "lost" comet, we usually ob-

Figure 5–33. *The appearance of the tail of a comet in the part of its orbit near the sun.*

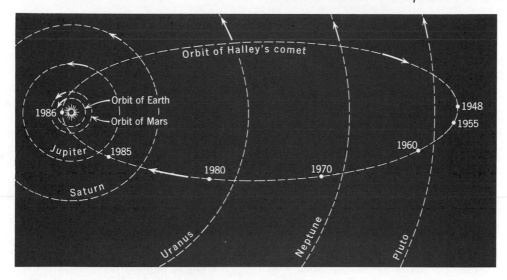

Figure 5–34.   The orbit of Halley's comet.

serve a large number of "shooting stars," or meteors. This indicates that the material of the comet has been spread all around its orbit (Figure 5–35), so that there is no longer a concentration which we can see and call a head. Occasionally, one of these particles is large enough to survive its trip through out atmosphere, and when it is found on the surface of the earth it is called a meteorite. Chemical analysis shows that meteorites are composed of familiar elements: most of them are stony, and some are made of an alloy of iron and nickel.

SUMMARY

1. Jupiter is the largest planet. It has twelve satellites. Our first determination of the speed of light resulted from a study of the moons of Jupiter.
2. Saturn is particularly notable for its system of rings.
3. Uranus was the first planet discovered with the telescope.
4. Neptune was discovered through its gravitational effect on Uranus.
5. Pluto is much smaller than the other outer planets. Of the known planets it is farthest from the sun.

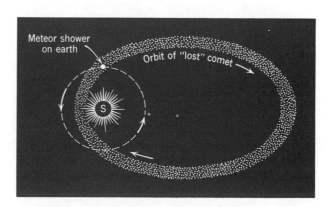

Figure 5–35.   An explanation of the appearance of meteor showers on earth at regular intervals.

6. Comets are members of the solar system, and have highly elliptical orbits. They consist of a swarm of small particles traveling as a group.
7. Meteorites are particles which survive the trip through the earth's atmosphere from outer space. They are always either stony or an iron-nickel alloy. The frictional resistance of the earth's atmosphere heats them glowing hot, so that we see them as "shooting stars," or meteors.

QUESTIONS AND EXERCISES

1. The longitude of New York City is approximately 75° west of Greenwich, England. On a clock set on Greenwich time, what time would the sun be directly south at New York?

2. Why are the eclipses of the four moons of Jupiter more useful for setting a mariner's clock than those of the moons of Mars?

3. How do we know that Saturn's rings are not solid, like a washer?

4. During an eclipse on Uranus what would be the angle between its axis of rotation and a line joining the planet to the sun?

5. If Jupiter is observed to be on the meridian at 1 A.M. on a certain day, at approximately what time will it be on the meridian at this same station one year later?

6. Make a rough calculation estimating how far Halley's Comet will travel in each of the decades 1960–1970, 1970–1980, and 1980–1990.

7. The Doppler effect can be used to measure the rate of rotation of Jupiter. What is the magnitude of the shift in wavelength observed?

Chapter 6

Beyond the Solar System

To ANYONE but a city-dweller, the Milky Way should be a familiar sight. On a moonless summer evening this gorgeous carpet of star dust stretches from near the North Star to the southern horizon. Hundreds of individual stars can be seen, and in places they are so tiny and so numerous that they look like a glowing stream. The Milky Way seems to be a luminous river flowing across the sky. Why is it that such a large proportion of all the stars are seen in such a small fraction of the whole dome of the sky?

OUR GALAXY

The answer to this question became clear after we found a way to measure the distances to the stars (see below). When the results were analyzed, it turned out that our solar system is a part of a vast collection of stars that are organized in a shape resembling a pocket watch. In this arrangement the sun is about where the pivot of the second hand would be (Figure 5–36). In most directions in which we look there are relatively few stars, but we see a concentrated belt of them as we look toward the center of the main mass of this system.

Each star shines by its own light, like our sun. Some stars are larger than the sun, some smaller; some are hotter, some cooler. Frequently we find two or more stars moving close together in a common system. In some stars the particles are as scattered as they are in the tail of a comet,

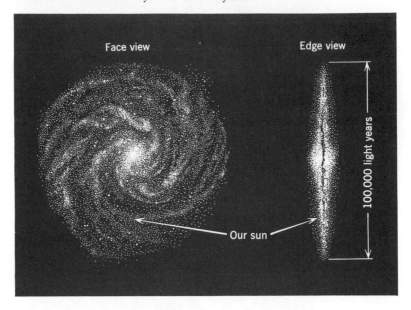

Figure 5–36.   The position of the sun in our galaxy.

and in others the matter is packed together so closely that a cubic inch of it would have a mass of many tons. In fact, our sun is a very ordinary, unspectacular member of the family of stars.

Another way in which the sun may be an ordinary star is in its possession of a family of planets, on some of which the conditions are right for the existence of life. There are so many stars that are similar to the sun in other respects that it is reasonable to suspect that our situation is not unique. The distances to even the nearest stars are so great that we cannot expect to see their planets with a telescope, but we might be able to communicate with distant intelligent beings by radio. The prospect and the problems involved are intriguing.

We must use a new measuring stick to talk about the distances to the stars. Light traveling from the sun reaches us in about 8 minutes 20 seconds. It travels on for 4 hours before reaching Pluto. It then travels for more than 4 years before it reaches the nearest star, called Alpha Centauri. The light year, the distance light travels in 1 year at its speed of 186,000 miles per second, is approximately 6×10^{12} miles. Even with such a large unit, we find that the system of stars of which our sun is a part is about 100,000 light years in diameter. This system is called a galaxy.

EXTRA-GALACTIC NEBULAE

Here it will be possible to give only the briefest of descriptions of the objects and events that are observed beyond our galaxy. When light from the sun leaves our galaxy it goes through vast regions of nearly empty space for about a million years in every direction, and then it reaches other galaxies much like our own. To a person observing with any but the best telescopes these galaxies look like hazy spots and were first called nebulae (clouds) because of their appearance. When better telescopes were built and photographic techniques improved, it was seen that the nebulae were systems of individual stars like our own galaxy. They are now called extra-galactic nebulae, or nebulae outside our galaxy (Figure 5–37).

The distant galaxies differ considerably in appearance and size, and there seem to be higher orders of organization among them. All the distant galaxies are receding from ours and the greater their distance, the faster is their motion relative to us. Some galaxies contain much dust and hydrogen between the stars, others are practically clear of this.

Radio telescopes give us information about some members of the solar system (the sun and Jupiter), the structure of our galaxy, and events in distant galaxies. In our own galaxy the large amount of hydrogen in the spiral arms becomes observable and the central region is the source of intense radiation in the radio spectrum.

Another fact that develops from a study of stars both in our galaxy and in other galaxies is that stars differ greatly in their ages. There are stars that are probably as old as the universe itself (about 10 billion years old), there are middle-aged stars, and there are many that cannot be more than a million years old. These latter ones were still part of a dark cloud of cosmic dust when early man first cast his glance upward to the heavens.

Figure 5–37. An extra-galactic nebula. The great spiral nebula in Andromeda. (Mt. Wilson and Mt. Palomar Observatories.)

DETERMINING DISTANCES
TO THE STARS

The emerging architecture of the universe reveals such a multitude of stars and such vast distances that we tend, on one hand, to feel insignificant by comparison and, on the other, to feel proud to realize that the human brain is able to penetrate such mysteries. Details of this picture could not be sharpened until the discovery of dependable methods for determining the distances to nearby stars, to the whole of our galaxy, and to other galaxies. The story of this development is a good case history of how science proceeds by steps, each one building on the previous one.

Somewhat over a century ago telescopes and their mountings were improved to the point where parallax could be observed and measured. Using the diameter of the earth's orbit as a base (Figure 5–38) and measuring the two adjacent angles, a triangle could be constructed and its altitude (the distance to the star) calculated. This method has been applied to thousands of stars and is reliable for those out to a distance of at least 100 light years.

The next step in measuring the distances to the stars makes use of the law describing the decrease of intensity of light with increasing distance (page 80).

For this purpose it would be convenient if all the stars have the same intrinsic brightness, but this is far from true. Sirius is several times brighter than Alpha Centauri although it is nearly twice as far away. A study of the stars whose distances can be measured by parallax shows that their intrinsic brightness can be related to details in their spectra. This is the step that takes us out beyond 100 light years. From the spectral type of a star, its intrinsic brightness is obtained and then from its observed brightness we can calculate how far away it must be (see page 84 Problem 11).

When this spectral luminosity relationship is used and the resulting distribution of stars is studied, their population seems to thin out in all directions with increasing distance. Thus it would seem that the sun is at the center of all the stars. If this were true it would be a most amazing coincidence. The unequal distribution of one type of star grouping, the globular clusters, did not seem consistent with a sun-centered galaxy. These globular clusters are ball-shaped aggregates of about 100,000 stars. There are over a hundred of them, nearly all located in one small part of the Milky Way. Is this unequal distribution real, or are we off at one side of the picture looking toward the main part of it? When faced with those alternatives, scientists have found

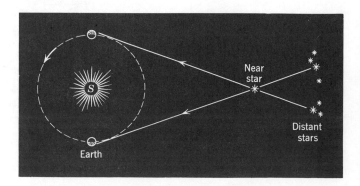

Figure 5–38. Stellar parallax. At six-month intervals we should see different distant stars behind a near star.

it safer to assume that nature is uniform until there is convincing proof to the contrary.

If the globular clusters are fairly evenly distributed around the center of the galaxy, then something is interfering with our luminosity measurements in that direction. A possible explanation for the abnormal dimming of distant star light could be the presence of dust in interstellar space. If we make the assumption that the stars are distributed evenly (but not necessarily so in all directions), the effect of dust can be allowed for, and we can proceed with the measurement of distance. This pragmatic solution may seem unjustified, but it is not really so arbitrary as it seems. The wise scientist is always aware of the assumptions on which he is working and is alert for evidence that they are not true. If such evidence turns up he then revises his assumptions and starts over again. After a working hypothesis has proved to be consistent with a large variety of accumulated facts then we begin to feel confident that it is valid.

This new study of our galaxy showed it to be the lens-shaped structure pictured in Figure 5–36. As we look up toward the Milky Way we are looking toward the main part of the system. It is about 100,000 light years across with our solar system some 25,000 light years from the edge, and the dust near the center section effectively obscures the parts beyond. Although light waves are stopped by the dust, radio waves are not. Recent studies with radio telescopes are revealing details of this region near the center and beyond.

A study of Cepheid variables provided a most useful tool for extending the study of stellar distances. These variable stars pulsate in brightness over a period of from one to forty-five days. They are found in our own galaxy and in all the galaxies that have been resolved into individual stars. When Cepheid variables were observed carefully it was discovered that their average brightness is proportional to their period. The ones that take the longest time to complete their cycle of variation are the brightest. The period is easy to measure so we have a simple measure of brightness. The only catch is that it was necessary to measure the distance to a few of these variables in order to determine their intrinsic brightness. Once this is done the luminosity-distance relationship (with allowance for dust) can be used. Unfortunately none of them is close enough to be measured by parallax. A study of the Andromeda nebula (Figure 5–37) from a number of different viewpoints fixed its distance at 2,500,000 light years. With all the Cepheid variables in this galaxy being at essentially the same distance from us, their observed brightness can be related to their absolute brightness, and our new measuring stick is calibrated. If we apply this to our own galaxy, we arrive at the same dimensions that had been calculated previously.

When the light from distant galaxies is analyzed by the spectroscope, it is observed that the lines of familiar elements are measurably displaced toward the longer wave length (red) end of the spectrum. This phenomenon of apparent shift in wave length is another example of the Doppler effect discussed on page 98. The only interpretation that we have for this is in terms of the relative motion of the source and the receiver. Since in every instance the shift is toward longer wave lengths this would mean that the distance between our galaxy and the others is increasing. The red shift is not the same for all galaxies. Without exception it is greater for the more distant ones. The greater the distance to the galaxy (as determined from Cepheid variables) the faster it is moving away from us. This, of course, gives us a new criterion of distance and it can be applied to the more distant ones that cannot be resolved into individual stars. The picture that is presented of an expanding universe is an intriguing one and we can only guess at its meaning.

The final step in our study involves estimating the distances to galaxies that are at the limit of observation of our present techniques. The total amount of light coming from the galaxies differs almost as much as that from individual stars, so we cannot assume that the dimmest ones are necessarily the most distant. In this situation we must settle for an average estimate. While we realize the limits of error introduced, we can say that the dimness of the far galaxies is a measure of their distance. By applying the criterion of red shift versus distance, we find confirmation for our working assumption and we apply it to measure the population density at the farthest reaches of our present means of observation.

This is a story which is typical of the way science proceeds into the unknown. One after the other, a series of well-established hypotheses are set up to serve as base camps for further exploration. Each one is tied in with the previous one as securely as possible so that we feel we know where we are as we proceed.

SUMMARY

1. Our sun is but one of many millions of stars organized in a watch-shaped system called a galaxy. Our galaxy is slowly rotating about a point near its center.
2. The stars shine by their own light, like our sun.
3. A light year is the distance that light will travel in 1 year.
4. Our galaxy is but one of many millions of galaxies. They differ considerably in the numbers of stars they contain—our own is one of the largest.
5. If the red shift is interpreted as a Doppler effect, the universe seems to be expanding.
6. Stars differ greatly in their ages.
7. The distances to the stars are measured in the following series of steps (this presentation is greatly simplified):
    a. Measurement of parallax. This is useful out to at least 100 light years.
    b. Spectral-luminosity relationship. This is useful out to about 20,000 light years and, combined with the following techniques, it is used to the limits of our means of observation.
    c. Period-luminosity relationship of Cepheid variables. This is useful for distances in our own galaxy and for distances to other galaxies up to 4 million light years.
    d. Red shift-distance relationship. This is useful to the limit of our means of observation.
    e. Whenever possible a cross-check of two independent techniques is obtained and the criterion of consistency is applied.

QUESTIONS AND EXERCISES

1. Would the constellations with which we are familiar appear about the same, or very different, if viewed from near Alpha Centauri?
2. If you look through even the biggest telescope at an extra-galactic nebula, it appears as a fuzzy spot, but a photograph will reveal its many individual stars. Explain.
3. Would we observe a shift toward the red in light from the stars in our own galaxy?
4. How does our galaxy compare in size with the others?
5. In the following list, which ones shine by reflected light, and which shine by their own light: comets, nebulae, planets, stars?
6. How fast would a distant galaxy be receding from the earth for a spectral line of $\lambda = 3900$ to be just barely visible?

Chapter 7

History of the Development

of Our Ideas about

the Universe

T ANY point in the history of civilization the current theory of the structure of the universe is an important part of the culture. Men have gone to prison and have died for daring to challenge the accepted point of view. Any broad philosophy will be influenced by the position that man thinks he has in the general structure of the world around him.

for their motion. The sun, moon, and planets moved independently across the dome. By 424 B.C. the Egyptians had determined that the year was 365 days long, and later the Babylonians figured that it was 365 days and 6 hours. The best modern measurement of the length of the year is 365 days, 5 hours, 48 minutes, and 46 seconds.

PRE-GREEK

In all the early civilizations the earth was pictured as a flat disc with a dome-shaped sky supported in various ways above it. The stars were lights or holes in the dome, whose revolution accounted

ARISTOTLE AND ERATOSTHENES

The prevailing opinion among the Greek philosophers was that the earth was flat and that the heavenly bodies circled around it. Aristotle (384–322 B.C.) taught that the earth and all the heavenly bodies were spheres and that the earth was the center of the whole system, with the sun, moon, planets, and stars moving around it in circular paths. He reached his conclusion by a method that science has since shown to be untrustworthy. He assumed that circular motion is the most perfect form of motion and that the heavenly bodies were obviously perfect objects, and from that assumption he concluded that they must travel in circular paths.

Somewhat later Aristarchus (flourished about 280–264 B.C.) said that the earth, moon, and planets all revolved around the sun and that the stars were located at a great distance from the solar system. About 250 B.C. Eratosthenes used this theory to calculate the circumference of the earth (Figure 5–39). He knew that at Syene (Aswan), in southern Egypt, the sun was directly overhead at noon on June 21. Alexandria is almost directly north of Syene, and at noon on June 21 the edge of a shadow at Alexandria makes an angle of 7½° with the perpendicular.

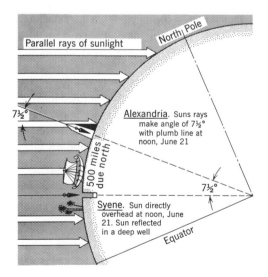

Figure 5–39. Eratosthenes' experiment in which he measured the circumference of the earth.

Assuming that the rays of light from the sun are parallel, a plumb line at Syene would be at an angle of 7½° with one at Alexandria. Since both lines point to the center of the earth, the distance between Syene and Alexandria must be 7.5/360, or ¹⁄₄₈ of the circumference of the earth. This distance was measured and found to be 500 miles (in modern units), which gives 24,000 miles for the circumference of the earth. This is within 4% of the value accepted now. (If one assumes that the earth is flat, this experiment can be interpreted to give the distance to the sun. This comes out to be about 3800 miles.)

PTOLEMY

Claudius Ptolemy, a Greek astronomer working in Alexandria during A.D. 200, elaborated Aristotle's picture of the universe into a scheme which, with slight modifications, was used for 1500 years. Aristotle's assumption that all celestial motion must be circular was the untouchable, unquestionable center, the "sacred cow," of the Ptolemaic system. The motions of the sun, moon, and stars were easy to explain. They all traveled circular paths, with diameters and speeds calculated to agree with experience. The motions of the planets called for a more complicated explanation. They were assumed to travel in circular paths around a point which, in its turn, followed a circular path around the earth (Figure 5–40).

Even though every motion had to be circular, by varying the size of the circle and the speed of revolution, a very complicated apparent motion could be accounted for, and the Ptolemaic system was extremely successful in predicting the behavior of the planets. It was useful for

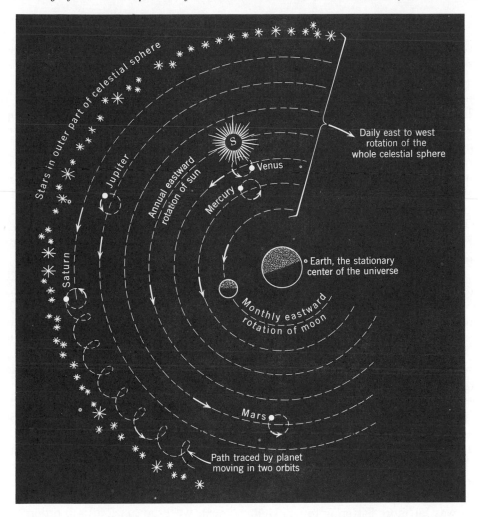

Figure 5–40. Ptolemy's picture of the structure and relative motions of the members of the universe.

navigation and in making calendars, and it had the psychological advantage of putting mankind at the very center of the universe. The church officially approved, and none questioned the system for many centuries.

In the fifteenth century, it was still not decided whether the earth was flat or spherical. Columbus thought it spherical, and used for the circumference the value of about 18,000 miles which had been calculated several centuries before from an experiment like the one of Eratosthenes. Knowing the distance from Spain to India going eastward by way of Arabia, he figured that it would be as close and much more convenient to sail westward across the Atlantic. He did this in 1492, and when he discovered land he thought it was India. This is where we get the names "the West Indies" for the islands and "Indians" for the natives.

COPERNICUS

The original Ptolemaic picture of the universe was not completely perfect; to bring it into line with observation, adjustments were made, cycles were put on cycles, and by 1500 a bewilderingly complex structure had resulted. Nikolaus Copernicus (1473–1543), a Polish astronomer, was one of those rare intellectual giants who are able to break the bonds of their times and question the basic assumptions, instead of patching up existing theories. He came to the conclusion that the behavior of the planets could be more simply explained if he assumed that the sun was the center of the rotating system and that the planets, including the earth, circled around it, with the moon revolving around the earth. The stars were pictured as being fixed and very remote in space.

By the use of the model of the solar system that Copernicus developed it was possible to predict the future positions of the heavenly bodies with about the same accuracy that had been achieved with Ptolemy's theory. In other words it was hard to decide between them on the experimental evidence available at the time. The idea of an earth-centered universe was far more flattering to mankind than one in which the earth was just one of several satellites revolving around the sun. Copernicus anticipated the antagonism that would be aroused by his theory, and he delayed publication of his book, *De Revolutionibus Orbium Caelestium*, until he was on his deathbed.

There was one critical experiment which would have settled the question of whether the sun or the earth is the center of revolution of the solar system. If you hold a pencil at arm's length and look at the wall beyond it, closing first your right eye and then your left, you will see a dif-ferent part of the wall beyond the tip of the pencil each time. Similarly, if the earth revolves around the sun and we observe the distant stars behind a near star, they should appear to shift back and forth every 6 months (Figure 5–38). This effect is known as parallax, and its importance for settling this question was realized by Aristarchus. He explained the failure to observe parallax by assuming that even the nearest star was so far away, compared to the diameter of the earth's orbit, that the effect was too small to observe. It was not until the development of a fairly good telescope that this crucial test could be applied (1838).

Copernicus had also pointed out that his theory required that Venus should go through a series of phases—new, half, and full—like the moon. In his picture of the solar system Venus shone by light reflected from the sun and revolved in an orbit smaller than the earth's, so when Venus is between the sun and the earth we should see only a part of its lighted surface. When the sun is nearly between us and Venus we should see the lighted side in full. According to Ptolemy, on the other hand, the sun, moon, and all the planets revolved around the earth. The moon was the closest, Mercury and Venus next, with the sun fourth in order. If this were true, we should never see Venus as a disc. It would vary between a crescent and a half-full phase, because it never gets very far away from the sun in direction, and it lies between the sun and the earth (Figure 5–41). This test, too, had to wait for the telescope.

BRAHE AND KEPLER

Copernicus was followed by two men who, together, combined the qualifications of the ideal scientist. Tycho Brahe

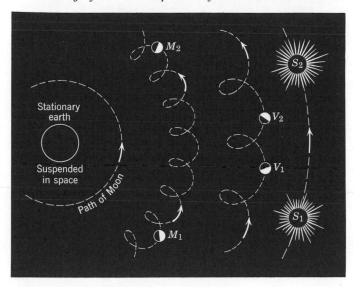

Figure 5–41. According to Ptolemy we should never see as much as half the lighted side of either Mercury or Venus.

(1546–1601) was a painstaking investigator who made many thousands of observations. His patience and accuracy were outstanding, but he did not attempt any generalization from his data. It was indeed fortunate that he had Johannes Kepler (1571–1630) for his assistant. Kepler was an excellent mathematician and he had a consuming passion for demonstrating that the solar system was organized according to a logical, symmetrical pattern. He set up a model of the solar system, from this calculated where the planets should be in relation to each other, and then compared these results with the data accumulated by Brahe. One after another of these models was discarded because it did not agree with the facts. Kepler was under the influence of the Aristotelian ideas, which were still dominating European thought, and so it is natural that he chose circular orbits for the planets in his model. After years of work in which his models were always faulty, he turned reluctantly to the consideration of elliptical orbits. These fit the data much better, and he was soon able to correlate Brahe's findings with three simple yet comprehensive general statements. Kepler's three laws which describe the motions of the planets are:

1. Each planet moves in an elliptical orbit about the sun, with the sun at one focus of the ellipse (1609).
2. As each planet moves around the sun, an imaginary line joining it and the sun will sweep out equal areas in equal intervals of time (1609).
3. The squares of the periods of revolution of any two planets are proportional to the cubes of their mean distances from the sun (1619).

To get an idea of what an ellipse looks like, knot a string so that the doubled length is 6 inches. On a piece of typewriter paper (8½ × 11 inches) place two thumbtacks 5 inches apart, with the loop around them. Place a pencil in the loop and draw a figure around the tacks (Figure 5–42). This is an ellipse. The sum of the distances from any point on the ellipse to each of the tacks is 7 inches (12 − 5).

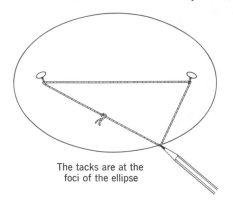

The tacks are at the
foci of the ellipse

Figure 5–42.   Drawing an ellipse.

Move the tacks so that they are 3 inches apart, knot the string so that its doubled length is 5 inches, and again draw an ellipse. As before, the sum of the distances from any point on the figure to the two tacks is 7 inches (10 − 3) but this one is more nearly circular. Each tack is at one focus of the ellipse. The second ellipse is said to be less eccentric than the first. The orbit of the earth is only very slightly eccentric; that of Pluto is much more so;

and the orbits of comets are highly eccentric with the sun at one focus.

Kepler's second law is illustrated in Figure 5–43. The eccentricity of this ellipse is much exaggerated to make the point clear. When the earth is closest to the sun, it travels more rapidly than when it is farther away. Referring to Figure 5–34, you can see that Halley's comet takes only 2 years to travel the same distance near the sun that it covers in 30 years at the far end of its orbit.

The third law states in precise terms the general fact that, the farther a planet is from the sun, the more slowly it moves. In a way, this is a repetition of the second law.

GALILEO AND NEWTON

While Kepler was working out the architecture of our solar system, the great Italian scientist Galileo (1564–1642) was discovering the experimental evidence that would help confirm it. In 1608, he

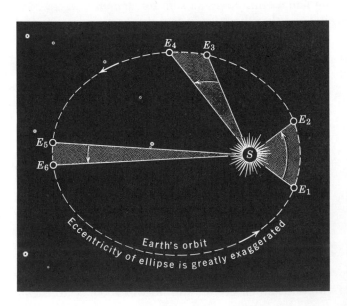

Figure 5–43.   An illustration of Kepler's second law. The earth takes the same time to travel from E_1 to E_2 that it does to travel from E_3 to E_4 and from E_5 to E_6.   The dotted areas are the same.

heard of a spyglass, invented by a Dutch optician, which made it possible to magnify objects at a distance. From his knowledge of optics, he figured out what sort of a lens system was necessary to do this, and he built one. His first telescope magnified 3 diameters, and later he made one that magnified 30 diameters. He examined the skies with this instrument and discovered:

1. Sunspots, and surface features of the moon. These showed that heavenly bodies are not so absolutely perfect as Aristotle had claimed.

2. The moons of Jupiter. This system of moons going around another planet exploded the idea of the earth as the center about which everything revolved.

3. The phases of Venus and Mercury. This showed that the basic idea of Copernicus was correct.

Galileo encountered powerful resistance to his new notions. People denied his facts by saying that his telescope was enchanted. He had an aggressive personality and pushed his ideas whenever possible. He came into conflict with the church, was put into "protective custody," and was forced to recant his heretical views, but it was too late. The work of Galileo and Kepler swept away the old theories, and the sun-centered picture of the solar system gained acceptance. Newton put the capstone on this edifice with his law of gravitation (page 259). This showed the reason for the motion of the planets which Kepler had deduced by trial and error.

SUMMARY

1. In early days, the earth was pictured as flat, with the sky as a dome above it.

2. Some of the Greeks thought that the rest of the solar system revolved about the earth, and some thought that the sun was the center of the solar system.

3. Using the earth as the center of the universe, Ptolemy invented a system of cycles and epicycles for the paths of the heavenly bodies. This system was tolerably good from a practical point of view.

4. Copernicus invented a system much simpler than Ptolemy's, which was equal to it in predictability. He placed the sun at the center of the universe and had the planets follow circular paths around it.

5. Using Brahe's observations, Kepler was able to work out his laws describing the motions of the planets. They are: (a) Each planet moves in an elliptical orbit about the sun, with the sun at one focus of the ellipse; (b) as each planet moves about the sun, an imaginary line joining it and the sun will sweep out equal areas in equal intervals of time; and (c) the squares of the periods of revolution of any two planets are proportional to the cubes of their mean distances from the sun.

6. Galileo's invention of the telescope provided much evidence in support of the theories of Kepler.

QUESTIONS AND EXERCISES

1. What is the latitude of Syene, Egypt?

2. What was the principal advantage of Copernicus' theory of the structure of the solar system over that of Ptolemy?

3. At what time of the year is the earth traveling fastest around the sun?

4. With the planets and comets traveling in ellipses, what is the changing force that is responsible for their changing speed?

5. What crucial test that would help decide between the ideas of an earth- and a sun-centered solar system was not carried out by Galileo?

6. When Eratosthenes measured the angles of elevation of the sun at two different places: (a) Did he have to do it on a certain day of

the year? (b) Did he have to do it at a certain time of day?

7. What is there about the apparent motion of the planets that is different from that of the stars?

8. To what extent can we say that an inaccurate scientific measurement led to the discovery of America?

9. Compare the length of time in which it was generally assumed that the earth was the center of the universe with that in which it has been generally accepted that the earth revolves around the sun.

10. What part of Copernicus' theory of the structure of the solar system was faulty and later corrected?

Chapter 8

The New Era in Astronomy

THE COMING of travel by rocket ships in interplanetary space has opened up a new era in astronomy. More specific questions about the composition of the solar system, its age and history, the variety of living things to be found under extreme conditions, etc., can now be asked. The great popular interest in the subject of space travel (spurred on by the substantial fraction of our national budget and the scientific manpower being devoted to space travel) has introduced new words into the general vocabulary—"weightlessness" and "escape velocity," for instance.

Let us explore some of the background of this subject and see some of the vistas it opens up.

ACCELERATION DURING FREE FALL

In this connection it will be well for you to review the sections on velocity and acceleration and Newton's laws of motion. Table 5–3 gives the data for a typical experiment involving a uniform force acting on a body under conditions where friction is negligible. The figures given above the double line are the observed data. At the end of 1 second the object has traveled 16 feet, at the end of 2 seconds a total of 64 feet, etc., and after 6 seconds it was 576 feet from its starting point.

The values in the rest of the table were calculated from the data. During the first second the object traveled 16 feet, during

Table 5-3

	0	1	2	3	4	5	6	7
At end of time t seconds	0	1	2	3	4	5	6	7
Total distance traveled (in feet)	0	16	64	144	256	400	576	
Distance traveled during a 1-second interval	16	48	80		144			
Average velocity in ft per sec during this interval	16	48	80		144			
Velocity in ft per sec after t seconds	0	32	64	96			192	
Acceleration in ft per sec² during each 1-second interval	32	32	32			32		

the next second it traveled 48 feet, etc. Some spaces are left empty here and below for the student to fill in. Since the time intervals are 1 second, the average velocity for the first second is 16 feet per 1 second = 16 feet per second, for the second interval it is 48 feet per 1 second = 48 feet per second, etc.

How can one calculate the instantaneous velocity at the end of the first, or any other time interval? At this point in the calculation it is only possible to make an intelligent guess, follow it through consistently, and see how it works out. As a preliminary guess we will assume that the average velocity, V_{ave}, is half way between the initial, V_i and final, V_f, velocities.

$$V_{ave} = \frac{V_i + V_f}{2}$$

This gives us the figures in the fifth horizontal row. We can now calculate the change in velocity for each successive second and this will be numerically equal to the acceleration in feet per second². The

numbers in the bottom row indicate that a uniformly acting force gives a uniform acceleration. The internal consistency of the results tends to justify the assumption made, but it can be checked further by using the results to calculate where the object should be at the end of 7 seconds and then testing it experimentally.

Assume a uniform acceleration $a = 32$ feet per second²; the velocity at the end of the first second is $V_t = at$, or more generally, $V_t = V_o + at$. The distance traveled during any given interval of time is the average velocity multiplied by the time, or

$$S = \frac{V_o + V_t}{2} t$$

Substituting $V_o + at$ for V_t we get

$$S = \frac{V_o + V_o + at}{2} t$$

or $\quad S = V_o t + \frac{1}{2} at^2$

If the object starts from rest $V_o = 0$ and at the end of 7 seconds it should be

$$S = \frac{1}{2} \times 32 \frac{\text{feet}}{\text{second}^2}$$

$$\times 49 \text{ seconds}^2 = 784 \text{ feet}$$

from the starting point. When the experiment is carried out it is found that the object does, in fact, travel 784 feet in 7 seconds. The prediction was based on the assumption that a uniform force produces a uniform acceleration. The experiment supports the assumption and other lines of evidence confirm that this is the case.

The particular experiment described above was chosen because it describes the behavior of a body in free fall in the gravitational field at the surface of the earth. Any object near the surface of the earth is subject to the force of gravitational attraction that is tending to accelerate its motion toward the center of the earth at a rate of 32 feet per second². Since this force varies inversely with the square of the distance, the acceleration due to gravity is only 16 feet per second² at a height of 1640 miles above the surface, and at a height of 4000 miles its value drops to 8 feet per second².

SPEED IN A STABLE ORBIT

Consider the problem of how fast a satellite must be moving in order to remain in stable orbit around the earth. Such orbits are actually ellipses, but for simplicity of calculation we will assume that they are circles. The inertia of the satellite gives it a forward motion tangent to the surface of the earth; the force of gravity, acting toward the center of the earth, gives it an acceleration in that direction of 32 feet per second². It will fall away from the straight line path by 16 feet in the first second, 64 feet at the end of 2 seconds, etc. (refer to the second horizontal row of figures in Table 5–3). The object must be moving so fast that

its straight-line path is 16 feet above the surface at the end of 1 second. A satellite is always put in orbit 100 miles or more above the earth's surface to avoid the frictional drag and heating of the atmosphere.

Figure 5–44 shows part of a circular orbit EHE' located 4000 miles from the earth's center, C. The satellite is in stable orbit, so it will have sufficient forward speed to carry it from E to H while it drops toward the center of the earth by the distance FH. The line CHF is the diagonal of the square $CEFE'$. We need to calculate how long the object takes to fall the distance FH and that will be the time that it takes to travel the path EH.

$$EF = CE = CH = 4000 \text{ miles}$$
$$(CF)^2 = (CE)^2 + (EF)^2$$
$$(CF)^2 = 4000^2 + 4000^2$$
$$(CF)^2 = 32 \times 10^6 \text{ miles}^2$$
$$CF = 5657 \text{ miles}$$

$$FH = CF - CH$$
$$FH = 5657 - 4000 \text{ miles}$$
$$FH = 1657 \text{ miles}$$
$$EH = \tfrac{1}{8} \text{ circumference of}$$
$$\text{circle with a radius of 4000}$$
$$\text{miles}$$

$$EH = \frac{4000 \times 2}{8}$$

$$EH = 3142 \text{ miles}$$

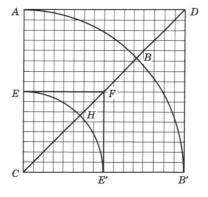

Figure 5–44.

Rearrange the equation $S = \frac{1}{2} at^2$ to

$$t^2 = \frac{2S}{a};$$

when $S = 1657$ miles and $a = 32$ feet per second^2

$$t^2 = 2 \times 1657 \text{ miles} \times$$

$$5280 \frac{\text{feet}}{\text{mile}} \times \frac{1 \text{ second}^2}{32 \text{ feet}}$$

$$t^2 = 54{,}680 \text{ second}^2$$
$$t = 740 \text{ seconds}$$

The speed of the satellite is then

$$v = \frac{3142 \text{ miles}}{740 \text{ seconds}}$$

$$v = 4.25 \text{ miles/seconds} =$$

$$15{,}300 \text{ miles/hours}$$

In Figure 5–44 the orbit ABB' is drawn for a distance of 8000 miles from the center of the earth. Verify that the speed in this orbit is 3 miles per second.

WEIGHT AND MASS

When a rocket is in stable orbit around the earth, everything in the rocket is following this curved path. The inertial tendency to fly off in a straight line is precisely balanced by the gravitational pull toward the earth. Imagine yourself in such a rocket. You have a glass of water in your hand, you turn the glass upside down (that is, with the open top pointing toward the earth) and the water does not run out. You lift up the over-turned glass and the water remains as a blob in mid air. You let go of the glass and it, too, remains suspended in air. Now, if you should strike quickly at the glass with your knuckles you would feel the expected pain. You would begin to sense the difference between weight and mass.

In our everyday life we have little occasion to be aware of the difference between weight and mass. Mass is the amount of matter in a body, that is, the total of electrons, protons, and neutrons. This does not change as the body moves (except at speeds close to the speed of light) so that when we measure the inertia of the body we always come up with the same answer. The weight of a body is the measure of the gravitational attraction between that body and the earth. We can also talk about the weight of a brick on the moon, or Mars, etc. The weight, as measured by a spring balance, will be different at the equator and at the south pole. The weight of a brick on the moon would be about one-sixth of its weight on the earth.

In a rocket in stable orbit the tendency to fall toward the earth and the tendency to move away from it in a straight line are exactly balanced so that everything aboard has no weight although it has all of its original mass. The psychological and physiological implications of this situation are interesting to think about.

ROCKET PROPULSION

The only way we can travel to other members of the solar system and obtain first hand information about them is to travel by rockets. Airplane wings need air to support them, gasoline engines and jets use air as an essential part of their fuel. Rockets do not glide and they carry all their fuel with them. Many bizarre combinations of fuel are used but they all produce the same result: a vigorous chemical reaction produces a tremendously hot stream of gases that is directed out a nozzle. The reaction to this (Newton's third law) sends the rocket in the opposite direction (Figure 5–45). Ion propulsion (page 161) works the same way. No atmosphere is needed for this action. Rocket ships that are speeding to the

Figure 5–45.   The Air Force ATLAS thunders aloft on its first successful fully powered flight. Propelled by twin booster rockets and a main sustainer engine, the intercontinental ballistic missile was reportedly fired a distance of about 2500 miles to test engine components. (Air Force photo.)

moon or from it to another planet can be steered, made to revolve as they travel, or slowed down by rockets fired in the appropriate direction.

It is a mistake to speak of a space ship "escaping" from the gravitational field of the earth. First of all the attraction is a mutual one, and second, it extends indefinitely. How fast must a rocket ship go in order to travel from the earth to the moon? Any speed that it maintains throughout the journey would do, but this would require a tremendous fuel consumption. A more practical solution is to accelerate as quickly as possible to a high speed, cut off the power and coast the rest of the way.

Galileo, in his experiments with motion, observed that a ball rolling down one arm of a V-shaped trough tended to roll up the other side to the same height from which it started. The greater the height that it fell through, the greater was its

speed at the bottom, and this speed was just sufficient to carry it back to the same height on the other side.

The speed that a moon-bound rocket ship must have at "burn-out" is the same speed that it would achieve in free fall to the earth's surface from the distance of the moon. This necessary initial velocity is sometimes called the escape velocity. It is different for each member of the solar system because of their different masses and diameters. For the earth it is 25,000 miles per hour $\simeq$ 7 miles per second. If a rocket ship is accelerated to this speed the power can be turned off. Although the forward velocity will then decrease steadily, the ship will still be drifting away from the earth at the point where it begins to be accelerated toward the moon (Figure 5–46). It is estimated that the trip under these conditions will take about 4 days. The effort of starting the return journey will be much easier.

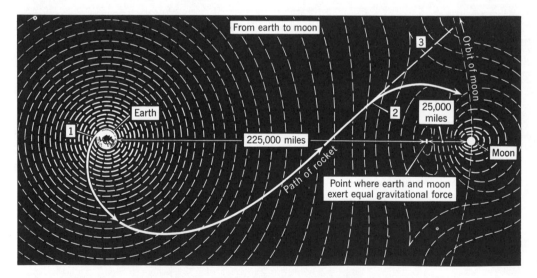

Figure 5–46. "Man to the Moon—the Paths and a Peril on the Way." Diagram above shows gravitational pulls of earth and moon. To reach moon a vehicle must be aimed precisely and accelerated (1) to 25,000 miles per hour, the velocity needed to escape earth's gravity. The vehicle, past the resistance of earth's atmosphere, travels in free flight until its course is altered by moon's gravity (2). Rocket guidance may be added for more accuracy. Without moon, rocket would travel course indicated by dotted line (3). (Redrawn from The New York Times, May 28, 1961).

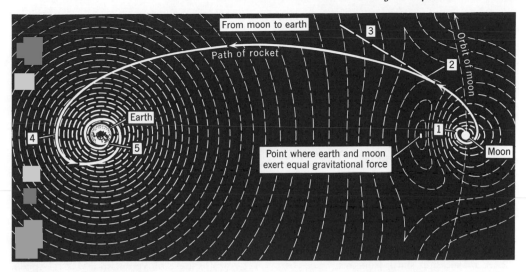

Figure 5–47. *Moon's gravity pull is about one-sixth that of earth. For return trip to earth, vehicle must be boosted to an escape velocity (1)—4100 miles per hour compared with 25,000 for earth. Vehicle then comes into pull of earth (2). Dotted line (3) would be path without earth's gravitational pull. On nearing earth, rockets would slow vehicle into a close circular orbit (4). Additional rockets would then dampen speed further (5) so vehicle would fall to earth. (Redrawn from* The New York Times, May 28, 1961.)

With the mass of the moon about 1% of the mass of the earth (Table 5–1) the escape velocity from the moon is only 4100 miles per hour (Figure 5–47). It is probable that any interplanetary exploring expedition will be "staged" on the moon because of its more favorable escape velocity.

We will be able to study many interesting problems from a base set up on the moon. The significance of many of the markings on the surface of the moon can only be studied in this way. A study of its rocks should provide information helpful in solving the question of the origin of the solar system. The lack of atmosphere on the moon will be a great boon to the astronomer. One of the most exasperating limitations on earth-bound telescopes is the atmosphere through which the light must travel to reach them. The turbulence of the atmosphere produces irregular refraction and reduces the clarity of the view. Some wavelengths of the electromagnetic spectrum are absorbed before they penetrate the atmosphere. When observatories can be set up on the moon we shall be able to study many problems that can not be attacked from the surface of the earth.

SUMMARY

1. For uniform acceleration

$$V_t = V_o + at$$

and $$S = V_o t + \frac{1}{2} at^2$$

2. At the surface of the earth the acceleration due to the force of gravity is 32 feet per second^2.

3. Weight (as measured on the earth) is a measure of the gravitational force between the earth and the object being weighed.

4. A body appears to be weightless when it is being accelerated toward the center of the earth with the acceleration of gravity.

5. Rocket propulsion can be explained in

terms of action and reaction as described in Newton's third law of motion.

6. The "escape velocity" from the earth is approximately 7 miles per second and from the moon about 1.15 miles per second.

7. There are many important scientific problems that can be attacked by laboratories set up on the moon.

QUESTIONS AND EXERCISES

1. An object starts from rest and is given a uniform acceleration of 5 feet per second^2. How far will it travel in 10 seconds? Repeat the calculation assuming an initial velocity of 2 feet per second.

2. A rocket ship starts from rest, receives a uniform acceleration of 320 feet per second^2. (10 gravities) and just reaches the earth's escape velocity when the fuel burns out. How long did this take?

3. For what practical reasons will the rocket to the moon from the United States be launched from established bases in Florida rather than California?

4. Does a person jumping out of an airplane experience weightlessness before his parachute opens?

5. Would the "kick" of a rifle against your shoulder be as severe on the moon as on earth?

6. It has been predicted that the surface of the moon is covered with a layer of dust at least several centimeters thick. What could be the origins of this dust?

7. Is it likely that sedimentary rocks will be found on the moon? If so, what kind would they be?

8. From an observatory on the moon could we make a more sensitive analysis of the atmosphere of Venus and Mars? Explain.

9. If you used an equal arm balance to measure weight, what would you find, on the surface of the moon, to be the weight of a brick that weighs 3 pounds on the earth?

10. Give several reasons for the fact that rockets are designed to accelerate rapidly.

Unit Six

Story of the Earth

Chapter 1

The Earth as It Is Now

Every landslide, every tree growing from a cracked rock, and every muddy river tells us that the surface of the earth is constantly changing. However, we shall be concerned with more extensive changes, such as the appearance and wearing away of mountain ranges, arms of the sea that once covered millions of square miles of what is now dry land, and the development, dominance, and disappearance of strange types of animals. These events are the long-term results of the familiar forces that we see daily altering the landscape. Let us take a preliminary look at the evidence and see some of the reasons that compel us to think that such drastic changes have occurred in the past.

EVIDENCE THAT THE SURFACE OF THE EARTH HAS CHANGED

In many parts of the United States, particularly in certain limestone and shale deposits, there are fossils of marine animals. They are found, for instance, high up in the Rocky Mountains. The rocks containing those fossils were undoubtedly formed at the bottom of the sea. Any explanation of this fact requires a considerable stretch of the imagination, but it seems more reasonable to assume that the rocks at the bottom of the sea were lifted up to make the mountains, rather than that the rocks were moved to the mountain tops from the bottom of some distant seas, or that the sea was once deep enough all over the earth to cover mountains as high as the Rockies.

The occurrence of fossils in general is evidence of the changing forms of life on earth. Fossils may be thought of as entombed life. Sometimes only an impression of an organism is left in the rock; sometimes the hard parts, like bones or shells, are preserved; and sometimes the entire organic structure has been petrified (Figures 6–1, 6–2, and 6–3).

The basic principles that guide the study of fossils are surprisingly simple. Geologists merely carry on the same kind of study that has revealed to archeologists what life was like in ancient Greece, Egypt, Palestine, and among the early cave dwellers in Spain and France. Geological research has revealed that there is a uniformity among fossils found in any one layer of deposit, and that there is a smooth sequence of small changes and an increase in complexity from the lower layers to the upper ones. It is assumed that the lower layers were deposited before the upper ones, in those situations where the rocks have not been greatly disturbed. Marine type fossils are found in deposits that are similar to the kinds

now found at the bottom of the sea. Fossil land animals and plants are found in deposits like the La Brea tar pits and in rocks formed from the mud of shallow lakes.

A very special and unusual set of circumstances must have occurred for a plant or animal to have been preserved as a recognizable fossil. When we consider that most animals die a violent death, and that most dead plants lie on the surface of the ground until they decompose, any fossil remains that we do find must have been preserved by some lucky chance. A dead plant or animal, exposed to both air and water, usually decomposes entirely; but if either one or both influences are excluded, a fossil may result. These conditions are fulfilled when the remains are covered quickly by mud or tar, or drop to the bottom of the sea. We would expect a particular type of marine animal to be widely distributed, and we would also assume that land animals and plants would have a much more limited range. This is true now, and it is also true of the plants and animals of the past, as recorded in fossils.

The fossil record tells us a story of

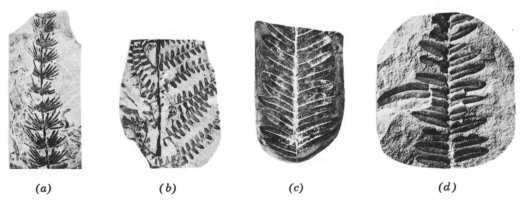

(a)   (b)   (c)   (d)

Figure 6–1.   Pennsylvanian plant fossils, about one-third natural size. (a) Calamites folliage (Ohio). (b) Fern (Oklahoma). (c) Seed fern (Illinois). (d) Seed fern (Michigan). (Reproduced by permission of McGraw-Hill Book Co. from Chester A. Arnold, 1947, An Introduction to Paleobotany.)

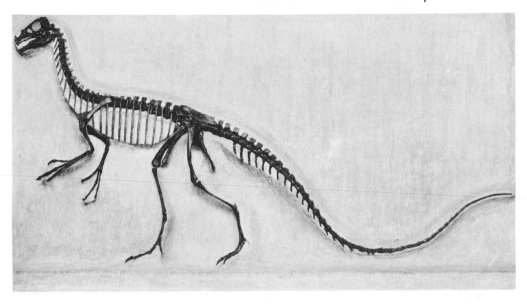

Figure 6–2.   Skeleton of theropod. (American Museum of Natural History.)

a time when life was found only in the sea, and of a later time when life appeared on dry land in a few forms. These forms became more numerous and more complex, and many species developed, flourished, and died out. Specialization increased, and finally man appeared on the scene at least a million years ago.

The Colorado River has gouged its way through thousands of feet of rock in the Grand Canyon. This river has, in effect, cut the leaves of a book that starts with the roots of a mountain range formed over 1500 million years ago. It carries us through ancient layers of rocks that are tilted and contain no fossils, and, finally, through many horizontal layers of limestone, shale, and sandstone. The lowest of these contain only marine fossils; the upper ones are rich in increasingly specialized marine and dry-land remains. This is an unusually complete and extensive record.

Many apparently isolated facts have stimulated us to construct a consistent

Figure 6–3.   Fossil lepidophyte stump. (Geological Survey of Canada.)

story about the changes that have taken place on the surface of the earth since it was formed. For example: beds of coal containing well-preserved fossils of temperate zone plants are found in Alaska and Antarctica; Long Island is covered with the type of deposit formed at the end of a glacier; the Hudson River has a channel far out to sea. Also, marine sediment many feet deep was excavated from around the columns of the Temple of Jupiter Serapis in Pozzuoli, Italy; these marble pillars contain holes bored by salt-water molluscs. During the past 2000 years the ground on which this temple stands has apparently sunk and risen again above the water of the Mediterranean. (You might give some thought to the problems such a situation would create in New York City.)

We are going to survey very quickly what we know about the structure of the earth as it is now, then study some of the agents that are changing it, and subsequently have a look at the story of the past.

PRESENT STRUCTURE OF THE EARTH

The earth is surrounded by a blanket of air called the atmosphere. This consists of 78% nitrogen and 21% oxygen, with the remaining 1% composed of carbon dioxide, water vapor, and rare gases. The higher we go above sea level, the less concentrated are these gases. At 10,000 feet altitude mountain climbers find themselves short of breath, and jet planes must have pressurized cabins as they cruise at 30,000 feet. At 20 miles above the surface of the earth the atmospheric pressure has dropped below 10 cm of mercury. Two hundred miles up there is enough air to heat up moving meteorites and rockets; the glow of the northern lights shows the presence of

ionized air molecules as high as 600 miles; and the Van Allen belts of ionized particles extend for many thousands of miles from the earth. Thus the atmosphere gradually thins out and there seems to be no point in saying that it extends to some specific height and ends there.

The ups and downs of the surface of the earth seem considerable to a man climbing a mountain with a 40-pound pack, but, when reduced to proper scale on a 12-inch globe, they would be hard to see. The highest mountains are less than 30,000 feet above sea level; the greatest depths in the ocean are 35,800 feet below sea level. The extreme difference is about 12.3 miles, which is only 0.3% of the earth's radius.

As you look at the globe, you should notice that slightly more than one quarter of the earth's surface is dry land, and that this is massed around the North Pole. The emblem of the United Nations takes advantage of this fact (Figure 6–4). In many parts of the world there is a gentle slope on both sides of the shore line, so that a difference of a few hundred feet in the level of the water in the ocean would make a considerable differ-

Figure 6–4. Emblem of the United Nations showing concentration of land masses around the North Pole.

ence in the area of dry land. Beyond the continental shelves and continental slopes lie the ocean depths. Here the scenery is scarred by deep trenches and marked by thousands of mountains and mountain ranges.

Since the deepest wells go only a few miles below the surface, our information about the bulk of the earth must be inferred from circumstantial evidence. The vast interior of the earth must be very hot. Although shallow mines and caves are cool, all deep mines show a steady increase in temperature with depth of about 1°C per 100 feet.

We must also assume that the material deep in the interior of the earth has a much higher specific gravity than the rocks that are common on the surface. The earth as a whole has a specific gravity of 5.5, yet that of the surface rocks is only 2.7. Therefore, well below the surface there must be some material that has a specific gravity much greater than 5.5. A clue to the nature of the heavier material concentrated at the center of the earth comes from meteorites. The great majority of these are stony, but about 10% are an alloy of iron and nickel with a specific gravity between 8 and 10.

Could the earth have a large core of metal with a thick layer of rocks around it? How thick would these layers have to be to explain the facts?

Further clues to the structure of the interior of the earth come from a study of earthquake waves. Abrupt movements of the crust of the earth send out both longitudinal and transverse waves that travel out from the site of the disturbance (the focus) in all directions through the earth. Their intensity and time of arrival can be observed by a seismograph. Part of this instrument moves with the shaking of the earth and part remains relatively stationary during the quake. Figure 6–5 shows how this is accomplished.

The great inertia and the pivoted support of the heavy mass keep it from acquiring the jiggling motion passed on to the U-shaped generator from the quivering bedrock. Most of the time, the light beam marks a straight line as the drum revolves. During a quake it gives a record such as you see in Figure 6–6.

It is observed that three different waves are sent out by an earthquake. They travel at different speeds and are recorded successively by the seismograph. The fastest (p in Figure 6–6) is a longitudinal-

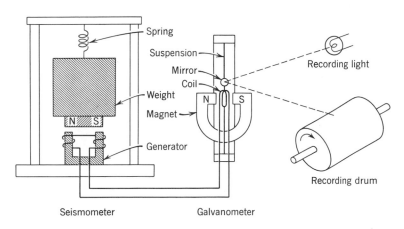

Figure 6–5. Schematic representation of an electromagnetic seismograph. (Courtesy, Dr. Hugo Benioff.)

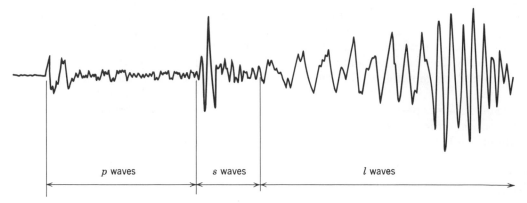

p waves   s waves   l waves

Figure 6–6.   A seismogram. The record starts at the left with the p waves.

type wave and is called the primary wave. The second wave, *s*, is a transverse-type wave and travels more slowly. The slowest is the *l* wave, which travels around the surface of the earth and is responsible for most of the damage from earthquakes. The difference between the time of arrival of these waves is a measure of the distance of the earthquake from the observing station. When each of these observatories in different parts of the world draws a circle on the globe showing where the quake could be, these circles will intersect at the point (epicenter) above where it was (Figure 6–7).

A study of innumerable seismograms has shown that the speed of earthquake waves varies with the depth as they race around the earth. Figure 6–8 summarizes those results. The most curious result that emerges from this study is that over a third of the earth on the side across from the quake receives no seismographical record of the *s* wave. There seems to be a central section that casts a "shadow" for the *s*, but not the *p*, waves. You will remember (page 90) that transverse waves are not transmitted through liquids and gases. It is most improbable that the earth has a gaseous core, but a reasona-

ble estimate of the temperatures and pressures present shows that it might be a viscous liquid. We have not yet been able to duplicate these conditions in the laboratories so we must fall back on educated guesses. By a study of several ex-

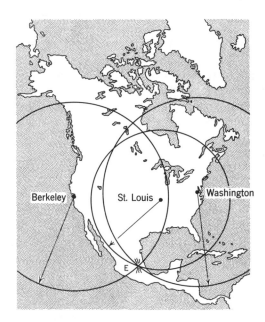

Berkeley   St. Louis   Washington

E

Figure 6–7.   Epicenter of earthquake near Mexico City can be located from observations made at three different stations.

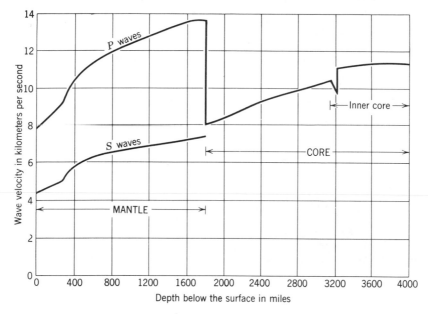

Figure 6–8. *Graph showing the change in velocity of p and s waves at different depths below the earth's surface. (Based on a diagram in P. Byerly, 1942, Seismology, Prentice-Hall.)*

amples of the "shadow" cast by the core we can get an idea of its size. It lies at a depth of about 1800 miles (Figure 6–9). Significantly, at this same depth there is an abrupt decrease in the speed of the *p* waves. There is another abrupt change in the speed of the *p* waves at a depth of 3200 miles that is currently interpreted as meaning that there is a small inner core that is solid. Further along in this unit it will become apparent that the distinction between liquid and solid is not sharp and absolute.

Most of the 1800-mile-thick mantle around the iron core behaves like an iron and magnesium silicate (olivine) that is a common mineral in stony meteorites. Very near the earth's surface there is another abrupt change in composition revealed by seismic and explosion waves. It is named for its discoverer, Mohorovicic, and this name is frequently shortened to Moho or M discontinuity. This is the sur-

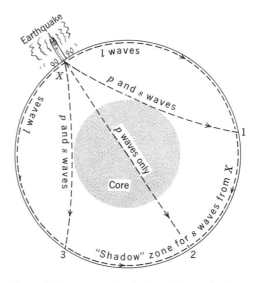

Figure 6–9. *Cross-sectional view of the earth, showing how different types of waves are transmitted.*

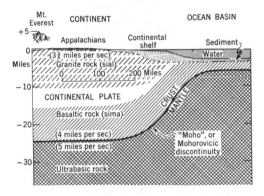

Figure 6–10. The earth's crust is much thicker under continents than beneath the ocean basins. (From Physical Geography, *Second Edition, by Arthur N. Strahler, John Wiley and Sons, 1960.)*

face between the deep, dense olivine mantle and the layer of basalt that is laid like a skin over it. The basalt layer is covered with thin sediment and water in the ocean basins and with a thicker layer of granite that forms the continents (Figure 6–10). A project is under way to drill (a Mohole) through the M layer to learn more about this situation.

SUMMARY

1. Fossil remains tell a consistent story of the history of the past.
2. In an undisturbed deposit the lower layers are assumed to have been laid down before the upper ones.
3. The atmosphere contains 78% nitrogen, 21% oxygen, and small amounts of carbon dioxide, water vapor, etc.
4. Dry land covers only about one-quarter of the surface of the earth.
5. The specific gravity of the surface rocks is considerably less than that of the earth as a whole, so the earth must have a core made up of material more dense than the surface rocks.
6. From a study of the refraction of earthquake waves we learn that the earth has a shell-like structure with at least three layers. There is a plastic metal core which may have a solid kernel, a thick rocky mantle, and a thin basalt crust upon which we find the surface rocks.

QUESTIONS AND EXERCISES

1. What are the facts about fossils that make us think that there has been an orderly development in the forms of life through the ages?
2. In what way could a person untrained in geology destroy the value of a fossil that he might find?
3. List some of the facts mentioned that indicate that conditions in the world many years ago were considerably different from present day conditions.
4. What is the weight in pounds per cubic foot of a substance with a specific gravity of 5.5?
5. Determine, in a rough fashion, the specific gravity of a rock, by weighing it and dropping it into a graduated cylinder containing water.
6. If the surface temperature is 50°F, what would be the temperature at the bottom of a mine 3 miles deep?
7. Why is the Mohole being drilled from a barge in the ocean instead of from a much more convenient location on dry land?
8. What clues do meteorites give us to the nature of the interior of the earth?
9. What would be the shape of the longest possible path for an *s* wave?
10. In a seismograph (Figure 6–5), why must the mass be a heavy one?

Chapter 2

Wrecking and Rebuilding

THE EARTH, like a city, is never finished: wrecking or building is going on wherever we look. The floors of oceans and lakes are carpeted with mud and sand from rugged mountain peaks; many of the present mountain ranges were once the beds of ancient seas or their substance was spewed forth from subterranean reservoirs of molten rock; the old material is used and reused. Let us look at this process of tearing down and rebuilding through the ages.

CUTTING THE ROCKS DOWN TO SIZE

Our first problem is to find out how great masses of rock arc broken down into pieces small enough to be moved. In this whole sequence of weathering and erosion we are going to find that water plays a major role.

We can discuss only a few of the many types of chemical reactions by which rocks can weather. An example of hydrolysis is the decomposition of olivine

$$MgFeSiO_4 + 2HOH \rightarrow$$
$$Mg(OH)_2 + Fe(OH)_2 + SiO_2$$

The student should realize that chemical equations like the previous one have only qualitative significance. In olivine, for instance, there are varying proportions of magnesium and iron, and the products of hydrolysis will be various intermediate silicates. However, equations such as these do give a useful representation of the kinds of chemical reactions that are

Figure 6–11.   A specimen of granite. (From Elements of Geology, *by W. J. Miller, D. Van Nostrand Co., 1939.)*

occurring. The iron in olivine and other igneous rocks is mostly in its lower valence state and when it is exposed to the air it is oxidized by some such reaction as

$$4FeSiO_3 + O_2 \rightarrow 2Fe_2O_3 + 4SiO_2$$

A combination of hydrolysis and hydration of the feldspar fraction of granite (Figure 6–11) breaks up the rocky material and forms a type of clay called kaolinite ($H_4Al_2Si_2O_9$). These and many other types of reactions aid in the disintegration of large rocks.

Carbonic acid (H_2CO_3) and soil acids increase the chemical action of water. As surface water seeps into natural cracks it enlarges and deepens them. Plant roots will take advantage of these crevices and

Figure 6–12.   Granite rock being split apart by a tree growing through it. (U.S. Forest Service.)

Figure 6–13.   Blocks of granite sprung apart by frost wedging. Sierra Nevada, California. (F. E. Matthes, U.S. Geological Survey.)

will accelerate the change from rock to soil (Figure 6–12). The fact that water expands about 10% on freezing is another important factor. Frost wedging will break up resistant rocks into rather small pieces (Figure 6–13). Clear running water has only a slight cutting action, but if it carries sediment, its abrasive power is greatly increased. Fast-moving mountain streams erode rapidly and then carry away the debris.

MOVING THE PIECES

Running water is by far the most important agent for transporting the debris that results from the processes described in the previous section. It has been estimated that the Mississippi River carries 1 million tons of sediment each day. This comes from the land surfaces of the Middle West and is dumped into the Gulf of Mexico. In carving out the Grand Canyon, the Colorado River carried away 2000 cubic miles of debris, and it is still going strong. Farmland is being denuded of topsoil; reservoirs for irrigation and hydroelectric power are being filled up; ship channels must be kept dredged; giant deltas are being built up—running water is indeed a major factor in our economic life as well as a geological agent that is changing the face of the earth.

The faster the water is running, the larger are the rocks it will move, and the greater is the load it can carry. As these streams slow down in their rush to the sea the sediment they are carrying drops to the bottom—the heavier particles first, then the light ones and finally the silt. River-borne deposits are typically graded by size with allowance made for the complication of springtime floods (Figure 6–14).

Between flood seasons these deposits

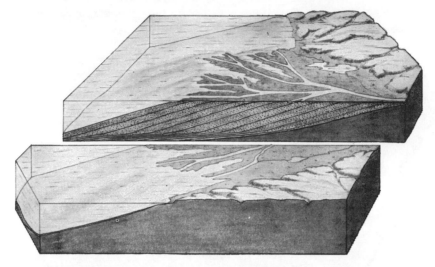

Figure 6–14.   Ideal small delta in three-dimensional view. On the surface appear "delta fingers" formed by deposition from distributary streams. The block has been cut in two and the pieces pulled apart to reveal a vertical section of the delta. Thick, inclined foreset beds are underlain by bottomsets and overlain by topsets. The topsets are represented only by the thickness of a single line, because they are commonly very thin. The slope made by the uppermost foreset bed is shown in phantom view, through the water. (Vertical scale greatly exaggerated.) (From Physical Geology, Third Edition, *by Chester R. Longwell, Adolph Knopf, and Richard F. Flint, John Wiley and Sons, 1948.)*

have time to settle into layers. Chemical reactions and pressure from the layers above consolidate the lower ones, and a typical sedimentary rock is formed (Figure 6–15).

Ocean and lake currents running parallel to the shore have the transporting action of streams, and storm waves eat away cliffs above the high tide mark

Figure 6–15.   An outcrop of sedimentary rock consisting of shale and sandstone near Oxnard, California. (From Elements of Geology, *by W. J. Miller, D. Van Nostrand Co., 1939.)*

(Figure 6–16). The occurrence of wave-cut terraces above the present water line, or high upon a mountain side, gives us a clue to changing water levels and ancient lakes that have now disappeared (Figure 6–17).

When the summer temperatures of a region are so cool that not all the previous winter's snow melts, the snow accumulates. As the snow deepens year after year, the lower part is compacted into ice, and the pressure forces it to flow slowly downhill. This river of ice is called a glacier (Figure 6–18).

Glaciers are common in the high mountain regions of the world. There are many in the Himalayas, the Alps, the Andes, in Norway, and in Alaska. Greenland is one vast ice sheet and so is the continent of Antarctica. As we shall see later, a large continental ice sheet spread down from eastern Canada into the northeastern part of the United States many thousands of years ago.

A solid mass like a glacier moves very slowly; the usual speed is a few feet a day. But even this is sufficient to move rocks, scour out valleys, and make characteristic changes in the landscape. At the head of a glacier a semicircular area called a cirque develops (Figure 6–19). Since the cutting action is greatest at the bottom and sides, a glacial-cut valley has steep sides and a broad, flat bottom like a U (Figure 6–20). The bottom is marked by many parallel scratches in the direction of flow of the glacier, showing where rough rocks have been pushed along (Figure 6–21). These rocks and the soil are incorporated into the ice and are carried

Figure 6–16.   Wave-cut cliffs along the Oregon coast. (Oregon State Highway Department photo.)

Figure 6–17.   Remains of the shoreline of old Lake Bonneville in Utah. (U.S. Geological Survey.)

Figure 6–18.   Aerial view of a glacier. (U.S. Forest Service.)

Figure 6–19.   Glacial cirques. (U.S. Geological Survey.)

down to where the melting of the glacier balances its advance. Here the material is dumped into an unsorted pile called a glacial moraine (Figure 6–22). Since this material was carried in suspension, it still has rough edges. Hence an unsorted de-

posit of rough material is readily recognized as glacial till. A careful study of pictures and a geological survey map of Yosemite Valley will reveal many of the characteristics of a region that has been glaciated fairly recently (Figures 6–23

Figure 6–20.   A glaciated valley. Notice U-shaped cross section. (U.S. Geological Survey.)

Figure 6–21.   *The scratches on this rock were made by a glacier pushing other rocks over it. (U.S. Geological Survey.)*

Figure 6–22.   *An exposure of a ground-moraine sheet left by the great glacier of the Ice Age. (From* Elements of Geology, *by W. J. Miller, D. Van Nostrand Co., 1939.)*

Figure 6–23.   Yosemite Valley before glaciation. (After Matthes.)

and 6–24). Many of the states in the north-central and northeastern part of the United States bear the marks of the continental ice sheets that last retreated only eleven thousand years ago. Figure 6–25 diagrams the more typical features of such a landscape, and Figure 6–26 shows how some of them appear after the inevitable changes brought about by erosion and plant growth.

Although the wind is a relatively minor agent of erosion it is responsible for some characteristic features of the landscape. The stark beauty of sand dunes and wind-carved rocks is found in deserts and along shore lines. Only fine-grained material can be carried any distance, but the periodic dust storms that have swept our western plains have had catastrophic eco-nomic effects (Figure 6–27*a* and *b*). The dust is scattered over a wide area, and in the United States it has accumulated into the loess deposits that occasionally reach 100 feet in depth (Figure 6–28) in our north-central states.

MOUNTAIN BUILDING AND EARTHQUAKES

The eroding effects of wind and water would eventually wear down the continents almost to sea level if it were not for opposing forces that are pushing up mountain ranges. Mountain building forces are imperfectly understood, but we do know about some aspects of the process. Volcanism, treated in the next section, is

Figure 6-24.   Yosemite Valley after glaciation. (After Matthes.)

one obvious type of mountain building. The theory of isostasy attempts to account for another type. As rivers carry sediment down and dump it at coastal regions, the downward pressure at these points on the earth's crust is increased and the pressure under the mountainous regions is decreased. What readjustment would you predict in this situation if the rocks a few miles under the surface of the earth are subject to the plastic flow, somewhat like the flow of a glacier? The coastal region should sink gradually under its increased load, and the mountains should be pushed slowly upward as erosion lightens them. This would keep the downward pressure approximately equal in both places. The theory of isostasy assumes that there is a tendency toward equal downward pressure at all portions of the earth's surface, and it predicts a slow buckling of the earth's crust (Figure 6-29) following extensive transfer of material.

There is increasing evidence for slow, vertical circulation cells in the mantle. The central Atlantic Ridge and the East Pacific Rise may be indications of such a phenomenon. Where this upwelling takes place beneath a continental crust one would expect to find the kind of vertical thrust that is observed to be occurring in the Sierra Nevada. The possibility of this kind of mountain building force has only recently been suspected and it is being studied actively.

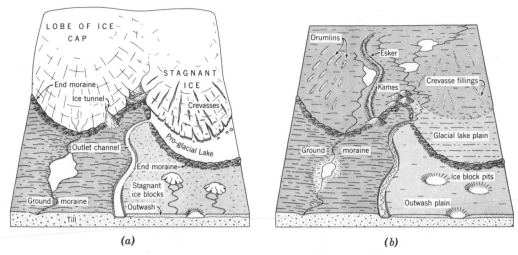

(a)

Glacial deposits and their relationships to a retreating ice cap.

(b)

Glacial deposits and land forms after disappearance of the ice cap.

Figure 6–25.   Block diagrams showing the conditions that prevail during the retreat of an ice cap (a), and the glaciated landscape after the ice has disappeared completely (b). (From Elements of Geology, by James H. Zumberge, John Wiley and Sons, 1958.)

Figure 6–26.   Morainal topography consists of many small hills and depressions. (From Physical Geography, Second Edition, by A. N. Strahler, John Wiley and Sons, 1960. Photograph by Douglas Johnson.)

Figure 6–27a.   The approach of a dust storm. (Soil Conservation Service.)

Figure 6–27b.   Wind-borne topsoil has ruined this farm and nearly buried the buildings. (Soil Conservation Service.)

318

Figure 6–28. Loess deposits which have been deeply eroded in Helena, Phillips County, Arkansas. (U.S. Geological Survey; photo by A. F. Crider, 1905).

Rocky layers are subject to many kinds of deforming forces. The effect that these have on the structure depends partly on the nature of the rocks and partly on how fast the forces are acting. If the conditions are right for a wave-like folding, the troughs are called synclines (Figure 6–30) and the crests are called anticlines (Figure 6–31). Surprisingly complex folding is possible (Figure 6–32). A huge trough extending for many hundreds of miles is called a geosyncline.

Under other conditions the rocks break, and the surface where the break occurs is called a fault (Figure 6–33). The formation of a fault is probably accompanied by an earthquake. Once a fault has

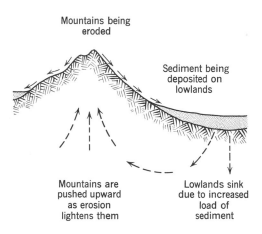

Figure 6–29. Movements of the crust of the earth as explained by the theory of isostasy.

Figure 6–30.   A syncline. (U.S. Geological Survey.)

Figure 6–31.   An anticline. (U.S. Geological Survey.)

Figure 6–32.   Sedimentary rock which has been folded extensively. (U.S. Geological Survey.)

Figure 6–33.   A vertical fault. (U.S. Geological Survey.)

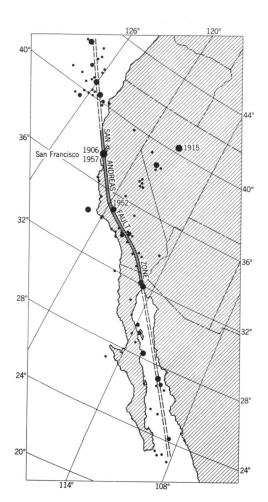

Figure 6–34.   The black dots show the distribution of earthquakes in California and Nevada. The majority, but not all of them, are related to the San Andreas fault zone. (After H. Benioff and B. Gutenberg, 1955, Earthquakes in Kern County, California during 1952, California Department of Natural Resources, Division of Mines, Bulletin 171.)

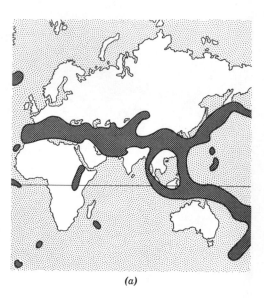

(a)

Figure 6–35a.   Regions of most intense earthquake activity in the eastern hemisphere.

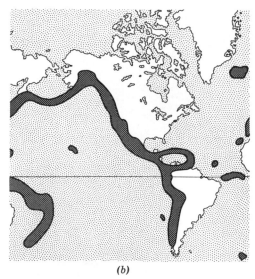

(b)

Figure 6–35b.   Regions of most intense earthquake activity in the western hemisphere.

Figure 6–36.   An example of the horizontal displacement which took place during the earthquake of 1906. This picture was taken near Pt. Reyes Station, California. (U.S. Geological Survey.)

formed, future stresses tend to be relieved by further movements along this surface. Many important faults have been traced, the most spectacular being the San Andreas fault in California (Figure 6–34).

One finds the greatest stress in the earth's crust in the neighborhood of very high mountains, particularly where mountain ranges are close to the sea. We find these conditions along the shores of both sides of the Pacific Ocean, in India, around the Mediterranean, and in the Caribbean. Compare this with Figure 6–35*a* and *b* which shows the regions of the earth where earthquakes occur with the greatest frequency.

Many earthquakes occur every day, but nearly all of them are so minor that they are remembered only as wiggles on a seismogram. An earthquake in a heavily populated region can cause serious loss of life and property. On April 18, 1906, there was a horizontal displacement along the San Andreas fault line in California that caused damage to property over an area of hundreds of square miles (Figure 6–36). The water pipes in San Francisco were sheared off, and a fire raged out of control. Millions of dollars of damage was done, and nearly a thousand people were killed. During the winter of 1811–1812 three earthquakes centered near New Madrid, Missouri. They were among the greatest in history. The region was so thinly populated that there was little loss of life or property, but an area of 30,000 square miles sank from 5 to 15 feet. Great rolling swells were seen to cross the prairie. Earthquakes and landslides in the ocean floor are the causes of destructive "tidal waves" or tsunami (Figure 6–37).

VOLCANISM

Are active volcanoes, geysers, and hot springs surface features that indicate isolated pockets of hot rocks deep in the earth's crust, or are they connected through the M discontinuity to the great mass of hot mantle rocks? No certain answer can be given to this question but it seems more probable that local concentrations of radioactive minerals in the crust furnish the heat to melt the rocks. This magma, or molten rock, tends to flow toward the surface through fault-line cracks, so that a map of recent volcanic activity would closely resemble the one of earthquake activity (Figure 6–35).

Sometimes the magma solidifies before it reaches the surface. Its presence is re-

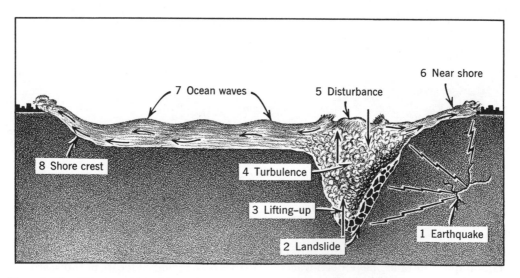

Figure 6–37.   *How an earthquake causes a tsunami is not fully understood. It is believed an earthquake (1) causes either an underwater landslide (2) or a rise of a few feet in ocean bottom (3). Result is turbulence in ocean depths (4) and rise or fall of ocean surface (5). Waves from this hit the near shore (6). Tsunamis cross the ocean (7)—much like ripples from a rock dropped in a pond—at speeds up to 500 miles an hour. Waves rise only a few feet and crests may be hundreds of miles apart. At the far side (8), when tsunami hits shallow water, its great mass and velocity produces giant waves that crest on shore. (Redrawn from* The New York Times, *May 27, 1960.)*

Figure 6–38.   The grand eruption of Lassen Peak, California, May 22, 1915. The volcanic cloud is fully 8 miles high. (From Elements of Geology, by W. J. Miller, D. Van Nostrand Co., 1939. Photograph by Myers and Loomis.)

vealed when erosion removes the overlying rocks. When magma emerges at the surface it is called lava. The rocks that solidify from the molten state are called igneous because of their fiery origin. Granite and basalt are two common types of igneous rocks. The action of air and water on the igneous rock alters part of it, and other parts are carried away to be deposited and formed into sedimentary rocks. The further action of heat, pressure, water, and air on either sedimentary or igneous rocks occasionally changes them so much that we find it convenient to give them a special name—metamorphic rocks. Rocks are thus divided into three broad classifications: igneous, sedimentary, and metamorphic.

Lava may come to the surface in spectacular central eruptions, or it may ooze out through a great crack in the earth's surface and flow over the ground like cold molasses over a pancake. A lava flow that covered several hundred square miles occurred in Iceland in 1783.

We owe the existence of many beautiful mountains to volcanic activity. The Hawaiian Islands are the tips of volcanoes that stand on the floor of the Pacific Ocean; Fujiyama, Vesuvius, Pelee and Ranier are well-known volcanoes. Mt. Lassen (Figure 6–38), in northern California, should be mentioned as one in the United States that has been active recently (1917), and Paricutín, in Mexico (Figure 6–39), is one of the most recent additions to the family (1943).

The intermittent spouting of geysers is often found in a region of recent volcanic activity. Old Faithful is the most famous example but there are hundreds of others. We would expect hot springs in a volcanic area, but the alternate quiet and eruption of a geyser suggests a special set of circumstances. When a sinuous cavity in volcanic rocks fills with water from underground flow, the water is under an additional pressure of one atmosphere for every 34 feet of depth. Its boiling point is correspondingly higher (page 25). After the water has been heated to this higher point some of it rises as steam, pushing a little water out ahead of it. This lowers the pressure and the rest flashes into a great volume of steam and blows the whole cavity free (Figure 6–40). The geyser then quiets down until it is again filled and heated.

Figure 6–39. Paricutín, the world's youngest volcano, in violent activity. (From Physical Geology, *by Longwell, Knopf, and Flint, John Wiley and Sons, 1948. Photograph by Otto Brehme.)*

SUMMARY

1. Large rocks are broken into smaller pieces by a number of processes. These include chemical reaction, splitting by plant roots and ice, changing temperature, and abrasion.
2. The smaller pieces are transported by running water, winds, and glaciers.
3. A typical glacial-cut valley has a U-shaped cross section, parallel scratches on the walls and bottom, cirques at its head, and a moraine at its mouth.
4. The theory of isostasy states that there is a tendency for the downward pressures on different parts of the earth's crust to equalize each other by a slow transverse movement of the material under the crust.
5. A syncline is a down folding in layered rocks.
6. An anticline is an upfolding in layered rocks.

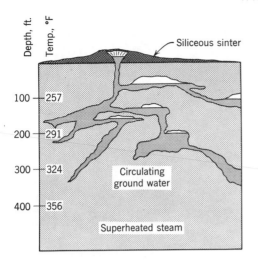

Depth, ft.   Temp., °F

100 — 257

200 — 291

300 — 324

Circulating ground water

400 — 356

Superheated steam

Siliceous sinter

Figure 6–40. Vertical section to show the conditions necessary for geyser action. White areas represent large cavities in which steam accumulates. (From Physical Geology, Third Edition, by Chester R. Longwell, Adolph Knopf, and Richard F. Flint, John Wiley and Sons, 1948; drawing modified from E. T. Allen and A. L. Day.)

7. A fracture in the rocky structure in which there has been displacement is called a fault.

8. Earthquakes occur most frequently in parts of the earth where there are the greatest differences in elevation.

9. Igneous rock is rock that has solidified from the molten state.

10. Sedimentary rock is rock formed by the cementing together of small particles or by chemical precipitation.

11. Metamorphic rock is either igneous or sedimentary rock that has been more or less altered after it was formed.

QUESTIONS AND EXERCISES

1. State the different ways in which a large rock may be broken up into small fragments.

2. What are some of the signs that indicate water erosion in the past?

3. If you live in a section of the country where there is a particularly muddy stream, take a glass full of this water and let it stand to see how much sediment settles out.

4. What are the main differences between glacial till and river-borne sediment?

5. Does a wave-cut terrace above the present shore line of the ocean necessarily indicate that the level of the sea has dropped? Explain.

6. How do we explain the fact that the surface of the delta of the Mississippi has remained at about the same level for many centuries?

7. Would you be more likely to find fossils in marble or in sandstone?

8. Would you find particles of igneous rock in a sedimentary deposit or of sedimentary rock in an igneous deposit?

9. How would you explain a situation where igneous rock is found lying on top of a sedimentary deposit?

10. Mention two examples where the level of a part of the earth has changed by thousands of feet.

Chapter 3

Progressive Changes

in the Landscape

IT MAY be well to pause at this point to organize somewhat differently the information in the previous section. The subject is so large that only the most obvious phases can be mentioned, but even these will be enough to make your trips more meaningful.

SOME THINGS TO LOOK FOR

The ability to identify rocks and minerals can be developed only by careful study and actually working with materials. You could no more learn practical geology without laboratory work than you could learn typing without a typewriter. However, Figure 6–15 will give

you some idea of what a sedimentary deposit looks like, and Figure 6–11 shows a typical igneous rock. Slate is an example of a metamorphosed shale; marble is metamorphosed limestone; metamorphosed granite is one type of gneiss (Figure 6–41).

A good place to start looking is where a highway has cut deep into the earth. Here the vertical surfaces will be fairly clean and the rock formations observable. Notice whether the rocks are igneous (granite or basalt) or sedimentary (sandstone, shale, limestone, layered, gravelly, etc.). Sometimes you will observe sedimentary deposits resting on igneous rocks or an igneous intrusion breaking through layers of sedimentary rocks (Figure 6–42). In some places the sedimentary layers are

Figure 6–41. Banded gneiss. (Geological Survey of Canada.)

practically flat, in others the folding is extensive. Many of the rocks in lava beds are porous and spongy (Figure 6–43) and hot springs may be present. From all this you can infer something about the history of the region.

It will be practically impossible to date the strata unless you are a geologist with a working knowledge of fossils. However, several of our national parks have excellent displays that point out salient features of the landscape, and the rangers are only too happy to answer informed questions.

In an area of extensive limestone deposits look for caves that can be visited. Water seeping through the ground contains dissolved carbon dioxide.

$$CO_2 + H_2O \rightarrow H_2CO_3$$

This leaches out great caverns in the rocks by the reaction,

$$H_2CO_3 + CaCO_3 \rightarrow Ca(HCO_3)_2$$

Figure 6–42. An igneous intrusion (dike) cutting horizontal sedimentary beds at right angles (Alamillo Creek, Socorro Country, New Mexico). (U.S. Geological Survey; photo by N. H. Darton, 1915.)

Figure 6–43.   An outcrop of volcanic breccia showing a coarse fragmental texture: ten miles west of Reno, Nevada. (From Elements of Geology, by W. J. Miller, D. Van Nostrand Co., 1939.)

At this stage in the life history of the cave the roof may fall in leaving a huge quarry-like hole in the ground called a sink. If the roof does not collapse, the solution of $Ca(HCO_3)_2$ that is dropping from above

tends to lose CO_2 and the series of reactions mentioned is reversed. The limestone is again deposited in the spectacular shapes of stalactites (hanging down and dripping), stalagmites (the droppings from above), and other bizarre formations.

Where organic remains are buried below the water table the particles of organic material may be dissolved and replaced by silica. This has occurred with such precision that petrified trees can be found that retain every detail of growth rings and bark structure.

Next observe whether the sedimentary rocks are uniform and sorted (deposited by rivers) or unsorted and angular (deposited by glaciers). A glaciated valley will be characterized by its U-shaped cross section, waterfalls from the sides, and cirques at its head. The characteristics of a river-cut valley will be described in the next section. Strata may be traced across

Figure 6–44.   The Grand Canyon of the Colorado River is a mile-deep gash in the Colorado Plateau. The initial cutting of this magnificent canyon probably began in late Pliocene time. (Fairchild Aerial Surveys, Inc., Los Angeles.)

a road cut, or even across a valley, and fault lines can sometimes be followed for miles. A vein of a valuable mineral will usually be broken off at the plane of a fault, and it then becomes the job of the geologist to predict in which direction to dig to find it again. Grand Canyon National Park offers an unrivaled opportunity to follow the geological history of a single region over hundreds of millions of years (Figure 6–44).

THE SEQUENCE OF CHANGES

We are fortunate to be able to visit, within the limits of the United States, examples of nearly all types of geological formations in all stages of progressive changes they undergo. In the Sierra Nevada Range we find young mountains still being raised; the Rockies are older; the Appalachians are more than two hundred million years old; and the Adirondacks of northern New York are the stumps of a range raised up about a billion years ago. Eleven thousand years ago a great ice sheet retreated from the northeastern part of the United States, and we can still see much evidence of its work. In 1917 Mt. Lassen last erupted, and the trees killed by that action are still stand-

Figure 6–45. A very narrow, steep-sided canyon 1500 feet deep. The Narrows, Zion Canyon, Utah. (From Elements of Geology, *by W. J. Miller, D. Van Nostrand Co., 1939.)*

ing. As you read these lines, the Great Bear sand dune in the eastern shore of Lake Michigan is engulfing and smothering another grove of trees that are in the path of its relentless march.

Among our rivers, the lower Missouri is old, the Tennessee is middle-aged, and the Columbia is young. Let us now fol-

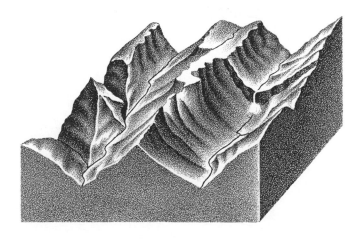

Figure 6–46. First stage in the development of a landscape, characterized by newly formed mountains and young rivers.

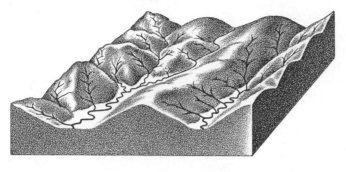

Figure 6–47.   Second or mature stage in the development of a landscape.

Figure 6–48.   Monadnocks near Moosehead Lake, Maine. (From Physical Geology, by Longwell, Knopf, and Flint, John Wiley and Sons, 1948. Photograph by McLaughlin Aerial Surveys.)

Figure 6–49.   The third or old-age development of a landscape.

Figure 6–50.   Meanders of the south Saskatchewan River. (Royal Canadian Air Force.)

low through some of the changes that take place after an extensive mountain-building period.

In young mountains the peaks are jagged, the ridges sharp. The streams run over waterfalls and cascades and cut deep, steep-sided valleys (Figure 6–45). They run through small lakes and have few tributaries (Figure 6–46). Since these streams have a steep gradient, they carry their sediment along. Their burden of abrasive material carried at high speed enables them to cut downward rapidly.

The downward cutting eventually reduces the gradient of the stream, and more and more tributaries are formed. The tributaries are younger and pour a large burden of rocks and sand into the main stream. A point is reached at which the main stream is not able to carry away all the sediment that is brought into it.

Shoals develop, and the river begins to form a flood plain and meadows (Figure 6–47). By now, most of the waterfalls have disappeared and fertile valleys mark the place of former lakes. The rugged peaks have had their slopes reduced, trees, bushes, or grass have covered the soil formed, and the mature stage has been reached. At the mouth of a river, sedimentary layers are laid down for thousands, and possibly millions of years.

The passage from the mature state to old age is gradual and poorly marked. The higher ground is subject to the greatest erosion, but it can never be worn down to sea level. The process of washing away becomes slower as the heights are reduced, until a gently rolling pene-plain landscape results. Here and there, a particularly resistant mountain root may stand out (Figure 6–48). The flood plain of

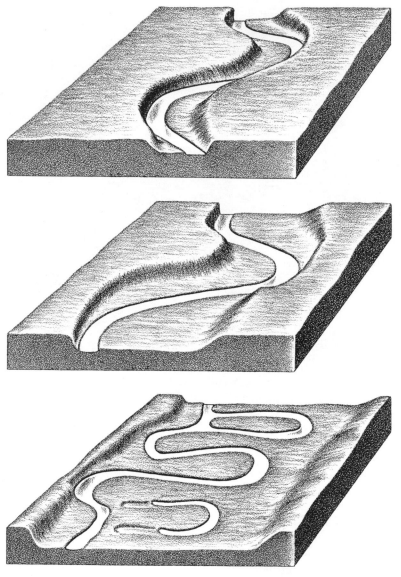

*Figure 6–51.   Three steps in the development of a river, show-
ing how it cuts away its banks and forms oxbows as it matures.*

the river is very wide, with numerous
meanders (Figures 6–49 and 6–50). An oc-
casional spring flood may change the
course of the river so that one of the meanders is cut off and is left to form a type of
lake called an oxbow (Figure 6–51). At
present the Mississippi River is threaten-
ing to return to an old path to the sea that
would by-pass New Orleans completely.

Not always does the life of a river follow this uninterrupted course. Mountains
grow by fits and starts, so that a river may
have reached the flood-plain stage when a
new thrust starts it flowing more rapidly. It

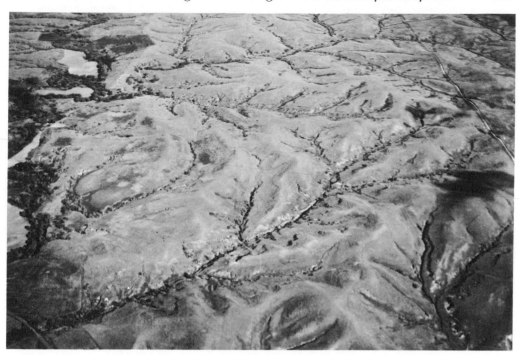

Figure 6–52.   Rejuvenated streams. From the well-rounded contours of the landscape one would expect to find a mature stream with meanders and a flood plain. Instead, these streams have steep walls and nearly straight courses. (U.S. Geological Survey.)

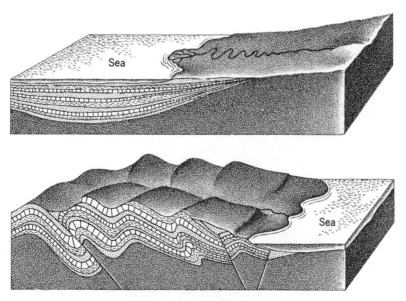

Figure 6–53.   Sedimentary layers laid down at the mouth of a river (above) are folded and faulted as they are lifted to form a new mountain range (below).

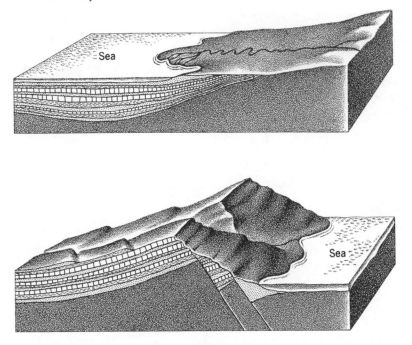

Figure 6–54.   *The lifting of a new mountain range may result in the breaking of the strata, forming block faults.*

Figure 6–55. *An unconformity separating horizontal layers above from steeply tilted layers below. Gaspé Peninsula, Quebec. (From* Fundamentals of Physical Science, *by K. Krauskopf, McGraw-Hill Book Co., 1948.)*

then cuts a new channel (Figure 6–52).

As layer upon layer of sediment is deposited at the mouth of the river (which probably forms a delta), the rocks underneath sag into a trough. For some reason, not yet well understood, a new period of mountain building begins. This time, the filled trough is elevated, either in complex folds (Figure 6–53) or in great tilted blocks (Figure 6–54). The former peneplain sinks and is covered by the sea.

The material eroded from these new mountains is placed in layers of horizontal sediment on the irregular outline of the old peneplain to produce an unconformity (Figure 6–55). An unconformity necessarily represents a very great difference in age between the lower and upper layers.

SUMMARY

1. Limestone caves are formed by solution, and either collapse or are partially filled by redeposition.
2. Petrified fossils are formed by replacement of the organic structure with inorganic material (usually silica).
3. A young landscape is characterized by jagged, rocky peaks, flat uplands, swift streams with waterfalls, cascades, and lakes.
4. A middle-aged landscape is characterized by mountains that are mostly covered with soil and vegetation, streams in a dendritic pattern, and rivers with shoals and meanders.
5. An old-aged landscape has developed to a peneplain with sluggish, meandering streams.
6. An unconformity is the surface separating two layers of rocks in certain special conditions. These conditions are that the lower layer appears to have been extensively eroded, before the upper one was laid down.

QUESTIONS AND EXERCISES

1. What are the signs indicating that a stream has passed from youth to middle age?
2. In a situation like the Columbia River, in which a river cuts directly across a mountain range, what is the relative age of the river as compared to that of the mountain range?
3. Write a paragraph tracing the story of a grain of sand that was first part of a mountain range, was then carried away by erosion, and later returned to be deposited as part of the upper layer of an unconformity.
4. What would you expect to observe if you placed a drop of dilute HCl on a piece of limestone and on a piece of petrified wood?
5. What would be characteristic features of the landscape of the Sierra Nevada?
6. List some of the more obvious differences between sedimentary and igneous rocks.
7. Yosemite Valley now has a river running through it. What makes us think that this valley was once occupied by a glacier?
8. How many different unconformities can be seen in the Grand Canyon of the Colorado?
9. Can a river show signs of being both old and young at the same time? Explain.
10. Explain briefly but precisely the basic reasoning involved in interpreting geological records.

Chapter 4

Up from the Sea

S WE look across almost any broad landscape we observe a wealth of detail in the foreground; the middle distance reveals several clear features with things hidden by trees or buildings; and the distant scene extends indistinctly to the horizon. Similarly, the geologist stands at the present and looks backward across a vista of time and events. Near at hand and rich in detail, he observes the last sixty-five million years, which he calls the Cenozoic era. In the middle distance he can discern the Mesozoic era that reaches back to more than two hundred million years ago and the Paleozoic era that started about six hundred million years ago. In both of these there are many well-defined landmarks and much

evidence for supporting details in the picture. The more distant view is, however, extremely fragmentary. What evidence there is has been subject to rough handling in the succeeding years and efforts to date it have only recently met with any success at all.

GEOLOGIC TIME

The answer to the question "How old is the earth?" requires a definition of terms. As this is being written, the oldest rocks that have been definitely dated (see next section for the method) are 2.7 billion years old. These, however, are intrusive into metamorphosed rocks that are considerably older, so that age is not even a minimum one. The rocks originally crystallizing on the surface of the earth have been so thoroughly worked over by erosion and recrystallization that they may be unrecognizable. There is a distinct probability that meteorites were formed at the same time as the earth, and several of these have been shown to be 4.6 billion years old. In the light of the discussion above the question can be answered by saying that the beginning of geological time is probably close to 4.6 billion years ago.

The great bulk of geological time is lumped together under the name Precambrian. The major divisions since then are called the Paleozoic, Mesozoic, and Cenozoic.

The direction in which science is advancing at any one time in history is determined by economic and social pressures to a much greater extent than most people realize. This is nicely illustrated by the combination of circumstances that lead to the understanding of how to put geological strata in the correct sequence. Josiah Wedgwood, the eighteenth-century pottery maker, was having trouble transporting his fragile wares to the London market from his factory in Staffordshire. He was successful in agitating for a system of canals for inland transportation. One of the surveyors laying out routes for the canals was William Smith. Smith must have been an unusually observant person, because he noticed and studied the surface strata of the country and even the fossils they contained. He found out that each layer contained characteristic fossils and that there was a regular succession of layers that was repeated at widely separated places. Since the order of these layers was never inverted, one could say with confidence that the lower ones had been formed before the upper ones. He also pointed out that

the two strata in different parts of the country that contained the same types of fossils must be the same age. His intense interest in strata led to his nickname "Strata Smith," and to a tremendous advance in our understanding of the history of the earth. All this started with a fragile teacup.

By the middle of the nineteenth century, Charles Lyell had made a convincing case for the modern point of view that past changes in the earth's surface are adequately explained by processes now in operation. This replaced the catastrophic theory, which held that a few world-wide catastrophes, such as floods and volcanic activity, were responsible for the present surface features of the earth. Darwin's theory of evolution (1859) did for biology very much what the theory of uniform change did for geology. In fact, the two theories strengthened each other, just as two quarter circles fit together to make a strong arch.

By 1900 geologists were making good progress at the task of arranging formations in correct sequence, but they had no way of giving these layers an absolute date. The discovery of radioactivity (page 208) provided the clue that is solving this problem. In the simplest case, a long-lived radioactive isotope will be mixed with its stable disintegration product (uranium 238 and lead 206, for instance). If each atom of lead 206 came from an atom of uranium 238 we know what fraction of the original uranium has disintegrated. The half-life of U 238 is 4.6×10^9 years and, using the relationship

$$t = 0.3 \, T \log \frac{N_0}{N}$$

we can calculate the age of the uranium-lead deposit. Here t is the age of the mineral, T is the half life of the radioactive isotope, N is the number of radioactive atoms remaining, and N_0 the number originally present.

Clearly, there are many precautions that must be taken in using this method. Some of the observed lead 206 may have been present in the original mineral or some of the radioactive decay products may have been removed mechanically, or by leaching. When this technique is applied with due care it can furnish absolute dates with an accuracy of better than 5%. There are several radioactive isotopes with half-lives of the order of magnitude of a billion years that can be used with

Table 6-1

ERA°	PERIOD	PHYSICAL EVENTS IN NORTH AMERICA	CHARACTERISTIC LIFE
4.6 billion years ago—formation of the earth's crust			
Precambrian			2 billion years ago the first "living" thing appeared. Granite and limestone deposits.
		Laurentian mountains formed. Erosion from Cascadia and Appalachia.	Algae and primitive invertebrates.
600 million years ago—first rocks containing abundant fossils			
	PERIOD		
Paleozoic	Cambrian	Continent gradually sinking after previous mountain building. Extensive erosion.	First trilobites.
	Ordovician	Large part of North America covered by sea.	Dominance of trilobites, corals, and other invertebrates. Early vertebrates.
	Silurian	Climate hot and dry. Salt deposits formed.	First land plants. Rise of fishes. Dominance of trilobites.
	Devonian	Most of North America above sea level.	First land animals. Large land plants.
	Mississippian	Center and eastern part of continent a shallow marsh that rose and fell several times.	Complex invertebrates. Extensive forests.
	Pennsylvanian	Same as Mississippian	Coal deposits of east. Many amphibians. Dragon flies.
	Permian	North American continent rose above sea level.	Last of the trilobites. Rise of the reptiles.

° Notice that the space given to the eras is not related to the length of time they lasted.

different minerals and that can frequently serve as a cross-check in any one deposit. Uranium 235 ends up as lead 207, thorium 232 as lead 208. Rubidium 87 decays to strontium 87, and potassium 40 changes to argon 40.

The major divisions of geologic time (and it should be re-emphasized that they vary greatly in length), eras, have already been mentioned. There is not a consistent system for naming the shorter subdivisions. The seven parts of the Paleozoic and the three of the Mesozoic average about 60 million years each and are called

Table 6-1 (Continued)

ERA°	PERIOD	PHYSICAL EVENTS IN NORTH AMERICA	CHARACTERISTIC LIFE
		230 million years ago—Appalachian revolution	
Mesozoic	Triassic	Dry climate; much volcanic activity along west coast.	Rise of dinosaurs.
	Jurassic	Sierra Nevada thrust up. Mild climate.	Dominance of dinosaurs. Flying reptiles and earliest birds. Earliest mammals.
	Cretaceous	Rocky Mountain area pushed up above sea level. Cooler, drier climate. Western coal and oil deposits formed.	Early mammals and birds. Last of the dinosaurs. Many flowering plants, and insects.
		65 million years ago—Laramide revolution	
	EPOCH		
Cenozoic (Tertiary Period)	Paleocene	Coastal plains submerged.	Reptiles giving way to mammals.
	Eocene	Mild climate and general erosion.	Mammals dominant. Modern plants.
	Oligocene	Mild climate and general erosion.	
	Miocene	Lava extrusions cover Columbia River basin. Renewed upthrust of Cascades and Sierra Nevada.	Many modern animals well developed. Modern grasses.
	Pliocene	Continuation of mountain building.	Manlike ape.
Cenozoic (Quaternary Period)	Pleistocene	Four great ice ages.	Appearance of early man. Social behavior of man.

° Notice that the space given to the eras is not related to the length of time they lasted.

periods. In the Cenozoic there are six shorter epochs. Left over from a discarded system of naming there are the terms Tertiary and Quaternary: the Tertiary period includes the first five epochs of the Cenozoic and the Quaternary corresponds to the most recent epoch, the Pleistocene. Table 6–1 outlines the divisions of geologic time and the more significant physical events and forms of life.

PRECAMBRIAN

There is so little deciphered evidence presently available from the first 85% of the earth's past that it is best considered as a unit. There were many periods of widespread erosion, there were several periods of mountain building, and there are deposits of organic origin. However, it is not yet possible to put these together into a connected story, so only a few highlights will be mentioned. At some time about 2 billion years ago, chemical reactions taking place in the warm ocean produced the first living things. There was very little free oxygen in the atmosphere so that ultraviolet light from the sun could penetrate to the surface of the water in greater amounts than it does now. With this source of energy many fairly complex organic molecules could be built up. The more stable ones increased in concentration and some served

Figure 6–56. Spriggina floundersi glaessner. *(Courtesy, Dr. M. F. Glaessner, University of Adelaide and South Australian Museum.)*

as catalysts for the production of their own kind and of others so that a complex "broth" accumulated. When a combination that was sufficiently complex and well integrated to exhibit the behavior of metabolism, growth, and reproduction occurred, life was on its way. (It was probably to this period that Pooh Bah was referring when he said, in *The Mikado:* "I am in point of fact a particularly haughty and exclusive person of pre-Adamite ancestral descent. You will understand this when I tell you that I can trace my ancestry back to a protoplasmal, primordial, atomic globule.") Extensive graphite and limestone deposits are evidence of life during this period.

In Australia there are some Precambrian deposits that have remained relatively undisturbed and from which recognizable fossils have been obtained. These are shallow-water plants and animals that lacked hard shells (Figure 6–56). A few examples of blue-green algae are found in other Precambrian rocks.

The mineral-rich rocks of Canada and the Vishnu schist through which the Colorado River is now cutting in the Grand Canyon were formed about 1.5 billion years ago. The areas that are now the Rocky and Appalachian Mountains were great geosynclines being filled with sediment from the west and east respectively (Figure 6–57). The east-coast and west-coast parts of this continent have changed from high mountain ranges to below sea level more than once.

PALEOZOIC

A dramatic change is observed in the rocks dating from about 600 million years ago. There is an abundance of fossils so that the story in various parts of the world can be connected into a sequence. This is the opening of the Paleozoic (old

life) era. It lasted for over 300 million years and has been divided into seven periods. During this time, living things conquered the difficulties of existence on dry land and evolved many complicated forms, including seed plants, flying insects, and reptiles.

The first period in this era is the Cambrian. By this time the animals had developed the ability to surround themselves with hard shells, and it is thought that this factor is responsible for the sudden appearance of rocks rich in fossils. The most frequently encountered fossil in this period is the trilobite (Figure 6–58). It also serves as the most important index fossil for the whole era. It was widely distributed and evolved through hundreds of different forms that assist in correlating rocks from different localities.

During the second, or Ordovician period, the middle west was a vast, shallow sea abounding in trilobites, corals,

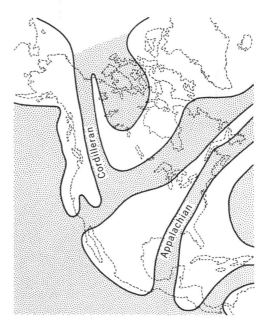

Figure 6–57. Map of North America during the Precambrian era. Sediment was being deposited in the Appalachian and Cordilleran geosynclines.

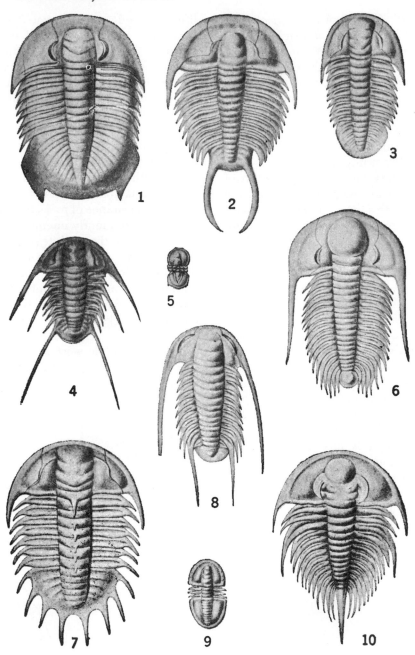

Figure 6–58.   Cambrian trilobites. All natural size except 6, which is about one-sixth natural size. (From Historical Geology, by C. O. Dunbar, John Wiley and Sons, 1949. Drawn by L. S. Douglass.)

oysters, and many other marine inverte-brates. Cephalopods, an early form of squid (Figure 6–59), reached a length of 15 feet, and the first vertebrate, a primitive fish, put in its appearance.

The third period in this area is called the Silurian. During this period, the various marine invertebrates evolved increasingly complicated forms. Many areas in North America that had been under water were lifted gently (without much faulting or folding). The drier climate resulted in the formation of extensive salt deposits in New York and Michigan. Plants which had been growing in shallow water either developed so that they could survive on dry land or perished. This emergence of the plants from the water to dry land is probably the most significant event in this period, because the animals had to stay in the sea until there were land plants for them to feed on.

In the next, or Devonian period, the land plants developed rapidly. Ferns, club mosses, and even primitive trees (Figure 6–60) were abundant. Although an early type of air breathing scorpion is found in late Silurian deposits, the first true land animals (amphibians) are thought to have appeared in the Devonian. In the sea the trilobites and cephalopods, although more complex in structure, were becoming less important. They were being supplanted by the fishes. These developed a great variety of forms, one of the most interesting of which is the crossopterygian (Figure 6–61). This fish is remarkable in two ways. It is the most likely ancestor of the amphibians, and it has existed in the ocean with very little change for the last 350 million years. The modern coelacanth (Figure 6–62) strikingly resembles the crossopterygian fossils from the Devonian.

Figure 6–59. An Ordovician sea beach, on which specimens of the great cephalopod, Endoceras, are stranded. (Chicago Natural History Museum. From a mural painting by Charles R. Knight.)

Figure 6–60.   Reproduction of a middle-Devonian seed-fern tree. These grew to a height of 25 to 40 feet. (Courtesy of the New York State Museum and Science Service.)

After the Devonian came two periods, the Mississippian and the Pennsylvanian which have so much in common that it is convenient to consider them together. The climate was temperate and uniform for a long period of time. At the close of the Devonian nearly all North America was dry land, and it returned to this state by the opening of the Permian; but in the interval a shallow sea covered most of what is now the continental United States west of the Mississippi. The scene of the present Appalachian Mountains had many ups and downs. For long periods, our present eastern coal beds must have been a huge swamp resembling the Dismal Swamp in Virginia. Luxuriant, primitive vegetation flourished and fell

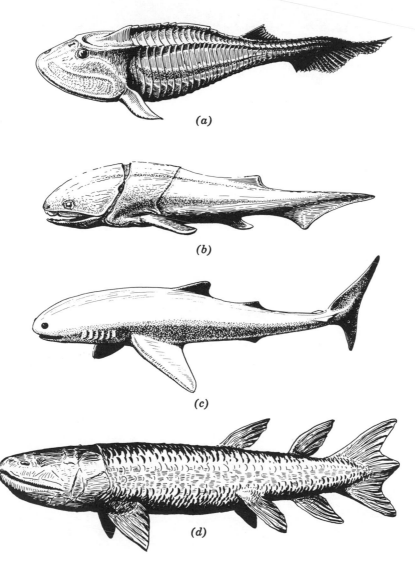

Figure 6–61. Devonian fishes. (a) Ostracoderm. (b) Placoderm. (c) Shark. (d) Crossopterygian. (From Evolution of the Vertebrates, by Edwin Colbert, John Wiley and Sons, 1955.)

Figure 6–62.   Cast of the coelacanth (Latimeria). (Courtesy of the American Museum of Natural History.)

Figure 6–63.   Reconstruction of a Pennsylvanian landscape. (Yale University, Peabody Museum of Natural History.)

Figure 6–64.   Restoration of Permian reptiles. (Chicago Natural History Museum.)

into the water to be turned into coal. Giant dragonflies and cockroaches flew through the air; amphibians developed, flourished, and gave way to reptiles (Figure 6–63). Myriads of one-celled animals died and left their shells to form the limestone deposits of the midwest.

The last period of the Paleozoic is the Permian. The North American continent rose above sea level, never again to be so extensively invaded. The climate became cooler and drier, and this change put the dry-land animals and plants to a severe test.

From the amphibians, which had to breed in water, came the reptiles that could lay eggs on the ground (Figure 6–64). The plants had developed a sexual method of reproduction, which made for more variety in each generation and, hence, for more rapid evolution. The characteristics that did not contribute to success were more rapidly eliminated and a greater variety of responses became possible as conditions changed.

As the climate turned progressively colder during the late Permian, this period saw the most extensive ice age of

any period before or since. Strangely enough, most of this glaciation took place in the neighborhood of the present Equator.

The close of the Paleozoic era is marked by the Appalachian revolution. The Appalachian Mountains were being slowly pushed up, and there was a great amount of folding, faulting, and erosion as the process continued. With the Appalachian revolution the curtain falls on this era, which saw so many significant changes taking place. As erosion once more lays down sediment we open the next act.

SUMMARY

1. Under favorable circumstances rocks can be dated by a study of their radioactive decay products.
2. The date of the initial formation of the earth's crust can only be guessed at, but it may have taken place as much as 4.6 billion years ago.
3. Geologic time has been divided into four major eras called the Precambrian, Paleozoic, Mesozoic, and Cenozoic.

4. In a sequence of strata, unless there is reason to suspect otherwise, it is assumed that the lower layers were laid down before those above them.

5. We find a consistency among the fossils in any one stratum and an increase in diversity and complexity from older to younger strata.

6. It is now agreed that past changes of the earth's surface are adequately explained by geological processes now in operation.

7. The Precambrian era lasted about 4 billion years. It saw extensive changes in the face of the earth, but few of these have yet been dated. The first form of life appeared, and there are some recognizable fossils and much unrecognizable material that is undoubtedly of living origin. Erosion was filling up the Appalachian and Rocky Mountain geosynclines. Important mineral deposits were laid down in Canada and the United States.

8. The Paleozoic era lasted about 370 million years, from the formation of the first rocks rich in fossils to the Appalachian revolution. Trilobites developed, flourished, and died out. There occurred the earliest appearance of vertebrates, land plants, land animals, insects, amphibians, and reptiles. The eastern coal deposits were formed.

QUESTIONS AND EXERCISES

1. What is the present ratio of U 238 to Pb 206 in the mineral used to date the oldest meteorites? What would this ratio be in a suitable mineral formed at the end of the Permian?

2. Arrange the following forms of life in the order in which they developed: fishes, land plants, reptiles, trilobites.

3. What is the nature of our oldest fossil deposits?

4. Would you expect to find fossils in the rock of the Laurentian Mountains? Explain.

5. Why do we suppose that there was extensive erosion during the Precambrian era?

6. What kind of evidence indicates that the Appalachian geosyncline was being filled up by erosion from a mountainous area located east of it?

7. What would be a particularly useful type of fossil in dating Paleozoic sedimentary rocks?

8. Name several factors that make it more difficult for plants to live on dry land than in the sea.

9. What was the first living creature to fly and when did it develop?

10. What is an important difference between amphibians and reptiles? Name a living example of each group.

Chapter 5

From Early Mammal

to Early Man

THE MESOZOIC (middle life) era began 230 million years ago and lasted for about 165 million years. It is divided into the Triassic, Jurassic, and Cretaceous periods. The rigorous climate of the Appalachian revolution eliminated many of the star players in the previous act of our drama and left all but part of the far west above sea level (Figure 6–65). The trilobites have disappeared; the cephalopods and amphibians have been reduced to a minor role; the reptiles and seed plants have taken over. Just as the Paleozoic was outlined as the rise, heyday, and decline of the trilobite, so the Mesozoic was the scene for the reptiles. This era ended with an extensive mountain building period known as the Laramide revolution.

MESOZOIC

The Triassic period was one of transition from the cold, dry climate of the Appalachian revolution to the warm, moist conditions that characterized the Jurassic. Large areas of the west were under water, but, in the eastern two-thirds of the continent, sediment was being deposited on what is now the continental shelf. Although the reptiles had not yet become unusually large, their number and variety were increasing rapidly.

The Jurassic rocks were the principal ones studied by "Strata Smith." During this period the reptiles developed into complex and fearsome beasts. To anyone

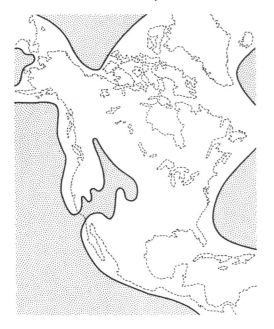

Figure 6–65. Map of North America during the Triassic.

but a scholar of Greek their names are equally impressive. The ichthyosaur (fish-lizard) (Figure 6–66) and the plesiosaur (near or semi-lizard) (Figure 6–67) swam the seas; the brontosaur (thunder-lizard) (Figure 6–68) and gigantosaur (giant-lizard) were so ponderous that they spent most of their time partially immersed in swampy water, munching the lush vegetation; the stegosaur (lizard-with-a-roof)

was a plant eater and depended for protection upon its heavy armor plate; the pterosaur (winged-lizard) (Figure 6–69) was a flying dragon with a wingspread of as much as 25 feet. Along with the flying reptiles appeared the first true bird with feathers, the archaeopteryx (ancient-bird) (Figure 6–70). The first mammals also date from this period. These primitive animals had hair on their bodies, laid eggs, and suckled their young very much as the duck-billed platypus (Figure 6–71) does now. In the plant kingdom the gingko tree and the metasequoia (a deciduous form of redwood) developed and are still to be found as "living fossils."

Igneous activity, mainly by intrusion of granite, pushed up the Sierra Nevada. With these mountains were formed the gold ores that later drew the forty-niners to the west.

The Cretaceous period was one of slow change in climate from mild to cold. It saw the start of a mountain-building program (the Laramide revolution) that was probably the most extensive the world has ever known. Along with these events came the rapid development of some types of life and the equally rapid disappearance of others.

Although the thrusting up of the Rocky Mountains marks the end of the Cretaceous period (and of the Mesozoic era), it was a process that was going on gradually

Figure 6–66.   Skeleton of Jurassic ichthyosaur. It is about 12 feet long. (American Museum of Natural History.)

Figure 6–67.   A pair of plesiosaurs in the foreground, with ichthyosaurs in the right background and fish in the left foreground. (From Historical Geology, *by C. O. Dunbar, John Wiley and Sons, 1949. After E. Fraas, Stuttgart Museum.*

Figure 6–68.   Skeleton of a brontosaur. This specimen measures 67 feet from nose to tip of tail and stands about 18 feet high at the hips. (Yale University, Peabody Museum of Natural History.)

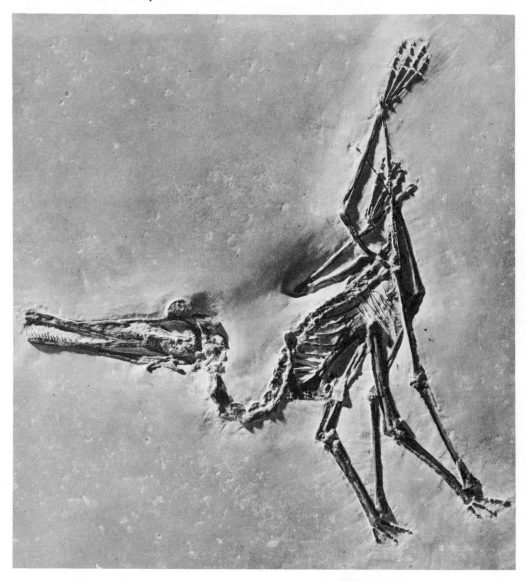

Figure 6–69.   Skeleton of a pterodactyl. (American Museum of Natural History.)

during most of this time. We have a repetition of the situation during the Permian period. There was a change toward a cooler and drier climate and an increased complexity in plants, and the giants among the animals gave way to the smaller and more clever creatures.

The most dramatic event in the plant kingdom was the appearance and phenomenal development of flowering plants. In this one period they rose from first beginnings to dominance. The ancestors of our present-day hardwoods, conifers, palms, and grasses were all present.

Among the reptiles, the terrifying flesh-eater Tyrannosaurus rex (tyrant-lizard) (Figure 6–72) represents their last fling in size and might. The dinosaurs decreased rapidly in importance and disappeared altogether by the end of the era. A number of factors contributed to the decline of the dinosaurs. One wonders whether some of these have a modern-day parallel. Since reptiles are cold-blooded (their body temperature changes with changing air temperature), the cooler climate made them more sluggish. Both the coolness and dryness cut down the luxuriant vegetable growth so necessary for feeding their huge bodies. They had such small brains they must have been unbelievably stupid. They laid eggs on the ground, then went off and left them. At this point the life threads of the dinosaurs and the mammals cross.

Egg-laying mammals appeared during the Jurassic, and marsupials and placentals developed in the Cretaceous. The placentals were the most successful of these experiments in evolution and they rapidly increased in variety and number. Mammals are warm-blooded, have a rela-

Figure 6–70.   The oldest known bird, Archaeopteryx. *The bird was about the size of a crow. (From* Historical Geology, *by C. O. Dunbar, John Wiley and Sons, 1949. After G. Heilmann.)*

Figure 6–71.   Duck-billed platypus. (New York Zoological Society.)

Figure 6–72.   Restoration of Tyrannosaurus rex. (Chicago Natural History Museum.)

tively large brain for their size, and nurse their young. Although the Cretaceous mammals were so small that Tyrannosaurus rex would have needed several for a mouthful, he could not catch them, and they found dinosaur eggs a convenient and delicious meal (Figure 6–73). It is small wonder that the mammals began to displace the reptiles in importance.

The Laramide revolution involved the formation of the mountainous spine of two continents. From Canada through

Figure 6–73.   A nest of fossilized dinosaur eggs. (American Museum of Natural History.)

Central America, the Rockies were forming, and in South America the Andes continued this range. The Appalachians had eroded nearly to a peneplain, and they, too, were pushed up again. In Virginia and Pennsylvania many old rivers cut directly through the more recently-formed ridges. These events, which happened about 65 million years ago, mark the end of the Mesozoic and the start of the Cenozoic.

CENOZOIC

When the curtain goes up on our final act (which is still going on), we find the scenery and the players surprisingly familiar. The North American continent is about its present size and shape; the mountains are rather more rugged than we know them; important changes have yet to take place in the West; but, by and large, we would recognize it readily.

The trees and flowering plants look vaguely familiar. The animals would not be any more surprising than those we see on our first visit to the zoo (Figure 6–74). Instead of a widespread, uniform climate, there is our present distribution of hot, moderate, and cold.

This era has lasted only about as long as one of the average periods of the two previous eras. It started about 65 million years ago and has been divided into two periods, the Tertiary and the Quaternary. The Tertiary period is subdivided into five epochs: Paleocene, Eocene, Oligocene, Miocene, and Pliocene. The terms Pleistocene and Quaternary both refer to the last million years and the latter name is gradually being replaced. Since all these are so recent we have a wealth of detail in the fossils. This era will have to be treated in terms of a few high spots.

In the Paleocene the present coastal plains were submerged into continental shelves. All the mammals from this period were small, but they diversified rapidly.

In the Eocene the flowering plants and mammals were the dominant forms of life. The ancestors of our present important mammals were all small and swift—the early horse was running on paws. In the sea, the seaweed, fish, oysters, crabs, etc., were practically the same as their present-day descendants.

During the Oligocene the climate was rather mild and general erosion was taking place. A sample of the type of evolution that was occurring can be further shown by the horse. In the Eocene it was a terrier-like animal with paws (Figure

Figure 6–74. Some animals of the early Eocene. (Chicago Natural History Museum and Charles R. Knight.)

6-75). By the Oligocene it had grown larger and was developing hoofs (Figure 6-76). As it grew larger, it attained more speed, a larger brain, and more specialized teeth.

The Miocene was a time of mountain building in certain areas and of gentle uplift in others. The Columbia River plateau was covered by igneous extrusions. These lava fields are about 200,000 square miles in extent and reach a thickness of 3000 feet. The Cascade Range and the Sierra Nevada were renewed by vertical thrusting. The earliest of the present grasses and cereal grains appeared during this epoch. This development was crucial for the evolution of browsing animals.

During the Pliocene the thrusting up of these mountains continued and there is evidence that their growth is not yet finished. A man-like ape had developed, and recent fossils suggest the possibility of a definite human as much as 10 million years old.

The Pleistocene covers the last million years. During this relatively short period of time there were some rather striking changes taking place. There were four great ice ages which left their marks on the northern part of this country and which presented a challenge that speeded up the evolutionary process.

From a center in Canada, sheets of ice, thousands of feet thick, ground and scraped their way across New England and the north central and northwestern states

Figure 6-75. Restoration of Eohippus. *This horse was about a foot high at the shoulder. Restoration by Charles R. Knight. (American Museum of Natural History.)*

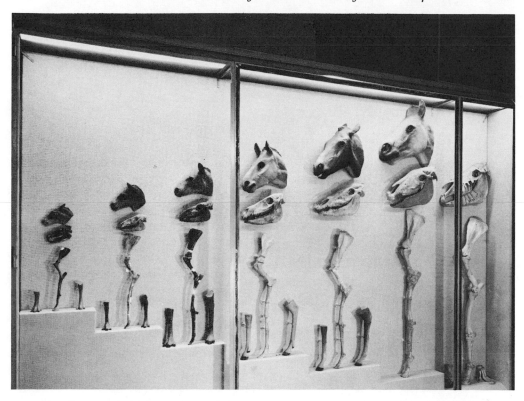

Figure 6–76. Stages of evolution of the horse as shown by limbs and skulls from successive zones in the Cenozoic rocks of the western United States. (Yale University, Peabody Museum of Natural History.)

(Figure 6–77). They advanced and retreated four different times, leaving the lakes of Minnesota and Michigan and the rolling hills of Ohio and New York to mark their passage. They carried topsoil from New England into a moraine we now know as Long Island. Many small local glaciers left their marks in the Rockies and the Sierra Nevada. The Yosemite owes its flat, central valley and its waterfalls to this period. With all this water tied up as continental ice, the sea level fell and the rivers cut valleys far out into the continental shelf. The last major ice sheet started to recede about 11,000 years ago.

The generally cooler climate put a premium on the smaller and more adaptable forms of life. At approximately the begin-

ning of this period, the earliest form of man put in his appearance. By modern standards, he was not particularly attractive, and, compared with the rest of the animals, he was poorly equipped physically. His fur was inadequate; neither his claws nor his teeth were sharp; nor could he run very fast. His brain and the shape of his hands were his two main assets. In a period of change he was better suited to meet the challenge than were some of his more specialized competitors. Figure 6–78 shows some early men. Pithecanthropus erectus lived about a million years ago, Neanderthal man at least 100,000 years ago, and the Cro-Magnon man about 40,000 years ago. There is no evidence that the Cro-Magnon man developed from these earlier

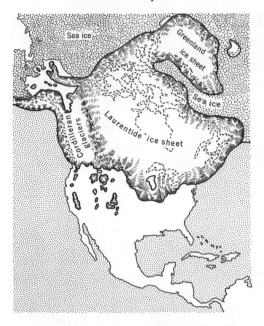

Figure 6–77.   *The continental glaciers of the Pleistocene.*

types. Since the study of these early human remains is only about a hundred years old, it is not surprising that there are many gaps yet to be filled in our picture of the past.

ANOTHER ICE AGE?

Considering the drastic effects of the last ice age, one may well wonder whether we are entering a new one or are still on our way out of the last. Many guesses have been made to explain the change in climate that led to these great sheets of ice. Two recent theories, neither of which is generally accepted, will be presented here.

One theory, based on data from the field of astronomy, seems to account very well for the repeated fluctuations of glaciation during the Pleistocene. The

Figure 6–78.   *Restorations of early man. From left to right: Pithecanthropus, Neanderthal, and Cro-Magnon. (American Museum of Natural History.)*

accumulation of snow is due to unusually cool summers, not to abnormally cold winters. When the air temperature is below freezing, the moisture precipitates as snow, no matter how cold the air is. But, if the summer is cool, not all the previous winter's snow melts. As the snow accumulates year after year, it pushes forward in the form of a glacier. You will remember that the reason for the seasons is the inclination of the earth's axis of rotation to the plane of its orbit around the sun. In January the sun's rays are falling more nearly perpendicularly on the southern hemisphere (Figure 5–2). In its elliptical path around the sun, the earth is closest to it in January, so that the seasons of the northern hemisphere are less extreme than those in the southern hemisphere. The difference in distance is only about 3%, but the chill of the northern winters and the heat of the northern summers are somewhat tempered. In Australia both the angle of the sun's rays and the distance to the sun combine to accentuate the seasons.

Has the situation always been as it is now? We know that the axis of the earth's rotation is swinging around just as a spinning top wobbles. The gravitational effect of the rest of the planets on the earth is not great, but it is enough to make small changes in the eccentricity of the earth's orbit and to change the angle between the orbit and the axis of rotation. At times in the past, all these factors have worked together to make summers abnormally cool over a long period of time. At other times both the eccentricity and the angle of the earth's axis of rotation were great; consequently, summers were particularly hot and winters cold. These changes can be calculated from the known orbits of the other planets. Figure 6–79 shows the calculated and predicted summer temperatures from astronomical data and the records of glaciations from geological data over a period from 60,000 years ago to 100,000 years in the future.

The coincidence of calculated and observed glaciations is so close that it seems that the astronomical factors must be important ones. It predicts that we are emerging from a glacial period and that the climate will continue to grow milder for about 20,000 years before we find ourselves headed for another time of glaciation about 50,000 years from now and a really severe one 100,000 years hence.

The other theory concerning Pleisto-

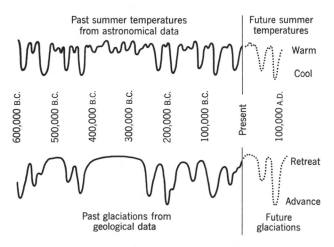

Figure 6–79. *Graphs showing the correlation between calculated summer temperatures and glaciation in the past and a prophecy for the future. (Redrawn from* Scientific American.)

cene glaciation holds that it is when the Arctic sea is free of ice that there is enough moisture in the air to supply the heavy snowfalls needed to build up the continental glaciers. When the glaciers increase in volume, the ocean levels all over the world drop and warm Atlantic ocean water stops flowing into the Arctic ocean. When this happens the Arctic ocean freezes over, snow stops falling and the glaciers melt and retreat. The water from the glaciers flows back into the oceans, the Atlantic ocean (and the others) rise in level, warm water flows northward and again melts the ice cover of the Arctic. This interesting rhythmical theory dates the last freeze-over of the Arctic (and correspondingly, the retreat of the glaciers) as having occurred 11,000 years ago, and it puts us in a period of rapid warm-up and melting. It is possible that the Arctic will be an open ocean within a hundred years and then the cycle would start over again. These two theories do predict a very different time for the next glaciation and it may not be too long before we have evidence to judge which (if either) has put its finger on the crucial conditions.

The many theories attempting to explain the widespread glaciation occurring at the times of the Appalachian revolution and earlier would take too much time to present here. None has been generally accepted, but the theories would make interesting reading and would be worth your critical examination.

EVOLUTION

The evolutionary process rests on two observed facts. The first is that offspring are never identical with their parents, and the second is that offspring are somewhat similar to their parents. In other words, we have variations from one generation to the next, and some of these

variations tend to be inherited by future generations. If an individual is helped to survive by a particular variation, then it will have a better chance to live and to pass on that characteristic to its children. In this way, a useful variation will be encouraged, and what we call evolution will be the result. Many variations will be harmful, and the individuals bearing them will be weeded out gradually by the struggle for existence. The trilobites and the dinosaurs are just two examples from the many dead ends in the evolutionary process. Some variations have no noticeable effect on the struggle for survival. It is important to realize that evolution is a chance process; it is not purposeful.

The role of environment in heredity is becoming clearer, although there is still much to learn. We have come to realize that the word "environment" of a plant denotes more than the soil and the climate in which it is growing. We must consider minute changes in the concentration of the elements in the soil, the complete electromagnetic spectrum of radiation to which it is exposed, winds, drought, the presence of other plants, and many other factors. In fact, the division of the situation into plant, on one hand, and environment, on the other, is an artificial distinction that is useful for some purposes but confusing for others.

In a plant (or animal) there are certain extremely small (submicroscopic) structures called genes, that are principally involved in inheritance. Although these genes are extraordinarily stable they are subject to permanent change when attacked by certain chemicals, by radiation, etc. Any individual plant may be considered to be the result of the interaction of these genes and their environment (in the larger sense). Some of the variations between one plant and its offspring may be inherited by future generations, and others may not. Genetic changes brought about by cosmic rays and the challenge of the environment are two of the most important factors in evolutionary development.

In this unit we have followed the 3-billion-year-long story of the changes of the surface features of the earth and of the living things that populate it. We have seen how the landscape goes through a cycle of changes of mountain building, followed by erosion, and how the cycle may be repeated many times in any one region. We have seen how living things, on the other hand, have taken the path of progressive change. The few and simple gave rise to more variety and more complexity. The highly specialized prosper only so long as their environment remains stable. Abrupt change favors the versatile organism over the specialized one and accelerates evolution by increasing the frequency of variations and by intensifying the struggle for existence.

SUMMARY

1. The Mesozoic era lasted for 165 million years from the Appalachian revolution to the Laramide revolution. The Triassic period saw the rise of the dinosaurs to dominance among animals. In the Jurassic period the earliest birds and mammals appeared. The ancestral Sierra Nevada was formed. During the Cretaceous period the dinosaurs declined in importance and disappeared, mammals and flowering plants flourished, and western coal and oil deposits were formed.
2. The Cenozoic era started 65 million years ago. Mammals and familiar plants were the dominant forms of life. The Cascade Range was formed, and four great ice ages during the last million years left their mark on the northern part of the United States and Canada. Man developed and learned social behavior.
3. Recent studies indicate that we are still in a period of cyclical appearances of continental ice sheets. There is still no generally accepted theory to suggest the most signif-

icant factors involved and to predict the onset of new glaciation.
4. Genes are extremely small units in a living organism which are principally concerned with inheritance.
5. Some variations are inherited from one generation to the next, others are not. Some variations have survival value, others are injurious; and still others seem to make no difference.
6. Evolution is a chance process of progressive change that results from the interaction of the genes and their environment.

QUESTIONS AND EXERCISES

1. It is incorrect to say, "During the Silurian drought, plants changed in order to be able to live on dry land." How should this change be described?
2. What are some important differences between reptiles and mammals?
3. Trace the major steps in the evolution of plants during the Paleozoic and Mesozoic eras.
4. Trace the major steps in the evolution of animals during the Paleozoic and Mesozoic eras.
5. Take some region, such as the present Appalachian mountains, and trace it through its various ups and downs.
6. Which of the following mountain ranges consists principally of sedimentary deposits: Appalachian, Cascade, Laurentian, Rocky, Sierra Nevada?
7. Explain how it happens that several lakes which have a short geological life are found in the Adirondack mountains, which are very old.
8. What conditions are favorable for evolution in the direction of large size?
9. Explain how each of the following factors would affect the winter temperature of North America: (a) the earth's orbit nearly circular; (b) the earth's orbit fairly eccentric; (c) the earth's axis of rotation perpendicular to the plane of its orbit; (d) the earth's axis of rotation at a considerable angle to the plane of its orbit.
10. What are the various ways in which the environment affects evolution?

Chapter 6

Speculation Concerning Beginnings

Iт seems appropriate to conclude this unit by examining some of the speculation concerning the origin of the earth —how did it all get started? If this text has been successful in making you aware of the way scientists work and think you will realize that this chapter will give no final answers, and that we can come to grips with only a few of the many parts of the problem.

Was there a beginning, and if so, what was it like? What was the course of cosmic events after the beginning? Even within the limits mentioned in the first paragraph, this is a tall order for one chapter. It would have to cover the story from the first huge primordial atom that contained all the ele-

mentary particles through all astronomical and geological time up to the present, with implications for the future. Remember that we are going to examine only a small part of the speculation about these events. One limitation is that we shall restrict ourselves to those parts of the sequence for which a background has already been built up in this text.

The evidence from the red shift seen in distant galaxies suggests a beginning in time and space. If all the observed galactic motions are projected backward, they are seen to be diverging from a common source about 10 billion years ago. Let us assume a compact cluster of matter, consisting only of elementary particles. There would be no galaxies, no stars, and not even any elements. This would be an unstable situation and the whole cluster would expand rapidly. Parenthetically, this raises the question of how such an improbable concentration could have occurred. One answer is to assume a pulsating universe.

In this expanding ball of elementary particles that contained all the matter of the universe, the electrons and protons soon combined to form atomic, and later, molecular hydrogen. Whether the other elements were formed at this time is not important here. There were local concentrations and eddies in which the molecules tended to travel as a unit. These were the beginnings of the galaxies. Within the galaxies there were inequalities of distribution. Thermal motion tended to dissipate these, and gravitational attraction tended to concentrate them so that only those with a certain minimum mass survived.

As gravitational concentration proceeded, the pressure and temperature increased to the point where thermonuclear reactions were possible, and over a long period of time the elements were formed. There are many possible evolutionary paths that a star might take, and there are many different types of stars. There may well have been near, or actual, stellar collisions leading to local scattering of matter.

The whole story of stellar evolution is too long to go into here, but it turns out that in any one local eddy there will usually be more than one center of condensation. This can lead to double, or multiple stars, and nearly half of the known stars are found in such combination. Another possibility is that one center will sweep up most of the mass and the others will get only a minor fraction of it. As they condense their surface temperatures will be low, and even in the deep interior, it is probable that the temperature has never exceeded 10,000°C.

Our solar system seems to have developed according to this latter pattern. The sun accumulated most of the matter in its neighborhood (this was nearly 99% hydrogen) and near it were several minor aggregations that also consisted principally of hydrogen. When the interior temperature of the sun rose to the point at which hydrogen was turned into helium, the sun assumed a definite size. The radiation from the interior balanced the gravitational pressure.

Just as the radiation pressure from the sun blows the tail out of a comet, so did it blow away the atmosphere surrounding the inner planets. The mystery of the missing $_{18}Ar^{36}$ is one result of this. In all the elements with an even atomic number from carbon through calcium, the most abundant isotope is the one with an equal number of protons and neutrons. Argon is included in this list, and in the stars, Ar 36 is the most abundant form. But on earth Ar 40 accounts for 99.6% of the argon. Argon 40 is produced by the radioactive decomposition of K 40. Apparently all the argon was lost at an early stage in the earth's formation and the argon in our present atmosphere is of radiogenic origin. The moon may well have condensed at this same time around a separate nucleus near the earth. The outer planets were far enough from the sun and cold enough to retain their hydrogen, helium, methane, ammonia, and water in either liquid or solid form, and these substances make up most of the bulk of Jupiter and the planets beyond. Whether the asteroids are chunks that never congealed or are the debris of a broken up planet is not clear, but the latter alternative seems the more reasonable. The sun settled down to radiating at a rate that has remained essentially constant for perhaps the last 5 billion years.

Gravitational pressure inside the contracting earth would have raised the temperature above the melting point of the rocks. After the contraction was completed, the earth started to cool, and the various substances crystallized out. We have not been able to reproduce, in the laboratory, the high temperatures and pressures prevailing deep in the earth, so we cannot predict what to expect under these circumstances. Some details, however, are clear. The important radioactive elements, thorium and uranium, formed ions that are too large to fit into crystals of silicates, so they were progressively rejected as the mantle crystallized and were concentrated in the thin layer of the crust. Heat from radioactivity is sufficient to furnish the energy for volcanic activity and it is an important factor in mountain building. The crystallization of the earth's crust is estimated to have occurred no longer than 4.6 billion years ago.

After the formation of the crust there was erosion, sedimentation, sinking, remelting, and recrystallization. Volcanoes spewed forth the gases that furnished a new atmosphere and water for the oceans, and mountain ranges were thrust up. The early atmosphere consisted mainly of H_2, H_2O, CH_4, NH_3, and H_2S, and there was water in the ocean basins. Laboratory experiments have demonstrated that when energy in the form of ultraviolet light or electrical discharges is supplied to such a mixture a complex array of organic compounds is formed. With nothing to destroy these substances, they would accumulate and react with each other in all possible ways. Metal catalysts like iron and copper ions were abundant, and some of the organic compounds are capable of catalyzing their own formation. In this way certain complicated molecules would increase in concentration at the expense of other possible ones. This is a chemical analogy to biological evolution.

Another important reaction that was taking place was the photodecomposition of water vapor to form hydrogen and oxygen. Both atmospheric oxygen and ozone absorb ultraviolet light and form an effective blanket that protects the surface of the earth. Some aggregation of molecules sufficiently complicated to metabolize and reproduce formed in the broth that was the sea, and then the newly formed oxygen in the atmosphere blocked off the source of energy that had made this possible. Biological evolution took over and the rest of the story has been outlined in the preceding chapters.

Is this proposed sequence of events too completely fanciful? Is it so improbable that it happened only once in the whole universe? Without doubt, many of the above details will be revised in the light of later knowledge, but some such process seems not only possible, but inevitable. Considering the number of stars that have an appropriate size, output of energy, and other crucial factors, Harlow Shapley estimates that there are probably 10^{12} stars (10^8 as an absolute minimum) that have planetary systems that are presently supporting organic life. This idea has tremendous philosophical implications. Nowadays there is a tendency to consider a person with a "global" point of view as being unpatriotic. The day may come when he will be thought of as provincial.

Answers to Numerical Problems

Chapter 1

2. 1.19 ft³.
3. 1 ounce (approximately).
4. 23.2 in.
5. 1050 cm.
6. 212°F; −17.8°C; −40°F.
8. 5.17 ft³.
9. 1.149 ft³.
10. 14.4 ounces.

Chapter 2

3. 5.88%.

Chapter 3

4. 11 ft.
5. 252 cal/Btu.
6. 3000 g cm per sec.
8. 11,250 g cm² per sec².
9. 3 newton meters.
10. 1.4 m per sec.

Chapter 4

4. 93°C; 98°C.
5. 717.8 mm.
6. 131.25 g.
8. Speed H_2 molecule is three times that of H_2O molecule; 2100 m per sec.
10. 10°C.

Chapter 5

9. 50°F.

UNIT 2—PHOTOGRAPHY

Chapter 1

1. 35 in.
5. Greater in water.
8. 41%.
10. 985 g.
11. 4*f*.
12. 2*f*.
14. 2 in.

367

Chapter 2

1. 55.5 ft candles.
2. f 11.
3. ½ inch.
4. Twice as much.
5. ¹⁄₁₀₀ second.
7. 1.8 ft candles.
8. 4.1 ft from dimmer bulb.
9. f 16.
10. 14.1 ft.

Chapter 3

2. ¹⁶⁄₁.
6. $f = 5$ per minute, $p = 12$ seconds or ⅕ minute.

Chapter 4

2. 4.2 ft.
3. 22.4 per second.
4. 2200 ft.
5. 10,000.
6. 1100 ft per sec.
7. 1.7 seconds.
9. 2750 ft.

Chapter 5

1. 9/8.02 or 8.98/8.
4. D♯ = 309.4, F = 343.8, F♯ = 366.7.
5. True tone scale 1.25, eqaul-tempered scale 1.26.

Chapter 6

1. ap.
9. o-p would be greater.

UNIT 3—ELECTRICITY AND MAGNETISM

Chapter 3

4. 4.17 amperes.
5. 120 ohms.
6. Approximately 1 cent.
10. 7.5 volts; 1.5 volts.

Chapter 5

1. 1200 watts; 1200 watts.
5. 20 turns.
6. 0.6 amperes.
8. 48 ohms.

Chapter 7

1. Speed of light 186,000 miles per second.
2. 1.8×10^4 cm or 0.335 miles.
8. 2.58 seconds.
9. 15,750 lines per second.
11. 1860 miles per second.

Chapter 8

5. 5.72 minutes.

UNIT 4—ATOMS IN ACTION

Chapter 1

1. $Na_2CO_3 + 2HCl = 2NaCl + H_2O + CO_2$.
2. SiO_2 60.06; Al_2O_3 101.94; $CuSO_4 \cdot 5H_2O$ 249.69; C_2H_5OH 46.07.
3. 31 g; 20.6 g.
4. $CH_3CH_2CH_2OH$, $CH_3CHOHCH_3$, $CH_3OCH_2CH_3$.
5. $Cl^- = 0.401$ g per 100 ml.

Chapter 3

4. 2.67×10^{-23} g.
5. 6.02×10^{23}.

Chapter 5

1. 1.36×10^{21} atoms.
2. 3 protons, 4 neutrons, 3 electrons.
3. 10 neutrons.
7. ⅛ would be left.
10. Diameter of sun is 1/8000 of solar system, diameter of nucleus is 1/10,000 of atom.

Chapter 7

9. Kinetic energy of proton is 1838 times that of electron.
10. For $_{50}Sn^{119}$ ratio is 1.38, for $_{92}U^{238}$ ratio is 1.59.

Chapter 8

4. 303×10^{12} calories.

UNIT 5—THE SOLAR SYSTEM AND BEYOND

Chapter 1

3. 90°.
4. $90° \pm 1°$; $90° \pm 6.5°$; $90° \pm 16.5°$.
5. Angle to sun = $90° \pm$ (degrees N latitude —23.5°).
9. 13.
11. For 40°N maximum length is 20 ft, minimum is 2.97 ft.

Chapter 2

10. I Earth/I Mars = 1/0.43.

Chapter 3

5. About once a week.
7. Midnight.
8. 1/10; 1/10; yes.
9. Sun-moon force is greater.

Chapter 4

1. Approximately 16/1.
6. Earth 1540 miles per minute, Mars 903 miles per minute.
8. 360,000,000 miles.

Chapter 5

1. 3 P.M.
4. Approximately 90°.
5. Slightly before 3 A.M.
6. 1960–1970, 880×10^6 miles; 1970–1980, 1×10^9 miles; 1980–1990, 2.3×10^9.
7. Frequencies at two ends of equator will be displaced by this fraction of their true values 1.0000417/0.999583.

Chapter 6

6. For $\lambda = 3900$ to shift to 4000 A, speed is 4650 miles per second.

Chapter 7

1. 23.5°N.

Chapter 8

1. 250 ft; 270 ft.
2. 115.5 seconds.
9. 3 pounds.

UNIT 6—STORY OF THE EARTH

Chapter 1

4. 343.75 pounds.
6. 2901.24°F.

Chapter 4

1. U 238/Pb 206 = 28.6/1.

Index